The Civil War in North Carolina

Volume 2 : The Mountains

ALSO BY CHRISTOPHER M. WATFORD
AND FROM MCFARLAND

*The Civil War in North Carolina:
Soldiers' and Civilians' Letters and Diaries, 1861–1865.
Volume 1: The Piedmont* (2003; paperback 2009)

*The Civil War Roster of Davidson County,
North Carolina: Biographies of 1,996 Men
Before, During and After the Conflict* (2001)

The Civil War in North Carolina

Soldiers' and Civilians' Letters and Diaries, 1861–1865

VOLUME 2 : THE MOUNTAINS

Edited by CHRISTOPHER M. WATFORD

McFarland & Company, Inc., Publishers
Jefferson, North Carolina, and London

To my friend,
Lucas R. Clawson

The present work is a reprint of the illustrated case bound edition of The Civil War in North Carolina: Soldiers' and Civilians' Letters and Diaries, 1861–1865; Volume 2: The Mountains, *first published in 2003 by McFarland.*

LIBRARY OF CONGRESS CATALOGUING-IN-PUBLICATION DATA

The Civil War in North Carolina :
soldiers' and civilians' letters and diaries, 1861–1865.
Volume 2: The Mountains / edited by Christopher M. Watford
p.   cm.
Includes bibliographical references and index.

ISBN 978-0-7864-4595-0
softcover : 50# alkaline paper ∞

1. North Carolina—History—Civil War, 1861–1865—Personal narratives.
2. North Carolina—History—Civil War, 1861–1865—Social aspects.
3. United States—History—Civil War, 1861–1865—Personal narratives.
4. United States—History—Civil War, 1861–1865—Social aspects.
5. Soldiers—North Carolina—Correspondence.
6. Soldiers—North Carolina—Diaries.   7. American letters—North Carolina.
8. American diaries—North Carolina.   I. Watford, Christopher M., 1978–

E464.C484 2009   973.7'82'0922756—dc21   [all vols.: 2002152909]

British Library cataloguing data are available

©2003 Christopher M. Watford. All rights reserved

No part of this book may be reproduced or transmitted in any form or by any means, electronic or mechanical, including photocopying or recording, or by any information storage and retrieval system, without permission in writing from the publisher.

Cover photograph: James Thomas Weaver of Buncombe County rose to the lieutenant colonelcy of the 60th North Carolina (Library of Congress)

Manufactured in the United States of America

*McFarland & Company, Inc., Publishers
Box 611, Jefferson, North Carolina 28640
www.mcfarlandpub.com*

Contents

Acknowledgments vi
Preface vii

Introduction 1

1861 7
1862 33
1863 87
1864 139
1865 187

Appendix 1: Distribution of Letters, Diary Entries, by County and Author 201
Appendix 2: Units with at Least Four Companies from the Mountains 203
Appendix 3: Companies Organized in Mountain Counties 204
Appendix 4: List of Employees at Asheville Armory 208
Appendix 5: Letter Writers and Diarists Herein Who Died in Service 212
Appendix 6: A Poem Composed by Private Harvey Davis 213

Notes 215
Bibliography 241
Index 245

Acknowledgments

Like its predecessor, this volume owes its existence to those state agencies and private and public institutions that have preserved these firsthand documents for posterity so that their words may be heard again, and to those who treasure these words for their honesty, humor, and tragedy.

I wish to first thank the institutional contributors of diary entries, letters, and images: the Rare Book, Manuscript and Special Collections Library at Duke University, Durham; the Southern Historical Collection, Wilson Library, University of North Carolina at Chapel Hill; North Carolina Division of Archives and History, Raleigh; the Library of Congress, Washington, D.C.; the United States Army Miltary History Institute, Carlisle, Pa.; the W. L. Eury Appalachian Collection, Appalachian State University, Boone; Western Carolina University, Cullowhee; Pack Memorial Library, Asheville; and the Smith-McDowell House Museum.

I also wish to thank those organizations which helped to promote the project and suggest sources: the North Carolina Civil War Roundtable, the Davidson County Civil War Roundtable, the North Carolina Collection, the High Point Public Library, the Macon County Historical Society, the Old Buncombe Genealogical Society, the John W. McElory House Museum, and the Zebulon B. Vance Camp #15 Sons of Confederate Veterans, along with the Asbury T. Rogers Chapter, Military Order of the Stars and Bars, Asheville.

My special appreciation goes out to all those individuals who helped make this endeavor much easier: William Best, Laura C. Brown, Bill Butcher, Francis Dedmond, Lisa Harizjan, Steve Massengill, Janie C. Morris, Jeanette Wilson, and the search room and institutional staffs who assisted me.

My continued appreciation goes to all those previously mentioned, and especially to the following individuals who have supported me in very diverse ways: Lucas R. Clawson, to whom this work is dedicated, who provided me with insight, respect, and friendship; Richard Conrad, Lee Crook and Sim Delapp, whose encouragement helped more than they will know; W. Keith Alexander and Mark Bradley, whose advice and comments on the project were invaluable; Lee Sherrill, for providing me with several excellent opportunities; and to all my friends and family, co-workers, and students.

Preface

This work is the second of a four volume series anthologizing letters and diary entries that document the Civil War experiences of soldiers and civilians of the Old North State. Compiling firsthand accounts from citizens of the 29 counties in the Piedmont region of North Carolina, the initial volume commenced by considering several fundamental questions: What were the common experiences of North Carolina soldiers? What types of difficulties did civilians face on the home front, and was the response adequate or appropriate? To what extent did revolts and disorder occur within the state and what was the government's reaction? How did the average soldier or civilian view his or her life under North Carolina's Confederate government, along with the conflict's key military, social, and political figures? Assuming reliability, how can such firsthand accounts offer perspective on North Carolina's ability, or lack of ability, to wage war while at the same time provide for the needs and well-being of its citizens?

I have always had an interest in, perhaps a reverence for, the culture and history of the North Carolina mountains, making use of the wealth of sources that exist to document the region and its role in the Civil War. In fact, it is the letter from Colonel Isaac Erwin Avery to Major S. D. Tate of the Sixth North Carolina Infantry that still offers one of the most intriguing, if not poignant, firsthand accounts from a soldier, North or South. This brief message, from a Morganton businessman turned soldier, continues to be my favorite. Recent scholarship enables the student of the region's history to examine the events of the war, their root causes and consequences without resorting to archaic stereotypes and long-held misconceptions. Historiography on the region is ever-growing, as the regional conflicts in western North Carolina and East Tennessee provide the historian with a way to analyze a fascinating microcosm of the war within the boundaries of two Confederate states.

The indigenous population of the mountains seems to possess a keener knowledge of that region's role in the American Civil War. Indeed, many descendents and scholars share with me their interpretations of "bushwhacking" and the military conduct of key figures such as William Thomas, Harvey Bingham, George W. Kirk, Goldman Bryson, William Walker, David Coleman, George Stoneman, and John B. Palmer. Key locations including Camp Patton, Quallatown, Burnsville, Camp Vance, Camp Mast, the "Globe," and Deep Gap remain in popular memory, if not in physical existence. Within western North Carolina, even the staunchest historians cannot avoid careening into subjectivity at times, especially when discussing events such as the now infamous Shelton Laurel Massacre, the court-martial of Col. William H. Thomas and his conduct during the war, the response of the state to economic, social and political disorder, and, depending on who one asks, the heroism or villainy of Union and Confederate commanders.

As with the first volume of the series, this book is truly written by the men and women who penned these accounts of their daily lives, and events surrounding them, nearly 140 years ago. These primary sources chronicle, in well-nigh narrative form, the experiences of western North Carolina soldiers and civilians during the American Civil War. Once again, it remains my privilege to have collected, transcribed and edited this latest volume of primary sources from the soldiers and civilians of the Old North State. The mountain region of western North Carolina and its people, culture, and history hold a special place in my heart and memory, and perhaps always will.

Christopher M. Watford
February 2003

Introduction

For most scholars and enthusiasts who study the Civil War in North Carolina, the 21 westernmost counties of the mountain region boast one of the most interesting histories for study. Accomplished historians always look upon events and personalities from this theatre of the war to provide a microcosm for the study of the American Civil War as a whole. Indeed, some of the Appalachian region's most preeminent scholars continuously publish and release new studies that document the true society and environment of the North Carolina mountains during the great American conflict. However, the role of legend and oral tradition cannot be discounted, and doubtless remains one of the main contributors to the legacy, and on occasion the mythology, of the Civil War in the mountains.

The mountain region of North Carolina contains elements of a past and heritage distinct from the rest of North Carolina, and it is necessary to examine this past in terms of the Civil War experience. To what extent did the culture of the region shape the way the war developed? How did the circumstances and events of the war shape the region? This work confronts such questions. Other inquiries must also be considered. Were the mountain counties exposed to a different set of circumstances that distinguish them from others of the state? Were the mountains truly the Unionist bastion of popular history, or did local and clannish loyalties contain Unionism to certain townships and communities? What effect did the presence of a large Federal force in East Tennessee have upon the Confederate forces and civilians in the area? Did partisan warfare, guerrilla attacks, and depredations visited upon civilians fuel the concept of "bushwhacking," or was that part of an art perfected long before the war? How did the mountain elite, such as the Averys, Vances, Browns, Silers, and others regard themselves? As the landed gentry and pioneers of an opportunistic wilderness, or the forlorn children of the east who hoped to create the same society in the backcountry as in eastern North Carolina? Finally, how did the mountaineers see themselves? When seeking to resolve such questions, the answers are often vague, hypocritical, and hard to come by. Perhaps discoveries lie within the reports and opinions of those who inhabited the peaks and valleys during the conflict, shielded with a sense of clarity that modern observers are unable to discern.

In many ways the experiences of the soldiers and civilians of the North Carolina mountains were indeed unique. Beginning with the military aspect, cavalry and infantrymen from the mountains provided service on three fronts—the Army of Northern Virginia, the various armies of the west, and in the Department of East Tennessee and Western North Carolina. The region is also well known for furnishing several thousand forces to the Union army, including two full regiments of mounted infantry, along with many companies in the service of Tennessee's loyal forces, and the scores of detachments of Union partisans, scouts, and raiders. In later years, Haywood County could boast about sending men to fight at such various places as Richmond, Virginia; Murfreesboro, Tennessee; Jackson, Mississippi; Sharpsburg, Maryland; Chattanooga, Tennessee; Atlanta, Georgia; Plymouth, North Carolina; Petersburg, Virginia; Mobile, Alabama; and, of course, Waynesville, North Carolina.

Divided loyalties and national politics played out on a much smaller stage in the mountains. The region remained strongly Confederate and provided nearly 190 company-level military units to the Confederate war effort. Many of the region's staunchest anti-secessionists, including one of the most prominent, Zebulon B. Vance, changed their position when President Abraham Lincoln issued a call for troops to put down the rebellion. Unionism, or perhaps more aptly named conservative anti-secessionism, existed alongside stout Confederate patriotism. Unionism in the mountains seems to have had two varieties—passive and active. Most who opposed secession did not volunteer to fight or actively support the Confederacy during the early stages of the war. The arrangement proved adequate, and while some confrontations did occur, they were marginal; however, conscription in the summer of 1862 only irritated the already tenuous situation, and for some, forced an elevation in animosity. Active Unionism and pro-Unionist sentiment seemed organized at local, almost township, level. Indeed, in Watauga County, Boone was called a "secessionist hole," providing many recruits and volunteers for the Confederate army. In a stark contrast, just a few miles to the west, Zionville, a township which borders Tennessee, provided large numbers of its men to serve in two companies: Company A, 13th Tennessee Cavalry, and Company A, 4th Tennessee Infantry. In fact, at Zionville Baptist Church, all veterans buried in the cemetery were part of Mr. Lincoln's army.

Despite active and open Unionism, Confederate civil officials were not driven from office nor were official Union governments established in any part of the mountains. In addition, anti-Confederate sentiment was present in all of North Carolina's regions. Where the mountains stood out, and especially where its pro-Confederate population was concerned, were the seemingly never-ending raids and attacks from within and from across the border. Guerrilla raids and partisans such as George W. Kirk, Goldman Bryson, and the Blaylocks were emboldened by a large Federal presence in East Tennessee following Burnside's seizure of Knoxville. Each of these partisans, whether formally endorsed by the Union Army or not, developed their own system of communication, secure routes of travel, and scouts and spies to further the cause. By far the most successful of these raids was conducted by Colonel Kirk, who attacked Morganton and Camp Vance in July 1864. In addition, Confederate Home Guard responses were often tardy, inappropriate, and ill-coordinated. The responsibility of defending most of western North Carolina after the capture of General Robert Vance fell to Brigadier General J. W. McElroy, whose defense of the region, undeniably a daunting task, was nearly abysmal. Among the most successful Confederate defenders were battalions of Thomas' Legion, the assortment of regular units, and the little-known commander of the Eleventh Home Guard Battalion, Major Harvey Bingham. In retrospect, however, their successes seemed marginal at best, as a result of the lack of a strong Confederate presence in support. While Union partisans and raiders certainly did not function without opposition, they did function with a substantial degree of impunity.

With several pre-established exceptions, the Civil War experience of the mountains offers no major contrast to the rest of North Carolina. The presence of Unionism, civil problems, economic inflation and speculation on the home front, and the contribution of fighting men to the ranks of Lee's Army and forces protecting the eastern part of North Carolina provide a substantial common thread.

While the mountain region is remembered as a bulwark of pro–Union sentiment, it is necessary to take into account that significant opposition to secession and civil war also emanated from the Piedmont. Key Whig politicians such as Jonathan Worth, a mainstay in state politics, controlled many of the region's counties. These conservatives were often vocal advocates for peace. In fact, following the state's declared secession, Worth remarked to his brother, "I do not have a particle of confidence in the wisdom of the new rulers to whom we submit." Worth echoed many of his fellow party members' opinions when he said that the South would be unable to manage the war and the only course left was to "manfully go down with my companions." Quaker opposition is well-documented in nearly four counties of the Piedmont for its pacifism; however, several peace protests of a more secular sort are also well-documented, including an early-war demonstration in Davidson County.

Crime and other depredations emerged in all regions of the state. Upon his inauguration, Governor Vance's office often received reports of atrocities and unjustified violence against citizens. While violence in the mountains remains a matter of fact, the presence of insurrection and civil disorder in the Piedmont region cannot be ignored. The murders, abductions, and violence of the "Randolph insurrection" spread to nearby counties of Moore and Montgomery and risked spreading even further. In addition, "outlaw bands" existed in nearly every North Carolina county, from the famous Lowry Band of Robeson to random groups in Person, Surry, Columbus, and Onslow counties. Efforts to arrest these men and their compatriots often involved vigilantism and cruel tactics inflicted upon innocent civilians including women and children.

The difficulties of the Southern homefront were faced throughout the Confederacy including the North Carolina mountains. Inflation ran rampant throughout the state, creating a problem in the purchase and distribution of consumer goods. Government contractors deprived civilians of leather, salt, and other raw materials, which under normal circumstances would have been relatively abundant. Daily complaints were made to local officials regarding issues of impressment and the confiscation of property, while pleas for tax relief and control of speculation fell upon apathetic ears. The women's raid of Burnsville, in order to make use of government stores reserved for the military, appears in its scope very similar to the famed "Salisbury Bread Riots" and other women's protests throughout the state and country. Conscription also took away the only remaining source of income potential from many families, and throughout the state many civilians sympathized with the deserters. Some even offered direct aid and assistance.

Despite the large contribution of mountain soldiers to the Confederate and Union efforts in the western and Appalachian theatres, large numbers of mountaineers served alongside their fellow citizens in the east. Of the state's regiments, the 25th North Carolina was composed entirely of mountaineers. One company of the 16th North Carolina came from outside the region. In addition, at least four companies from the mountains of western North Carolina formed parts of the 9th (1st Cavalry), 22nd, 26th, 34th, and 37th regiments. In addition, the region contributed 42 companies to service, spread across 11 Confederate brigades.

Most of the historical and social differences center on the region's development and geographic challenges. Prior to the Civil War, the mountain region of North Carolina (for the purpose of this study, composed of 21 of the westernmost counties) was still developing. While internal improvements lagged behind those of the remainder of the state, the region was moving forward in road building and construction of a spur of the NC Railroad. Owing to many geographical and economic reasons, plantation agriculture did not take a firm hold; instead, other diverse industries including livestock grazing, gold and other mineral mining, professional occupations, real estate development, tourism, and retail industries began to explode. While many writers and thinkers have dismissed the region as backward, or the victim of concentrated political power and influence, the natural tendency is to skim over or omit the delayed settlement of the region. For example, New Hanover County developed steadily since the early 1700s, whereas in portions of the mountains, significant settlement, for all practical purposes, began during the 1830s and 1840s. To the established east and Piedmont, the region inevitably seemed less developed. All economies, however, develop and emerge over time.

Geographic isolation and sparse population continue to be cited to explain the different nature of the mountain region. However, the same sparse population and separation of white inhabitants from one another may also be seen in North Carolina's extreme eastern counties. In the east, large landholdings, broad rivers and swamps, and other natural and social barriers prevented widespread population growth. In addition, many of the region's economic and trading partners could be found more often in Tennessee and Kentucky than eastern North Carolina. While the mountain region certainly faced a more challenging topography, it was by no means insurmountable, and as the region developed, such challenges were overcome with more efficiency.

Stereotypical views of how "educated" the citizenry of the mountains were prior to the Civil War prevail unjustly, perhaps fueled by a sense of paternalism. North Carolina, the mountains included, was not an uneducated, backward place with only a handful of intellectuals. Many reasons exist for this exception to the stereotype. First, communication, including written communication, was a method of survival economically speaking. The professional occupations demanded literate workers, and were much more stringent on writing skills than the modern world. Even farmers kept records of crops, receipts, and credit extended to them. Reading and writing were methods of entertainment and information. The letters contained herein demonstrate this concept perfectly. In these letters, the soldiers often inquire about relatives, friends, gossip, and the weather, along with providing information on business and current events. Without modern forms of communication, the arrival of a letter was very exciting! Religion, especially an emphasis on Scripture, played a major part in emphasizing basic comprehension. North Carolina's common schools had been valuable in shaping the state since 1848. In the mountain region, local schools, usually one or two per township, provided basic education during off months in the agricultural year. Of course compulsory attendance laws did not develop until the 1880s, but the majority of students were exposed to some form of rudimentary public education, in addition to family-based instruction prior to the Civil War. Some soldiers learned to read and write in service from other soldiers who were literate. In Company A of the 37th Regiment, Calvin Childers often helped his messmate Thornton Sexton compose letters home. After a falling out between the two, Sexton was, judging by the grammar and spelling and personal admission, forced to write his own letters. Numerous colleges, academies, and common schools invested in readers and other literary instructional texts. In fact, a popular novel among students and the Southern aristocracy was Victor Hugo's *Les Misérables*.

No official surveys have analyzed literacy rates in the region as a whole, but preliminary studies conducted for this work judged a sample of over 500 inhabitants between the ages of 18 and 50 in Ashe, Mitchell, Burke, Buncombe, and Haywood counties, with the conclusion that 38 percent of the population was unable to read or write. The most literate county population in the state—Watauga, at well over 90 percent—was not included in this study. The reader and student should keep in mind that literacy has different definitions over the course of time. While no typical citizen could be expected to quote Homer, Shakespeare, or contemporary writers, the typical citizen did possess the ability to communicate and understand in a written fashion.

For a soldier in North Carolina, a letter from home was a welcome sight. It brought news of home, information about crop prices, encouraging words, truths, an escape from the fighting for a few minutes, a break in the monotony and boredom, and hope. Soldiers on any side in any war read the same letter from home repeatedly. For a civilian at home, the letters provide a reassurance that their loved one is still alive. Corresponding with other friends and relatives throughout the county, region, state, or even country, offered valuable information, and sometimes very entertaining speculation and reports of scandal and rumor.

While some letters give in to raw, unending emotion, most letters to family and friends possess a certain formality, but often some facts were obscured, omitted, or overembellished. In diary entries, the notes and inscriptions that were intended to remain private reveal daily life and events in the army. Sometimes the entry is short, just a few summative lines for the day. Despite a desire to continue exploring the soldier's mindset, the reader and scholar must remember that picket duty, days in camp or in the field, and endless marching became second nature to the men in service. Daily chores and responsibilities also became automatic for civilians; therefore, such happenings could be easily dismissed by their performers as unworthy of note.

What is important, though, is that these documents do survive to a large extent. Many of the letters come from larger collections. For example, the dozen letters of the Love family from Henderson County are just the tip of the iceberg; nearly 115 surviving letters have been deposited in two major archives. While it is believed that each North Carolina soldier sat for at least one picture, there is no end to the number of letters that could be written during the course of four years. If a soldier wrote one letter or diary entry everyday, that would total approximately 1,460 pieces. If each soldier wrote at that pace, the total letters from soldiers alone could possibly total 182,500,000. This, of course, is simply multiplication, but it does suggest the large body of information that exists for the state of North Carolina.

The mountain region of North Carolina, for purposes of this book, includes Allegheny, Ashe, Buncombe, Burke, Caldwell, Cherokee, Clay, Haywood, Henderson, Jackson, McDowell, Macon, Madison, Mitchell, Polk, Rutherford, Surry, Transylvania, Watauga, Wilkes and Yancey. Eighty-one different men and women, soldiers and civilians, from varied and diverse backgrounds, recorded brief glimpses of their lives in writing. Their simple words, though now faded with age, document their struggles to understand their roles, their lives, and the events in which they found themselves playing a part.

1861

They tore up the flag of the U.S. & made a new one with seven stars, 2 red & white each Stripes and dropt the glorious old Eagle. It makes the heart sad to see & dwell on it.
> —Mr. William J. Brown, Asheville, Buncombe County, 29 April 1861

I didn't like much to see all the boys go off but I know that it couldn't be helpt and so I took it very easy, but there is a good many yet. There would have to be a bust up of some kined to take all the boys out of henderson.
> —C. P. Gash, Hendersonville, Henderson County, 5 June 1861

We have been in no fights yet, neither am I able to tell you when we will. There has been heavy firing heard in the direction of Washington city yesterday and today.
> —Private William H. Proffit, "The Wilkes Valley Guards," Company B, 1st Regiment North Carolina State Troops, Ship's Point, Virginia, 20 September 1861

We have very cold weather at this time & our men being thinly clad suffer much on picket. We have 120 of the regiment sick and a death about once a week. I am enjoying fine health & am quite comfortable.
> —Major James Byron Gordon, 9th Regiment North Carolina Troops (1st N.C. Cavalry Regiment), Centreville, Virginia, 3 December 1861.

1. April 26, 1861

Mr. William John Brown, Asheville, Buncombe County, letter to his son, James E. Brown, Canterbury, New Zealand. Source: William Brown Papers (2603), Southern Historical Collection, Wilson Library, University of North Carolina at Chapel Hill. (Part of multiple-day letter.)

Many of the families of western North Carolina descend from Pennsylvanians who migrated down the Great Wagon Road and settled in the mountains. One such family, the Browns of Buncombe County, originally from Pennsylvania, were among the most extensive landowners in western North Carolina. The Browns quickly became friends with the Vance family. William John Brown and his wife had three sons: John E., William Caleb, and Samuel. John and William had gone to California during the gold rush of 1849. Afterwards, John continued his travels and went to New Zealand, while William returned home to a law partnership with Zebulon Vance. Samuel Brown worked as a surveyor, and even coached Vance on using pistols when Zeb was challenged to a duel.[1] In this letter, which is only an excerpt from eleven typewritten pages, William talked about his two other sons enlisting in the "Rough and Ready Guards," the new Confederate flag, the breakup of the family, and the Baltimore Riots.

Samuel Brown was one of William Brown's sons who died while in Confederate service. (Library of Congress.)

> 26th April '61
> My Son
> Just think of this "if ever it reaches you" is very probably the last letter you will receive from any of us & from the old mansion, as citizens of these United States of America. On yesterday, Zeb, Will and Sam joined the vol company for good. In a few days, the Legislature meets to pass a law calling a convention to pass an ordinance dissolving our connection with the once happy & prosperous, but now broken, Union. They tore up the flag of the U.S. & made a new one with seven stars, 2 red & white each Stripes and dropt the glorious old Eagle. It makes the heart sad to see & dwell on it. When you left us in March, 1849, we were a whole family & I distinctly remember your poor dear Ma saying at the Breakfast Table as we sat around it, "Pa, this is most likely the last meal & time we shall all eat together or be seated at our own table again." She & I cast our eyes around the group & alas how true it was. Your poor dear Ma & Mary are lying in the cold & silent tomb, the

· 1861 ·

Despite the opinions of Unionists such as William Brown, these men volunteered for Confederate service in Asheville during the summer of 1861. (Pack Memorial Library, Asheville, N.C.)

eldest and youngest. Elizabeth in Tennessee. You in a far off & foreign land. Will & Samuel gone to prepare to battle for one section of the country vs the other section & that section contains all our blood relatives save our four selves. It is awful. It makes my heart ache to contemplate it as I sit in a large & silent house alone writing these few additional lines. I left W. & S. in town last evening drilling. They leave in a few days for Va or Md. I had a letter from Z. yesterday. Her & Ed were quite unwell and all excitement & confusion. Tennessee has tendered 50000 men to Va to aid her & to protect the South vs the Black Republicans & Lincoln. It is only the beginning, where it is to end no one knows. The Md troops and NY troops had a fight NE of Annapolis a few days ago. The NY tried to slip around to Washington City as they could not go through by R. Road to Baltimore. The Marylanders had burnt the RR ferry boat at the time & tore up the bridges to keep the NY troops back. They then tried to go around & the Md's got wind of it, met & defeated them driving them back. You will see the accounts in the N.Y. papers before you get this. S & W again write in love to you. Adieu & accept of this from a troubled & affectionate father. I have sent this by Lexington, Ky to get it out. The mail cant go by Washington City & North. Lincoln has ordered them stopd.

W. J. B.

2. May 23, 1861

Corporal Lewis Warlick, "The Burke Rifles," Company G, 1st Regiment N.C. Volunteers, letter to Laura C. McGimsey,

Pleasant Hill, Burke County, North Carolina. Source: Laura C. McGimsey Papers (2680), Southern Historical Collection, Wilson Library, University of North Carolina at Chapel Hill.

John Lewis Warlick, a 27-year-old Table Rock farmer, volunteered for service at Morganton on April 18, 1861. Warlick was mustered in as a corporal in the "Burke Rifles," the first volunteer company to leave Burke County. When the First North Carolina Volunteers organized, the Rifles were mustered in as Company G.[2] Throughout his term of service, Warlick maintained a regular correspondence with his sweetheart, Laura Cornelia (Corry) McGimsey, who lived at Pleasant Hill. The large cities of Richmond and Petersburg must have been an intimidating sight for a simple farmer from the mountains such as Warlick.

> In Camp near Richmond Va
> Dearest Cornelia;
> I have not received but one letter from you since I left home. Why is it? I would like very much to hear from you weekly. I have written you every week since I left with the exception of the last. We left Raleigh on the 21st Inst., and arrived here, in Camp, Yesterday morning about 3. On our way to this place at every turn out and depot we were met by large crowds and especially by the ladies, who presented us with many boquets, cakes, etc. Richmond is a beautiful city it is splendidly layed of streets paved, and many superb buildings. I have to laugh at part of our company when they get into a city. They look at every thing and in every direction and their fingers pointed at every curiosity, which their eyes may behold; it shows at once they never traveled a great ways from their native place. There is now in the vicinity of Richmond about fifteen thousand troops. The 2nd regiment of Louisiana left this morning for Yorktown by orders from the Gen.
>
> Our regiment (so says report) also two others from S. C. will leave for the above named place tomorrow. It is thought that, that place will be invaded shortly. Men women and children in this State are alive with excitement. Everybody is under arms and it seems they are anxious for the contest. It will be impossible for the enemy to entrap this State and keep their ground because the South has men that will defend their rights or die in the attempt. I think we have force strong enough to drive back a powerful enemy. There is now over a hundred thousand troops in the state ready to move at a moments warning to any place which they may be called to.
>
> The city of Petersburg has sent out ten companys and are getting up two others; it is not who shall go to war but who it is will stay at home. I was sorry to leave two of our company in Raleigh sick one of them was G. W. Anthony,[3] he has Catarrhal Fever, he was left in the hospital; but one of our officers made arrangements before he left to have him taken to a private house where he will be well taken care of. Cornelia, it is only about a month since I saw you and it seems to me to have been a much longer time than that.
>
> Often have I thought of the many happy hours we have spent in each others company; shall we be spared to meet again? I hope and trust we will, if that will be granted us. What a happy time that will be, it will be happiness beyond expression to make each other happy during life. I feel there is no one beside you who could confer upon me happiness and a peaceful life, [and my] devotion for you never changes. It is fixed firm and I hope yours for me is the same. Give my best wishes to Puss, Susan, Hattie[4] and accept the largest portion for yourself.
>
> Your Devoted Lover
> Lewis
>
> Cornelia I wish you to write to me often

Robert B. Vance was a prominent Asheville merchant. Two years after writing the letter quoted on this page and the next, Vance became a successful regimental commmander, and brigadier general in charge of western North Carolina. (North Carolina Division of Archives and History.)

do not wait to get a letter from me to answer but sit down and write every week for you do not know how pleased I am to receive an epistle with your signature.

PS Direct to Richmond in care of Capt. C. M. Avery[5]

3. May 28, 1861

Robert Brank Vance, Asheville, Buncombe County, letter to brother, Captain Zebulon B. Vance, "The Rough and Ready Guards," Company F, 4th N.C. Volunteers. Source: Governor's Papers (Zebulon Vance), North Carolina Division of Archives and History.

David Vance II and his wife, Mira Margaret Baird Vance, would raise two of the most dominant political figures in western North Carolina history. Public service was synonymous with the name Vance in 1860. Robert Brank Vance, the oldest of the Vance brothers, was born in 1828 and named after his uncle, who had been killed in a duel in 1827. Robert Vance was a successful Asheville merchant, but was overshadowed by his dynamic little brother, Congressman Zebulon Vance.[6] On May 6, 1861, Robert's brother, Zeb, had taken the "Rough and Ready Guards" to Statesville and they continued on to Raleigh. The company reached the capital city on May 25, 1861. Robert wrote to his little brother about several new companies forming in the mountain region, as well as a rumor about an unruly soldier.

Asheville NoCa
May 28th 1861

I wrote you Sunday to Weldon & directed Hattie's letter there also. If you wish those letters you can direct PM at Weldon to return them to Raleigh. We did not know that you were to remain in Raleigh any length of time. But now we hear thro Dr Hilliard that you, Love, Peek, Shipp, & McElroy[7] await the arrival of the troops here, including the McDowell & Polk Co to form a Regiment. I suppose this is all correct. Dr. H said you were urgent for the companies to go on for the purpose named. Hyman & Hilliard do not agree in their statements. Hilliard says Hyman made the impression along the route that no more

Volunteers would be accepted—that men must now join the State troops of N. C. or be drafted. Hilliard says they still take them for 12 months. Who is right? We learn here that Harkins declined to join your company, and to day it is reported that he was trying secretly to raise a mutiny in your camp. Is this all so? I trust not for decency's sake, and for the honor of old Buncombe!

The Mail has come and brought your letter. There never was a baser falsehood than that Jos Randal's wife has nothing to eat. She has shoes 2 or 3 dresses and plenty to eat and so with every man's wife left behind. Charge the men to believe no lie, for I am here and I say that none shall suffer. Newton Pattons wife was here to day. I gave her Bacon & flour. I particularly now want you to send to Weldon for the letter I wrote you. That has details in full about these matters & that before I knew of Harkins miserable conduct. He is an ass and a scoundrel and if I were you he should not disgrace my company. I will try and write you often. Wm Brown[8] will leave in a few days and I will send the recruits.

Robert B. Vance

4. June 1, 1861

Captain Clarke Moulton Avery, "The Burke Rifles," Company G, 1st Regiment N.C. Volunteers, letter to wife, Lizzie Avery, Burke County, N.C. Source: Edward G. Phifer Collection (1368), North Carolina Division of Archives and History.

Lewis Warlick and the "Burke Rifles" were under the command of Captain Clark Moulton Avery, a substantial planter, and a member of one of Morganton's elite families that produced a state Supreme Court justice, and four Confederate officers, two of whom would not survive the war. Clark Moulton was born in 1819 to Isaac and Harriet Erwin Avery, and was the grandson of Waightsill Avery. Moulton grew up in Swan's Pond, Burke County, and graduated from the University of North Carolina in 1839. In 1860, Clark Moulton lived on a 900-acre plantation along with his wife Elizabeth Walton Avery, who he married on June 23, 1841. They had nine children: Louise, Martha, Harriet, Adelide, Clara, Mary, Isaac, Lizzie, and Moulton W.[9] In this letter, Captain Avery described the conditions on the peninsula for the 1st N.C. Volunteers, who participated in the war's first major action at Bethel, Virginia, on June 10, 1861.

Yorktown
1st June 1861

My Dearest Lizzie,

I failed to write yesterday for the fact that we were ordered to prepare several days provisions and march at 5 o'clock in the direction of Newport News, a point on the bay about twenty one miles from this point. The enemy have landed troops there and are engaged in throwing up breastworks. We started and marched five miles and were overtaken by an order to march back into Camp. I cannot give you any idea of what will be our future movements.

Col. Magruder is in command of this brigade. He does not give satisfaction. He ranks our Col. Our Col[10] is universally esteemed and we all have the utmost confidence in him also our other field officers. I had no idea of the hardships of seniority. If, however, I had known that, I could not have been deferred from the discharge of duty. The greatest trouble is to keep our persons clean. John Woodard is doing his whole duty we could not get on without him. I wish you could make me at least two pair of drawers and ask some of our friends to assist you in sending them to me. We have a bad day to have washing done and it has been so dry that the dirt is almost suffocating.

I was delighted to receive the joyous letter from my dear little Daughters also from my father. I hope this will find you my dear Lizzie in enjoyment of improved health. Should you become weak from nursing do go to the Doct and have some bitters made and take them as you would do if I were at HOME (that precious word) to urge it upon you. I do fear the debilitating effect of warm weather on you. Say to William Avery "Harrison is now in camp and will be able for duty tomorrow." I was glad to hear through Pa's letter that cousin J. Avery was likely to visit us here.

At present my men are all able for duty and quite cheerful under the many hardships incident to a soldier's life. I regret we could not remain at Richmond. We were comfortably situated and I think in a much more healthy locality. The days here are awful hot but the nights so far have been cool. This old Town is entirely depopulated and the country below on the Bay is rapidly becoming so. The females everywhere are fleeing at the approach of Lincoln's army.

I wish to God I could once more behold your lovely face and the cheerful countenances of my dear little Miss, but trusting that a kind providence may yet return me to you all. I bear my lot with becoming manliness. It is reported that federal troops have been landed in N.C. soil. If this is so I would like to be there to defend it.

Kiss my dear children all, give my love to my friends & also to my negroes. Tel the negroes I think of them often and only hope that I and they may be spared to meet once at Magnolia to recount on my past the incidents of my travel and receive from you a good account of their deportment towards you. Tell Martha to write we giving all the news even the most trivial to dear father. Now May the choicest blessings God almighty rest your head is the prayer of your own devoted Husband.
Moulton

5. June 5, 1861

Addie Patton, Pigeon Valley, letter to her sister, Mary A. Gash. Source: Mary Gash Papers (59), Private Manuscripts Collection, North Carolina Division of Archives and History. (Excerpted.)

Addie Gash was born in Henderson County (the part that became Transylvania) on September 30, 1831. She belonged to the prominent Gash family of western North Carolina which spanned several counties. Their relatives and cousins were among the widespread upper middle class of the mountains: the Silers of Macon County, Carpenters of Madison, and Osbornes of Haywood. The family also maintained a regular correspondence with relatives in Missouri. Addie married her husband, Eli Patton of Buncombe County, prior to 1861.[11] This correspondence between sisters provides an interesting look at the early stages of the war, as well as concerns about family and their spiritual health.

Pigeon Valley
June 5th 1861
My Dear Sister
Brother Jules letter was received a few days since and I have been in great trouble every since—though I thought my troubles were great enough before when I wrote last. I thought you would be in less danger than we of the war but have learned through the papers that I was very much mistaken and Brothers letter still confirmed my belief and now I write to you instead of him for fear he will be killed before this letter reaches you. If he is living tell him to prepare for death not only with arms but the heart more particularly. Brother Roland[12] has volunteered and many

others. Mr. Lane is their captain but the company is not made up yet and some think it will not be but I think it will. One company has gone from Haywood and another will start in a few days. Mr. L is the 3rd. One has gone from Franklin, one from Jackson, 2 from Buncombe and one has gone from Henderson. Jule Gash[13] went from M with Mr. Ship. We cant help what is past but I wish you had never gone, and that brother had remained with us and then I would like to have aunt Eliza and all her children with us. Tell them if they think they can come safely to gather up and come anyway and you and Brother can come with them.

We cannot talk or think of anything but war, but we must not forget to pray. There is more power in prayer with those cannons and guns therefore we should be engaged all the time. If Brother was only a Christian I could feel much more reconciled to hear of him falling on the battle field but how can I bear it just as it is and how many souls in the same condition and many of them my relations and friends, God save them is my prayer.

I am glad to hear that you are no worse and hope to hear that you are improving. Take good care of yourself, be prudent, take exercise as much as possible smoke Mullen. That is Cousin Kate's medicine. Put it in your whiskey and boil it then use a table spoon 3 or 4 times per day. Make mullen syrup in candy for your cough. Keep your bowels regular, use cream of tarter if you will take nothing stronger. Cousin Kate is poorly but not confined to her bed.

I was at Franklin about that time the friends were generally well. The volunteers left while I was there. Cousins Jesse and Willie Siler and three Robinson boys went. It was a very serious time with mothers, fathers, sisters and brothers and friends in general. Cousin Rufus went to Texas just before the war and they have not heard from him in 7 weeks. Father is waiting on me and I must close. Excuse this paper as I could not find any other when I commenced. Write to me as soon as this is received and tell brother to write as long as he lives for that may not be long. Tell him his letter was good except one word that liked to have spoiled it which he must not use any more. Give my love to cousin Pauline and all my relations. Sister trust in God and he will bring us out more than conquerors.

Your sincere and affectionate sister
Addie

6. June 22, 1861

C. P. Gash, French Broad, Henderson County, to cousin Mary A. Gash, Buncombe County, North Carolina. Source: Mary Gash Papers (59), Private Manuscripts Collection, North Carolina Division of Archives and History.

Not only was the Gash family prominent in western North Carolina, but they had relatives as far away as Missouri. C. P. Gash was born in either Henderson or Buncombe County and moved to Missouri sometime prior to November 28, 1864, when he was married in Clay County, Missouri. Gash returned home for months at a time,[14] and during the early stages of the war, he commented on young men going into service, sickness, a gentleman his cousin once admired, and other relations.

French Broad
NC June 22th 1861
Dear Cousin

This evening while I am resting my mind from studying, I seat myself to write a few lines to you. I have been anxious to hear from you for sometime and could not hear. I will tell you before I commence that you need not expect to hear anything of importance, for that is what I cannot write, but I will tell you a few things concerning home. We are all well, and enjoying ourselves finely. We are going to school, and have not much time to play. I didn't like much to see all the boys go off but I know that it couldn't be helpt and so I took it very easy, but there is a good many yet. There would have to be a bust up of some kined to take all the boys out of henderson.

There has been a great deal of sickness in this neighborhood this spring. Miss Hawkins died last week. Well Love you might have been here this summer. Your sweetheart came down here to go a fishing. We had a great deal of fun, but it was not as fun to me as the rest for I could not catch anything but mud turtles, but when I fish on dry land I am going to do better than that. You had better believe you must write and tell me if you have fallen in love with my Missouri gentleman. I think that it is a bad time to marry but they are uniting in the bonds of wedlock just as soon as war.

Arthur has just come from uncle Johns. They are all well. Aunt Lou is very anxious to hear from you. She wants you to write to her. She hasn't heard anything from you since you left Georgia. Give any love to all of my relations, and more particularly to cousin Lou, Sort and Arthur sends their love to you. Cousin Mollie is up here going to school.

I recon you heard that Bud is married. They had a big time. Your old sweet heart was one of the waiters. I will tell you he looked as slick as a peeled onion. He started to war, but his health failed and he could not go, and I expect he was sorter glad of it, but I must not talk that way about him. Excuse my bad penmanship, write soon,

Your cousin,
C. P. Gash

7. July 4, 1861

Private Calvin Leach, "The Wilkes Valley Guards," Company B, 1st Regiment N.C. State Troops, diary entry. Source: Diary of Calvin Leach, Calvin Leach Papers (1875-z), Southern Historical Collection, Wilson Library, University of North Carolina at Chapel Hill.

Wilkes County provided hundreds of recruits to the war effort in 1861. One of those recruits was Calvin Leach. He was born in 1843 to Daniel and Rebecca Leach of Wilkes County, North Carolina. On July 1, 1861, Calvin, the oldest of seven children, volunteered for service at age 19.[15] Private Leach joined this company in late June and was present to witness all the Independence Day festivities in Warrenton.

> This memorable day long hailed by the citizens of the "United States" was spent with grate pleasure to me. The noble citizens of Warren co & town provided the soldiers with an excellent dinner. Col Stokes rigiment[16] marched out to and through town. The tables was sat close to the court house. The court house was occupied by the ladies. I then ate a hearty dinner. The soldiers then made a long ring before the court house dome. Prayer by Rev. J. B. Solomon. Then speeches by Col Stokes, Ranson, Cheeck Gordon etc. Then went to the Academy. March around jentlemen & ladies of the town came also. Then marched back to the camp. This was a pleasant day to me and will long be remembered by me on behalf of the noble citizens of Warrenton and surrounding county.

8. July 25, 1861

Laura G. McGimsey, Pleasant Hill, Burke County, letter to Private Lewis Warlick, "The Burke Rifles," Company G, 1st Regiment N.C. Volunteers. Source: Laura

C. McGimsey Papers (2680), Southern Historical Collection, Wilson Library, University of North Carolina at Chapel Hill.

The Warlick brothers of Burke County survived their first battle at Bethel, Virginia, on June 10, 1861. In the following letter, Cornelia McGimsey talked about times back at home with her friends and family. Cornelia was raised by her much older step-brother, John Wakefield. Cornelia described several antics which the younger folks used to entertain themselves, relations with William Avery, and her cousins from the Alexander family.

>Pleasant Hill, N. C. July 25th 1861
My dear, dear Friend,
>   Day before yesterday I returned home from Canoe creek, Hattie Jewell and I went down to Canoe Hill Last Friday evening. We stopped at Theodore's, and Matilda Roderick went with us; when we arrived at Mr. Averys we found Puss and Laura Alexander there and to our great joy the old folks were not at home. There was eight girls, and not a gentleman on the place if we didn't have some fun Oh! Hush. Hattie Jewell and Puss Alexander were the life of the crowd. Hattie first acted like one of the old South mountain women come to <u>town</u> to sell eggs, berries, etc. She said her husband had gone to the war, and she was left alone she seemed to be in great distress, about him; but while she was talking who should step in but her husband home from the war. Such a meeting and so much joy I never saw you cant imagine how they did take on. Hattie then went out and put on Mr. Avery's coat, hat and a mustache, of soot. She came in and introduced herself as Mr. Port Warlick just from Yorktown, you ought to seen us rejoicing over him, We soon began to interrogate him about those left behind we ask if you ever said anything about the girls in the camp. She said no that you did not care a red cent for any of us and that you had all sort of fun over our letters, she said some rich things about you sure, but time will not permit me to tell you all. I think it would take about a week to tell you all that was said. You know I could never write it. I was afraid to look at the carpet next morning I expected to see it threadbare; but as luck would have it there was no holes in it. Liz Parks and Jane Sisk came down Saturday evening we all stayed at uncle Bobs that night, I cant tell you what all we did Saturday night, suffice it to say we had a fine time. Hattie Jewell came home Sunday her <u>Sweetheart</u> from S. C. (Mr. Nichols) came up Saturday and of course she had to go home with him. Tell Port he had better keep awake and write fast or Mr. Nichols will slay him. I dont want him to do that for I would hate so much for Hattie to go back to S. Carolina. Will Avery came out to uncle Bobs to call on us Sunday you know it is a treat to have a gentleman call on a lady <u>now a days</u> for they are as scarce as beggars dimes. Will kept me posted in news while I was down there and I have come to the conclusion that he is right clever after all. What think you?—Laura Avery had a beau while I was down there. I suppose you have seen him. The Rev. Mr Mason I think he is very nice and very polite indeed. Aunt Sophie requested me to give you her best wishes and kind regards and to tell you that she was fattening a pig and raising a heap of chickens said she intended to give her friends and relatives a big dinner when they come home from the war.
>   Since I commenced writing I received a letter from you dated July18th. You cant imagine how glad I was to see it I was getting uneasy about you as I had not heard from you for a few days you are not as well pleased to receive a letter from me, as I am to get one from you I know, if you could see me taking on when I get a letter from you you would think me crazy sure enough. You are

not good at guessing J C B sends all his letters to the post office he is an ardent admirer of Miss Hatties Camp Bragg is near Suffolk Va my letter was from one of my Buncombe friends who belong to Capt. Vances company. Tell John Suddreth if he dont treat Sue better I intend to scratch him off my book I know he could have written her ere this I dont suppose he cares a straw for my friendship, but I might say something in his favor. Sue told me she didnt intend to write to him until she received a letter from him. I heard Hattie Avery speaking of Mr. Haynes when I was there I think she said he had measles the last she heard from him I was sorry to hear of H Avery and S Wakefield being in the hospital I do hope they will get well soon it seems like Harrison is unfortunate this is two spells of sickness he has had. I will tell Hattie that Port is a candidate for County Court clerk she surely will exert her influence in his behalf I fear he will not be elected as so many seems to be tied to Kincaid he did not announce himself soon enough! We have heard of a hard and bloody battle at Manassas Junction great loss of life on both sides the confederates whipped the Yankees and run them to Hampton. It is stated that our men got their big cannon the loss, on our side is over five thousand. Col Fisher was killed and nearly all his Regt there is not enough left to form one complete Company Jo and Sam Brown belonged to that Regt and many others from about here. Surely old Abe will see that he never can subjugate the South. I do hope they will be compelled to acknowledge the independence of the Southern Confederacy soon, and that we may conquer a speedy peace. I believe it is about three months now since you left Morganton surely it has been the longest three months that ever was; it seems to me to have been six and just to think you cant come home for three months more, who knows, but before that time you may be killed I know we ought to be very thankful that your lives have been spared, while so many have fallen in Battle Surely the Lord will have mercy upon us, and avert the dire calamity I hope He will incline his ear to our humble petitions and save us from destructive war. Suppose I turn over and change the subject.

We have had very little sickness in our neighborhood this summer Mr James Hunter is sick now he has been confined about a week I do not know whether he has fever or not, as he has not sent for a physician yet. I think Mary Ann McGimseys health is improving some, but very slowly. Have you ever been sick since you left home. I know that you never have written to me that you had been sick; does your weak eye ever pain you now, I was fearful it would hurt your eyes to be exposed to the sun so much. I have heard you say that you had weak eyes. What have you done with my old ugly type you surely have not kept it all this time I know if I had been you I would have disposed of the ugly thing long ago How many in camp have you showed it too? I know even one that would look at it is it not so. Uncle John has gone fishing this evening and will not come back tonight Puss and I will have to stay by ourselves unless some one comes to stay with us. We are great soldiers not afraid to stay alone but I am inclined to think we are like most braggarts the greatest soldiers in time of peace. I expect you will be sadly disappointed when you see this letter, you will think you are getting some news of interest; but it all amounts to very little, judging you by myself I thought you would be pleased to hear any thing that comes from Burke. You gentlemen will not condescend to write such simple things as we silly girls do. You will not write any thing short of a battle or somebody being sick or killed. I assure you the

9. August 14, 1861

Major James B. Gordon, 1st N.C. Cavalry Regiment (9th N.C. State Troops), letter to his mother, Wilkesboro, Wilkes County, North Carolina. Source: James G. Hackett Papers (112), Private Manuscripts Collection, North Carolina Division of Archives and History, Raleigh, N.C.

Trade and commerce in the North Carolina mountains were anchored by three cities: Asheville, Morganton, and Wilkesboro. One of Wilkesboro's professionals, attorney James Byron Gordon, became a major in the First North Carolina Cavalry on May 16, 1861, after a brief period commanding a volunteer company raised by Montfort S. Stokes which became Company B, 1st N.C. Troops.[17] Gordon and the 1st Cavalry were posted in Ridgeway, Northampton County, North Carolina, at a camp of instruction designed for cavalry training. Gordon described his relationship with his commanding officer, Colonel Robert Ransom, and a visit to a nearby lady's home.

James Byron Gordon, a prominent citizen of Wilkes County, left the "Valley Guards" for a commission in the cavalry. (Library of Congress.)

Camp Beauregard
Augt 14th 1861

My Dear Mother,

It has been some time since I wrote to you. I have been changing my location and am at last settled down for a few weeks. I come into this camp Regularly on Saturday last and I am very well satisfied and pleased. Though it was very hard for me to give up my old company. I regret so much to leave Allen[18] believing that I could be of great service to him in many ways, But I find he is doing very well and succeeding in commanding the company finely. I believe the Regt left Richmond on Thursday. I expect there is some hard work before them but hope they may be equal to the task.

My present position is one of more responsibility and danger than the former one, but I feel assured of my

most simple thing that occurs in your camp would be interesting to me. Your letter is before me now the only fault I can find with it there is not enough of it; but do not trouble yourself for my gratification. I am very glad to receive a letter from you regardless of length. Laura Avery told me that she was going to write to Port and give him the news. I suppose she will keep him well posted in the news and times in Burke. We all wrote to Charly McGimsey from Canoe Hill. Tell him he must answer every one that wrote to him I thought I would finish out this page, but I fear you will be wearied before you get this much read and I concluded to not write any more this time. Please do do do write soon and often

to your unchanging friend
Cornelia

determination to discharge the duty required of me. The Colonel of this Regt is a true military man,[19] gallant & generous and we are getting along finely. The Col and myself had a delightful ride into the country yesterday to call on the wives of some of the officers. If you had seen the rappid hedlong pace ... you had thought we could have charged any battery. He is a splendid rider and you know I am. It is understood that as Cavalry officers we ride any way only in a race. I think there is more danger of our men getting their necks broken than being Killed. I have received two letters from Foster since I have a few here the last one yesterday. Tell him I will write him to morrow. Tell him also to say to Crumpler that taken the corn will do well to feed & to have all the hogs that will do to fatten up till about the 1st of September will be the usual time. I will write more freely in regard to it in a day or two. I am glad you have heard from Tom. Write me on how I shall direct a letter to find him. Could you send Miss Cunninghams letter to me that I may form some idea of her. Have you heard from Ann lately. Give my love to all the relatives. Tell Ellen & Octavia to write to me. How are Carrie and the Baby? Tell Mr. Brown that he must keep up his spirits & be ready to hear the news of peace after the Cavalry regt gets into a fight.

     Your Son,
     James
Direct your letters to Ridgeway, N. C.

10. August 23, 1861

Private Walter L. Jones, Company A, 22nd Regiment N.C. Troops (12th N.C. Volunteers), letter to his father, Edmund Jones, Clover Hill, Happy Valley, Caldwell County, N.C. Source: Edmund Jones Papers (3543), Southern Historical Col-

Despite a speech impediment, Hamilton "Allen" Brown commanded his company successfully, eventually rising to command of the First Regiment. (North Carolina Division of Archives and History.)

lection, Wilson Library, University of North Carolina at Chapel Hill.

 State Senator and prominent Caldwell County citizen Edmund W. Jones and his wife, Sophia Davenport Jones, had several children: William Davenport, John Thomas, Walter L., Edward L., Preston Harper (died in 1856 after falling down a well), and Mary. Walter or "Wat" Jones resided in Caldwell County prior to volunteering for service at eighteen on April 30, 1861. The first letter from the Jones boys finds Wat Jones in his unit, the 12th

N.C. Volunteers (later the 22nd N.C. Troops), part of the force defending the Southern side of the Potomac.[20]

> Camp Bee Aquia Creek Aug 23
> Dear Father
> I would have written to you before but the mails all so uncertain that it is doubtful that you would have got it or not. There is no certain regular mail to this place. We are all well and in fine spirits and are spoiling for a fight. We are stationed about three miles from the Potomac river and some of our batteries firing at the Yankee vessels every day or two when they venture too far. We have the North Point gun which was taken at Manassas. They threw two shells on board the Pawnee with her yesterday and killed several. We are about fifteen thousand strong here under the command of General Holmes[21] of North Carolina. I saw him today and he is a very hard looking case it would make the Yankees men [afraid] to look at him. We were inspected by him this morning and he sayed our was a very fine company indeed. We had also another compliment paid us the other day by the Col of the Second Georgia regiment. He sayed ours was the best drilled company in the skirmish drill he had ever seen. We drill it entirely by the bugle. When we left Richmond we expected to be in a fight before night and we heard they were fighting at that time at the mouth of this creek and you may imagine how badly we were disapointed when we arrived to hear that there had been but a few shots fired at the vessels. I have no idea how long we will stay here or anything about the movements of the troops as we have not seen a paper since I got here. We are encamped in a beautiful place on the top a young mountain and can see the river and the yankees too sometimes that is their vessels.
> We are off about a mile from any other regiment and it is found to be a healthy place although there is a good deal of sickness moving through the troops on account of the marshes but there is no other kind of sickness as I know of. There are five North Carolina regiments at this place. Col Tew and Col. Stokes among the number.[22] We live pretty hard now. I tell you we have not had a mouthfull of bacon in two weeks but live entirely on fresh beef without salt as we cannot get it any where but will weigh nearly 175 pounds and every man in the company looks better than they did when we left home. If you do not hear from me as often as you expect you must not imagine there is any thing the matter with me as it is very seldom we can get the chance to send letters off from here.
> How are all of the friends in the Valley and your own health and little Marys? I think of her fifty times a day and would give any thing to see her. Kiss her for me and tell her she must not forget brother Wat. Give my love to Will and Mary and tell them I would like to hear from them and know how they are navigating. I suppose they stay at Clover Hill most of the time. I hear that Coot[23] has got entirely well. Give him my love and telll him he must make haste and get big enough to fight the Yankees. Also give my love to aunt Connie and uncle Finley and all of the rest who ask about me. Send love to all.
> Your affectionate Son
> Wat
> PS Write soon and direct to Richmond VA Care Col. Pettigrew Co A 12th Reg N.C. Vols.

11. August 31, 1861

First Lieutenant John T. Jones, Company I, 26th Regiment N.C. Troops, letter to his father, Edmund Jones, Clover Hill, Happy Valley, Caldwell County, N.C. Source: Edmund Jones Papers (3543),

Southern Historical Collection, Wilson Library, University of North Carolina at Chapel Hill.

On April 6, 1861, the Orange Light Infantry was raised in order to form a company of one of North Carolina's first volunteer regiments. Among those men who joined was young John Thomas Jones, a fourth-year student at the University of North Carolina, and the son of Edmund Jones, a prominent senator from Caldwell County. Jones was assigned to Company D, 1st N.C. Volunteers, and in July 1861, Jones transferred to a company from his native Caldwell County with the rank of first lieutenant.[24] By the time of this letter, all regimental officers had been elected, and Jones faced his first test as one of them.

> Camp Carolina
> August 31/61
>
> Dear Father
>
> I have been so busy since my arrival here that I have hardly had a moment of leasure to write you before. I had a very pleasant trip of it down to Chapel Hill where I stayed two days and where of course, I had a very pleasant time of it. I found the delectable Mollie looking as pretty and as sweet as ever. The Doctor looks better than I ever saw him. From the Hill I went straight to Yorktown. There is a great deal of sickness. There was as much as I expected, mostly chills and feaver. I found no difficulty in getting my discharge. We are now as you know in the 26th regiment, Vance is Colonel, and an old college mate of mine, Burgwin is Lieu. Col and Bynum Carmichael is Major.[25]
>
> I would like very much if you could get us some recruits so I could bring them down when I go up. I have been advanced one post in senior. I am now 2nd Lieu. Blair[26] is third and makes a very good officer. Oxford has resigned and gone home since he found that he did not have sense enough to fill the office. We have not got a full company yet, and I fear unless we do soon we may be left out of the regiment. I have received the [commendation?] of my commander and other officers for the proper manner in which I suppressed a rebellion. I was officer of the guard and had the guard house full. I came down on them though too hard and about 300 men determined to take them out but I showed them different.
>
> I think may be Vance will give me Adjutant. I wish you could see him and suggest it to him. He is not here yet but we look for him in a few days. There are several applicants for the post but I think he ought to give it to me on account of the letter I wrote him last winter.
>
> Write soon. Affectionately
> J. T. Jones

12. September 11, 1861

Corporal Lewis Warlick, "The Burke Rifles," Company G, 1st Regiment N.C. Volunteers, letter to Laura McGimsey, Pleasant Hill, Burke County, North Carolina. Source: Laura C. McGimsey Papers (2680), Southern Historical Collection, Wilson Library, University of North Carolina at Chapel Hill.

The First North Carolina Volunteers passed their first test at Bethel on June 10, 1861; however, much more soldiering remained for this now famous unit. Along the peninsula, Corporal Warlick kept a constant watch for Federal movements and performed a series of duties. On September 11, 1861, Warlick wrote an interesting story about apprehending a lighthouse keeper whose loyalties lay with the Union to his sweetheart, Cornelia McGimsey.

> Camp Fayetteville, VA
> Sept 11th '61
>
> Dearest Cornelia
>
> Your note by the Captain came to hand a few days since which was gladly

received though short. It found me suffering with a severe fever as I had had a shaking chill a few hours previous, which is the last I have had and I hope it will be the last so long as I am in Va; that was on Sunday I had one the day before.

I had the chills checked on me at Ship Point and I was imprudent enough a few days alter to go out on an expedition for the purpose of blowing up or burning up a lighthouse 6 miles above Fortress Monroe, we started about three hours before sundown (twenty three in all) in small boats and was gone the whole night, did not return until daylight the next morning was traveling all the time, had no way of lying down to rest being exposed all the while to the night air that was I believe what brought the chills back upon me.

After all our trouble and danger to which we were exposed we succeeded only in part, which was that we arrested the light-house keeper and brought him prisoner to Ship Point; the lighthouse we could not burn nor could we blow it up as it is solid masonry from the base for forty feet. Therefore we had to leave that fine piece of property to benefit on by the Yankees who plough the rough billows of Hampton Roads with their freighted ships men-of-war, etc. This is the reason we wanted to destroy it as it is of no use to us at all now, for we have no ships upon the bay and if we had, the great navy of the North would soon capture the last one. They (the Yankees) are greatly helped by that light to guide them along the channels and roads at night. They would have missed it very much if we only could have destroyed it, but failing to do so we heaved a sigh, set sail and rejoiced only over the capture of our man who was sent to Yorktown from Ship Point to stand a trial for being a traitor which I suppose he is as he visited Fortress Monroe often and received pay from the Lincoln Government for keeping up the lights. That shows he was not true to his country.

We keep moving, we only remained at Ships Point two weeks, and then we were ordered here for what purpose I cant tell. We are now six miles from Yorktown, in a pine grove and have the best water we have had since we have been in Va., and for that one thing I would like to remain here until our time expires, if we could get to stay here I think we would all get good health again. I got the cheese you sent me for which I am very thankful. The socks I have not got yet but Bob says he will give them to me at any time and for those I am under many obligations to the donor and wish her long and happy life.

I understand that Sid Conley[27] has got a discharge from the army and will start home tomorrow. It was on account of bad health. Several more in the company ought to be sent home as they will not do any good while we stay here on account of their inability. Say to sister I will answer her letter as soon as possible. Write soon and often to your best friend and something else.

Lewis

13. September 20, 1861

Private William H. Proffitt, "The Wilkes Valley Guards," Company B, 1st Regiment N.C. State Troops, letter to his brother, Alfred Proffitt, Wilkes County, North Carolina. Source: Proffitt Family Papers (3408), Southern Historical Collection, Wilson Library, University of North Carolina at Chapel Hill.

William H. Proffit was born in 1839 to William and Mary Proffit of Reddie's River, Wilkes County. William and Mary raised five children at their Wilkes County home: four boys—Andrew, William H., Alfred, Calvin L.—and one daughter, Rachel. All four brothers would fight in the war—Alfred and Andrew in the 18th North Carolina and Calvin in the 13th North Carolina. William worked as a teacher before volunteering at age 21 on May 30, 1861.[28] Private Proffit, a soldier in the "Wilkes Valley Guards," was with his company holding a battery at Aquia, Virginia.

> Aquia Creek, Va
> September 20th 1861

AJ Proffitt, Dear Brother

Your very kind and interesting letter of the 6th inst is at hand to which I hasten to reply. Your letter gave me much satisfaction by informing me that you were all well, and that times there were good, etc, etc. I have very little interesting news to write to you at this time that will be of much interest to you, more to inform you. I wish the rest of your relations and friends in camp are all well, hoping when you receive these few lines you will all be enjoying health and prosperity.

I suppose you are aware of our company's being at the mouth of Aquia creek, and having charge of a Battery at that place. We have been here near a week and are far better accommodated here than we have been since we have been in camp. I cannot say that we are encamped as this time for every one of us is living in a house, though some of them are small, any of them are preferable to tents. This is the prettiest place I ever saw. The river at this place is said to be five miles wide and the creek one. When we go to the spring, we get in a boat and cross the creek, as the spring from which we get our water is on the opposite side of the creek to where we are stationed. We spend many of our leisure hours in fishing, which at this place is not an uninteresting business you may suppose. T. C. L.[29] makes the fishing business pay. You can see ships, boats, and schooners at almost anytime. Some are sailing up and down the river while others are motionless.

We are improving our fortifications at this place which will be very soon sufficiently strong or, however, we think, it will be. We have been in no fights yet, neither am I able to tell you when we will. There has been heavy firing heard in the direction of Washington city yesterday and today. We have not heard the result, but there is no doubt that there is a dreadful battle being fought near that place.

I was very happy in receiving a full account of your School which indeed is one that is worthy of your time and attention, and I feel quite confident that the citizens of Beaver creek will continue to furnish you with a good school as long as you wish to Teach, and I recommend you to remain there until you have taught at least two or three sessions. I was informed by C. L. P. [his brother Calvin] that he did not know whether or not he would have the opportunity of returning to school with you. If his opportunities are bad at present, I want him to remain there with you during the winter. He informed me that he was requested by E.K. Walsh to teach a school in his district. I think it would be a good idea for him to teach a few months sometime in the Winter, but not to neglect going to long on account of doing so. He wrote me a few weeks ago concerning his interest in volunteering in Mr. Barber's company. I would be glad for Mr. Barber to succeed in getting up a good company, but if C. L. wishes to volunteer, if he will wait until I came home he can come back with me and join this company. I would prefer that all my relations and particular friends should be with us. I would be glad to recieve a letter from A. N. and know what his intentions are. I was informed by C. L. that he was riding over the country and taking his pleasure. I would be happy in hearing of his going to school this Winter, but I know it is impossible for you all to be gone from home long at a time.

I would be glad to know if R. L. P. [his sister, Rachel] is going to school any this fall or not. I was glad to hear that Father's crop was so good and that his and Mother's health is as good as usual. You said in your letter that you would be glad if I could take charge of your School so that you could accomplish some valuable pieces of work at home. I will assure you that I would be as happy in occupying a seat in that school as in almost any place I ever saw for I have spent probably the happiest days of my life at that place.

As I commenced your letter on yesterday and did not have any opportunity of finishing it, I have received some news of the Battle near Washington city. I heard this morning that news was brought on the 12 o'clock train last night that General Beauregard had taken Arlington heights with the loss of an immense number of men, perhaps 14 or 15000. The above is a mere report, and I am unwilling to vouch for the truth of the same though we are unable to give you the particulars, it is unnecessary to doubt that a tremendous battle has been fought for we heard the report of cannon a large part of two days. About sunset last night four or five large guns were fired a few miles down the river. We heard the report distinctly and saw the smoke ascend and some said they saw the place where the balls struck the water. I am unable to inform you why the guns were fired. I will very soon close by asking you to write me soon after the reception of this letter, and give me the news. Please direct your addresses to Fredericksburg, Va. in care of Capt. Brown, 1st Reg. N.C. State Troops.

SC Land, DM Carlton, Wm and Alfred Walsh, LW Laxton, WH Witherspoon,[30] and your relatives and friends in camp are well and doing finely. Please give my love and respects to all inquiring friends, particularly to AM Foster and family to all your students, etc. Tell John J. Foster that I was glad to hear that Mr. West's drum was as good as it was when we last saw it, and that there is a great need of Mr. West and his drum in the army. Give him my best respects, and tell him "it is all right on the Goose."

I hope to see you all very soon and tell you some good jokes and then it will "be all right on the Goose." You said Wm and Alfred's likeness had reached home and that they were a very exact resemblence of them. You said you would be glad to have mine, I will send it to you as soon as I have an opportunity of sending it to you. I think I will go to Fredericksburg very soon and have one taken.

Write me soon

I remain now as ever yours, etc.

W. H. Proffit.

14. October 17, 1861

Colonel Zebulon B. Vance, 26th Regiment N.C. Troops, letter to his wife, Harriet Espy Vance, Asheville, Buncombe County. Source: Zebulon B. Vance Papers, North Carolina Division of Archives and History.

The little brother of Asheville merchant Robert Vance was the dynamic Zebulon. When the war commenced, Zebulon Vance was one of the foremost political figures in the South. The 31-year-old member of the House of Representatives was known for his frankness and powerful opinions. Before entering politics, Vance attended Washington College and the University of North Carolina. He was admitted to the bar in 1853, and in August of that year, he married Harriet Espy at Quaker Meadows in Burke County. At the opening of the war, Vance took command of the Buncombe Rough and Ready

Guards, a local militia group, which would later become Company F of the 4th N.C. Volunteer Regiment. On August 29, 1861, Vance was elected to command a newly organized regiment, the 26th North Carolina.[31]

> Camp Wilks near Fort
> Macon Oct 17 1861
>
> Your long letter was recd yesterday and I was deeply grieved at its contents in more respects than one. My poor child it seems gets no better but rather worse. Dear little fellow how my heart bleeds for him. I will try to get permission to visit you by the 1st November at least, but it is very uncertain as to my getting permission. We are in constant doubt here, immense naval preparations have certainly been made by the Yankees for attacking the Southern Coast, but where they will strike no one can say. We may be here till Spring without being molested, and then a days carelessness might see us surprised and ruined. We have to watch & be patient.
>
> I regret exceedingly Mothers conduct towards you about Herndon.[32] She is certainly very inconsistent. Whilst in my company I paid every attention to Herndon and tried to wear off every thing unpleasant between us. But he would not reciprocate any of my advances—the truth is he is a low bred fellow and cant appreciate what is genteel & becoming & I soon gave up all attempts to put us on a brotherly footing. I should regret bitterly to see that Mother was determined to trample on the feelings of the whole family for the sake of a fellow who clearly proves his unworthiness—But it is often so— Hannah has more complete control of Mother than all the balance of the family; she, that has been most undutiful and brought most distress upon her Mothers grey hairs, is not only forgiven, which was right enough, but is made to control all the rest. It is very hard for any shadow to come between me & my mothers love, but I never can & never will sacrifice my self respect for a dirty puppy as I believe Herndon to be, nor do I want you to do it. This is all private darling, you must not let any of them see this letter, it would do no good; I write my sentiment to you that you may Know how I wish you to do in the matter. Of course I desire you to treat my Mother with all Kindness, but let Herndon & his wife be a forbidden subject between you. In fact dont talk about them to anybody, not your best friends.
>
> Kiss my darling Children & receive my blessing upon you all In haste most truly your husband Can you spare me a pair of good bed blankets? I begin to need them now.
>
> Z. B. Vance

15. October 29, 1861

Private James H. Baker, Company B, 2nd Battalion N.C. Troops, letter to his father, William, Siloam, Surry County, North Carolina. Source: J. H. Baker Papers (288), Manuscripts Department, Special Collections Library, Duke University, Durham, N.C.

The Second North Carolina Battalion, also known as General Daniel's "Little Mob," suffered 153 casualties at Gettysburg. Among the 29 killed was a Surry County private, James Baker. James H. Baker was born in 1840 to William and Polly Baker. James worked as a farmer and lived with his parents and six sisters prior to enlisting into service on September 22, 1861.[33] In this letter, James was resting in the hospital, a change that is not recorded in his service record, and asked for some money from his father, William.

> October the 29 1861
> Richmond Va
>
> Dear Farther
>
> Your kind and very welcome letter dated the 23d came to hand yesterday

Like James H. Baker, cousins Nathan Gwyn (left) and Alex Chatam were among nearly three hundred Surry County men who volunteered for service in either the 21st North Carolina or the Second N.C. Battalion. (Library of Congress.)

perity and will find you at home. I am treated very well here at this hospital.

Dear farther I want you to send me some 4 or 5 dollars in the next letter if you can possibly spare it. I need some very bad. I want you to rite me as soon as you get this and rite me all the news you have as I cant get much news in here. I must come to a close by saying rite soon and direct your letter the same place as before. So nothing more at presant but I remain

Your affectionate and loving son until death

J. H. Baker

16. November 2, 1861

Private John H. Kimzey, Company I, 16th Regiment N.C. Troops, letter to his father, Henderson County, North Carolina. Source: Kimzey Letters (148), Private Manuscripts Collection, North Carolina Division of Archives and History.

After the victory at First Manassas, Confederate hopes for an offensive mired down in western Virginia. John H. Kimzey, a 21-year-old Henderson County resident, volunteered for service on April 30, 1861. The 16th North Carolina (6th N.C. Volunteers) was part of a command which was posted in western Virginia. The regiment was present, but did not take part in, Robert E. Lee's Cheat Mountain Campaign. After this debacle, the 16th continued its duties in the Kanawa Valley, Valley Mountain, and the areas along the Greenbrier River. After Kimzey wrote this letter, he was promoted to sergeant, then he was appointed second lieutenant on August 3, 1862. Kimzey

and gave me much satisfaction hear from you and hear that you was well and at home. I can say to you in reply that I am getting on tolerable well at this time. I was as glad to hear from you as I ever had been in my life as I hadent heard from you since the 5th of September and I couldent hear whether you were at home or in virginia.

I have written several letters to you and have receaved no answers except the one I got last night. I hope when these few lines may come to hand that they may find you in good health and pros-

served as second lieutenant until he was killed in action at the Battle of Second Manassas.[34]

    Camp at Greenbrier Bridge
    Nov 2/61
Dear Father

 We are yet at Greenbrier winding our way along as usual waiting for order[s] to make an ordeal ... what they will be or whom they will be given to nobody knows. Cabins are being built by the score but whether for our regiment or not I cant say. Colonel Love thinks we will go to the coast.[35] Our duty is much lighter than it has been previously but it is made upon us by the reduction of rations. We scarcely get half enough to eat particularly in the Bread Line. Consequently we have to apply almost daily to our purses for assistance in the Bread Line. One ham being worth $2.00, apple pies 40 to 50 cents. The citizens keeps up a market for us. Apples $3, Irish potatoes $1.50 per bushel, Cheese $5.00 per cake, Butter 50 cts per lb., Chestnuts 30 cts a quart, Milk 80 cts per quart. We make or receive payments occasionally which affords the necessary means to procure these articles of food.

 I suppose you have heard much ridicule about western va, but I think there is not better country this side of the Southern pole. Indeed I think the application once belonging to the isle of Sicily would be an improper one for western va. That was the Land of Milk & Honey. All the elements of food adapted to the temperate zone are found in abundance and fullness of growth. The citizens here live better here on less labor than any people I ever seen. The scarcity now is all together attributed to the demands of these ten thousand soldiers that have been quartered here during the year. But notwithstanding my exaggerated opinions of the Country as you may take it, I would if I could get foot loose strike a bee line for old Henderson and do without the milk and honey of Va.

 I cannot give you any information respecting the engagements of our forces at different places from the fact that you already know more about them than we do in camp. We scarcely ever see a Knews paper here though as far as have any information. Our arms have been crowned with greatness which is a strong manifestation of the mercy of providence.

 If our Regt. Goes to eastern v.a. I will probably be close to your brother. You will please send me the number of his regiment & the letter of his company, the Col commanding, & the initials of his name & do write to me oftener or make some of the family write. Tell Mr. Barnette I am waiting to hear from him. Give my respects to all.

    Your Obedient Son
    John N. Kimzey
    Poe Jim & Co. is well

17. November 3, 1861

 Private Roland C. Osborne, "The Haywood Highlanders," Company F, 25th Regiment N.C. Troops, letter to his sister, Addie. Source: Mary Gash Papers (59), Private Manuscripts Collection, North Carolina Division of Archives and History

 Roland C. Osborne, a Haywood County farmer, volunteered for service on June 29, 1861, leaving behind his wife, Jane Cathey, and a young daughter at home. Osborne's regiment, the 25th North Carolina Troops, arrived at Camp Davis off Mitchell's Sound on September 29, 1861, and was issued weapons the same day. On November 5, 1861, the 25th moved to Charleston, and then to Coosawatchie and Grahamville, South Carolina, where it remained until March 15, 1862.[36]

Camp Davis
Nov the 3/ 61

Dear Sister

I received your note to day and was somewhat surprised, and why, because I had not heard from home in so long. I received this last letter in two days from Asheville. I have received one letter every week from my Dear wife. Well Sister A, I am convinced that I have the best Ladie of the land. Don't you believe it? I think I hear you say yes. One thing I can say I never can pay to hur what is due to hur and her sister.

I suppose she is gowing out there to stay a while. I want you to treat hur the very best you can. I want you to strive to make hur comfortable and cheepe hur comfortable there as long as you can. Sister you will pleas excuse me for braging so. I want you to give my best respects to Unckle Joseph and Aunt Nep. When you git to see my little Boy I want you to tell if you don't think he is the best looking of the Osborn Race. I think in your heart you will say yes. You might tell me how father is getting along these times.

Sister we have just received marching orders tonight to leave heir and gow to Charleston from there to Beaufort South Carolina. We will leave heir tomorrow morning at seven oclock. I have just bin talking to friend [original marked out]. He says that is a better place than this is and if it is I am glad that we are gowing there and so if we gow to fight we will not be so much exposed as we are heir. So if we should gow I will let you know where we are as soon as we land. You will pleas excuse my hastily writing. If we do not gow or if our order is Counter manded, I will stop writing for the night. So good buy for the present. I will remain

Your brother,
R. C. Osborn

18. December 3, 1861

Major James B. Gordon, 1st N.C. Cavalry Regiment (9th N.C. State Troops), letter to his sister, Carrie, Wilkesboro, Wilkes County, North Carolina. Source: James G. Hackett Papers (112), Private Manuscripts Collection, North Carolina Division of Archives and History, Raleigh, N.C.

After completing its training, the 1st N.C. Cavalry moved to the vicinity of Centreville, Virginia to establish winter camp. After the summer's victory at Manassas, the area around Centreville became the front lines of the war in the east. In this letter, Major James B. Gordon described the physical aspects of the regiment's camp, an outbreak of disease, and a small action and victory over Federal troopers.

Camp Ashe
Near Centreville Va
December 3rd 1861

My Dear Sister,

I have intended writing to you for several days but knowing that some one at home received a letter every week from me I knew you heard through them where I was and what I was doing. We have now a very pleasant camp in a thicket of pines and cedars all small and scrubby so that we are well protected from the wind. The ground is rolling so as to drain the camp and we have to cut out roads to pass from one row of tents to the others. We are still 1½ miles from Centreville.

We have very cold weather at this time & our men being thinly clad suffer much on picket. We have 120 of the regiment sick and a death about once a week. I am enjoying fine health & am quite comfortable.

We have been expecting an advance of the enemy for some weeks, but they have not yet advanced. It is now believed by our Generals that a fight is inevitable within a short time but dont [know] where the main attack will be wether on the right, left, or centre and there are designs for our regt to find where it will be. The battle flags have been distributed to the various regts & they have been impressed with the believe that a tremendous battle is inevitable and soon. We have a large number of troops near here & if the attack is made at this point I have no fears of the result. We had a little fight with Cavalry the other day of 180 to 200 on each side & we scared them so badly that very few of them fired. We chased them for 3 miles & such yelling & firing & reckless riding by our boys you cant imagine.[37]

I dont much blame the poor creatures for running. I was placed in front and ordered to lead the column of attack & saw more of the fight than any one else. I felt calm and quiet during the whole affair. Though most of the time in close proximity to the enemy & fireing at them. I wrote Foster, giving him an account of the affair. The Col was kind enough in making out his report to head quarters to mention my name very kindly & flattering in conversation with the officers.

Well my dear sister I have nearly completed this sheet and have not given you anything of interest either. I have to write but war news. You must write me often Carrie and tell how you all are and how the baby grows. Tell Frank also to write. My love to all.

    Your brother,
    J. B. Gordon

19. December 10, 1861

Mrs. Mary Gray Bell, Franklin, Macon County, letter to her husband, Captain Alfred Bell, Company B, 39th Regiment N.C. Troops. Source: Alfred Bell Papers (417), Manuscripts Department, Special Collections Library, Duke University.

On October 19, 1861, a company under the command of Captain Alfred Bell left Franklin, the county seat of Macon County, for Camp Patton in Asheville. Mary Gray Bell was the wife of Alfred W. Bell, local dentist turned captain. Bell, despite his outward roughness, was an intelligent and respected man. His pride and individuality caused many problems for him during the war; however, his company seemed to hold him in very high regard. The Bells were from a modestly wealthy background, and by 1860, the couple had two children, Mary and Sarah,[38] and raised them on a small plantation outside the Franklin limits.

    Franklin Dec. 10th 1861
My Dear Husband

I received your letter this evening. I am glad you are so prompt about writing and was so glad that you did not have to go fight those Tenesseeans. I was so uneasy until I got your note by Mr. Cabe. I did not know what to do. There is no news of importance here. I believe some men [are] in town this week as it is court week. I see several of your men here. Mr. Moore has gone as far as Mr. Elmores tonight. Mr. Owens also starts in the morning. I did not have time to write by either after I received your letter but I will send this by Frank Poindexter as he starts to Asheville in the morning. I sent those shirts for Mr. McDowell in that box, they were in the bottom of the box with paper over them. I do not see how you missed finding them.

Do as you please about me coming to Asheville. Dee says he will go with me, and so does James Roane. He told me today that he wanted to go and if I would let him know when I wanted to go we could get Pa's buggy and he would find one horse or two if I could not get one. I will send your soap by Frank. I recon you will not want another blanket as you bought one from Arnold. One of my hogs in the pen had the quinsy but I have doctored it up until I think it is out of danger. I was very uneasy for fear it would die. I was afraid I would have to beg my meat next year and you know I am a poor hand to beg. I recon you have plenty to eat in the camps yet. I see your men all look like they had plenty to eat.

I will close as it is late. Fannie said to tell you howdy for her and Sallie and tell you to send howdy to her and Sallie. She does not like it because you do not send them some word. Sallie asked me this morning when would her Pa come back and sleep on her arm. She is of her Ma's notion. I know you can not miss us half as much as we do you. I am sorry to my very soul that you ever did volunteer but regrets are in vain. I want you to come back soon if you can. Good night, may you have pleasant dreams of home and friends.

Your ever true devoted wife,
Mary

20. December 29, 1861

Private Robert M. Blair, "The Caldwell Guards," Company I, 26th Regiment N.C. State Troops, letter to mother, Abigail Blair, Deal's Mill, Caldwell County, with additional notes to brothers, Caldwell County, North Carolina. Source: Blair Letters (1206), Private Manuscripts Collection, North Carolina Division of Archives and History.

The Twenty-Sixth North Carolina contained two companies of Caldwell County men. One of the later volunteers was the Caldwell Guards' Robert A. Blair. Robert was the oldest son of John and Abigail Blair of Caldwell County, North Carolina. On October 21, 1861, this 24-year-old farmer volunteered for service and was assigned to Company I of the 26th North Carolina.[39] In this letter, Private Blair talks about the arrival of several gentlemen from back home with much appreciated boxes of gifts and provisions. Blair also makes a brief note to his brothers who remain back at home.

Camp Vance
Dec 29/61
Dear Mother
I this night seat myself to rite you a few lines to tell you that I am well, hoping these lines may find you all enjoying the same blessing. I have nothing new to rite to you. J. M. West, C. D. West, and Caldwell Blair arrived safe to our company this night a week ago, with all there boxes. I received mine very gladly. It had some apples some butter and my slips in it. But I have got so big or something else down here that my slips is to small for me. I had to let them out the full bigness and then they were as tite on me as the skin. Every time I go to draw a long breath I can hear them tear. So if you are very plenty of cloth you may make me another pair and send to me but make them larger round. They are long enough. I am happy to inform you that our company is generlay well. We have but one in the hospitle at this time. That is J. Teague.[40] He is down with fever. Some men are complaining in camp. I would be the gladest in the world to see you all once more and will hope that I will sometime. So I will bring my letter to a close.

Yours affectionately,
R. M. Blair to Abigail Blair

Monday Morning
The 30th
Dear Brothers
I this morning seat myself to rite you a few lines. I have bought me a bull dog this morning and gave $7 for it and intend to send it by Harvey & C. D. West and I want you there to take good care of it for me if it ever gets home. I

would not tooke ten dollars for it if they get it home.

     So no more yours truly
     R. M. Blair
To A, W, and J. P. Blair

 If you have plenty of cabage I would be glad that you would send me some heads by Solmon Heartly when he comes or some other person. Clint Lee[41] will be at home in a few days. You could send them by him. You need not be surprised at my wanting cabage for almost any thing is good down here. So no more at present, R. M. Blair

1862

I stode gard nite beefore last and it give me a hurten in my brest and my head and I Cofte all day and nite but I went to the docktor and got some medicen and it helpt me.

> —Private Jordan S. Council, "The Watauga Marskmen," Company B, 37th Regiment North Carolina Troops, New Bern, North Carolina, February 4, 1862.

Whar has bin hard for many days we ort to think that death is on ever sid of us. God is our friend. We ort to pray to god fer the many Blesing he has Be stod upon us. I think we all ort to pray.

> —Private Marion Sexton, "The Ashe Beaureguard Riflemen," Company A, 37th Regiment North Carolina Troops, Richmond, Virginia, July14, 1862.

In all probability our regiment will be stationed here permanently for the winter to guard the bridge across the Watauga River against the incendiary attacks of the tories of this unfortunate state.

> —Private John H. Phillips, Company E, 62nd Regiment North Carolina Troops, Cater's Depot, Tennessee, October 13, 1862.

We have been hearing heavy cannonading in the direction of Nashville for the two past days and it was reported that our forces were gradually falling back before a large force of Yanks until this morning when the rascals were reported to be within eight miles of town.

—Second Lieutenant Thomas W. Patton, Company C, 60th Regiment North Carolina Troops, Murfreesboro, Tennessee, December 28, 1862.

21. January 1, 1862

Private William H. Proffit, "The Wilkes Valley Guards," Company B, 1st Regiment N.C. State Troops, letter to his brother, Alfred Proffit, Wilkes County, North Carolina. Source: Proffit Family Papers (3408), Southern Historical Collection, Wilson Library, University of North Carolina at Chapel Hill.

After almost seven months in service, William Proffit had yet to see combat against Yankee forces. Company B, 1st North Carolina left Camp Bee, Virginia, in September 1861, and stayed at Game Point, Virginia, until March of 1862. During that time, Company B improved Game Point's defenses and fortifications and manned a piece of coastal artillery. In this letter, former teacher William Proffit described to his brother Andrew how he spent his time during Christmas.

Game Point, Va, Jan 1, 1862
Mr. AJ Proffit
Dear Brother,

These lines will inform you that yours of the 23 December was gladly received on yesterday morning, and I hasten to reply. I had been expecting to have received letters from you or some of my friends on Lewis Fork for two or three weeks but as I did not receive any I wrote A. N. [his brother Andrew N. Proffit] a few days ago which I hope he will get. I am unable to interest you on the War question, as there is but little news in this part of Virginia. We seldom get an opportunity of firing upon the Yankee steamers, but when one approaches within 3 or 4 miles of our Battery we are shure to give them a sign by which they may know that we are yet a living and wide awake.

I would have been glad to have taken Christmas wish for you, but as some 12 or 15 of the company had gone home on sick furlough, I made no application for a furlough, but thought I would content myself until those who were absent returned. The manner in which we spent the Christmas holidays, compared with former ones, presented a contrast that is more easily imagined than described but we spent the day or at least a portion of it quite agreeably, particularly while seated at the dinner table partaking of an excellent Chicken Pie, etc, etc, which had been prepared by mess no.5.

On yesterday morning, one of my messmates and I took a small row boat and went up Aquia Creek about four miles, where we called at a private house and took dinner and bought some articles for the mess and returned to camp a little before night. I tell you we enjoyed our trip very much, as we have not, until lately, been allowed such priviliges, since we have been stationed at this point. I would have been glad if you could have been here to have taken a New Years dinner with us, as we dined upon a fat Turkey well baked and other delicaces, but I would advise you to stay on Lewis Fork, at least until spring.

I was glad to hear that those East Tennesseeans were being compelled to walk up to the chalk. The only thing to be regretted concerning those traitors, is that they had not been hanged long since. Tell mother that I received her letter long since and answered it immediately after its arrival.

I will soon close for the present by informing you that I am quite well at present, hoping these lines will find you all well. Please give my compliments to all inquiring friends. T.C. Land and TC Miller[1] say they would have written you long since, had they rec'd answers to the ones they sent you. They say they are not sent you a letter as you supposed.

I remain

W. H. Proffit

22. January 22, 1862

Colonel Clarke Moulton Avery, 33rd Regiment N.C. Troops, letter to wife, Lizzie Avery, Morganton, Burke County, N.C. Source: Edward G. Phifer Collection (1368), Private Manuscripts, North Carolina Division of Archives and History.

After leading his company to victory at Bethel, Captain Clark Moulton Avery was assigned to the 33rd North Carolina Troops, with the rank of lieutenant colonel. On January 17, 1862, Avery was elevated to colonel and took command of the regiment. On January 22, Avery sat himself down to write his wife, Elizabeth, to inform

After serving as an officer in the 1st N.C. Volunteers, Burke County's Clarke Avery commanded the 33rd North Carolina for almost thirty months. (North Carolina Division of Archives and History.)

her of his status. Avery also referred to an element of "prejudice" against him in Burke County.

Head Quarters 33d Regt
NC state troops
Camp Branch Newbern NC
22 Jan 1862 11 o'clock

My Dear Wife,

I wrote you a humble note this morning acknowledging the receipt of yours and Martha's letters. Everything is quiet here at present. I will keep my letter open until morning and advise you if there is any danger from the news tonight of an attack at this point. I do not believe as much as I did two days since that we will be attacked here. Of course, this is only my individual opinion. Very much to the gratification of my Regt, my comission arrived as Col Commd today and I have just concluded my speech in answer to a Seranade in this occasion.

I suppose before this reaches you, you will have received a letter from Capt. Englehard enclosing a check in favor of Mr. Houck. This I intend to be applied to the payment of Mr. Shull.

I hope you will make Mr. Jerry do all the painting necessary. Do not let any part of it off for I know how hard it is to have a small job done. I am disappointed and quite mortified that my friend Armfield[2] has failed to report a company for my Regt. I fear it is the result of prejudice against me in Morganton. But thank God I have a position in the Army gained by my own industry and attention to my duties and feel no obligations to none of them.

Gaston H. Lewis[3] of Edgecombe County who was in the 1st Regt is Major and present in the tent with me. He is every gentleman and a good officer. I have no one in my Regt from my immediate county and perhaps it is best. I have heard nothing from Erwin except through yours and Martha's letters. Tell Martha I will answer her letter tomorrow or the next day.

The Exodus of the people of this town still continues. We have very variable weather part of the time it is like May. I am sorry I did not bring my blouse.

23rd January 1862
Your precious [?] of the 19th was received this morning. I wish you would send to Dr. Happoled and get something for your Boil. I fear it may be a carbuncle and you are so unselfish, I know you will neglect yourself.

We have had a dreadful blow during the night and its raining now in torrents. I have a good stove and am quite comfortable. In the future I will write at least every other day and whenever I can every day.

Urge Mr. Houck to attend to my request of him. Give my love to your Ma and all my friends. Kiss our dear ones and whenever your duties prevent tell my daughter Martha (who you think is the idol of her father) to write me. God bless you my dear Lizzie.

Your own husband
C. M. Avery
PS I have my commission as Col.

23. February 4, 1862

Private Jordan S. Council, "The Watauga Marksmen," Company B, 37th Regiment N.C. Troops, letter to his mother, and wife, Mary A. Council, Boone, Watauga County, North Carolina. Source: Source: Mary A. Council Papers (1259), Special Collections Library, Duke University.

The small town of Boone was home to the Council family. On September 14, 1861, their 19-year-old son volunteered for service.[4] The 37th Regiment was trained at Camp Fisher, near High Point. After completing its training the regiment was ordered along with several other units to the command of General Lawrence Branch in defense of New Bern, one of the largest cities in eastern North Carolina. Among the problems faced by this force included inadequate food and disease. Jordan also talked about working on several defenses in and around the area.

Near Newberne Camp _____ NC
February 4th 1862
Deare Mother
I seat my self with grate Plesure to drop you a few lines to inform you that I am well at this time but I aint bin well

fore the last day and nite. I stode gard nite beefore last and it give me a hurten in my brest and my head and I Cofte all day and nite but I went to the docktor and got some medicen and it helpt me. I hope when these few lines come to hand they may fin you all in Joying all the blessing that can beestod on woman kind. I beegan to get out of hart to think that I was not goin to get a letter. I receved your kind and afectionit letter to day the 4 of February 1862 and it give me mutch sadisfaction to here from you all that you was well.

Deare mother give my Respects to all the famely and to all of my friends and I want you to rite to me as soon as you git this letter. Do not fail to rite. I want you to rite to me wonse a week. Deare mother I will tell you what I have bin doing. I have bin floring the gard tent today and I have bin at work on the forte. I work there for days and they work us day and nite but they have quit it now. They do not work us so hard but Solgers see harde times. I ashore you I have seen harde times. We are in too miles beelow Newbern on the neus river clost to three fortes. One is in it the other is in about too miles from us that is the one that we have bin at work. One I think the yankes cante git it. I think if they come here that we can whip them. I think that we will stay here till spring and then we will leave here and gow to Currtuck or tenisee. The officers has Rasd a patetion to leave here. This plase is in a vary low plase and the water is bad and we have to take it agan.

You stated that you wanted to now who my messmates were. I will tell you all of them Will Daner & Cousin Henry & Cousin S. G. Tmares & David Cook Johnny Cook & J. V. Benfield J. C. Benfield & Luther Fenly Bill Brinte Jesy Brown J. D. Council C. H. Davis[5] and I and I am at the head of the mess and I like them all vary well so far and they all like me so far and if they dont mind I will make them leave my mess. The officers like me vary well so far as I now. I like them so far as I have obey them. They all seem vary kind to word me and I will try to please them just as long as I can not be contrary to them and the Company all like me. I quit them boys that I had bin sleepin with and went to bill taners tent. They is oneley five of us in it. We haev plenty to eate. I drawde enufe to do me sevral days to day. Pork and rice an sugar and pees and molases and soape. I aint got time to Rite mutch.

Deare wife I will drope you a few lines. You said something about clothing. I have gote as mutch here as I want. I wish I had Cavelid at home for I have got as mutch as I can take and I can git any Chance I will send it home. I have gote as mutch as I neede at this time. I want to now what you have gote that likeness or not and ten dolars or not and wether Pa caried my coates home or not. I want you to tell me what you have herd since I left home. I think som of the boys will come home with sore heads at the end of my time. Plese rite to me wonce a week and I will do the same. I will rite about 3 days a gan. Direct your letter to the same plase the same way. I am very well sadis fide at this time. Excuse all bad riten and spelling. Remanin your affecton husban.

J. S. Councill

24. February 8, 1862

First Lieutenant John T. Jones, "The Caldwell Guards," Company I, 26th Regiment N.C. Troops, letter to his father, Edmund Jones, Patterson, Caldwell County, N.C. Source: Edmund Jones Papers (3543), Southern Historical Collection, Wilson Library, University of North Carolina at Chapel Hill.

John T. Jones and his company, the "Caldwell Guards," were posted along with

Branch's command in the vicinity of New Bern in the late winter of 1862. In this letter, Lieutenant Jones talked about the prospective re-enlistment of the volunteers into state service for the duration of the war, as well as his ambitions to possibly become an officer in the cavalry under the command of Mr. Faucett.

>Camp Branch
>Feb 18th/ 62

Dear Father

I take this oportunity of droping you a few lines. There is no news I reckon which you have not heard. It is generally thought that Burnsides fleet will pay us a visit sooner or later. I don't know myself whether they will come or not; hardly think they will. There is some talk of trying to get our regiment in for two years longer, but I don't think it can be done. There are not more than 20 of my company that will go without going home. I hear that Mr. Faucett is trying to get up a company. I hope he will succeed. If he can make up a good company and will give me the place of first lieutenant I will go with him, otherwise I will not. I think I can get me a company after we go home. All the men in the company that will go again will go under me.

I wish you would inform me whether the State will receive any more cavalry companies or not and if so on what terms as I think I could raise a cavalry company with all, that is if they will furnish us with horses. I heard that there was a draft in Caldwell Co a week ago. I expect you are almost ready to leave Raleigh by this time.

I was much disapointed that you would not come down when you were at Goldsboro. I wish you would inform me where Mary is as I owe her a letter. As the drum is beating, I have to go for drill.

>Your aff son
>JT Jones

25. February 12, 1862

Thomas W. Patton, letter to his mother, Harriet Kerr Patton, Asheville, Buncombe County, N.C. Source: Patton Family Papers (1739), Southern Historical Collection, Wilson Library, University of North Carolina at Chapel Hill.

Thomas Patton was vacationing in Alabama, far from the building garrison at New Bern. Thomas Walton Patton was born in 1841 to Asheville merchant James W. Patton and Harriet Kerr Patton. Thomas lived with his family, which included two brothers, William Augustus and James, and a sister, Frances. Also living in the household were his aunts Charlotte and Margaret Kerr. After serving in the Buncombe Rifles, Company E, 1st North Carolina Volunteers, Patton was mustered out in November 1861. Patton used that time to relax and visit several relatives in Tennessee and Alabama.[6]

>Lowdens County Ala Febry 12 1862

My Dear Mother,

I arrived here last week and every day until yesterday the rain poured down incessantly and a big swamp between here and Hayesville was so high as to render it unsafe to cross it, and this accounts for your not hearing from me sooner. I have only received one letter from you since I left home.

I found things going on much better here than I expected. Mr. Barlow seems to be an energetic and honest man. He treats the negroes well and I think will do what is right. The negroes were generally well, but had had much sickness all through the summer. One of Susan's twins had died. They were all very much in need of clothes and I am going to have some clothes made, as for the shoes, they must do without them as it is impossible to get them. Patty and Mary have fine babies, the former only three weeks old.

John E. Patton[7] left here last week

for Bowling Green to join Fagg's company. He said he only went because he had no other way of making a living. I am very sorry for Cousin Sue. I did not stop in Montgomery on my way here, but intended to spend a day there on my return so as to see our friends. I wrote to Mr. Fagg by John E. The people here think he will come home shortly on a furlough. If so, I think I had better stay to see him. If I do not hear from him I will probably start home next week. I received a letter from Fannie the other day. She seemed to be in good spirits and getting along well.

What terrible news we have from the war now. Fortune seems to be turning a little. First Zollicoffer's defeat and death, and then the capture of Roanoke Island & three thousand prisoners by the Yankies. I have only heard rumors of the latter and hope they may be exagerated. Mr. Miles' family are generally well. I have been to see Mr. Moose, he says he remembers you and Aunt Charlotte perfectly. I did not know that she had ever been out here. He is a very gentlemanly old man and has two very nice daughters.

I hope Brother James' health is improving and that all are well. With much love to all, I remain

Your affec Son
Thomas W. Patton

26. March 11, 1862

Private Thornton Sexton, "The Ashe Beaureguard Riflemen," Company A, 37th Regiment N.C. Troops, letter to his parents, Pryor and Mariah Sexton, Ashe County, North Carolina. Source: Thornton Sexton Letters (4749), Manuscripts Department, Special Collections Library, Duke University.

Thornton Sexton was born in 1842, and resided in Ashe County, North Carolina. Thornton and his bother Marion volunteered for service and served as privates in the "Ashe Beaureguard Riflemen," which became Company A, 37th Regiment N.C. Troops.[8] The Sextons were posted outside of New Bern when he sat down to dictate this letter to Calvin Childers. Three days later, the 37th North Carolina was part of a command under Gen. Lawrence O'Brien Branch that defended New Bern against Burnside's Union forces. Thornton's expectations of a fight came true, and the Confederates suffered two major losses in two months with the fall of Roanoke Island and a defeat at New Bern.

Newbern NC Craven County
March the 11 day 1862

Dear Father and Mother

I take the oppertunity to right you a few more lines. I am not well but is beter than I have bin & hoping when these lines comes to hand tha may find you all well. I have got out of the hospitle and is back in Camp and I think that I will be able to drill in a few days. Maryon is beter. I receved a leter from you last night Stating that you was all well which gave me much satisfaction to here from you. You want to no whether I sent a leter to Susanna Sexton[9] or not. I did and I want to no whether she got it or not and what you wanted to no fur and what shed sed about it.

I can inform you that we are expectin a battle here now every day. They have had a battle at nofolk last weeke. They fout four days and Sunk three yankey vesels.[10] I wood like to see you all very much but I dont expect that I will tel [till] my time is out fur they wont give a furlow without we inlistin fur the war and I dont intend to do it. So I must close my leter. Give my best respect to all of my friends and tel them to right to me and I will right to them. So I remane your efectionate sone un tel deth so farewell

From Thornton Sexton
to Pryar Sexton and Moriah

27. March 20, 1862

Private James W. Love, "The Edney Greys," Company A, 25th Regiment N.C. Troops, letter to his sister, Elizabeth J. Love, Henderson County, North Carolina. Source: Matt Love Papers (3276), Special Collections Library, Duke University.

The Love family of western North Carolina was concentrated in Haywood, Jackson, and Henderson counties. One of the Henderson County Loves, James, was one of the several brothers in the 25th and 56th regiments, and was the brother of company commander Matthew N. Love. James volunteered for service at Edneyville, Henderson County, on May 15, 1861.[11] On March 20, 1862, the 25th was posted at Kinston, and Private Love wrote his sister Elizabeth about the spread of disease in another Henderson County unit and requested information on his two brothers, George and Samuel, who were reported in the service.

> State of NC Lenor county
> March the 20 1862
>
> Dear Sister
>
> It is with pleasure that I take my pen in hand this morning to ancer yours that James Mc brought and to let you know that I and Matthew is well and all of my mess is well. The helth of the company is very good at presant and I truly hope these few lines may safely reach and find you all well. One of the coners that come J. A. Poor is ded. He wasent sick but a few days. Lieutenant Garon in Jordons com[12] is ded tho he is at home by this time. I have nothing that is very interesting to write to you at this time more than we have had no fighting yet and I don't believe we will very soon. We are in 30 miles of newbern tho I don't beleave we will go to virginia. They say the law is now to press us and make us stay 2 years but they will give us a furloe but if they do that I don't know when I will be at home. Tho I would like the best kind to be at home a few days but do not know when I will be there. You sed that Erwin and Robert[13] had volunteered in Lanes company. I declare I don't know what to say to them for the best this war looks like will never end. Tell them to do the best that they can. We will all get threw this war. I hope you did not write like you think that I had got so far off from home that I had forgot my friends but I think of them all evry day.
>
> We have plenty of meat and Bread to eat. That is all we get. We drill 5 hours evry day and one fourth of that is Double quick & dress parads. They keep us stirring around. I can stand it very well. I will tell you I received a letter from cousin Sarah chambers. It was full of news but I have no time to tell you the news. The talk is now they are a going to stop the male and if they do this may be the last letter you will get from me. I will write evry chance. The will shorley will not stop the male.
>
> I would of wrote oftener but I have a bad chance and they is so much camp news that we do not know what to write but I think I will be at home in May. Write Sue and tell me if Erwin & Robert is at home and when they are going to try the camps. You can thell the 2 maryes howdy for me and give them my best respects and tell all Sally that I will write to her soon. I gave my best respects to all inquiring friends. So I must bring my lines to a close by saying take care of your self.
>
> J. W. Love
>
> Direct your letter to Lenor Cty Kineston PO

28. April 19, 1862

Lieutenant Colonel James B. Gordon, 1st N.C. Cavalry Regiment (9th N.C. State Troops), letter to his brother-in-law, Frank, Wilkesboro, Wilkes County, North Carolina. Source: James G. Hackett Papers

(112), Private Manuscripts Collection, North Carolina Division of Archives and History, Raleigh, N.C.

Ransom's promotion to brigadier general allowed James to be promoted to the rank of lieutenant colonel on March 1, 1863. A couple of weeks later, Gen. Theophilus H. Holmes, in response to the fall of New Bern, ordered the First Cavalry back to the state on March 22, 1863. In the following letter to his brother-in-law, Colonel Gordon discussed his desire for some gloves and other items of clothing. In addition, Gordon referred to the recently adopted Conscription Act, the Battle of Corinth, Mississippi, and meeting several of his fellow Wilkes County officers, William Barbour and Charles Hickerson, of the 37th North Carolina Troops.

> Camp Ransom
> Near Kinston
> April 19th 1862
>
> Dear Frank
>
> I wish you to write me immediately and let me know how Ben is and when you think he will be able to return to camp. I wish his health to be entirely restored before he comes. I think there will be no advance of the enemy on this road. I regret very much leaving the army in Va. It will be exceedingly hot here this summer, and nothing to eat but bread & bacon. If Crumpler passes through Wilkesboro on his return to camp send me 2 pair of red gloves size 8½ and some towels. I wish you would have me 2 pair of drawers made by Ann Hines if you can get any suitable material. Let them be made of the size of some of my old ones you will find in my wardrobe.
>
> How did the draft fall upon our peoples? The conscription Act I think is the very thing for the occasion. It will bring into the service many men who have been shirking the cause. I suppose you have heard of the fight at Corinth. We have news here that there is a fight going on at or near Richmond. Our troops so far from home are prepared for the enemy. There will be much fighting during the next 2 months. I think we will have but little to do here on this line. Our horses are improving rapidly and soon we will commence picket duty. Lt. Col Robinson of Spruills Cavalry,[14] who was said to have been killed in a skirmish some days since. He was only wounded and taken prisoner.
>
> I spent a day with Col Barber[15] a few days ago. He is quite well and seems quite pleasant with the service. He has gotten over his pnumonia in regards to himself. Charles Hickerson[16] is in love as usual with some girl in Kinston. The same Charles of old. Write me soon and direct to Kinston Lenoir Cty NC. I have recd my commission for lt. Col. My love to Carrie and tell her to kiss the baby for me.
>
> Yours truly,
> J. B. Gordon

29. April 21, 1862

Private George L. Cunningham, Company L, 16th Regiment N.C. Troops, letter to parents, George and Polly Cunningham, Haywood County, North Carolina. Source: Cunningham Letters (1455), Private Manuscripts Collection, North Carolina Division of Archives and History.

Private Cunningham of the 16th North Carolina was one of thousands of young Tar Heels holding the Yorktown line against McClellan's army in the spring of 1862. Cunningham was born in Haywood County, N.C., to George and Polly Cunningham and worked as a farmer prior to volunteering for service with his brother, John, on May 4, 1861.[17] In April 1862, George wrote his father about the enforcement of the Conscription Act, the bonuses of re-enlisting in Confederate service and the reorganization of his company.

Yorktown V a
April the 21 1862

Dear Father

It is with pleasure I take my pen in han to drope you a few lines to in form you that we ar in tollerable good health considern the long march we had to March. I hop when these few lines comes to hand they may find you and all the rest of the famley enjoying good health.

We ar eccspecting a big fight every minit at this place. The yankeys has a bout one hundred & eighty Thousand men. We have from one hundred & forty Thousand men at this place. We ar fortyfied on the line seven or eight miles seven men deep a long the line. I eccspect we will have the hardest fight that ever has bin heard of. I would be glad to see you all but I am a freid it will be a long time if I should liveto git through this battle.

They say that Congress has past a law to ceap all men in serves from eightteen to thirty five. We have ninty days to stay after our time is out. We can reorganis our Company and elect our officers as we did before but remain as we are until the ninty days is out. They say they will pay fifty dollars bounty money & sixty day furlow & go to any company or regiment we pleas, but I think if they ceap us that long they will ceap us on the guns and canons roar this morning. It may be that we will be call out be fore night. I think it is hard for free men who volunteer their servis freely. If I cood had the pleasure to come home when my time is out and stay thirty or forty days I wood bin better sadisfied but, after bein put up with as it is I want you to do the best for yours and also do the best you can for elizabeth & margaret for they ar the children you have at home for gods saik don't de prive them of a home for all the boys you have ar here to defend the rights of our Country. It may be that we all three may fall in defending our rights so do the best you can for yourself and the rest.[18] I want to sell my bacon. I want to ceap my mair till fall if I should have the luck to live till fall and don't git to come home I want you to sell her for me. If you can git from one hundred fifty to seven five dollars. You can do so and it will be all right with me. It may be that I will git a furlow when our ninty days ar out. We have never received the things you started to us and I don't eccspect we will ever will git them. I don't eccspect to see home for any thing if I should stay in war five year. So I must bring my letter to a clouse. Give my best resspect to my friends. I still remain your son untill death.

G. L. Cunningham

30. April 27, 1862

Private Jordan S. Council, "The Watauga Marksmen," Company B, 37th Regiment N.C. Troops, letter to his wife, Mary A. Council, Boone, Watauga County, North Carolina. Source: Source: Mary A. Council Papers (1259), Special Collections Library, Duke University.

Private Council saw his first combat at New Bern, N.C., on March 14, 1862. In the letter to his wife, Mary, Council talked about "joinde the regelrs" as well as the conscript law coming into effect. Upon regimental re-organization, the men were offered a choice to be elevated to "State Troops" status (somewhat higher than volunteers) which came along with a $50 bounty and a soldier's promise to serve for three more years or the duration of the war.

Camp Holmes Kinston
Aperil 27 1862

Dear wife

I agane imbrase another operttunity of love and of plesure today to answer your kind and affection letter which came safely by they hand of Mrs. More. I can say to you that I was glad to here from you and to here that you was well and doing the best you can. I red it with some sadesfaction but not as mutch as I did with the other. Dear companion I am afraide that they is something the matter in the famely but I hope that they aint Poley. You rote to me to no if I was not willin for you to go and see your kinfolkes. I can say to you that when you want to go to go alonge and see them and then go back if you are sades fide. I tolde you beefore I left home that if I was not sades fide that I would Cary you a way but I aint there no more. I dont no when I will bee if ever but I hope that I will see the smiles of your red ruby lips wonse more in this world. If they is any thinge the matter any way I want you to tell me of it if you please. I would like to see you I could tell you a heape.

Calvin Miller of Watauga was one of the county's two hundred man contingent in the 37th North Carolina. (North Carolina Division of Archives and History.)

Dear wife you rote that if you had my con sent that was all that you wanted I dont recon that you want to go vary often that they need to be a grombling at you. I dont think they have any rite too. I all ways con sent you to go when I was there and I expect too when I aint there. I will stope that subject. Dear wife I can say to you that I have joinde the reglers and has gote $50 bounty but I can say to you that it was aganste my will but I had to go in or do with the money and I thought that I had just as well have it as any body else who stays on with out it. It was not for the money that I went in fore they posted a law that all that from 18teen and 35 five had to come in to the field in 30 days after this law was past and if they is any body who wants to come to this Company had better come bee fore the 30 dayes is out. If they will come they will git the $100 dolars bounty. The law was past on the 15th of this month if they wate till then they will have to stay in the Company they are put in. I can say to you that I was down at ransoms Cavraly yesterday and J. C. Councill[19] was well and all the rest was well.

The Cornal[20] sayes that when time will obenit he will grante furlows. I will come home if I can get off. I can say to you that they is a good deal of sickness here in Camp. I halled one off tusday last week and has died three in too days.

The nuse is here that the yankes has taken new orleanes. We dont now if it is so or not. I will stope. I can say to you these few lines leaves me well at this time and I hope when these few lines comes to hand they may find you injoying good health. Give my best respectes to all in quirers frindes and save for your self. I will close this by saing good by Dear wife

I remain your affection Husban unitl seperated by death

        J.S. Councill[21] to his dear wife
PS You sent me your heart and hand. My hart you has got my hand too and it will bee with you as long as I live.

31. April 27, 1862

Private Isaac Whisenhunt, "Davis Dragoons," Company F, 41st Regiment N.C. Troops (3rd N.C. Cavalry), letter to Robert Perkins, Burke County, N.C. Source: Perkins Family Papers (3894), Southern Historical Collection, Wilson Library, University of North Carolina at Chapel Hill.

Isaac Whisenhunt served as a trooper in Company F, 3rd North Carolina Cavalry under the command of Captain Thomas G. Walton and Elisha Alexander Perkins.[22] In this brief note, Isaac wrote to his friend Robert Perkins, his lieutenant's brother, to let him know how things were and reported news of the safe arrival of a blockade-runner, the *Nashville*, at Wilmington.

        Camp Wyatt Apr 27th 1862
Mr. Perkins,
  Sir I drop you a few lines to let you know that I am well. I hope this note will find you in possession of the same. I have nothing of much interest to write you. The health of our company is not so very good at this time. We have several cases of the Diarear but none dangerous I think. Thirty-six of our men have bin sent to Onslow Cty. E. A. Perkins is with them. They left last Friday one week ago. We havent herd from them since they left. One of our vessels run the Blockade Friday night last called the Nashville. She has been to Europe and brought Eighteen Thousand stand of arms, Enfield Rifles, and a quantity of Powder. We gave her a hearty welcome in. I want to no if you have bought me my horse yet. If you havent you kneed not for I have bought one from the Captn. Altho if you have bought one I will take it according to my Bargain. I will close. I want you to let me no soon what you have don. Write as soon as you can. I remain your friend.

        Isaac Wisenhunt to Robt Perkins

32. May 4, 1862

John M. Walton, Pleasant Retreat, Burke County, N.C., letter to his mother, Burke County. Source: Thomas George Walton Papers (748), Southern Historical Collection, University of North Carolina at Chapel Hill.

At the start of the war, Thomas George Walton pulled both his sons out of military schools. John M. (Jock) and James T. (Jink) both served in the Confederate army. John served as a private in Company G, 1st Regiment N.C. Volunteers and was mustered out in December 1861. At the time of this letter, John was staying at a friend's home and had not yet re-enlisted, as many men of the "Burke Rifles" did. In May of 1862, his father, Captain Thomas G. Walton, faced re-election in Company F, 3rd N.C. Cavalry. Perhaps this is what is meant when John writes: "I am sorry his Co has been divided."[23]

        Pleasant Retreat May 4th 1862
My dear Mother
  I received your very interesting letter Thursday evening, and was very glad indeed to hear from home, as it has

been near three weeks since I had heard. I have never received Sis letter. I expect Stamy has forgotten all about it, and has never mailed it. I don't think you ought to blame me for not writing for I am sure I have allways been very punctual in answering all of your letters. The reason why I have been so long in writing this time is that I didn't think I ought to write until you answered the letter which I sent to Papy. I am sorry to say I have never written to Pa, or Jink,[24] it has been nothing but laziness, for I have intended to write and I have put it off, and off, until now, though I will write very soon. Please let me know where to direct a letter to Jink. I am sorry his Co- has been divided, though I suppose it is only for a short time. I came out here last Friday evening and couldn't go to church this morning on account of the rain. I have never seen as much wet weather in my life, I don't think.

Uncle John says he is completely worn out, he cant work on his farm, plant his corn or do anything scarcely. He and I went fishing yesterday. We had a very pleasant time, but we were not successful, as we didn't catch any fish. Cousin Clara sent us a very nice lunch down to where we were fishing. I think uncle J- is improving very fast, both in strength, and flesh. They are very kind to me indeed, as much so as they possibly can be. Cousin Clara received Aunt Mary's letter last night and gave me a great deal of news. She says she will answer it very soon. Tommy Patton leaves in the morning for Raleigh. He is going to join some Company. Cousin C- wrote to Grand Ma, Aunt Lizzie, and Ella. Cousin James got home from Charleston the other day. He has improved some though is still in very delicate health. Cousin C- says she will certainly expect you to come with the girls, and if you don't come you'll whistle for them before you get them back home again.

She says she will look for them next Tuesday, and will be very much disappointed if they don't come then. I will meet them if Mr. Holmes will let me off soon enough in the evening. Give my love to Aunt Mary and ask her please to excuse me from writing, as you know I am a very bad hand to write letters. Uncle John and Cousin C- send love to you and Aunt Mary, and all the children. Kiss all the children for me and tell Hugh I am getting very anxious to see him. Tell Bud he must write to me and let me know if he is fishing any now. Write soon to your devoted son.

John M. Walton[25]

33. May 18, 1862

Private Roland C. Osborne, "The Haywood Highlanders," Company F, 25th Regiment N.C. Troops, letter to his sister, Addie. Source: Mary Gash Papers (59), Private Manuscripts Collection, North Carolina Division of Archives and History.

Like the First Cavalry, the 25th Regiment returned to North Carolina following the Confederate defeat at New Bern. Soon, the 25th would depart for the fields of Virginia as part of a brigade commanded by Robert Ransom, but for now, the unit remained in eastern North Carolina guarding against any future Union incursion. By the time the smoke had cleared from the Seven Days Campaign, the 25th had proven its ability. They would undertake their next campaign without Private Osborne, who died of "febris typhoides" in a Petersburg, Virginia, hospital on August 5, 1862.[26]

Camp Near Kinston
May the 18th 1862
Dear Sister Addie

As I have not wrote to you for some time, I thought that I would drop you a few to let you know that I am well and trying to do the best I can. We have

South Carolinian and Flat Rock tourist Henry M. Rutledge was elected Lieutenant Colonel, then promoted to Colonel of the 25th North Carolina Troops. (North Carolina Division of Archives and History.)

hard living hier now, juts cornbread and Bacon & Pickel Pork. We can live most anyway to obtain the independence of our loved South, but I tell you it seams very hard. I saw yesterday for the first time three yankees. They ware stout healthy looking men. They seamed to be in fine spirits. The way I came to see them was my self and other men was sent a bout ten miles below hier to get some tools where our men had bin tarring up the Rail Road. We met the 4th Cavalry where they was watching three horses. Therefore I had a chance to have a talk with them. They had a yankeys Drum Majers drum staff. I tell you it was a pretty thing.

 I should like very much to see you all but it is rather uncertain when I get to see you all. But you may be shure as soon as I can get the chance. You wrote to me something about Drinking. You can rest very easy about that thing. I have not sean a man drink in six months. There is nothing hier to drink. I am trying to live the best I can under the present circumstances but I can tell you it is hard to live write in the armey. I have nothing more to write therefore I shal come to a close. Write soon to your friend and Brother
  R. C. Osborn

34. May 21, 1862

Captain Matthew N. Love, "The Edney Grays," Company A, 25th Regiment N.C. Troops, letter to sister, Elizabeth J. Love, Henderson County, North Carolina. Source: Matt Love Papers (3276), Manuscripts Department, Special Collections Library, Duke University.

Matthew Norris Love volunteered for service at Edneyville, Henderson County, on May 15, 1861. The same day, Matthew was appointed first lieutenant under Baylius Edney, and was later promoted to captain on April 30, 1862.[27] The 25th was not immune to the spread of disease; however, Love's company was in very good health at this time. Matthew described a wave of disease in the 35th North Carolina and a possible movement into Virginia.

> Kinston NC
> May the 21st 1862
>
> Dear Sister
>
> I once more take up my pen in hand to pen you a few lines which leaves us all in tolerable health hoping this may find you all enjoying similar blessings. I received a letter from Raleigh the other day. Capt Lanes Company is there and all well and were satisfied. I hope they may continue to be so for it must be a very hard life when one becomes satisfied. (My Company is in good health. I have narry a man in the hospital, but there is some complaining and there has been several deaths in this Briggade recently, several deaths in the 35th Regt to which Capt Jordans old Company[28] belongs. Leander Case and one of the Riterese, and others lying at the point of death. I think it is attributed to their lying out without tents after the Battle of Newbern.) You can tell all who have friends in my Co. that they are well, and getting along finely. I have just got through paying them their State Bounty which is forty dollars cash to the conscripts which received ten each at Asheville and I paid them their Confederate Bounty sometime since which was fifty dollars. I also paid them their monthly wages not long since and money is very flush in our camp. You can tell Cynthia Stepp[29] that her boys does not speak of coming home, they are going to take the places of some that are between the ages of eighteen & thirty-five and go on for the war.
>
> Gen. Ransom had the Commanders of Regts and separate companys summoned to attend at his head quarters this afternoon and gave them instructions to hold their commands ready to march at an hours notice and it is pretty generally the opinion that we will go to Richmond as they are expecting an engagement there soon. Others think we will go to weldon. We are having a power of rain here lately and the weather is extremely cold for this time of year. Hoping to hear soon I will add nothing more. Direct in care of Col. Rutledge.[30]
>
> M. N. Love

35. June 3, 1862

Private Lewis Warlick, Company B, 11th Regiment N.C. Troops, letter to Laura Cornelia McGimsey, Pleasant Hill, Burke County, North Carolina. Source: Laura C. McGimsey Papers (2680), Southern Historical Collection, Wilson Library, University of North Carolina at Chapel Hill.

Throughout most of April 1862, most men of the Burke Rifles, formerly of the 1st North Carolina Volunteers, re-enlisted in a variety of units. However, the largest concentration of Burke veterans volunteered in the 11th North Carolina Troops, or the "Bethel Regiment." Among these men was Lewis Warlick, who enlisted on May 15, 1862.[31] Lewis' regiment belonged to Pettigrew's Brigade and was posted in eastern North Carolina. In this letter to Cornelia, Lewis mentioned his intentions to fight on, a captured blockade runner, an unfortunate casualty, and recent health problems.

>Camp Davis near Wilmington
>June 3rd 1862

Dearest Cornelia

Yours of the 25th Inst. came to hand yesterday which was gladly received and now am about to respond but feel incapable of doing so. You say this is the first time in life you ever experienced a sad disappointment and was done by one who you thought would give you the least trouble, that I came off without telling you good bye or even tell you I was not going back; now you seem to think that it was intentional on my part that I knew very well when I left you that I did not expect to go back home but to remain.

I did not for a moment suppose that you would even sinuate, much less to say I had treated you badly; did I not explain to you in my last why it was that I did stay? I think I did. You say I ought to go home and hire a substitute, that I guess would be a hard job for men are so scarce at home I would not know where to get one that would be received in my place, and further more I would not get one if I could from the fact that it shall not be thrown up to my relations in future years that you had an uncle, brother, or that your father or perhaps grandfather would not go into the service when he was called on to assist his country in this great struggle for independence—was too cowardly, afraid of the Yankees & but hired a substitute to be shot at in my stead never never shall it be said of me or any descendants; death before dishonor. Dear Corrie you very well know that it is hard for me to leave you but I consider I am doing rightly. I think my first duties are to my country and then to you. I hope I may be spared to see the end of the war and then you and I will marry and try and live a happy life in the future. I pray do not sensure me for treating you badly if I have done so it was not intended it makes me feel badly to think that you blame me for every thing I do that is not according to your views. I have wanted to go into the service ever since last winter but you refused to let me come. I could have come against your remonstrances but did not want to do any thing to wound your feelings, which I have never done on purpose to my knowledge, but yet you say I have. Enough of that and I will write something else.

Before this reaches you you will have heard of the great slaughter at richmond Saturday & Sunday the particulars of which we have not got yet only telegrams all quiet there yesterday up to noon. We had marching orders last week but have never heard the word march. It was said by the Col.[32] that our destination would be Weldon.

Last week the blockading squadron captured the steamer Gordon off Fort Caswell from Bermuda bound for Wilmington her cargo consisted partly in five thousand stand of arms and twenty tons powder which would have been some little help to our army; we could hear the report of the guns very distinctly while they were firing on her.

Last week three of the squadron engaged the batteries at Fort Fisher. After firing over a hundred shots they withdrew, the only damage done was that of a shell killing a negro woman and a chicken the chicken being carried by the negro.

I have joined Armfields[33] company. Last week I had a sever attack of the diarrhea, am getting better I don't tink I'll have any more chills. You said you wanted some paper. I have plenty such as it is but I don't know how I will send it to you. I will send the first opportunity, in this I'll send some stamps. Jackson has been doing good service

Montford Sydney Stokes commanded the 1st North Carolina from its creation until he was killed in action at the Battle of Mechanicsville, Virginia, on June 26, 1862. (Library of Congress.)

don't you think so? I hope he is in Baltimore this morning and then right about march and come on Washington in the rear and burn it up and captured old Abe that would be too good.

This is so badly written I don't know whether you can read it or not. Write often to your devoted lover.
Lewis

Give my kindest regards to Puss and all my friends

36. June 11, 1862

Private William H. Proffit, Company B, 1st Regiment N.C. State Troops, letter to his brother Calvin L. Proffit, Wilkes County, North Carolina. Source: Proffit Family Papers (3408), Southern Historical Collection, Wilson Library, University of North Carolina at Chapel Hill.

After spending the winter in northern Virginia and spring in eastern North Carolina, William Proffit and the rest of the First North Carolina were sent to Petersburg. The First arrived too late to participate in the Battle of Seven Pines (Fair Oaks); however, within two weeks of this letter, the First received its baptism of fire at Mechanicsville, Virginia, the first of the Seven Days battles around Richmond.

Richmond, Va June 11, 1862
C. L. Proffit
Dear Brother,

This will inform you that I received a letter from you a few days ago which gratified me much by informing me that you were well. I suppose you have been informed of our leaving North Carolina and returning to Virginia. We camped a few days at Petersburg during which time we wrote you, but have not received no answer to your letters. I also had my type taken and started to you which I hope will be received. I guess you have heard of the recent fight near Richmond, and how our boys licked the yankees. I am not prepared to communicate any particulars of the battle. It will suffice to say that the Federals were repulsed with fearful loss—driven from their camps etc. It is said the Old North State stands first in honor of the battle.

We are encamped near the city of Richmond, and are getting along finely. The health of the Regiment is good at present and a spirit of unyielding resistance prevails among our soldiers. I had forgotten to tell you that the 1st Regt was ordered from Petersburg to the scene of action in the late battle, and arrived upon the field just as the battle of Sunday closed. As I was unwell, having another slight attack of chills, I did not accompany them but rejoined them a few days after. My health is now very good.

Our Regiment was on picket guard day before yesterday, and if I could see you I would recite several instances relative to it that would perhaps interest you, or at least it was interesting to me as it was the first time I had ever been on picket duty. Several shots were exchanged between our pickets and that of the enemy, with what effect, I am unable to say so far as in regards to the Yankees, but none of our boys were hurt. The Yankees were scared of our superior gunnery and by the hideous yells of a large spotted dog that eminated from the woods near the place where the enemy pickets were concealed. It also served to inform the owner that his appearance would be treated in like manner.

A. Walsh is in fine health and getting along nobly, also T. C. Land, D. M. Carlton, L. W. Laxton, and your friends generally.[34] The weather remains quite rainy and during the past few days has been very cool. The most intelligent men with whom I have conversed lately express the belief that the war will continue but a few more months. I hope it may be so, and I believe it will.

Give my compliments to the family and neighbors. Tell A. J. [his brother Andrew J. Proffit] that I have been looking, in vain, for along time for a letter from him. Tell A. N. [his brother Alfred N. Proffit] that his are few and far between. I shall expect to hear from you frequently. I would like for you to be a little more communicative in the future. Tell cousin William Walsh I would like to hear from him more frequently. Try to make good crops as they will be needed.

Yours til death,
W. H. Proffit

37. July 1, 1862

Private Calvin Leach, "The Wilkes Valley Guards," Company B, 1st Regiment N.C. State Troops, diary entry. Source: Calvin Leach Diary, Calvin Leach Papers (1875-z), Southern Historical Collection, Wilson Library, University of North Carolina at Chapel Hill.

Late on the evening of July 1, Clavin Leach commenced writing in a new diary. Like most young North Carolinians, Calvin avoided open combat until the opening of the Peninsula campaign in the late spring of 1862. Leach and the "Wilkes Valley Guards" participated in the battles of Mechanicsville (where they lost over two hundred men and their colonel, Montfort Stokes), Gaines Mill, and finally Mechanicsville on July 1, 1862. The recent carnage and suffering forced Calvin to re-evaluate his faith and his spiritual health.

Tues. 1st

This is the commencement of a new year with me in the history of this war. This day twelve months ago I left home for the field of war. During the past year the Lord has been with me and graciously delivered me from the hands of my enemys, but during the past year I have not been as faithful to my Lord and Master as I should have been, but the Lord who is righteous and juste to forgive is always with us to smile upon us in all of our troubles. Oh Lord thou art righteous, deliver me from trouble.

We also had a fight today, but I was sick and did not partake in the fight. I became so weak I could not go any further and my commander gave me permission to go to the rear. This was the battle of Malvern Hill. This was a sever fight. Great bravery was displayed on both sides and many of our co fell while in the engagement. The ball was opended about 1 oclock and continued untill after dark.

List of the Killed & Wound in the fight of Co. B, 1st Reg N C Volunteers

Killed	Wounded
Thomas Harley	Serg't Martin
J. E. Hendren	Serg't Carlton
Alfred Walsh	David Cockerham
Corp Land	John Estes
Corp Witherspoon	G. W. Spicer
Privates	F. Hemphill
R. S. Johnston	R. Brack
John Blaylock	Robert Chatam
Calvin Shores	Lucias Witherspoon
Cleveland Eller	William Mooney
G. W. Johnston	Joshua Johnston
Jesse Tylor	

38. July 14, 1862

Unknown private, Company I, 16th Regiment N.C. Troops, letter to brother-in-law, Charles Patton, Buncombe County, N.C. Source: Mary A. Gash Papers (59), Private Manuscripts, North Carolina Division of Archives and History.

The following letter was incomplete, missing the second page with the signature line. It is believed to come from one of three Gash brothers who served in Company I, 16th North Carolina Troops (Pender's Brigade, A. P. Hill's Division), whose family connection with the Pattons is well known. A note on this letter from a post-war source reports that the battle was Frayser's Farm, or Glendale, on June 30, 1862. The Battle of Frayser's Farm featured some of the fiercest hand-to-hand and small action fighting of the war. With the onset of darkness, the Union army withdrew to its stronghold at Malvern Hill.[35]

Richmond Va.
July 14, 1862

Mr. Charles Patton
Dear Brother

I received your very kind letter on wednesday the day that the battle commenced we was then on our march to attact the enemy we marched untill nearly midnight and halted untill two o clock the next day we started across the Chickahominy river and run in the pickets. The fighting commenced shortly afterwards and was kept up untill about 10 o clock in the night, we remained on the field till nearly day then went back to get our brigade formed, we was then placed in front trenchments, we Was then ordered to charge them. We charged through a large field and come to a steep bank which went down to a mill pond we went down the bank and got to the old run of the creek we was then halted. A battery of four or five peices was placed on the hill behind us they throde bumshells and grape shott on them so fast they had to get out if it had not bin for our artilery they would have killed over half of us before we could have got half way across the mill pond. We run them till about three o clock they called us to a halt our regt. was put as skirmishers to drive them in. We was going up a large hill when we saw them about two hunnread yards from us they commenced shooting and some of our boys did but I wanted to get a little clocer, I saw one raise up his gun I knew that he was going to shoot at me so I though I would be as fast as he was, altho I knew that my musket would not hold up unless I took very course sight and hold about his head. We fired about the same time his ball just did miss my left shoulder. He fell down I was surtin I had him but before I got my gun loaded he crawled up and took to his heels, we run them all in and went back to our Brigade we then went in another direction and had one of the hardest fights you ever herd tell of. We lost a good many men, but the Yankees was laying crost and piled. We like to have killed all their Zouaves. They turn as black as a negro in two hours after they are killed we took twenty pieces of artilery and a large number of small armes then on monday we had another very hard fight but we killed five to one it was on Monday that Miles Killian & Sam King[36] got killed, both of them was as good and brave boys as ever lived, they was awlways at their post. Miles was shot down on the field. Sam was carried of and dide the next day. We lost six killed and 15 wounded, well Charley we have had an awful time surtin but I am in hopes that we will get to rest a little while now. Our Regt. has bin engaged in five of the very hardest of battles there is not but four boys in our company that has bin through every one of the battles but what got killed or woundead, I am one and Tom Brittain[37] another that has went through the I have had men to fall on both sides of me On Thursday when we was charging their batteries the man may right and the one on my left both got shot also there was a cannon ball come in less than a foot of my leg. Well Charley it is not worth my while to try to give any discription whatever about our fights. All I can say is that I cannot see for my life how there is as many men gets through as does. when I get in to it I jest think if I am going to be killed that I will be killed anyhow and if not I will go through, so I go in with the detirmination to kill as many as I can

Well Charley I have bin plum completely worn out had have bin sick every since the battle, I am getting pretty stout again myself & Lieut Miller is staying at a private house in Richmond paying $2.00 a-day for board do write soon kiss all the babies for me, tell Ma I would be very glad if she could send me a pair of pants by some of the boys.

39. July 14, 1862

Private Marion Sexton, "The Ashe Beauregard Riflemen," Company A, 37th Regiment N.C. Troops, letter to his parents, Pryor and Mariah Sexton, Ashe County, North Carolina. Source: Thornton Sexton Letters (4749), Manuscripts Department, Special Collections Library, Duke University.

The Seven Days battles resulted in McClellan's retreat from his "On to Richmond" campaign. The victory was costly to the 37th North Carolina as well as other North Carolina regiments. This rough, yet earnest, letter from Marion Sexton, Thornton's brother, described the Seven Days battles around Richmond in June and July 1862. In this short message, Marion emphasized praying to God for deliverance and thought "we all ort to pray."

This is the 14 day of July 1862
State of Va richmond
Dear father and mother and Brother
 i tak my pen hand to let you now that i am well hoping that thes few lines may find you all injoying the same Blesing. We ort to be thank to god for thes many bless. He has got us through. i want to see you all But cant now but if i live i will come and see you all. i want you to rite to me as soon as this leter comes to hand. i hant got mutch to rite at presant. The fight comense in July. Hit last 8 day. We whip them and tuck ten thousand prisners. colonel Lee is dead.[38] he got shot. Isiah hast boy is dead he got Shot. Post welch[39] did with the fever in the hosse pittle at richmond. Sow farewell. Direct to richmond in cear of capt hartsog[40] in the 37 ridgement of N C trops in com A. This leter is from Marion Sexton and sent to pyrer sexton and mother.

Whar has bin hard for many days we ort to think that death is on ever sid of us. God is our friend. We ort to pray to god fer the many Blesing he has Be stod upon us. The first day of July & Second is sed 100 thousand men. I think we all ort to pray.

40. July 21, 1862

Second Lieutenant Thomas W. Patton, Company C, 60th Regiment N.C. Troops, letter to his mother, Asheville, Buncombe County, N.C. Source: Patton Family Papers (1739), Southern Historical Collection, Wilson Library, University of North Carolina at Chapel Hill.

After seven months, Thomas Patton re-enlisted into service and was elected first lieutenant on July 8, 1862. The unit in which Patton served as an officer would change names several times before being officially designated the 60th North Carolina. After completing its organization, the company moved along with Coleman's Battalion toward east Tennessee, through the Madison County community of Painted Rock.[41]

   Camp Smith July 21, 1862
My Dear Mother

We reached here in safety on Saturday morning after a rather tiresome march. My company marched from Alexanders to the springs on Friday and that was rather a forced march of twenty seven miles. On Thursday night we got shelter in Alexanders stable loft and so were sheltered from the rain, of which I was very glad as it would have been rather hard to have had the men to lay out the first night in such a rain. I found Guss here and succeeded in getting fixed up very comfortably in an old field about midway between the springs and Paint Rock. Our men are coming in tolerably well and by this evening I think all of our men will be here, as soon as we get them all together and regularly mustered in, it will be necessary for one of us to go on to Raleigh to get shoes and clothing. I suppose I will be the one to go, but don't much wish to as I have no particular love for Raleigh. If I do go I will pass through Asheville but it is doubtful.

If you write to me or have any letters or packages to send, direct them to the Warm Springs. I will write to Nannie today and hope that package has turned up safely and that you will forward it here—without opening it. Tell sister Anna, I tried to make a cup of cocoa today but failed rather. I will try again & hope for better luck. Love to all.
 Your Affec Son
   T. W. Patton

41. August 2, 1862

K., Asheville, Buncombe County, letter to her sister, Addie Gash, Henderson County. Source: Mary Gash Papers (59), Private Manuscripts Collection, North Carolina Division of Archives and History.

While the war went on, the effects of disease and combat began to tell on not only the soldiers, but also their families and extended families. Addie's brother Roland had been serving with the 25th Regiment for sometime, and had taken sick on several occasions. "K," believed to be Katharine Patton, expresses her concern as well as relaying a report she heard from Ben Edmonston, a Patton family friend.[42]

   Asheville, August the 2nd 1862
Dear Sister Addie

I can not consistently accept your kind invitation to be with you on the 9th. I feel compelled by some particular circumstances to stay at home unless something more urgent should call me away. I would love to be presant if I could consistently. Please give my kinest regards to Uncle Thomas Osborne, Mr. Siler and Cousin Matilda. I have heard so much of her that I should like very much to see her. Kiss little Rosie for me.

I received a note from Ben. F. Edmondston last Thursday. He said the Mr. Osborne was sick, not able to write, but he did not think him dangerous.

I suppose you have heard the same account of him. I fear he is much worse than Ben represented him or he would have writen himself. I do wish some one could go to nurse him. Could not Mr. Minigus er some one else go to him? Mother says she would keep any boy if I could go myself. I would love to go if it was posable or rather that he could not come home. Mr. Osborne, huggy, is mended, but is not at home. Rufus is well. Excuse this short note for my mind in on other things far way. May you be happy is the wish of

    Your affectionate Sister—K.

42. August 19, 1862

Captain John T. Jones, "The Caldwell Guards," Company I, 26th Regiment N.C. Troops, letter to his father, Edmund Jones, Clover Hill, Happy Valley, Caldwell County, N.C. Source: Edmund Jones Papers (3543), Southern Historical Collection, Wilson Library, University of North Carolina at Chapel Hill.

On April 21, 1862, John Thomas Jones was elected captain of the "Caldwell Guards." With his higher rank, Jones received additional responsibilities such as supervising earthwork construction. After the retreat from New Bern, the 26th briefly served with Ransom's Brigade during the Peninsula campaign. In this note to his father, Jones asked for some provisions as well as a pair of shoes.

    Camp Petersburg
    Aug 16th /62

Dear Father

I received your letter by Henry Holden[43] and will tend to the matter you spoke of. I hardly know how I will manage to get his State bounty as all of the rest have got theirs in his absence. I will attend to it though I have the 13 dollars. Would you like me to send the money in a letter?

I wish very much you would have me a good pair of shoes made and send them by Wat or some other person, size 6, sevens are too large. Anything in the shape of cheries or butter or dried beef would be very acceptable. Butter is one dollar per lbs.

My health has greatly improved. I have been at work all this week making breastworks. I am general superintendent of the works and have it left to my own judgement how I should make them. I had a dispute with an engineer how I should make a certain butting and the General decided in my favor. Govr Vance left us this morning very early. Last night he gave us his parting speech and it brought the tear to many an eye, this had long been a stranger to such a thing. Col Burgwin is now here and our Reg is in command of the trains Corps of Longstreet.

Has Miss Mollie Jones yet arrived? Please send my letter from Miss Maria to me as I have no idea of being at home soon. I don't see how she could have heard so. Your aff son

    JT Jones

43. September 4, 1862

Private Azariah Denny, Company C, 21st Regiment N.C. Troops, letter to his father, Joel Denny, and family, Surry County, N.C. Source: Jackson, Surry County in the Civil War, 1983.

Azariah Denny, the 18-year-old son of Joel and Nancy Denny of Pilot Mountain, was conscripted into service on August 14, 1862. In one of his first letters home to his father, Denny described traveling with a group of conscripts who were to be assigned to the 21st North Carolina regiment, a unit with three Surry County companies.[44] He alluded to the progress of Jackson, his tentmates, and advice to his brother-in-law, Jonathan Flinchum.

September the 4th 1862
Gordensville Va

Dear father, I now seat myself with pleasure to letting you know that I am well hoping that these few lines may find you all well. I am sorry to say that I have wrote this makes seven times and never heard the first word from Surry yet. I tent with Tyre Clasby, B. F. Kidd, William Ashburn, W. C. Banner, W. T. Lewis, L. Patterson, J. W. & Jonathan Creed, A. Denny, David Johnstone, Daniel McGee all agreeable boys.[45] Clasby is sick and is some better. We have bread enough and bacon plenty enough it is hardly fit to eat. There is no doubt but what Jackson has taken Manasses and Centerville back and I feel like taking my gun and whipping them and coming home to where I can get apples to eat—can get at $3.00 a bushel or 25 cents a dozen—small peaches at the same—a pie as large as your hand for 25 cents. Other things—have a good many friends here. I am sorry to say that Captain Shore[46] is dead. I am every hour expecting to start to Centerville. I want to see all but it is not worth my while to think of that so I will close giving you all my best respects until death.

Dear brother and sister, I now seat myself to let you know that I am well hoping that these few lines may find you well. I would be glad to see you, no I want Jonathan to stay at home as long as he can and come to me when [he] does come. I think that he would stand it well. I have gained 10 lbs. since I left home

to J. Flinchum[47] A. Denny Direct your letter to Gordensville Va 21 N. C. regiment Company C in ker of Lieutenant Whitlock[48]

44. September 8, 1862

Private Harvey C. Davis, "The Watauga Rangers," Company D, 9th Regiment N.C. Troops (1st N.C. Cavalry), diary entry. Source: Francis B. Dedmond, "Harvey Davis' Unpublished Civil War Diary and the Story of Company D, First North Carolina Cavalry," *Appalachian Journal* 13 (1986) 368–407. Catawba College Archives, Salisbury, North Carolina.[49]

Before the war, one of the well-known road junctions in Watauga County was Meat Camp. Farmers and those who raised livestock would drive their animals to this place to be sold or slaughtered or to rest before heading east or westward. Harvey Davis lived in the Meat Camp area and was the only support for his widowed mother and six younger siblings. Davis volunteered for service in May of 1861 and served in George Folk's Company D of the First North Carolina Cavalry. Davis and his regiment provided a scouting and screening force for General Lee's invasion of Maryland. Harvey recorded the incidents near Frederick in his diary and blamed the poor performance of some of the men on whiskey.

> On the 7th went to Sperryville. Here I will say I found some of the most noble clever people. Miss or Mrs Baughman in particular. She was a sister to the editor of the Southern Citizen, a paper published in Frederick City. They were whole souled Southerners & further they were Roman Catholics and until then I allways doubted whether there were any Christians in the Catholic church but since then never. Sept 8 the yankees charged our picket lines. They nearly run into our camp. Here some of the boys got some whiskey & was in a poor fix for fighting. But we soon turned the yanks and started them double quick the back track, but it was quite exciting to be roused from a good nap by yells, shots, &c.

45. September 9, 1862

Private Alfred N. Proffit, Company D, 18th Regiment N.C. Troops, letter to his brother, C. L. Proffit, Wilkes County, North Carolina. Source: Proffit Family Papers (3408), Southern Historical Collection, Wilson Library, University of North Carolina at Chapel Hill.

On August 22, 1862, Wilkes County brothers Alfred Newton and Andrew Jackson Proffit were conscripted into service. The Proffits, along with over twenty other Wilkes men, were assigned to the 18th North Carolina, a unit composed primarily of troops from eastern North Carolina. Alfred Proffit and the conscripts finally reached their command already engaged in the Maryland campaign. Alfred talked about his journey and referred to the stands of arms captured at the Battle of Second Manassas, August 28–September 1, 1862.

      State of Maryland Camp Thunder
      September 9: 1862
C[alvin] L. Proffit
Dear Brother,

These lines are to in form you that we are all well greatly hoping these few lines may reach you and will find you with the rest of my friends injoying the same blessings. I havent any news to write you of much importance more than we have had quite a frisky time since we left Richmond. We left Monday the 1st of September and have marched 8 days in succession and cooked our rashions every night. We waded the Rhappadan and Potomac rivers. We have passed many sights both pleasant and unpleasant. We passed many battel grounds though not exactly through any. We have passed many beautiful farms and villages.

When we left Richmond we expected to go to Gordons ville and stay thare some time but we dident dally thar and from thar we started to manassis and we turned before we got thar on account of a hard fought battel in which was fought a few days before we got thar and the loss was vary bad. The southern boys ware successful. It was somethun to see the armes that was taken from the yankis. We all have yankee guns of the best quality. The men in this stait are volunteering fast. We will soon have a larg army of marylanders. Then we may recross the Potomac but I dont no what the intention of Jackson is. He is unwell at this time. When he gets well he will do something.

We are encamped on a steep hillside without tents & so is all the army on this side of the P. We have plenty to eat and good water. The prospect for health is good but we expect to leave here in a few days. I wrote you while I was at Richmond which I suppose you have recieved the chance for sending letters here is bad on account of the railroad being torn up. We haft to haul our provisions from the rhappadan in wagons.

I must soon close. I will in form you how to direct your letters on a little scrap of paper and then I want you to write me as soon as you can. Give my respects to F. M. and Elisabeth and family. No more but remain yours
A. N. P.

Miss R[achel] L. Proffit—esteemed sister, these lines will in form you that we are all rite on the goods. I am now in maryland and injoying myself finely. We have plenty to eat and not mutch to do since we taken the march of 8 days. Thar was not mutch fun in that for the dust was so thick that you could not see on for 10 miles. Sis I havent taken off my cloathes since I left home and it will be something to git them clean. I wish you had the chance to wash them for me. I and some of the boys are goin to the crrek to wash now I must close for want of space. Write soon, A. N. P.

46. September 10, 1862

First Lieutenant Thomas W. Patton, Company C, 60th Regiment N.C. Troops, letter to his mother, Asheville, Buncombe County, N.C. Source: Patton Family Papers (1739), Southern Historical Collection, Wilson Library, University of North Carolina at Chapel Hill.

The final organization of the 60th North Carolina was completed by the first of September. At the time of this letter, First Lieutenant Thomas Patton was with his company in a grove outside of Greenville, Tennessee. Patton remarked on Mr. Fagg, who came to settle a debt, which was apparently a substantial one, and about not receiving a furlough.

                Greenville Sept 10 1862
My Dear Mother

I reached here in safety with my two deserters on Wednesday evening and was tired So tired too as my horse had to he slept at the spring and I had to walk over here. I stood the walk very well however and feel no ill effect, from it whatever.

Mr. Fagg reached here to day says he came all the way from Alabama to order to have a settlement with me. The ones on to Asheville tomorrow and I was anxious to go with him and I thought it very important that I should have some settlement with him if it were possible. But when I applied to the Col, he said that some of the officers had been talking about Frank[50] and myself being allowed more furlough and to be absent from camp more than the rest and he was afraid he would be charged with partiality if I went off again—of course I told him under the circumstances I would not insist upon going although I have never been away from camp since I left home except on company business—except a few days at the spring.

We are camped in a very pleasant grove and I like our present very well, it is the general opinion that we will be ordered away from here in a few days, but I see no reason to think so and you must not believe it until you hear it certainly. I will write oftener now after your scolding letter which reached me at the springs. I suppose Charlie is still with you. Mrs. Pritchard came down as far as the springs with me but I did not recognize her at all and consequently did not speak to her. I was very sorry when I heard it was she. Mr. Fagg seems to be very anxious to sell out his share of his property. He said he would take $27.50 for acre which for 600 acres amounts to $16500. I wish I could see any way clear enough to do something in regard to it but I think it is entirely too great indebted now for one to undertake during these war times it is true a portion of it would be dire to him to the estates but still my indebtedness would be the same or if it was all to him—when you write or have any letters so send to me direct from Greenville until further notice your affect son.

                Thomas W. Patton

47. September 11, 1862

Tolivar Davis, Cathey Creek, Rutherford County, letter to Governnor Zebulon B. Vance, Raleigh, Wake County. Source: Governor's Papers (Vance), North Carolina Division of Archives and History.

On August 16, 1862, Zebulon Vance delivered his inaugural speech which spiritedly refuted the claim he planned on taking North Carolina back into the Union, and stressed political unity. Of the many who received copies was Rutherford County planter and politician Tolivar Davis.[51] Tolivar Davis was a self-educated businessman who was a staunch secessionist, and in this letter, he confirms his patriotism.

Governor Zebulon Vance, of Buncombe County, was responsible for the state's conduct of the war and maintaining order within North Carolina. (North Carolina Division of Archives and History.)

Rutherford Cty N. C.
Sept 11th 1862

Although we have not agreed heretofore in Politicks, your speech at Raleigh was all I could have desired, and I feel it my duty to give whatever Influence & Support to your administration my limited Influence will permit. I feel shure the state will have & energetic Administration, & one that will endeavor to do Justice to all. I am aware Your administration will be Closely Scrutinized, but I think there is one road Chalked out by you, that will make you everything that you can or may desire, that is the active prosecution of the war, in that you have the advantage of any of your predecessors, during the time you remain in office I have no doubt this terable war will be terminated, & you will have much to do in enforcing Military obedience as well as Civil. I am sorry to say there are Citizens of our country that say they will not sirve as Conscripts, there are others that have got little mail contracts & Schools to keep them out of the war, while brave boys are pouring out their blood like water on the battle field, this is certainly rong. I think it is a common cause, and I think able bodeyd men ought to make common sacrifices, with out resorting to evry little means to evade the law. I am sory that the law made Such provision, I hope that it will yet be so amended as to Include every able bodeyd man in the Confederacy? If men because they happen to be a postmaster or School master or mail contractor can be excused from serving their country, then I think it time that the common citizen should be excused—but while our sons that are Just as good as those are undergoing all the Labour & hazzard of war, it is nothing but right that all should bear their part. There is enough over forty five to do all the business that is wanting with those that are unable to go by Infirmity of body, the boys under 18 years & the old men & women of the country can with the help of Negroes make with ordinary Seasons enough to eat if salt can be got to Save it, & I think if our people can whip the next call of the North it will end the war & that will depend uppon the energy & the Efficiency of the Confederate & State Governments. We must be as much united as possible, & we must expect to Suffer much before we get our Independence, hoping & praying that you may be Instrumental in assisting & carying out all the measures necessary under providence for our speedy deliverance from the grasp of the enemy and a safe return to piece, with this blessing we shall no doubt rejoice although a large a mount of our sons may find a premature grave far off from Home.

    Yours very Truly

PS Since writing the above I have read your Inaugural & it is all that could be desired, I think it will have a tendency to arouse some of your personal friends that have been lukewarm in the Cause & Make them active. I hope your Action will have the effect to unite us all as one. you may think this letter rather untimely from Me so soon but it breaths my best wishes for your welfare & that of the old North State, and may a kind providence smile on your Administration & make it just what you may desire.

    T. Davis

48. September 14, 1862

Private Calvin Leach, "The Wilkes Valley Guard," Company B, 1st Regiment N.C. State Troops, diary entry. Source: The Diary of Calvin Leach, Calvin Leach Papers (1875-z), Southern Historical Collection, Wilson Library, University of North Carolina at Chapel Hill.

Leach soldiered as a private in the Wilkes Valley Guards through the unit's combats during the Seven Days, especially the Battle of Mechanicsville, where the regiment lost nearly 154 men. The following diary entry describes the action by the 1st North Carolina (Ripley's Brigade), which belonged to D. H. Hill's Division defending Turner's Gap.

Sun 14th—Today was fought the battle of Boonsborer which was fought on the top of the where we crossed it on friday. Today at 10 oclock we mooved off from our position and marched to ward the roaring of the cannons. We marched about half way up the mountain and stoped for a moment, took off our knapsackes laid them by. Here I lost a testament which was gave me by a friend & loaded our guns. This was now an exciting time. Many of the wounded came down the road meeting us also the citizens were leaving out. Those that lived on the top of the mountain came riding down in a carrage with tears in their eyes whose faces I recollected seeing as we passed befor, who seemed gay and happy surround by home and its comforts waving the southern flag at us as we passed before. While we were stoped here they passed withe dead body Gen. Garland.[52] We now marched on to the top of the mountain where I could see the yankees in a line of battle and their artillery placed firing on us and our artillery was in position playing on them. The enemy were now trying to flank us on the right. We were now ordered by the right flank and marched on the top of the mountain keeping up withe the enemy going over rocks and cliffs, and some of the worst places I almost ever saw. We were march backward and forwar across the mountain and were marched to the top of it by the left flank in a line of battle and waited there till near sundown and then back again. There we waited till after dark & the infantry continue to fire at about 10 oclock in the night the fire ing stoped and about this time we marched silently off and left the field behind. We marched untill day. Our Reg did not fire in this battle.

Three days after the small but decisive engagement at South Mountain, both armies were prepared to do battle outside Sharpsburg, Maryland. Action commenced in the early morning and fierce combat broke out in the fields near the small Dunker Church. Ripley's Brigade of D. H. Hill's Division was sent in to counter advances made by the 19th Indiana and 7th Wisconsin (Gibbon's Iron Brigade) and Patrick's Brigade at about 8 o'clock in the morning. After conducting a successful charge, Ripley pushed back those Federals from the cornfield but was under a severe flanking fire from the 128th Pennsylvania, which had gone prone behind a fence.[53]

The handwritten page from Leach's diary detailing his account of the Battle of Sharpsburg (Antietam). (Calvin Leach Papers, Southern Historical Collection.)

49. September 17, 1862

Private Calvin Leach, "The Wilkes Valley Guide," Company B, 1st Regiment N.C. State Troops, diary entry. Source: The Diary of Calvin Leach, Calvin Leach Papers (1875-z), Southern Historical Collection, Wilson Library, University of North Carolina at Chapel Hill.

Wed 17th—Today a fierce engage ment followed, all the day, both by infantry and, artillery. Our Brigade was first in, soon in the morning the fight commenced, and very soon our Reg was under fire the balls whisin over us and wounding and killing many of our our brave boys. Here our gallant and much loved capt Boushell[54] got severely wounded in the mouth and had to be carried off the field. Olso Lieut Peden[55] was wound.

We were ordered by the left flank and were very soon into the engagement. I commenced loading and shooting with all my might but my gun got choked the first round, and I picked up the gun of one of my comrades who fell by my side and continued to fire. Here I could see the second line of battle of the enemy and when their men would fall, the rest would close in and fill their places. Their first line was lying by a fence and I could see the old "Stars & Stripes" waving over them. I fired as soon as I could aim at the men around the flag I do not know whether I killed any one or not.

During this time our Reg got cut up very severly, and the Reg was ordered to retreat back when we met reinforcements coming in and I was glad to see them for I was nearly tired to death, not having hardly any thing to eat for 4 or 5 days. We then marched up on a hill out of danger of the balls where we stacked arms and rested awhile. 66 men of our Reg stacked arms.

We received more amunition and was ordered back to our position in a line of battle, where we stayed till night. I often looked at the sun and longed for night to come so the fire ing would cease. As we marched back to our position Gen Lee met us and sayed "Go in cheerfull boys they are driving them back on the right and left and we need a little help in the center." Gen Ripley[56] our Brigadeer Gen. was wounded today.

50. September 18, 1862

Private John W. Reese, Company F, 60th Regiment N.C. Troops, letter to his wife, Christena, Buncombe County, North Carolina. Source: John W. Reese Papers (4417), Manuscripts Department, Special Collections Library, Duke University.

John W. Reese worked as a miller in Buncombe County, N.C. John and his wife, Christena raised their three children, Susan, Margaret, and John, in the Reem's Creek area in 1860. Two years later, John enlisted in service on August 22, 1862. He was reported absent sick quite often, due to, in no small part, the exposures suffered by men of the 60th who were undersupplied and underequipped since their first day in service.[57]

              Greenvill camp morting
              September the 18 1862

Dear wife

Its with pleasur that I tak the opportunity of riting to you by James Black. He has bin to the Cumberland Gap and is going to stay with us to nit. I am well onley I hav the hedack this eaving vary bad. Living on wheat Bread dont a gree with mee tena. I am in hops when these lins bring to you tha may find you and the Children well. God bless thar little sols. I no tha want to see mee and God nos that I want to see you and them. I dont sleep mutch hear. I am up lat at nit and up soon and as soon as my eys is open my mind is apon you and the Children. I hav to gut for a while and go on dress purrad.

I hav not got my money yet. The quarter master has not got back yet as soon as he cums I will send you sum money tena. I am a frad you hav dun had a bare sum thin to eat. I want you to rit to mee and let mee no how you hav mad out a bout Bread. I want me sum close. I got a pair of Blue long pants for three dollars and new shirt for one dollar and twenty five cent. If I dont git a fur low I want you to send mee two pair of socks. You can send mee any thing you pleas by taking it in a pak up and send it down to Elkans and tha will send it to me by some body.

My capton sed he intends mee to go home if thar is any chans but thar is no body out to send me after. I am hear with out a Blankit. I want you to send mee somthing to sleep on if you can. Tell the Boys that if tha doo hav to volunteer I want them to cum hear. Tha hav took men out of all the cumpanys and mad a new one and Goodson Robards is Capton[58] and he is one that will doo. Yet I belong to stevens.[59] I under stand that the quarter master has got back. The pay master will be in to day or to morrow then I will rite to you a gane. Tena I got a letter from John E. Barrett. He is well. James Black sed that thar was sevril of the Boys was bair footed and not mutch close on thar poor backs. I send you sum poetry in this letter.

                John W. Reese
            to Cris tena V. Reese

51. September 22, 1862

Private Andrew J. Proffit, Company D, 18th Regiment N.C. Troops, letter to his parents, Lewis Fork, Wilkes County, N.C. Source: Proffit Family Papers (3408), Southern Historical Collection, Wilson Library, University of North Carolina at Chapel Hill.

Andrew J. Proffit began 1862 as a Wilkes County teacher. In August, he and his brother Alfred were conscripted into service. Andrew marched along with the conscripts until joining their regiment at Harper's Ferry, Virginia (see letter for 9 September), in time to participate in the campaign which led to the fall of the town. Proffit chronicled his involvement in the overall Maryland campaign describing the fall of Harper's Ferry (14th), the short time in action at Sharpsburg (17th), and a hotly contested battle at Boetler's Ford.[60]

        Near Martins burg va
          Sept. the 22th 1862
Dear Father and mother

It is with great pleasure that I write you a few lines which will inform you that we are in the land of the living and enjoying reasonable position of health etc. I have indeed stood the trip well and have had no sickness. I have stood it better than the other boys. We have been gone one month & 2 days & have been in the battle the 15th at Harpers Ferry where we took about 10000 prisoners and in Maryland which was indeed a bloody battle. We did not get to fire there but was exposed to the fire of the enemy in an open field for about one half mile. Severil of our Reg were killed and wounded. We lay all day next day behind a fense exposed to their sharp shooters & A. W. Dunkin[61] was shot through the thigh. That night we crossed back into va. All though we ran the enemy from the field when we left they persued us and crossed day before yesterday. We turned on them and had a bloody engagement. We formed in line of battle about one mile from them and made a generil charge, exposed the whole way to the heaviest bombing said to be by old soldiers that they ever saw but we routed them and drove them back across the river about 9 or 10 oclock. I suppose we lost a great many but the yankees lay on the field in heaps and piles. We got all their arms, knapsacks, and all they had with many prisoners as they crossed the river.

We give them fits and I shot as long as we could see a blue coat. Exposed to the fire of 3 batteries the bombs burst round our heads with terrific fury and showers of grape and canister fell mingled with limbs of trees thick around us, but the God of heaven protected us from their power which I hope he will ever do. We were much exhousted from the fatigues of the charge that we threw away all our clothes & blankits only what we have on but that is all right. We will get more. A. N. [his brother Afred Newton Proffit] was slightly struck on the arm with a piece of shell or something. He dropped his gun. I asked him if he was hurt. He said not. He grabbed his and fought like a heroe while the sweat dropped fast from his brow. T. G. Walsh, A. Vannoy, John Ferguson, R. M. Blankinship, Vincent Hindrix & others were all engaged and fought like veterans.[62] Wm. C. Proffit[63] was struck on the knee with a piece of a bomb and knocked down so he did not go through but was not hurt much. He is not very well now but A.N. & W.C. have not stood it as well as I have but have kept up and done good service and for bravery can not be excelled. We have not been drilled exceeding 4 hours but our officers give us much praise for fighting.

Well Pa as it is all right on the goose about the war, I will now ask you a few questions. I want you to write me all the news about our domestic consensus. Have you bought you any land if so where & what price? Are you done fodering? Have you sold my Mare or Jack and what price? Have you made any trades of importance & what are they? DO we have any free school and who is teaching? Where is H. M. Stokes & what is he doing. If you have herd from Jesse Mills & how he is & how J. Betties family is doing and how the church is getting along. Please answer these interrogations and give me the news about all the connection and neighbors and if cousin fanny got well. Write if you have heard from harrison lately. He was broken down and not able to travel when his Reg left the Rhapadan and he was sent back to Gordonsville or Orange Ct. to rest. I saw some of his reg yesterday. I thought that William Walsh was gone home when I wrote before but he did not start then but I suppose he has or will go soon for he will not be retained in service. Tell H. Binghams connection that I see him almost every day. He is in our brigade & is doing well. Pa—I want you to keep Calvin at home if possible in an honorable way. I know he will stay if he will continue to teach school for he is not able for such service as is required.

I believe I have written about all I know. I am anxious to hear from you & to know what you are going to do about a home. I know not what plan to suggest if you could get that set of mules I would be much pleased, if not, I think you could do well on Gap Creek. If you get a good chance you must do the best you can. Sell any of my property and apply it to the most needful purpose. Write whether Capt Ball took my wagons or not and take it all in all. Get some man to write a day for you and write every thing that will be of interest to me. Tell all my friends to write often to me & I will write to them but my chance is bad. I have to send them to Gordonsville to be mailed which is about 150 or 200 miles. There fore if you do not get many letters from us you need not be uneasy. When you write direct this in writing thus they will follow me where I am "A. J. Proffit, 18th Reg. NC Troops, Branch's Brigade, A. P. Hill's division, Gordonsville va Co. D." I will now close by subscribing my self your most obedient son till death

J. Proffit

PS Please inform my friends how to direct their letters etc.

52. September 25, 1862

Anonymous writer, Columbus, Polk County, letter to Governor Zebulon B. Vance, Raleigh, Wake County. Source: Governor's Papers (Vance), North Carolina Division of Archives and History.

An anonymous, concerned citizen wrote this letter to Vance regarding the corrupt and incompetent officers in the Polk County militia unit which was designated as the 105th Regiment. Major problems existed in this system, and the particular situation in Polk County was confirmed by James E. Hannon.[64] Johnson L. Ward and Robert Lyles bore the brunt of the author's accusations.

Columbus N. C. Sept 25th 1862

I take the libbeter though a Stranger personally to drop you a line respecting affairs in our county with regard to the Conscripts in the first place Ward[65] & the oald Col is very obnoxious to the masses and when he got badly beaten for Shff. he started to make a company and has not got it full yet. He is gitting some accessions to it in this way he tells Maj. Liles[66] to arrest the conscripts and than he goes and gets them to Joine his company. Perhaps you may like to hear how Liles got to be Maj. Ward got one Capt & one Lieutenant in his office and elected Liles with three votes and not one other capt nor any of the commission officers knew any thing of the election it was not advertised as the law directs and Ward can make Liles do anything he wishes. They have got some of the captains riding in every direction and others will not go the people is willing to go under law full officers but the people will not submit much longer to such rule as Ward Mills & Com. We beat them all out last Election root & Branch and there is not a single Democrat in office in the Country except this miserobel Liles & George Mills one of the coart and we will set him out next march if time lasts Liles is one of the worst of fools in every respect in dating an order to Capt Hannons he dates it 9862

You may think that I am medling but I wish to see harmony but it is any thing but harmony in this County. As I Stated before Ward is one of the most obnoxious men in the County to a very large majority. He told Liles the other day that he had orders from you to take all men liabel to Conscript & tie them and bring them to Jail an carry them off in chains if necessary and that he had printed orders to that effect printed the morning he left Raleigh. They also tel the people that they have orders from you also to take the men from 35 to 45. Ward when the orders Came first for the Conscripts to enrole set his day to meet at Columbus and instead of being there himself he gose off to Richmond & the army Election & leaves Lils to manage affairs. Liles made arangements for transportation & had every thing arranged & the peopel though perhaps all right but Ward come back with new orders and then the Peopel began to think as before of Ward all rong and there has bin at least one half dozen meetings by them since and it leaves room for the peopel to dout the truth in any way that Ward & Liles may suggest or order. Ward is one of the most miserobel corrupt men in power in any way in N. C. or any whare els an honest man in my county will sustain me in what I say. He is of the worst Stock ever raised in our State his Father was whipe at the whiping post and Stood in the Pillery at Rutherfordton. Dont believe me but ask Gen Jones & John W. Hampton[67] for to sustain me in what I Say and about what I have ritten to you & if there was orders for an Election of pet officers in this the 105 the Regement N. C. melitia I think all coul be mange sattisfactorily to the peopel.

53. September 29, 1862

Major John T. Jones, 26th Regiment N.C. Troops, letter to his father, Edmund Jones, Clover Hill, Happy Valley, Caldwell County, N.C. Source: Edmund Jones Papers (3543), Southern Historical Collection, Wilson Library, University of North Carolina at Chapel Hill.

Two days after being promoted to major on September 27, 1862, Jones wrote this letter to his father in Caldwell County. This promotion allowed Jones to serve as a field officer under his good friend Colonel "Harry" Burgwyn. On September 29, Jones was again engaged in the tedious, non-combat duties of an officer that included sitting on a court-martial jury.

Petersburg, Va
Sept 29th/ 62
Dear Father.

I was very sorry to hear that you were quite unwell with diptheria a few days since. I hope it will not prove serious at all, but I shall feel uneasy until I hear from you. I have had it myself but had entirely recovered from its effects. I am again engaged upon court-martial which was interrupted by our trip down to Suffolk. I have been very much troubled very much with my bowels for the last two months but am better now than I have been in that time. The Doctor feared that it would prove to be chronic, but I think a few more days in the city where I can get something holesome to eat will sure me up.

There is a large force reported at Suffolk but I don't believe it. Some fear an attack on this place but I think it is all a ruse to draw our attention from other points. We have only two brigades here but I think it is plenty for all foreseeable purposes. You wanted to know if I wanted any winter clothing. I have provided myself with all I need. I would like to have a pair of pants made of good home spun cloth, grayish of hue or something of the sort. I have drawers and shirts enough.

Tell Mill I have just heard that Pete Rendall was dead. He had run the blockade at Wilmington but was taken sick and put into Charleston and from thence he came home where he died in a few days of yellow fever. Bill Adams was also killed at Sharpsburg. Give my love to Mary and tell my nephew howdey for me. Write soon and let me hear how you are.

Your affectionate Son
J Jones

54. October 13, 1862

Private John H. Phillips, Company E, 62nd Regiment N.C. Troops, letter to his cousin, Henderson County, North Carolina. Source: Matt Love Papers (3276), Special Collections Library, Duke University.

Organized during the early fall of 1862, the 62nd Regiment N.C. Troops mustered almost five hundred men. Third Sergeant John H. Phillips, a Transylvania County farmer who enlisted into service on July 14, 1862, was one of these soldiers. From Camp Carter, Sergeant Phillips wrote his cousin about the lack of provisions and his ideas about how Lincoln's proclamation would change the attitudes of east Tennessee loyalists.

Camp Carter
East Tennessee Octr 13th 1862
Dear Cousin

You will perceive by this that I am at least in the Confederate service and stationed in the above mentioned place. Since I have been here I have had a severe sickness but am glad to say at present I am well though I fear my sickness would have incapacitated me for active service. It has left me quite thin but I feel much stronger than I did some time ago. In all probability our regiment will be stationed here permanently for the winter to guard the bridge across the Watauga River against the incendiary attacks of the tories of this unfortunate state. I suppose owing to the warm and unprecedented dry summer, we will experience a very cold winter.

We are tolerably comfortable here but still there is room for improvement both in the Quarter Masters & Commissary's department as to our comforts. I do sincerely hope that this more than barbarous war will soon be over so that we all can return to our dear ones at home it has cost us a great deal of blood & treasure and will perhaps cause the hearts of many to bleed afresh yet. What is all this worth as compared to bondage & chains? No long as a true Southern

Along with John H. Phillips, privates Joseph Blalock (left) and Francis Burch served in the 62nd North Carolina. (U.S. Army Military History Institute, Carlisle, Pa.)

heart burns in defence of all that his dear & we will never be slaves to a licutious corrupt nation as our would be Yankee rulers wish to see Lincoln's proclimation has had the happy tendency of. I hear of uniting the people of East Tennessee together and causing them to stem the tide of Yankee invasion that may yet set towards our own fair Southern shores.

I wish I could see you once returned to old Henderson County, and having the plaudit ringing out from a grateful people well done through good and faithful service. When I last heard from home my wife and child was well. I have lost one. I do not suppose you ever heard about it. I hope this letter will be received and answered as an apology for my long silence. Write soon. I shall be delighted to hear from you and when you write direct your letter to me at Carter Depot E Tennessee Co "E" 62nd Regt NoCa Troops. I must now bring my letter to a close hoping this may find you enjoying good health is the sincere wish of your attached cousin

John H. Phillips

55. October 18, 1862

Colonel Isaac E. Avery, 6th Regiment N.C. State Troops, letter to his sister, Laura, Morganton, Burke County, N.C. Source: Waightsill Avery Papers (33), Southern Historical Collection, Wilson Library, University of North Carolina at Chapel Hill.

On October 18, Avery still held the official rank of captain, though he had served as the acting commander of the 6th North Carolina in the absence of any field officers. Captain Avery, the 32-year-old son of Isaac Thomas Avery, a Burke County planter, volunteered for service on May 16, 1861. He was wounded in action during the Battle of First Manassas on July 21, 1861. During most of late 1862, Avery served as regimental commander. Later, his promotion to lieutenant colonel was dated to June 1, 1862, the day he assumed active command, and his promotion to colonel was dated June 11, 1862. In this letter Avery talks about vaccinations, promotions among his surgeons, and the movements of Branch's Brigade, in which his older brother, Clark Moulton Avery, served as a regimental commander.[68]

     Camp near Winchester Va
     Octo. 18 1862

Dear Laura

 James Parsons arrived here a few days ago since and from what he said, I was very uneasy about brother Moulton. I was quite relieved when I got your welcome letter today, tho I still have some little apprehensions about him. I am very much distressed to hear of the situation of poor Nonie. It is with a good deal of difficulty that an officer can get leave to be absent from his Regt, even for a day. Thomas Alson [?] succeeded in getting another leave one day this made 2. I was again disappointed about seeing Willie. Their Brigade (Branchs) had been ordered off on fatigue duty (tearing up R. Rd track) several miles and Alphonso could not get there. He learned from sick men that Willie had been in camp and went with the Regt on horse back. He did not hear from Albert. If he could have seen Willie he would have advised him to send Albert home. My boy Albert has been complaining for several days. I hear nothing more about small pox. The Brigade in which it was prevailing has been sent to the rear in quarentine. I have had all my men re-vaccinated.

 Day before yesterday I recd an order not to allow any one to leave camp limits as we were likely to be ordered to march any moment. At 1 oclock am yesterday we had an order to prepare three days rations & be ready to march at day light. Laid on our arms all day when after dark we got a message that "there would be no move." This morning ordered to resume drill &c as usual. I have no idea what caused the sensation. I fear Bragg has met with a reverse as well as Van Dorn. It seems that this is the fighting army. It is the only army that can whip the Yankees.

 I wonder what Jed Hardy is doing. Dr Holt[69] has been appointed Genl Penders Brigade Surgeon. We need a surgeon very badly and I would have Jed appointed principal surgeon if I thought he would accept. I am very short of Officers. I haven't a single field or staff officer present. I heard yesterday that my asst Surgeon (Dr. Henderson[70]) was better-likely to get well. I haven't heard nothing from Sergt Erwin.[71]

 I can not tell how long we will stay here or what is the object of our remaining as we are. We cant stay for a great while, for it will be impossible to subsist our army. I judge from the fact that we have had a hundred ambulances running for some time transporting the sick from here to Staunton, and from our tearing up the track and burning the cross ties on the Harper's Ferry and Winchester Rl Rd, that we will fall back soon in the direction of Richmond.

 I am lying down under my tent in an awful smoke, which will account for the badly written letter. If an opportunity ever occurs, I would be glad if you would send my uniform. Give my love to all

     Your Affectionate Brother
     Isaac

56. October 23, 1862

Private William H. Horton, Company I, 58th Regiment N.C. Troops, letter to his sister, Mary A. Council, Watauga County, North Carolina. Source: Mary A. Councill Papers (1259), Special Collections Library, Duke University.

By October 23, 1862, William Horton had been absent from his Cove Creek farm for three months. The 27-year-old farmer from western Watauga County enlisted at Johnson's Depot, Tennessee, on July 15, 1862.[72] Horton was serving along with the 58th North Carolina defending Cumberland Gap, a strategic route which controlled southern Kentucky and east Tennessee. Horton's sister, Mary, married Jordan Council of the 37th North Carolina.

> Near Cumberland Gap Tennessee
> Oct the 23the 1862
>
> Dear sister it is with love and pleasure that I take my pen in hand this morning to send you a few lines to let you now that I am well at this time truley hoping when these few lines come to hand that they may find you enjoying all the pleasures that a woman could [hope] for. I dont see mutch sadisfaction in my life for I want to be at home with my little dutch gal. Well Polly I havent mutch news to rite to you. We went to kentucky last week but we didnot stay there long. I come back to our old camp and I have seen more men and more stock in the last week than I thought was in the war. They said at first the yankeys had run them out of there but the newse is now that Jeff Davis has ordered all the southern men out of the states that hant ceeded and some thinks that peace will be made before long and I hope and pray to god that it may be made so I can get to come home to live with my gal that I left at home. If I could have Carry with me I could do very well but I cant think of nobody elce only Carry and the rest of my folks.
>
> Well MA this company is the worst Co to swear and gambel you ever seen in your life. They play Cards day and nite but I havent played a game since I played in Camp and if I keep in the same notion I am in now I never will play another game while I live. I have quit swearing but near some times I get out of hart and get mad and I say dam before I think but I am going to try to do better than I ever have done before. Well Polly you must give my respects to the family and to all of Paul Shull family and to all of my friends and relations and tell them to rite to me and give me all the news. You must give my best love and respects to my Dear Carry Horton. Well Polly tell jordin he must come to see me before he goes back to va. Well I must stop for Amos Howell[73] is going to start to the gap so no more only I remain your brother til death. You must rite to me as soon as you get this.
>
> W. H. Horton
> to M. A. Councill

57. October 29, 1862

Private John W. Reese, Company F, 60th Regiment N.C. Troops, letter to his wife, Christena, Buncombe County, North Carolina. Source: John W. Reese Papers (4417), Manuscripts Department, Special Collections Library, Duke University.

Deeper in Tennessee, the 60th North Carolina reported 36 officers and 619 men present for duty on October 28, 1862. The regiment was the largest in Walker's Brigade (20th, 28th, 45th Tennessee and 60th N.C. Troops), and was assigned to guard the railroad running between Franklin and Nashville, Tennessee. In this letter, Private Reese is once again on sick call, in hopes of getting a furlough to return home and recuperate. On October 8, 1862, an invasion of Kentucky by Confederate forces was halted at the Battle of Perryville, Kentucky where, according to Reese, "the suthern Boys got a tree mends whiping."

October the 29 18 62
Mid dle tennesee
Ruther ford county
Murfeesburro [sic]

Dear Wife

With grat pleasure I am pur mitted to rite to you one more time in forming you that I am un well and has bin vary sick. On yester day I was vary Bad but thank God I am bet tur this morning. I am afflicted with Rumatis and cold. I am still on the sick list not able fur duty. The doctor giv me a puke yester day and I am rite smart bet tur this morning. I am in hope when thes lins cums to hand tha may find you and the children well and doing well. Tena you hav a Bad chance to do well. I sent you a letter by male the day aftur we got hear and I hant got any ansur yet. I suppose the letters all stops at Bridg Port ninty two miles a round where we crosst the tennessee river. I dont no what any news to pass. Tell this at Nashvill tena thar is all sorts of folks but the rite sort hear and the worst looking folks you ever saw in your life. Sum of them has bin out a long time in this un holy thing. Thar is lots of Cantuckens [Kentuckians] hear but I cant hear any thing from Will Reese. Thar is one thing shure—genaril Brag commanding the suthern Boys got a tree mends whiping over thar the other day.

Tena this is so no dout you will see if this rigment dont cum home or not. I dont lik to taulk a bout my offisurs but I hav herd lots of our men say the Colonel could not be rerelected. As to my Capton he may be a fine man to them that like him. He has past my tent door lots of times sence I hav bin sick but he dont cum in. He is Lit Jim Ray[74] and no smarter than he thinks he is. I askt him he will let me go home and let me see you and git my close but no I was not the man to go. He detailed Jack Marten[75] to take sum money fur the Boys home and to see his sick child and he hant cum in yet. I want you to rememeber him and your friends that he kept mee hear long and on the ground till rite lately.

Jess Black was in the fight at fishing Creek whar our Boys had to Run. He asked me the othur nite what the damed yankeys plade while tha was runing. He sed tha plad run niger Run. Dam them.

Tena I must close. I want you to rite to mee onst ar twist a week. Dear you had better not pay the letter you sent to me tha will cum. Better kiss my Boys for mee. May God bless you all thar. I am a long ways off from you my dear Rite Rite Rite Rite Tena to mee.

John W. Reese
to Cris tena V. Reese

58. November 2, 1862

Private Azariah Denny, Company C, 21st Regiment N.C. Troops, letter to his father, Joel Denny, and family, Pilot Mountain, Surry County, N.C. Source: Jackson, *Surry County in the Civil War* (1983).

After the Battle of Sharpsburg, the 21st North Carolina, along with the balance of the Army of Northern Virginia, began to wind down from the active campaigns of the summer and fall of 1862. Among those absent from the regiment at this time was Private Azariah Denny. Writing from a hospital bed, Denny mentioned the attitudes of soldiers regarding staying in the hospital.

Nov.2nd 1862
General Hospital No. 1
Richmond Va
in care of C. B. Gibson

Dear Father I now seat myself to let you know that I am still in the land of the living. My health is about the same, getting about half enough to eat I cant eat half I get this morning. I got 1 piece of sound bacon the first I have seen. We get bread plenty more water than we can drink and at dinner we get a piece of beef as big as two fingers, of a morning we get a piece of bacon as large as 2 fingers and generally rotten. I rather be here than in the battlefield some of them say they had rather be in hell. It is a hard place you may find that I had rather stay here till the war ends than risk my life in camp. 300 men came here the other day that makes times harder. I am fine in spirit for getting home. I think I am as near satisfied any where as any poor boy. I havent heard anything from home yet. I am tired awaiten for you to write. It would suit very well to hear from you all and suit me better to see you all. I will come home as soon as I can I though I would get a furlow but I think not now. I want you to come to see me. When you bring Gabriel[76] there is a good many fathers comes here. I have got clothing plenty. I must have shoes I am nearly barefooted. If I draw then I will have to pay $5.00 and there is none here to draw I dont think I will ever be able for service though I may take and start and soon get I want you all to do the best you can and I will try. I hope that peace will be made some way. I don't care how they say that. John will have to come. I say stay at home as long as you can and if you have to come do the best you can. I will bring my letter to a close by giving my best respects.

               A. Denny

59. November 3, 1862

David W. Siler, Franklin, Macon County, letter to Governor Zebulon B. Vance, Raleigh, Wake County. Source: Governor's Papers (Vance), North Carolina Division of Archives and History.

Thirteen months after the first volunteers left Franklin, the citizens of Macon County were required to come to grips with the war and its demands on the population. With the recent Conscription Act of September 25, 1862, raising the age of those liable for military service to forty-five years old, county leader David Weimar Siler sent word to his political friend to allow those men to volunteer instead of being taken as conscripts. Siler also pleaded for the retention of those men as the labor shortage in the mountains and Macon County, in particular, worsened with every new round of conscriptions.[77]

               Near Franklin
               Nov 3 1862

There are about enough men in Macon County between the ages of 35 and 40 to make one company? We have an opportunity as I understand of getting into Col Folks[78] battalion. This is preferable to going as conscripts. I am requested by a number of our most respectable citizens who are between these ages to ask you whether in your opinion any other alternative will be presented than conscription or going to that battalion. We have no hesitation in believing that it is our duty to stay here and provide for the helpless while it is in our power to do so. Consultations were held and it was agreed in family councils who should go & what one should stay. Those on whom the lot fell to stay in many instances made the greater sacrifice of feeling. But we have taken on upon us charges and responsibilities that we cannot throw off until compelled to do so—or until there is a certainty that we will be so compelled. Having acted conscientiously in the matter we feel that we have done nothing to deserve the punishment of going to the Army discredited by conscription. Before we are taken to a Camp of instruction discredited and scattered to the four winds we ask the privilege of doing what we should have done long ago, had it not been for the earnest appeals of brothers who have fallen in the service to stay and take care of those left to our charge.

I shall venture on a suggestion tho' it may seem to come from a party interested. For every able bodied man taken from this county, there ought to be an able bodied man retained. We have a number of men in the field now falling very little below the number of voters in the county. Our people having poor facilities for communication with other sections have learned to subsist mainly on the immediate productions of their own labor. Deprive us of that labor & and the innocent & helpless must perish though their pockets were filled with current money. You know all about men and their powers of endurance of their wives and children. They can turn away from the graves of comrades and brothers firm in resolve to die as they have died for the sake of objects coming to their recollections with thoughts of home, But what consolation or encouragement can come to a mans heart in an hour of trial from a home where the helpless are perishing for want of his hand to provide. We have but little interest in this connection about which we feel a very deep interest. We are opposed to negro equality. To prevent this we are willing to spare the last man down to the point where women & children begin to suffer for food & clothing. When these begin to suffer or die, rather than see them equalized with an inferior race will die with them.

Everything even life itself stands pledged to the cause. But that our greatest strength may be employed to the best advantage and the struggle prolonged let us not sacrifice at once the object for which we are fighting. I have not thought it worth while to dwell in argument upon the question as to whether the mountain people can subsist after taking out every man between the ages of 18 & 40. It will be sufficient for any one acquainted with this section to pass in imagination through almost any neighborhood and consider the matter over, In a short distance of where I now write there are several families living on adjoining lands and the only man to be left for them all is ninety years old. I have mentioned this case to no one who has not been able to point out one similar to it. The usual means of subsistence seems to be cut off from great numbers. I shall only ask you to reply to the questions presented in the first few sentences. Knowing the press of important matters that must be upon you it is with reluctance that I have written at all. And was only induced to bring matters to your notice which are not immediately under your control, by the request of a number of citizens that I should do so?

D. W. Siler

60. November 3, 1862

Quartermaster James R. Neill, 111th Militia, Bald Creek, Yancey County, letter to Governor Zebulon B. Vance, Raleigh, Wake County. Source: Governor's Papers (Vance), North Carolina Division of Archives and History.

James R. Neill seemed to have a proclivity for the work of the quartermaster department. The Yancey County carpenter and father of a young son volunteered for service on September 16, 1861. Neill served in Company K as its first sergeant before he was promoted and transferred to the regimental staff as assistant quartermaster (captain) on November 26, 1861. Neill resigned his commission on June 2, 1862, and returned home where he drafted the following letter to Vance asking for a political appointment. Vance complied and fulfilled this request and Neill received a commission as a quartermaster in the Yancey County Militia under Colonel John W. McElroy.[79]

Bald Creek N. C.
Nov 3d 1862

After my Compliments and good wishes for you and your family. I hope You will excuse me for troubling You When You are So presed with business. About fourteen Months ago I Vollenteered in the Servis of my County was advised at the same time not to do so as my health was quite bad Col. R. B. Vance promoted me to the office of Quartermaster of his Regt which I accepted and Served them faithfully for nearly a Year by taking the greatest care of my Self finely on account of bad health and nothing else I had to Resign my office and come home it was with great Reluctance that I left the Regt. for they cant be a better and Kinder man in the Army than Col R B Vance, he regretted very much to have to give me up but advised me to Resign, as he thought I could not stand it much longer.

I suppose in a short time all men to the age of Forty Years will be called out I am not quite that old it would make no difference with me about age If I could stand the hardships of camp life. If You Kneed any help in the way of Agents in this part of the State or any thing that you could give me to do that would release me I will be truly glad. I do not want you to think that I ask this of You merely because I was your warm and faithful friend in your Election for Governor. I Vote for all men that went in to this troublesome war as You did, do me a faivour if you can and it will be highly appreciated by your many friends in This section. Do Something if you can through the Legislature to put down the Rascal extortioners. Excuse this bad letter and write me Soon to Bald Creek
P O N C

61. November 4, 1862

First Lieutenant Thomas W. Patton, Company C, 60th Regiment N.C. Troops, letter to his mother, Asheville, Buncombe County, N.C. Source: Patton Family Papers (1739), Southern Historical Collection, Wilson Library, University of North Carolina at Chapel Hill.

Lieutenant Patton's first experience in battalion drill was altogether an unpleasant one. He had worked with his company for some time in company drill, and felt that Col. McDowell's failure to drill the company even once over the course of four months, represented both apathy and inability. Patton spoke about an effort to censure the colonel on the part of the company commanders, and the health of several acquaintances, and Sam Capps, his black servant who accompanied him into service and functioned as a cook for one of the officers' messes.

Murfeesboro [sic] Nov 4 1862
My Dear Mother,

I wrote to you on yesterday and mailed my letter but as the mail are very irregular indeed ans as I have an opportunity of sending this by hand I will write again today—Lieut Brevard[80] of our company has succeeded in getting a sick furlough he is in very bad health indeed being dipeptic—I expect he will resign and not return again—Sam's[81] throat is still very sore he is not yet able to cook or do anything. I hope he will get better before we are ordered away from here, for I would dislike very much to have to leave him here.

Our colonel becomes more and more unpopular every day—he is entirely unfit for his position & has never once attempted to drill his Regt (tell brother Jas—that the other day we had a general inspection the Regt was drawn up in line of battle and at order arms. The Col[82] took his position and commanded "the companies will right wheel" we guessed at his meaning and wheeled into column—after the inspection we were in column of companies and at open order and ordered arms—or Col Comanded "into line companies wheel"—when you remember that he has been in his present position for four months and that was the very first command he had ever attempted—Do you not think we had a right to be provoked at least eight of the captains or at least nine of them—had a meeting to decide what to do—but could come to no decision—but the Col heard of it and this morning instead of writing or acting himself he had Ed Clayton[83] to write them a letter whish is about as pointless as you would suppose one of his writing would be—it is very provoking that after we have labored to drill our companies we should have such an officer comdg us—the military part of this is for Brother James as he can appreciate it—I have rec'd more from home as get. They say that Bragg's army under command of Genl. Polk are within a days march of this place—when they arrive we may look out for some lively times.

Give much love to aunts N & C. Sister Anna Sister Julia & the Children & Believe me

Your Affec. Son
Thomas W. Patton

62. November 4, 1862

Reverend Robert L. Abernethy, Marion, McDowell County, letter to Governor Zebulon B. Vance, Raleigh, Wake County. Source: Governor's Papers (Vance), North Carolina Division of Archives and History.

The speculation and corruption which occurred generally in North Carolina was present in the mountains. This speculation, selective purchasing, and other questionable practices impacted the civilian population just as the losses from Sharpsburg had impacted Lee's army. In this letter, Reverend Robert Laban Abernethy, tax collector for McDowell County, informed Vance of such abuses.

Marion, N. C.
Nov. 4th /62/

Will your Excellency permit me a private individual, a Minister of the gospel of the grace of God; one who feels the greatest possible concern for the interest of your Excellency, as well as for the interest of the State at large, to address you in an unofficial way? If so, I proceed.

Your humble correspondent has always been an earnest and devoted friend of your Excellency; and though he has never enjoyed the privilege of seeing your Excellency but once, (when you past last through Marion to Asheville) yet he exerted all his limited influence in putting your Excellency in the Chair of State, and now he desires to lay some facts before you, which he conceives to be of vast importance to the interests of the people of Western N. Carolina. If it is Constitutional, and if your position as Governor of N. Carolina gives you the power to do so, in the name of God, of suffering humanity, of the cries of widows and orphans, do put down the Speculation and extortion in this portion of the State.

Here in Marion, beef is being sold to the poor wives of soldiers who get but $11 per month in the field, at the enormous price of 11 and 12 cents per pound! Leather at $4 per pound Bacon at 40 & 50 cents per pound; Corn from the heap, at $1.50 per bushel Salt at near 50 cents per Pound And every thing in proportion. If this thing is not put down, our Country is ruined forever. Many children of the soldiers in the Camps are nearly barefoot and naked without the possibility of getting clothes or shoes.

Here in Marion, Messrs Maroney and Halyburton have a large Tannery, and the tanner is allowed to remain by virtue of the Exemption Act, and yet one pound of leather cannot be bought of the concern by private purchase. The leather is put up in lots of 250 sides and sold to speculators at $4.00 & $4.50 per Pound! Your correspondent went himself in person to the concern of these gentlemen, and though he laid his case before them, that he had 6 little barefoot children that must have shoes, and offered to give any reasonable price for leather—just one side. But the reply was, if we sell to one man privately we must sell to others, and we will not do it.

In the name of the Great Gov of the universe, what are we to do? Pardon my presumption in addressing your Excellency, for I could not restrain.

Rev. R. L. Abernethy[84]

63. November 5, 1862

Private Calvin L. Proffit, Company H, 13th Regiment N.C. Troops, letter to sister, Rachel L. Proffit, Wilkes County, N.C. Source: Proffit Family Papers (3408), Southern Historical Collection, University of North Carolina at Chapel Hill.

A month after Alfred and Andrew Proffit were conscripted, Calvin, the 20-year-old youngest brother, enlisted on September 27, 1862.[85] Several things are interesting in the following letter—among them is that Calvin had not received arms by November 5.

Camp in Berry ville va
Nov 5 1862

Miss R L Proffit
Dear Sister,

I write you a few lines which will inform you that I am moderately well at this time hoping that this may find you all well. I have no very good news to write you. I have had a very easy time since I left home especially for a soldier. I have never stood guard yet. I have not yet received arms. I am vary glad that our Machine has done so well. I saw AJ & AN [his brothers Andrew J. and Alfred N. Proffit] a few days ago. They informed me that they recd a letter from you a day or two before. I want you to write me how many bushels they have thrashed and what conditions pa rented that farm, what he is doing, how much wheat you have sown, if the mules have mended much etc etc. And I want you to be certain to write where W. H. [his brother William H. Proffit] is and if you are going to school. Inform unkle McAlpins folks that Thomas is well & doing first rate. Wm West & Smith Cox went to the hospitle at Winchester a few days ago.[86] I think Wm will get a discharge. Smith had the measles. I will close. If you have any respect for a brother write one just as soon as you receive this. I remain,

C. L. Proffit

Direct to C.L. Proffit
AP Hills Division Penders Brigade,
Care Col. Ruffin 13th Reg. NC Troops,
Co H.

64. November 7, 1862

Colonel Isaac E. Avery, 6th Regiment N.C. State Troops, letter to Colonel Robert B. Vance, 29th Regiment N.C. Troops. Source: Waightsill Avery Papers (33), Southern Historical Collection, Wilson Library, University of North Carolina at Chapel Hill.

The following is an official dispatch from Captain Isaac E. Avery, acting commander of the 6th North Carolina, to Colonel Robert B. Vance, commanding the 29th North Carolina. The purpose of this dispatch was to alert Colonel Vance that a man may have enlisted in his company while listed as a deserter. Such actions were illegal. After his service in the 6th, William Buchanon seems to have disappeared.

6 Regt NC Troops
Camp near Culpepper
Nov. 7 1862

Colonel

On the 16th day of last July, a furlough of 30 days was given to Wm Buchanon, private of Co. E, 6th NC by order of Brig Genl Whiting. At the expiration of his leave of absence he failed to return to this command, and when steps were taken after his arrest, he secluded himself in the mountains of No Carolina until recently. I understand he joined Capt. Blalocks Company of your Regiment. I am sure Colonel you are not aware of this fact, or I think you would not only have had him arrested & sent back, but would also have dealt with Capt. Blalock, who had certainly laid himself liable to be cashiered, if he has allowed this man to join his Company, knowing him to be a deserter. If Buchanon was a member of your Regiment, I have this to request that you cause him to be arrested & sent to Castle Thunder at Richmond as a deserter.

 I am Colonel very respectfully
   Your obt srvt
   I. E. Avery, Comd,
   Co. E 6th NC
Col. Rob. B. Vance
Commanding 29th Regt NC Troops

Stephen Miller of Cherokee County was one of the officers in the 29th serving under Robert Vance. (United States Army Military History Institute, Carlisle, Pa.)

65. November 19, 1862

Sergeant Lewis Warlick, Company B, 11th Regiment N.C. Troops, letter to Laura McGimsey, Pleasant Hill, Burke County, North Carolina. Source: Laura C. McGimsey Papers (2680), Southern Historical Collection, Wilson Library, University of North Carolina at Chapel Hill.

In November of 1862, the 11th North Carolina remained in eastern North Carolina. Lewis was promoted to corporal the previous August and to sergeant shortly before the date of this letter. The force in eastern North Carolina was ordered to southeastern Virginia to support Confederate efforts there and to collect forage in close proximity to Union-occupied territory. Lewis described Pettigrew's Brigade in an action against Federal skirmishers and artillery.

Camp Nelson near Franklin Depot, VA
Nov. 19th 1862

My Dearest Friend

For the first time since my arrival I have undertaken to drop you a few lines I would have written yesterday or day before but was prevented by what I will relate afterwards in this. I arrived on last Thursday night tired and worn out as I had in charge twenty one boxes, and I can say that it will be the last lot of boxes of that number that I ever will undertake to bring through because it is so much trouble. I was lucky to get through as soon as I did and would not have gotten here when I did if I had have had no help. I found the boys generally well in camps but since I left there has been several men sent to Petersburg to the hospital some very ill among the members is John Duval[87]—has Typhoid fever.

Yesterday we had quite a lively time but I will pen what occurred the day previous. On Monday morning at 8 we were called up by the loud taps of the drum and ordered to get breakfast and be in readiness by 4½, at that time we were in line and at once marched to headquarters in town, Capt. Armfield, being in charge we halted, in a few minutes Col. Leventhorpe's loud voice was heard distantly all along the lines—we took up our march across Blackwater accompanied by three pieces of artillery and Col. Ferrebee's cavalry[88] with a train of twenty three wagons the object was to go over in Isle of Wight County after forage—we marched on in the direction of Suffolk five miles when we were halted—batteries put in position and every company assigned his—The wagon to therein loading of corn, fodder: etc; here we remained till all the wagons or nearly so were loaded, ail quietly. I was standing near Col. Ferrebee and others listening at their chat when I cast my eyes down the road and saw a courier coming at full speed. I will here state that there was two or three companies from the cavalry a mile and a half in advance at Carrsville, when the boy rode up he called out to Ferrebee to "bring your companies on they are fighting." I at once run for my rifle before the command "fall in" was given but before I got far all the officers were ordering "fall in" which was done quickly and off we went at double quick fight after the artillery; our gait was not slacked the whole distance but that did not seem to fire me as I thought there was some prospect of a fight but not so the cavalry drove them off before we arrived so we had a chase all for nothing; there was two persons taken—about all that was done; if there was any killed or wounded we did not find it out, after staying there awhile we commenced retracing our steps—reached our camps a little before night somewhat fatigued.

But yesterday was the time; before day the long roll called us again into line—marched to headquarters there the Col. assigned to each Captain his place two companies beyond the river to act as skirmishers, A & G, the remaining ones on this side. The report was the enemy was advancing in large force. Pretty soon after we got our position we heard heavy firing of artillery up the river 6 or 7 miles off while that firing was going on our scouts brought in nine prisoners and reported the enemy to be in heavy force two miles off; the Col. told us that from all he could gather from the scouts and prisoners that they had a very heavy force the lowest estimate he could get was four brigades but he thought it was quite probable that was two small, but said "I am determined to hold the place at all hazards and he hoped the Bethel regiment would still retain the reputation she had for valor" [and] further said our force was small but he was calling for help with all his might & after he got through three hasty cheers were given for our commander. We remained in our positions til 12 or perhaps a little after then the Yanks commenced shelling our scouts rapidly which was a shade too hot for them and they came in with five men wounded three very slightly the other two severely all from company A as soon as they and the pickets were driven in our batteries opened fire, but then the enemy had been shelling us for nearly an hour, our pickets and skirmishers prevented us from firing. When each side opened I tell you there was a thundering for two hours almost equal to the Bethel fight—bang; crash, sing went the shells and pieces all around us; you ought to have been there to have seen me dodge some time I would fall flat on the ground and then I would lie for some time and I would rise—here would come the shell down I would go again. We were all ordered to lie down but occasionally I would get up to look about but in that position I did not remain long as the shell made to much of a ratling for a man in a standing position when he could not defend himself there we had to lie and take it all and couldn't get a shot. There was no infantry firing at all. After two hours their batteries were silenced and they skedaddled for Suffolk which relieved me of a good deal of dread. Our cavalry followed them over some distance and along the road they learned from citizens, Gen. Peck was in command with two brigades and eight pieces of artillery. We had none killed and none wounded only those I have spoken of. The firing up the river was across the river at Col. Marshalls reg. at Joyners ford 6 miles above. The Yanks crossed up there but were driven back.

Collet Leventhorpe commanded the 11th North Carolina Troops during the engagement at Suffolk. (North Carolina Division of Archives and History.)

I am thankful I came out unhurt also all the rest of our boys. As ever your loving friend

Lewis

I saw a copy of the Southern Illustrated News in Weldon but hadn't time to examine it the first copy I can get I will send it and if you like it I will send it to you. If Bob Kerely is at Richmond yet write to him to send you a copy, for it may be some time before I see another If he should send you one you can write to me if you would like to take it if so I will subscribe for it I am on guard and must go to the guard house. I haven't got rid of my cold yet otherwise I am

In November, William H. Thomas, known for his leadership of eastern Cherokee, was at work building his legion of what he called "Cherokee Indians and Southern Highlanders." (North Carolina Division of Archives and History.)

No man was more loved and respected by the eastern Cherokee than William Holland Thomas. At a young age, Thomas made friends with many of the Cherokee chiefs, most notably chief Yonaguska, or "Drowning Bear," who gave Thomas the name "Wil-Usdi." Thomas was raised by his mother, Temperence Calvert Thomas, among the Cherokee people. The young William worked in a Quallatown mercantile store for three years until striking out on his own and becoming one of the most prosperous young men in western North Carolina. After the Indian Removal of 1838, Thomas worked continuously in Washington for the eastern Cherokees, acting as their lobbyist and land agent. In 1848, Thomas returned to the mountains and was the foremost advocate of improvements to the isolated region. With the opening of the war, Thomas, a staunch supporter of the South and secession, saw to the needs of the 16th N.C. Troops, and after, expressed his desire to create a legion of mountaineers and Cherokee Indians. Thomas achieved his goal on September 27, 1862, with the formation of the Thomas Legion.[89] In November of 1862, Thomas was aware of the strategic situation regarding the defense of the mountains, as well as the possibility of recruiting negro labor to finish the Western North Carolina Rail Road.

well. I fear you will not get this Saturday. We will get reinforced to-day by two regiments infantry 42 & 55 N.C. also from Petersburg. I understand the 55th camped in 7 miles of us last night.

66. November 22, 1862

Colonel William H. Thomas, Thomas Legion, letter to Governor Zebulon B. Vance, Raleigh, Wake County. Source:

Knoxville
Nov. 22 1862

In the progress of the war men and circumstances change. At the commencement you were in the military and I was in Civil positions. Now my position is what your position was then. I find myself at the head of a Regiment or Legion of Indians and mountaineers, entrusted with duties in East Tennessee and Kentucky. And as your duties relate principally to the defence of North Carolina permit me to submit for your consideration a few facts believed to be connected with the public services and the defence of the State.

1st Would it not be advisable to make an arrangement to have able bodied negro men belonging to the counties in reach of the enemy employed by the State and transferred from their present positions to work on the extension of the Railroad? They could, I presume, be employed for the cost on ensurance and food and raiment. By this two objects would be gained. 1st every negro would be a saving of $1000, to the owner.

2d Every able bodied negro kept out of the hands of the enemy would lessen the number of troops we have to raise in defence, equal to a saving of at least $1000 per year. Thus if North Carolina employed ten thousand negroes on the road where a small force could keep them in subjection, $10,000,000 would be saved to the owners, and 10,000 men more would defend our cause.

One consideration now animates us all. What will ensure success not what would be most agreeable to us. The Legislature appropriated two millions of dollars to defend Eastern North Carolina and the Western frontiers? Both are now in danger. The western Counties are in danger of being over run by deserters and renegades who by the hundred are taking shelter in the smoky mountains. The men between 35 and 40 west of the Blue Ridge should be furnished with arms and ammunition, and required to aid in guarding their homes And the Confederate should be required to place Military compys at every trap in the Smoky mountains from Ashe to Cherokee. As long as we can hold the Country encircled by the Blue Ridge and Cumberland mountains and their outside slopes we have the heart of the south, which commands the surrounding Plains. The loss of this country larger than England or France is the loss of the Southern Confederacy and we sink under a despotism.

W. H. Thomas

67. November 24, 1862

Colonel John W. McElroy, 111th Regiment N.C. Militia, letter to Governor Zebulon B. Vance, Raleigh, Wake County. Source: Governor's Papers (Vance), North Carolina Division of Archives and History.

Controversy plagued the leaders of western North Carolina. Colonel John B. Palmer, who at that time commanded the 58th North Carolina Troops, William H. Thomas, and Augustus Merrimon, are just a few examples of leaders in conflict with higher leadership and each other. John W. McElroy, commanding officer of the Yancey County Militia, avoided this strife and became one of the most influential civil officials in the region. McElory commanded the 111th Militia from May of 1861,[90] and performed his tasks with skill. In November of 1862, this 54-year-old commander was plagued with the same dilemma regarding conscription as other officials in the region.

Asheville Bla Mon
November 24th 1862

I received a letter from Col J. B. Palmer last week in which he requested me to write to you and ask you to write to him and give the charges made against him in a petition sent you from

Mitchell County as he is desirous of seting him self right before you and the community. I saw the Petition when in the hand of Solicitor Merrimon and am fully satisfied that there were many false statements in it and I have understood many of the names forged that were to the Petition.

I wish to know if it is my duty to enroll Mens names as Conscripts from 18 to 40 years of age, without a special order from the Adjt Genel of our State. We have no jail in our County and I find it will give me great trouble to take all the prisoners, one by one to the camp of instruction near Raleigh, and the number of deserters seems to accumulate rather than diminish, Please give me orders to lodge them in the nearest jail.

I hope you will write me soon on this subject and also tel me if a company was organized in this or in the county of Yancey If it would be received into the service of our state or the Confederate States.

Will you be so kind as to hand the enclosed two dollars to Mr. W. Holden and tel him to send me his weekly Standard, and to commence at the beginning of the present Session. I am at Roberts he is nearly well and will leave this week.

J. W. McElroy

68. November 29, 1862

Private Harvey C. Davis, "The Watauga Rangers," Company D, 9th Regiment N.C. Troops (1st N.C. Cavalry), diary entry. Source: Francis B. Dedmond, "Harvey Davis' Unpublished Civil War Diary and the Story of Company D, First North Carolina Cavalry, *Appalachian Journal* 13 (1986), 368–407. Catawba College Archives, Salisbury, North Carolina.

After the Battle of Antietam, the armies remained active in the East. The First Cavalry conducted multiple raids and scouting missions to assess the strength of Burnside's Union force. In this entry, Private Davis describes several of these victorious conquests, and tells about a humorous, if not eccentric, activity of some of the Tar Heel troopers.

During our stay in Culpeper (Stephensburg is in that county) we made some successful raids down the Oquaquon river. At one time we captured 49 wagons and loading and at another time 29 Sutlers stores and provisions and clothing. Being just before Christmas there were lots of fine delicacies for Christmas and new year. It was unusual to see our men making Rio coffee and eating fine cake, chees, oranges, lemons, and nuts of all kinds and strutting in fine Yankee boots. They were intended for yankee officers but our private soldiers made good use of them. A joke on one of our men was when he lay down before the fire in one of the yankee bear skin immitation overcoats, being too close to the heat the hair singed off. The cotton took fire when the wearer sprang to his feet crying "Burnside has attacked me in the rear," striking through the woods while others were after him to extinguish the fire.

69. December 2, 1862

Captain Julius Gash, Company E, 7th Battalion N.C. Cavalry, letter to his sister. Source: Mary Gash Papers (59), Private Manuscripts Collection, North Carolina Division of Archives and History.

Julius Gash, a native of Henderson County, resided in Transylvania County prior to the outbreak of the war. More than a year after the start of the war, Julius, or "Jule" as he was better known, volunteered for service in a cavalry company being formed in Hendersonville on July 15, 1862. Jule was appointed as first lieutenant of

Company E, 7th Battalion N.C. Cavalry.[91] The 7th, like other mountain battalions, operated in east Tennessee. These units were most often the poorest equipped and provided for in the Confederate service. Jule discusses this situation in asking for the large quantity of equipment. Leadership also appears lacking in the unit, as Col. George Folk's orders are condemned and the absence of Captain Spann is mentioned.

Camp on Little Doe River,
Johnson Co. Tenn.
2nd Dec 1862

Dear Sister

Your kind favor of the 7th has arrived last night with Capt. Gillespie[92] on a detail of fifteen days. You seem to think there were a few words, "Superfluous words," I think you called them. I reckon it must have been written to the Col. I don't think I ever use any superfluous words when writing you. I am very particular, knowing that I catch Thunder if I should fail to. Well if you wish me to write without using such words, you must quit cross writing or underlining. When you fill your sheet, get another or quit. I don't care much which.

I am very sorry sisters bird made its escape but I am not surprised and would not have been had both of them been killed or got away. I suppose there's no use fighting about things unavoidable but I would note had that bird to have got away for $50 in Confederate. Which one was it? I had much rather Frank had not been lost, Females not being so valuable as males, nor in so much demand, however, he will have to be replaced.

You say if I need anything I need not be any ways backward in asking. Well if I must tell you my wants, ill procured in the first place. I want a No. One Six horse wagon with six good mules to draw it. I then want it loaded with cooking utensils, axs, Blankets & clothing for the Co. Then I still want about fifty thousand dollars to keep the Co in horses and to keep them shod. There are a few of my wants. Can you do anything for me?

So far as I am individually concerned, I believe I need nothing particularly. I would like to have another good blanket or two, but I can make out very well. There are two men in the Co that I know have no blanket, and how they keep from freezing I cant tell, for this is a pretty cold country. Snowing or raining pretty much all the time. I intend coming home in about two weeks if I can get a furlough to see Thee and if I do come I think I will buy a two-horse wagon. We have about 72 tents and cooking utensils enough and cant get transportation for what we have. I'll give up that this Battalion is a little the worst managed concern ever I have seen. We have had 4 little one horse guns with the Battalion since we left Greenville and but three or four government horses, they are generally worked on the wagons. Our horses have never been valued, consequently the boys got tired of working their horses to the artillery. When they refused to put their horses in the guns, the Col[93] goes mad cusses every thing and every body unloads the wagons, tents, cooking utensils, trunks, and every thing else, puts the wagon horses to the guns, place a guard over the wagons. He will place a guard over the wagons and will not let the men hire horses and take their equipage, but goes off without anything. I am tired of such doings as this. Spann[94] wont do anything, in fact he is never here. I am going to get me a wagon & haul my own tent, cooking utensils, and haul what I can for the men. Tell the Col to please look around a little for a good light two horse wagon and a pair of heavy set mules. If he can ascertain by the time I get home where such a concern can be had, it will probably save my company.

I am certain to come if I can get a furlough and will be up there Christmas and I want something good to eat and no small quantity of it. I have two very particular reasons for coming. One and the prime one is to see Thee. The other is to get a wagon. When I left I was fully determined to never come home until the war was over and if that would not have come I guess I would not. I don't know that I will anyway but it shall not be my fault if the Col does not let me go now while Thee is there I shall not come at all.

We have lots of measles in Camp— 75 cases or more. Three or four have died and others will. Capt Gillespie started the remains of Parker[95], a member of his company, home this morning.

Baxter Headden is about well of them and Mant Hood is just taking them. John Orr is very low but I think not dangerous. Wesley Siniard[96] is also quite low & I think his recovery very doubtful indeed. The Doctor seems to think he may recover, but I don't, though I'm no Doctor.

I remain your brother affectionately
Jule

70. December 10, 1862

Private George F. Adams, "The Watauga Rangers," Company D, 1st Regiment N.C. Cavalry (9th N.C. State Troops), letter to his brother, Tarlton Adams, Sugar Grove, Watauga County, North Carolina, with additional note. Source: Alfred Adams Papers (19), Special Collections, Perkins Library, Duke University.

Cavalry trooper George F. Adams, a 17-year-old farmer, lived with his parents, Alfred and Elizabeth Adams, in the Cove Creek township of Watauga County. When he volunteered in Buncombe County on July 10, 1861, George left his two brothers, Tarlton and Abner, and his sister, Sarah, at home. Adams wrote about the condition of the 1st Cavalry Regiment and the location of the 37th N.C. Troops. Included is a note from Private B. C. McBride, Adam's friend and messmate.[97]

Rapidan Station Va
Dec. 10th 1862

Dear Brother
I seat myself to write you a few lines to let you know that I am still in the land of the living and in fine health and hoping that when this reaches you it will find you sharing in the same favor. I have nothing of interest to write to you at this time. We have very cold weather here and considerable snow. Forage is very scarce here and it is almost impossible to get any thing to feed our horses on at all. The health of our Regiment is very good at this time notwithstanding they are half naked and Barefoooted. There is some considerable grumbling about the way they are treated but my doctrine is submit to any thing rather than to Lincoln. In regard to war news there is nothing new or strange. Anyway the 37th Regt is stationed at Fredericksburg about thirty miles from this place. I would like to see you the best kind but cant tell when I will get the chance. I wrote to Jo day before yesterday at Richmond. Give my love to Father and Mother and to Sarah and Abner you must write to me as soon as you get this and give me all the other news. I will close for the present.
B. McBride words you his best love.
I remain your Brother until death. G. F. Adams to Tarlton Adams

Dear Friends in conclusion with this letter I send you a few lines to let you know that I have not forgot you also that I am in fine health hoping this will find you sharing the same favor. I have no news to write at this time. There is no war news. I have got no news from home since I was taken prisoner. You have no idea how bad I want to see you but I will have to committ them into the hands of God. I will write to you again soon. You must write to me as soon as you get this. I remain your true friend.

      B. C. McBride[98]
Direct to Richmond Va 1st NC Cavalry

71. December 21, 1862

Private Phillip P. Shull, "The Watauga Minutemen," Company E, 37th Regiment N.C. Troops, letter to his cousin, Mr. J.H. Council, Boone, Watauga County, North Carolina. Source: Mary A. Council Papers (1259), Special Collections Library, Duke University.

Just a couple of miles south of the Adams home in Sugar Grove, lived the Shull family of Valle Crucis. Phillip P. Shull, a 20-year-old carpenter from Valle Crucis, was part of the troops which held land near a marsh in the front of Jackson's Corps during the Battle of Fredericksburg. The regiment suffered significant casualties when troops from Meade's division were able to attack through the marsh. The breakthrough was contained, and the fighting shifted to Marye's Heights.[99]

    Camp on our Road
    to Fredrick Burge Va
    Dec the 21/62

Dear Cousin

I have found a faverabul oppirtunity of riting you a few short line which will inform you how wee are all giting along in Camp. The health of Camp is tolerable good at this tim. Several have been sent to the Hospitel on the march from furtige of marching and fitin. Cousin I can say to you that wee have had a nother vary hard batel but have bin suchsesful to drive the yankes back with a loss of 800 kild woundid and misin and a mong the kild I am sory to state the names of som of our Brave Boyes have fell on grat and bludy batel field the 13 of this instant. Cousin James M. Farthing and cousin N.C. Shull.[100] Tha both fout very bravly. James was shot in brest and kild instantly and a grat many woundid about 20 kild and a bout 75 woundid in the Rigement. Well I reakin you have hurd all about our travels in the Valley and as wee come on. Cousin it wuld take mee some time to rite it down and I have to gow to put on some of old Nead to cook to pursurve life.

Cousin I think wee have had some of the hardis times that we ever had sins we bin out I would like to see you coming back before long if you are abel for tha have bin bucking some of our boys down for 6 months for stayin too long but if I wasent well I would not come. Cousin I wish you could stay at home always and neaver haft to come back to this cold world around Fredricksburg. I hop and trust in him who holds the destines of our land undar the hollar of his hand will bring this turbel afar to a close and let us all gow home rejoyisen.

Cousin I hop you will have good luck and git well and com back and bring som Brandy and treat us all and have a big lafe. Well I will close. Give my best respects to all. Inqiror nothing more only I remain your Cousin ontel death. Rite soon and give me all the nuse.

    P. P. Shull to Mr. J. H. Council

72. December 27, 1862

Private John W. Reese, Company F, 60th Regiment N.C. Troops, letter to his wife, Christena, Buncombe County, North Carolina. Source: John W. Reese Papers (4417), Manuscripts Department, Special Collections Library, Duke University.

A day after his last letter, written on the 29th of October, Reese was transferred to a hospital in Dalton, Georgia, with continued fever. After a stay in Dalton, Reese was transferred back to the Army of Tennessee and was on sick call at the time he wrote this letter. With the year winding down, Reese reported his condition and what his regiment was ordered to prepare. Reese seemed very concerned about mail and packages reaching home: he had brought this up in his previous two letters and does so again here. A report of a military execution a day after Christmas ended this letter.

Murfees Burro [sic]
Tennessee december the 27 1862
Dear Wife

With pleasure that I am purmitted to drop you a few lines to let you no that I am still on the mend. I rote to you in my last letter how long I had bin sick. My dear I thout I had saw you for the last time. I wanted to see you and my dear Children. O how Bad you dont no. You hav no idey . You dont no how long it has bin fore weeks to day sence I have dun any dew ty. I am still mending and will be redy for dewty in a few more days. The times is squaley hear at this time. Tha wur fiting and has bin fur two or three days and hte news was yester day that the yankeys drov our troops back seven mils. Our loss was one thousand. Our Regt is order to cook 2 days rashings and be redy to march at a minutes warning. I am not able to go with them.

Tena I sent you a letter by male the other day but I expect this will beet it home. I rote Mary Edmonts one and I think I stated in hur letter that I wood send you fifty dollars but I will onley send you thirty dollars by franklin Parris.[101] He is on deatil and I will send you more by male or the nex one that gos home from hear. I want you to send me two pair of socks and one pair of suspenders and a pair of glovs. I hav shirts a nuff. I hav pants a nuff if I had a pair of warm slips I wood replace. But I dont expect hee can bring mutch. He will hav a good deal to bring fur his wife up the river and if you hant got any thing redy he can tell you when he will start back and you can fix them and send them down to Elexanders. Hav my name put on each pair and paper.

Tena there was fore men shot and hung. One man by the name of Gray. He had bin a pilet for the yankeys. He was hung or hung him self. He jumped off the gallos before they cood nock him off. William Little[102] was shot for running a way from us at greenvill. He was a brother to tom Little. He was in my mess. I saw him neel down by his Coffin and tha was puting a hanker chief on his hed and I left thinking. I did not no the other mans name. Kiss the Boys and tell the girls howdey.

John W. Reese to C V Reese
Send me a cake of soap

73. December 28, 1862

First Lieutenant Thomas W. Patton, Company C, 60th Regiment N.C. Troops, letter to his aunt, Charlotte Kerr, Asheville, Buncombe County, N.C. Source: Patton Family Papers (1739), Southern Historical Collection, Wilson Library, University of North Carolina at Chapel Hill.

On the 28th of December, Patton was performing duty as acting quarter master for the regiment, in the absence of his brother, William Augustus Patton. Patton seemed anxious to get in the fight; however, had he known the outcome of the impending battle and the conduct of the " Bloody 60th" in one of their first fights, perhaps Patton would have been happy staying in the rear. Patton talks about having to cook his own Christmas dinner, with his servant, Sam Capps, sick, and spending time with General Polk. Patton also describes the same execution that Private Reese of Company F talked about in his letter, December 27, 1862.

Murfeesboro [sic], Tenn
Dec 28 62

Dear Aunt C.

Your answer to my last letter only reached me yesterday and as it was written better than usual- I am glad to say I was able to decipher most of it. Brother B's exploit was certainly a glorious achievement and I hope the subscription it produced the desired effect. This a day of great excitement here. We have been hearing heavy cannonading in the direction of Nashville for the two past days and it was reported that our forces were gradually falling back before a large force of Yanks until this morning when the rascals were reported to be within eight miles of town and all of the forces in and around here were ordered to the front and have formed a line of battle. It is said extending fifteen miles across the country about three miles below here, so it is reasonable to suppose that "something is up." The "Bloody 60th" was marched off to its position early this morning and much to my chagrin, but I suppose to your joy. I, as quartermaster, was ordered to stay in charge of the camps, which is decidedly dull work, so please to hurry Gus up.[103]

Christmas went off much better with me than I had expected. Sam had nothing better to do than be sick, and so I had a fair prospect of having to cook my own Christmas dinner, but just after Breakfast Col Richmond rode over with an invitation from Genl Polk that I should take dinner with him which I was very gladly accepted and had a fine time of it. Gen. Polk is a very polite old gentleman but not much like a Bishop. He did not say grace before dinner.

It is said that on Friday last eleven men were shot in and around this place for desertion. I do not know how true that is but I know there was one executed from our Regt. The poor fellows name was Littrell. He deserted while our Regiment was stationed at Greenville and was arrested & brought back here about a month ago by Tom Stevens,[104] and in company with two others (one of them Spain) was tried by court-martial and all three sentenced to suffer death. The other two were pardoned by Genl Bragg and he was shot in the presence of all the troops of his brigade. It was an awful sight, but I am convinced it was necessary for the good of the service and will put a stop to our men running away. I send you a slip token from a Columbia paper which contained some very interesting news to me, in that there had been a fight at Murfeesboro [sic]. I think they treated us very badly to have so great a battle so near us and we not allowed to know anything about it.

Our Brigade has been torn to pieces and changed altogether. It is composed of the 60th NC Reg, 32 Ala, 4th Fla, and the 20th Tenn and we are put under command of Brig Genl Preston of Louisville Ky.[105] I do not like the change much as I much preferred Col Walker. Our division is annexed to Hardee's corps. I would much rather have remained under Genl Polk. Do not get scared about the impending battle for I believe it will all blow over yet.

My boots reached me in safety, and I was most happy to get them and also the papers by Col Richmond. Love to all, write soon to

Your affc nephew
T. W. P.

1863

The rest of us was marched at double-quick time to the field 2 miles off. We was marched to the right of the center division unattached to any brigade. On our approach to a fence the yanks had shelled us on our way. They wound several W. G. Thomas of my co was one. At the fence they give us a voley of minnie balls & wound several, Will Roane and Thompson of my co.

> —Captain Alfred Bell, Company B, 39th Regiment North Carolina Troops, regarding the Battle of Murfreesboro, January 11, 1863.

Major—Tell my Father I died with my face to the enemy.
I E Avery

> —Colonel Isaac E. Avery, 6th Regiment North Carolina Troops, written shortly before his death, Gettysburg, Pennsylvania, July 2, 1863.

Be fore I will parrish I leav if they hang me for when my life is gon what will this world be worth to me. I had as soon be hung or shot as to starv to death.

> —Sergeant William J. Smathers, Company C, Love's Regiment, Thomas' Legion, Freedom, Tenessee, August 21, 1863.

I hardly know what to think about our Hoam folkes turning our to Derleckting and incouraging dissertion from all acounts thay are but very trew Petreotical citizens in Macon.

—*Private William Tippett, Company B, 39th Regiment North Carolina Troops, Meridian, Mississippi, October 8, 1863.*

74. January 9, 1863

Captain Elisha Alexander Perkins, "The Davis Dragoons," Company F, 41st Regiment N.C. Troops (3rd N.C. Cavalry), letter to his brother and sister, Robert and Elizabeth, Morganton, Burke County, N.C. Source: Perkins Family Papers (3894), Southern Historical Collection, Wilson Library, University of North Carolina at Chapel Hill.

In May of 1862, Elisha Alexander Perkins became commander of the "Davis Dragoons." He replaced the respected Captain Thomas G. Walton. Perkins was born in 1823 to Alfred and Mary Perkins of Burke County. Alex served as a justice on the Burke County Court of Pleas and Quarter Session along with his brother, "Bob," prior to volunteering for service on October 17, 1861. Initially mustered in as a corporal, Alex was elected captain after defeating Walton.[1] Alex reported the situation within the company, including some soldiers' desire to leave the army, to his brother and sister.

Goldsboro N. C. Jan 9 1863
Dear Brother and Sister

I rec'd your letters last night but Stewart and Walton have not come up with the baggage for some cause. I think something happened to the car the baggage was in and it was left above Salisbury and Stewart and Walton waited for it there and the others came on. We got here last Saturday evening and expect to leave tomorrow for Wilmington instead of Swansboro. We are in pretty good health nearly all of us had colds. Part of our company are staying in an academy that has been used for a hospital the balance of us are staying in our tents in the fair grounds. I stayed one night and eat 3 or 4 meals with Mr. Gregory. He sends his respects to you. Dick is not at home. John Bristol[2] has returned home on account of his health. You can see him and he can give you the news. I have gained 4 or 5 lbs since I started. I have not been eating as much since we have been here as I can while traveling.

Col. Avery[3] and his regiment passed through this place last night and one or two more are expected this evening from Raleigh, all for New Bern. The latest is that 20 or more vessels are off cap Hateras, but I don't see many papers or hear much news these days. When we are settled if we ever get to that point we will take some papers and read the news. Esqr. Lisk is very tired of the service. He offers to give his horse and beading to any man that will take his place but if a substitute is [not] taken he must go in for the war. Lisk has found the man here that is willing and he may get off.

John McElrath started here last night and left this evening for Wilmington. McKesson[4] was here on Monday I believe. It is almost too dark to write any more direct your letters to Wilmington and I will write again when I get to some place.

Your affectionate brother
Alex

75. January 9, 1863

Private William H. Proffit, "The Wilkes Valley Guards," Company B, 1st Regiment N.C. Troops, letter to parents, William and Mary Proffit, Wilkes County. Source: Proffit Family Letters (3408), Southern Historical Collection, Wilson Library, University of North Carolina at Chapel Hill.

After the victory at Fredericksburg, Virginia, the two armies took position on opposite sides of the Rappahannock River and awaited the spring and its campaigns. Private Proffit commented on this arrangement and was confident in the army's ability to repel another Yankee assault such as the one on December 13, 1862. Proffit also reported news from his two brothers who had discovered several distant cousins, Ira and John Wesley, also in service.

>Camp near Fredericksburg Va
>January 9, 1863
>
>Dear father and Mother:
>
>I again drop you a note for the purpose of informing you that I am enjoying fine health, at presant, indeed. I am stouter than I have been perhaps, at any period of my life and I think I am much heavier than I ever was. C. L. Proffit came to see me yesterday. He is in elegant health. He looks the best I ever saw him. He says he weighs 140 lbs. He said he saw Andrew and Alfred the day before yesterday. They were in tolerably good health and improving. He said Thomas Walsh was also in tolerably good health.
>
>I am unable to interest you with news from the army. We have been very quitely encamped since the termination of the battle. Our forces are occupying the South and the enemy the North side of the Rappahannock river. Our forces are fortifying, very strongly, near the River. More, I suppose, as a matter of precaution than of necessity. It is not believed that they will ever make another demonstration in the vicinity of Fredericksburg, but if they should do so all seems to entertain the gratest confidence that they will meet with a much grater defeat than they did on the 13th Dec'r.
>
>I have become quite impatient in looking for a letter from you. I have not yet received a line from you since I left the Hospital. I hope you are not so unlucky in getting my letters as I am in getting yours. I am anxious to know what you have done in regard to buying land etc.
>
>I have written you my opinion upon the subject before, therefore, I shall decline offering any suggestions at the present, and be patient and answer to the letters heretofore sent. I learned yesterday from Calvin that Cousin John Wesley Proffit was dead. Calvin has also become acquainted with cousin Ira Proffit. He is a Lieut in a company from Madison co. Calvin said cousin Ira wanted you to buy land and move to Yancey county. I believe it would be a good idea to do so, when the war is ended. But for the present I could not recommend it. My love to all the family and inquiring friends.
>
>Yours as ever,
>W. H. Proffit

76. January 10, 1863

Second Lieutenant Thomas W. Patton, Company C, 60th Regiment N.C. Troops, letter to his mother, Asheville, Buncombe County, N.C. Source: Patton Family Papers (1739), Southern Historical Collection, Wilson Library, University of North Carolina at Chapel Hill.

The 60th North Carolina's performance at Murfreesboro, or Stone's River, on the 31st of December was a cause of great dissatisfaction and turmoil throughout the regiment and brigade. Preston's Brigade advanced toward the Cowan

House about 2 P.M. and encountered a large picket fence and numerous outbuildings which played havoc with the regiment's alignment and caused them to be continuously exposed to enemy fire. It was at this moment that companies A (which fought along with the 20th Tennessee), E, F, H, & K advanced forward under heavy fire into a skirt of woods. The balance of the regiment, not under the supervision of Colonel McDowell, bolted for the rear, nearly throwing the 4th Florida, also of Preston's Brigade, into confusion. The panic of these companies (B, C, D, G & I) tarnished the regiment's reputation for months to come.[5]

            Tullahoma Tenn Jany 10 63
My Dear Mother

   I am sorry not to have been able to have written to you sooner, especially as Augustus arrived on yesterday & told me how anxious you had been about not hearing from me. I wrote you a short note from Murfeesboro [sic] on December 31, saying that I as Qr Master would not be allowed to be on the field of battle and consequently would be in safety up to last Saturday morning. We were all certain that our troops had gained a great & decided victory when to our great surprise, we received orders to start with our wagons in retreat and had to travel through the entire night and reached Manchester about 10 oclock Sunday morning and we have been hauled about backwards & forwards every day since until yesterday when we arrived here & encamped. Our retreat is certainly a most shameful proceeding and I think it ought to kill Bragg.

   The Yankies commenced their retreat two hours before our troops commenced falling back, so that both forces where whipped. Our loss in the retreat must have been considerable. The road for thirty miles was lined with broken wagons & tents & cooking vessels thrown out. Our loss in the battle is estimated at about 5000 killed, wounded, & missing, while the Feds must have lost four times as many. Our Regt lost 2 killed 70 wounded & 10 missing. One of the killed was Stanhope Erwin (Captain Hardy's brother in law). He was shot through the head on Friday. His body could not be recovered. No man in the regiment would have been more missed than he. Guss reached here in safety, but could not get our boxes through so I fear my apples will be lost. All of Mr. Andrew Erwin's family have left home except himself & wife. Annie Robinson, I hear has gone to Buncombe. I cannot form an idea how long we will remain here but do not expect to stay long. You had best direct to me here until you hear further from me. I have not received a letter from any where since Christmas.

            Your Affec Son
            TW Patton

77. January 10, 1863

   Private John W. Reese, Company F, 60th Regiment N.C. Troops, letter to his wife, Christena, Buncombe County, North Carolina. Source: John W. Reese Papers (4417), Manuscripts Department, Special Collections Library, Duke University.

   The Union victory at Murfreesboro (December 31, 1862–January 1, 1863) halted the movement of both armies in Tennessee. The Confederates camped around Tullahoma. Private Reese returned to his company on January 7, 1863, after spending the greater part of six months on sick call and in and out of hospitals. In this letter, Reese talked about losses from the 60th Regiment and burying the dead, and requested items from home.

            January the 10 1863
Dear wife

   With pleasure I am purmited to drop you a few lins to let you no that I am still a liv and on top of the ground. I sed that I would rite to you as sson as the fite was over at murfeesborro [sic]. Thar has bin a turbil time down hear. The fite comenst the day be fore new years a wends day and ended on Friday. It was a grate slouter. Our los in the suthern armey is nine thousan wounded and kild. This is our statement. Our regment did not sufer like the others but thar was a bout seventy wounded and kild not many kild. Marien Piram and Will Pritchet is missing.[6] Tha was in the same company that I am in. I was not in the fite at all.

On Sunday nite be fore commenst Goodson Robbers was helping the doctor take the names of thos whoo was not able to go in to the fite and he came to mee and sed John you hav bin sick a long time. I dont think you ort to go. I will take your name and sen you off in the morning at fiv oclock up to Chat a nuga and I went and got to Chat a nuga a bout sun down and stad tell next day a bout sun down. The doctor sent mee to daulton in georgia and stad thar tell yesterday morning and I am now with my Regment and it is at Tul a homa thirty miles this cide of mur fees borro.

Tha whiped the yankeys but had to retreat as usual. On weds day the yankeys wanted to bury ther ded but ther request was not granted. But the boys tell mee that a heep of the ded yankeys was striped off and flat rocks laid on ther belleys. On Friday the yanks helt the battle ground and our ded fell in thar hands and I expect tha will rot on top of the ground. I dont no whar the next fite will be.

I sent you thirty dollars in money by Franklin Parris and a letter and for you to sen mee two pair of socks and a pair of sus penders. Tena I want you to rite to mee as soon as you git this letter and let mee no how you all ar and how you are dooing and if you hav got your hogg kild and at home and if you sault to sav them and so on. Tell Hrret Barrett that

I hav not saw John yet but I think he is well and all rite. I think we will make our next stand at Brigport 73 mils a bov mur fees burro. I saw a power of negras going thar yesterday to bild brest works. I think the yankeys will make us git a long out of tennessee. Yes you hear mee. Tena I sen you a hair brush for the galls to keep slick hair and tha must let Brug hav it to brush his curls and you and the children ten short peaces of candey sewed up in Ruperts apron by halen frisbey[7] to Elexanders. Tena I want you to eat sum of this candey and think of mee while you eat it and pray for mee that I may return home to you all. Tell all my friends howdy for me. Tell mother Eller howdy for mee. I want to see hur vary bad.

    J. W. Reese to C. V. Reese
Kiss my boys and rezerv one for mee.

78. January 11, 1863

Private Calvin L. Proffit, Company H, 13th Regiment N.C. Troops, letter to sister, R. L. Proffit, Wilkes County, N.C. Source: Proffit Family Papers (3408), Southern Historical Collection, University of North Carolina at Chapel Hill.

During the winter of 1862–1863, the Confederate Army of Northern Virginia was encamped at Guinea Station, Virginia. Winter camp was especially harsh on those soldiers who caught one of many diseases throughout the camp. Two such men who contracted illnesses during this time were brothers, William Proffit, who by his brother's admission, was well, looking as if he weighed 180 pounds, and Calvin Proffit, the author of this letter, who contracted brain fever and died on March 25, 1863.[8]

    Camp Near Guinea Station va
    Jan 11 1863
Miss R. L. Proffit
Dear Sister,
 I again seet myself for the purpose of dropping you a short note which leaves

me hoping this may reach you and find you all well. I have no news to interest you with. I visited W. H. Proffit [his brother William] last Thursday. He is vary stout weying at 180 or at least he looks like he ought. I saw AJ & AN [his brothers Andrew J. and Alfred N. Proffit] last Tuesday. They are doing finely. Furloughs are being given out now. I do not know wither I will get a furlough soon or not, though I hope to get one about march.

You spoke of my sending you my type in a letter some time ago. There is no chance for me to have one taken at this time though if an oppertunity presents its self I will be apt to have one taken.

I suppose your school is out by this time, if so you take a considerable portion of time in reading which will improve both your reading facultys and menity. Suppose you take your NC reader and read it through point and every place your read about and then think of the history of North and South america and the Indian captives and by tht time you can read with the best of them. I want you to write me a long letter. Write what H. M. Starke is doing, who is going to leve where Calph and Luther did, if he talks about buying some land and send me some thread and a kneedle. Give my respects to all of my friends. Tell them to write me for I have looked in vane for a letter a long time and etc etc.

C. L. Proffit

79. January 11, 1863

Captain Alfred W. Bell, Company B, 39th Regiment N.C. Troops, letter to his wife, Mary Bell, Franklin, Macon County, N.C. Source: Alfred Bell Papers (417), Manuscripts Department, Special Collections Library, Duke University. (Partial letter.)

Bell, a Franklin dentist and druggist, had served as commander of company B. By the end of 1862, little had occurred in his company except the public disagreement between Bell and Colonel David Coleman. By December, these arguments were apparently settled. The Battle of Murfreesboro (Stone's River), Tennessee, brought a clash between the Confederate and Union Armies on the last day of 1862 and the first day of 1863. During the early stages of the battle, the 39th North Carolina held position near the Nashville & Chattanooga Railroad. The regiment made two assaults—in the first it advanced with Donelson's Tennessee brigade and in the second with Anderson's Brigade. At the end of its duty, the 39th had performed "good service," as remarked by the colonel of the 16th Tennessee, and was allowed to paint a reverse cannon battle honor on its flag after capturing and enemy battery.[9]

Shelbiville Ten
Jany 11 1863

My dear wife

I again seat myself this nice Sunday morning to write you again. Well a history of our loss & defeat would probably interest you at this time more than anything elce at present to know that I am safe & the most of my boys. I wrote you from Loudon that we was ordered to Murfeesboro [sic]. We landed thare the night of 28th Dec & was ordered next morning to the battlefield & would be held in reserve. On starting Capt Crawford & co was detailed to the wagons of Amunition.[10] The rest of us was marched at double-quick time to the field 2 miles off. We was marched to the right of the center division unattached to any brigade. On our approach to a fence the yanks had shelled us on our way. They wound several W. G. Thomas of my co was one. At the fence they give us a voley of minnie balls & wound several, Will Roane and Thompson of my co.[11] Here Col. Coleman was wounded.[12] We pitched in our little

Regt & the 16 La[13] with not many more men than we had. The Yankees played on us with 2 batterys & had 2 Ky leagons & 2 Indiana Regt clost ot us & about 6 or 8 thousand in line of battle some 8 hundred yds from us. We commenced our fight at ? after 10 oclock & fought until 4 pm. We was reinforced about ? after 3. The 16 La then fell back & of course ours then fell back to the ditches about 4 hundred yds. Col Davidson[14] was wounded about 1 oclock & of course I had to take command.

Col Coleman was wounded in the right leg about the top of the boot then out the side just missing the bone passed directly through his leg. Quite a severe wound from a minnie ball. Col Davidson was wounded in the right elbo & rangin down about ½ way to the hand—a very painful wound & injuring to the bone. Coleman has gone to Knoxville & probably will go home. Davidson took fever & could not be moved. He was left at Murfeesboro [sic] & I reckon the yanks got him prisoner. I had 16 wounded & 4 taken prisoners. Wood Owens, Lish McConnel, K Gudger, & Thos. West are missing & I am satisfied they are taken prisoners for when we fell back they did not come out & I sent back for them when the yanks fell back & could not find them.

At 1:00 P.M. on December 31, 1862, Lt. Col. Hugh Davidson fell, wounded, and command passed to the senior captain, Macon County dentist Alfred W. Bell (above). Bell's mountaineers held their ground until 3 P.M., afterwards retiring to a defensive position. (Alfred Bell Papers, Duke University.)

Some of the boys hid & say they saw Owen & McClammock taken. I only had 5 severely wounded and needed medical aid. Thomas W. G.—left shoulder wounded by piece of shell. Roane Will left thigh minnie ball—flesh wound. Jess Gregory right elbo, John Guy left leg broke, Lt. Anderson right shoulder flesh wound the others are slight wounds.[15]

Captain Crawford joined us after we fell back to our ditches. He came to the field as soon after we did but could not find us. He was under a heavy shelling all day & but one of his boys was wounded. Ervin Moore, poor fellow, a piece of shell struck his arm and burnt it. It was taken off next day & he died the same evning. We lost 2 killed dead on the field—Lt. John Ray of Company F, Cherokee co, & Sergt Whitaker of Co D, Buncombe co.[16] We had 50 killed wounded & missing. My co had more wounded than any other it being the largest. I had 50 men & my self and Lt. Anderson[17]—all of my boys with but little exception acted bravely. I must confess that I am not as brave as I thought I was. I never wanted out of a place as bad in my life. The balls hurled, the shells sang & the grape shot rattled. I want in no more battles.

The last day of 1862 will long be remembered by many of us. We lay in ditches & behind breastworks in cedar thickets until Saturday night & the grape and shell rattled all around and & over us day & night. Thursday, Frid & Saturday the enemys left was drove 5 or 6 miles & many prisoners & 40 odd cannon captured. We drove them to a strong position by [?] & they had fortified. It was a desperet rainy cold time. We was nearly worn out & Genl Bragg on Saturday night ordered a fall back to Winchester. We left about 10 oclock at night & marched here by night falling next 30 miles through mud & rain. We rested here a day & then traveled 2 days & got to Arisona & rested thare one day & started back for this place some 25 miles. We got here last night. I gave out after our fight & fell out of ranks & rested untill morning & joined my comd that night. We retreated. I took billious chalck but come on to this place the day & have not been well since. I suffer with paines & bowel complaint. I am still unwell. I have got the Majs horse to ride or I could not have made the route.

80. January 23, 1863

Colonel Isaac E. Avery, Company E, 6th Regiment N.C. State Troops, letter to his sister, Laura, Morganton, Burke County, N.C. Source: Waightsill Avery Papers (33), Southern Historical Collection, Wilson Library, University of North Carolina at Chapel Hill.

In late January of 1863, an all North Carolina brigade was formed under the command of Robert F. Hoke, who was the colonel of the 21st North Carolina Troops. Colonel Avery's command, the 6th North Carolina, along with the 54th and 57th North Carolina were ordered out of Law's Brigade into this new organization. The 6th had a special attachment to Law's Brigade, serving with it through the battles of the Seven Days (where Avery himself was wounded), Second Manassas, Sharpsburg, and Fredericksburg.

> F& S Qtrs. 6 No. Ca. Troops
> Jan. 23, 1863

Dear Laura,

I recd. a letter of yours a day or two since in reply to mine by Sam Browns. It was a long time in the Mail. I was very glad to get it, I have I not hear of brother Molten's safe arrival at home soon. If I had not lung since made up my mind never to be dissapointed or put out by must anything that took place in the army would feel very badly now. But I have determined to make the best of everything & try to recollect that I am nothing but a part of the great machine that old uncle Robert Lee is at the head of. But I can't but feel a little a very little put out, by our Brigade being broken up again. The 6th 54th , & 57th Regiments (No Ca) are ordered to march tomorrow morning a distance of over 20 miles, to join Gen. Robert F. Hokes Brigade, in Gen. Earlys Division. Three Alabama Regts are to take our place in Gen Law's Brigade. Bob Hoke was appointed a Brigadier a few days since—I do not want this to leave this tent, I do not want to leave this Brigade (to go there) & I am dead against leaving this division, and I must say I do not care to join "old Jacks foot cavelry." I had just got my men comfortably fixed and may have to turn and in this weather & march over 20 miles thro the mud. I am in a few hundred yards of the Rl Rd Station & get the newspaper regularly, when I get this I will be 14 miles from the nearest point. Gen. Early maybe a very good man, but I would not give Hood for any of them. Besides I think that we all fare much better in Longstreet than in Old Stonewalls Corps. I have formed some very pleasant associations in this division & I do not like break them. I like Gen. Law[18] very much indeed, I know I never will meet with a Commander who I can get along more pleasantly than I have with him. I have no doubt Gen. Hoke is a very gallant officer, but he is so young, & besides it is perfectly natural, Cols. Godwin, McDowell & myself should dislike to go into a Brigade under an officers we "ranked" a few days since. But enough of this, I only set out to give you my address which will be Gen. Hoke's Brigade, Early's division, Jackson's Corps. Major Tate went down to Gen. Penders today. He saw Alphonso[19] & Miller, they now both well. I will perhaps see Alphonso tomorrow. I had enough socks I thought to last me two winters, but Albert has lost some & washed off & organized others, in taking them to wash so that I fear I may run short before Spring. There is a good deal of excitement here. Some persons think a fight is iminant. Furloughs have been suspended by order "Until the crisis is over". It is thought the enemy will go at two other points, one above & the other below Fredericksburg. Please write often, I was glad to get the newspapers.

Affectionately Yours,
IE Avery

81. January 25, 1863

Private Lewis Warlick, Company B, 11th Regiment N.C. Troops, letter to Laura Cornelia McGimsey, Burke County. Source: Laura C. McGimsey Papers (2680-z), Southern Historical Collection, Wilson Library, University of North Carolina at Chapel Hill.

The coming of the new year brought hope to the Confederate garrison in eastern North Carolina. The winter was used to build up troop strength through rest, conscription, and unit re-assignment. According to Warlick, the 11th was the best drilled regiment in Pettigrew's command, and would show off their skill in the spring campaigns. First, however, Warlick and his comrades had to fight boredom, high prices for provisions and some of the worst wood to be had in the army.

Camp near Magnolia,
Duplin Co. N. C.
Sunday, Jan. 25 1863

My dearest Friend

I received a letter from you last evening the first I have got from you for some time.

We left our camp last Monday and arrived here the following morning fatigued hungry and sleepy. Ever since then we have been expecting marching orders but luckily have not received any as yet—have made preparations for that purpose by storing up all surplus baggage that we could not carry. There is now in this vicinity a large force composed principally of Gens. Ransoms and

French's divisions and at Wilmington and Goldsboro there are also large forces. Should the enemy make an advance either on Wilmington or Goldsboro we are in striking distance being about halfway between the two points mentioned. The enemy were a few days since at Jacksonville in Onslow Co. but the impression is that he has retraced his steps towards Newberne doubtless it was a mere faint to draw our troops in order to make a strike at some other point my opinion is that Weldon will be the first place attacked as it would be more important to them than any place south of that from the fact, all communication from the south to Richmond would be cut off. Therefore our forces in Virginia would suffer much as there would be no way to get supplies from the South. There was a rumor afloat yesterday that we would go back to Weldon or Wilmington in a few days, may be so but I dont believe everything I hear in camp for there is always something going the rounds in camp for men to talk about. Today is the first time I have seen the sun since here we have been— has been cloudy and raining all the time.

We are encamped near a Baptist church and yesterday and today was their regular monthly meeting and of course our regiment made a good time out, if for nothing else to see the ladies who came to church; upon the whole I think they were a common looking assemblege, they will not compare with our mountain fair ones as to looks. We had only three cases of smallpox in our regiment when we left Weldon. I dont think it will scatter much as all have been vaccinated which is partially a preventative for taking it, and should one take it who has been vaccinated it will not hurt them much.

Our regiment is in very good health at present. Phillip Anthony was left at Weldon in the hospital with Pneumonia. I heard from him day before yesterday he was improving very fast and spoke of joining us in a few days. Tomorrow our brigade (Pettigrew's) will be ordered out to witness the execution by shooting of a member of the 26 N. C. for desertion. I understand there has been about fifty desertions in that regiment, perhaps by shooting one now and then it will put a stop to their leaving Say to cousin J. I was very well pleased with the cheese I could hardly keep them when I got to camp every body was wanting them—could have sold them for one dollar per lb. I wish I had some more of them.

We are the worst set of smoked men or rather a set of the worst smoked men I ever saw. We get nothing to bum but pine and the black smoke soon covers us. The reason why there is so much pine is that the turpentine makers skin the pines for fifteen feet up the tree which dies in a few years and all that part of the tree that is skined is as rich as it can be and that is what we burn [when] oak wood or any other kind cant be had.

You say that Miss Rack told your fortune and that it was very good. I want you to write me all she told you; did she tell you that you would marry soon? There is great excitement in camps now about furloughs, arose from the fact that there was an order for each company to furlough one man out of every twenty five for duty. I'll not get any until all those who have not been at home have that privilege.

Monday morning, there is heavy firing in the direction of Wilmington supposed to be at that place. We amuse ourselves now-a-days by playing ball. There was quite a large turn out of ladies at dress parade on last evening, some very hard looking ones. We have the praise of being the best drilled regiment in the service, which make us feel proud that we belong to the old "Bethel"

Write soon and often to your devoted

L.

82. February 1, 1863

Corporal James H. Baker, Company B, 2nd Battalion N.C. Troops, letter to his parents, Surry County, North Carolina. Source: J. H. Baker Papers (288), Manuscripts Department, Special Collections Library, Duke University, Durham, N.C.

On September 25, 1862, James Baker was promoted to the rank of Corporal in Company B. The 2nd Battalion was assigned to the brigade of Junius Daniel, a US Army veteran, and former regimental commander, along with the 32nd, 43rd, 47th, and 53rd N.C. Troops. This brigade suffered heavily at the Battle of Gettysburg, Pennsylvania, on July 1, 1863. Daniel's brigade came to the aid of Iverson's disintegrating brigade and was exposed to the same deadly fire. In the end, Daniel's brigade and the rest of Rodes Division surged forth, capturing thousands of prisoners and several stands of colors, including "re-capturing" the colors of the 20th N.C. Troops. The 2nd Battalion lost 29 killed and 124 wounded. Among the twenty-nine killed was Corporal James Baker.[20]

General Hospital No. 3
Richmond, Virginia
February the 1 1863

My Dear Father and Mother

I seat myself this beautiful night to answer your most kind and affectionate letter which has just come to hand and how happy I was to hear from you all and that you was well. I am happy to tell you that I am still on the mend. I think I will be able to come home in a short time. I would be very glad indeed if I could come home before you have to go back to the army and if I can not I wish and pray to God that we will meet at home one day or another. I do not think that this Cruel war can last all though I do think that there is a better chance now at this time more than any other time in the war. William Cook has just had a friend to come and see him from the army and he says the men is not going to stay in the field any longer and that they will not fight no more. Every night some leave and goes to the Yankees. I am in hopes that the end of the war is close at hand for we have lost a great deal of good men since this war has began and may it please God to see that the end of this is not far away.

Dear mother I can say to you that Miss Cordel sends her best respects to you and William Cook says you must not forget to pick out a nice little sweet [illegible] and send it in your next letter. So I will close. Write soon and give me all the news. Direct to General Hospital No 3 Richmond Virginia

From James H. Baker

83. February 20, 1863

Private Harvey C. Davis, "The Watauga Rangers," Company D, 9th Regiment N.C. Troops (1st N.C. Cavalry), diary entry. Source: Francis B. Dedmond, "Harvey Davis' Unpublished Civil War Diary and the Story of Company D, First North Carolina Cavalry, *Appalachian Journal* 13 (1986), 368–407. Catawba College Archives, Salisbury, North Carolina.

While cavalry was generally kept out of major engagements, no other branch of the military performed more day-to-day small action reconnaissance and skirmishing. All of this continued movement and action fatigued and took a large toll on the health of the men and their mounts. In the later winter, Davis was given permission to return home to gather better, more able mounts for the cavalry service.[21]

They were some of the muddyest men ever beheld. We were nearly frozen, but by applying to the fence we got fires and this being done next we set about to procure something to warm the inner man for a dram is good in its place. On the 19th we came to Conhouse Station. Here it was said we would stay some time. Our mess set about building a hut, for we had no huts all winter. Next morning boot and saddle sounded. Some predicted we would go back to the old picket line. We went back to Gordonville and took up camp in ? mile of there. On the next day I was detailed to come home to purchase a horse.

84. March 1, 1863

Private John W. Reese, Company F, 60th Regiment N.C. Troops, letter to his wife, Christena, Buncombe County, North Carolina. Source: John W. Reese Papers (4417), Manuscripts Department, Special Collections Library, Duke University.

On the first of March, the 60th North Carolina Troops remained in its post at Tullahoma, Tennessee. Soldiers, like Warlick and Reese, dealt with the monotony of winter camp as best as they could. Reese mentioned several things of interest, among them, the transportation of several items home including an apron and a pocket knife to his children.[22] He also believed that the Federals would reinforce their lines and a fight would be at hand.

Tulahoma march the 1 1863
Dear wife
It is with pleas ure that I am pur mitted this good sab bath morning to let you no that I am yet a mong the liv ing and in tolerbill healthe better than I hav bin for a long time hoping thes few lins may find you and the Chil dren all well. I deziar that thing a bov all things I hear in your letters. I hop and trust that healthe may be granted to us all tell I reach home. O what a happy meeting it will be for mee to meet you and set down and talk with you. I ust to lov to talk withe you when I had bin gon off any whar in the settlement. I loved to tell you what I had saw and learn while I was gon. I will hav something to tell you this time when I return. If I am pur mitted to doo so and I hope and trusr and pray that this privelig may be granted to me.

I recievd your kind letter last nite. O how glad it mad mee to hear from you and the children. It was rote the 23 of february. It giv mee a good deel of sats faction to hear from all you sed you had recievd. You did not say how mutch money was in any of them. I hav sent you in all one hundred dollars in all and I want you to rite if you hav recievd as mutch as a hundred or not. Tell John he shal hav a nife in his pockit if I liv to put it. I want to no if you ever got that letter I sent to Elexanders and that hair brush and candey and Ruperts a pron. You rite all a bout those things in your next letter with out fail. You ort to all ways rite a bout sutch things in time so I could at tend to it if thar was any wrong to take place and whoo you bout your corn off and whoo is doing your milling for you and cut ting your wood and how you are making out for cow feed. Dont be a fraid of riting two mutch to mee for I could reed your letters if tha was as long a gain as what as what tha ar if tha was a little better spelt.

The times is a bout as tha was when I rote to you the other day. This is the third letter I hav started sence James W. Ray left camp. The yankeys has taken Hunts vill in Alabama and reports say that thirty thousan has crost at the cum berland gap into east tennessee. The waters is all up for it rains hear every day. The feds has fixt up the railroad that run from luivill Cantuckey to nashvill and from nashvill to mur feesboro and can rein force hear as mutch as tha pleas.

Tha are seling flower at three dollars pur hundred and shugr at ten cents pur pound and Coffey at fifty cents pur pound. We will soon hav the yanks starv out if it favers it. If it dont this thing will hav to close. Doo your best to git sum body to a gree to cum to this regment so I can cum after them. Rite soon
    John W. Reese
    to Cristena V. Reese

85. March 2, 1863

Hattie Gash, Roseland, Transylvania County, N.C., letter to her sister. Source: Mary Gash Papers (59), Private Manuscripts Collection, North Carolina Division of Archives and History.

The extensive Gash family had relatives all throughout western Carolina, always referring to them by their first name. This makes it difficult to track their exact relation or identity. This letter comes from Harriet Gash, in the Roseland community of Transylvania County. Hattie expresses the usual interest in family and mentions that cousin Jule (Captain Jule Gash) was at home hunting deserters.

    Rose Land N. C.
    March 2nd 1863
My Dear Sister

It has been some time since I have heard from you and as I am getting anxious to hear, I will write to you although I have no good news to tell you. Cousin Matilda Gray has lost one of her little girls. It died last night. First it had measles, then took the sore throat which caused its death. It was Lelia the oldest of the two little girls. Poor cousin Mat. It seems like she has a full share of trouble. She had just heard of the death of cousin Mary Jane's husband and was very much troubled about that. Lelia will be buried tomorrow. Cousin Mary Jane too has had her share of trouble, has lost her dear husband & is left with two little children. I received a letter from sister Kate Saturday saying the yankees had taken Brother Dick prisoner & she had not heard from him in almost two months. I feel so sorry for her & do wish I could go & stay some with her. I know she feels lonely & distressed about Brother Dick. Oh how much more trouble is this wicked war going to cause us? I feel anxious about our dear brother Jule, but do hope he will be spared to return home safely.

Sister Kate was wanting to hear from you said he had not heard it a good while that you had almost quit writing to her since you was married and I think the same for I very seldom get a letter now. Tomorrow is Aunts birthday. She will be 64 & she has invited her children and a few others down to take dinner with her. Cousin Jule is at home and will be here. Cousin Thad would have been here but the river was up so last week that he could not cross it and he did not know we wanted him here particularly on that day. Cousin Jule & Capt. Dobson were sent home after deserters & recruits. Mr. Lee Allman has been home on furlough, but will start back next week. Cousin Roxie is still in Clarksville but is very lonely. Addie Moore has been staying with her but is speaking of coming home soon & if cousin Rox does not come with her I will have to go & stay with her.

Sister, what has become of my dear little Bud? I wrote to him and sent it to your office but received a letter from you soon after saying he had gone to Uncle Buds to go to school. How must I direct a letter to him? I would have written again before now but did not know where to direct. Uncle Jacob would write to him if he knew where to send it. Please tell me when you write. Aunt send her love or says she think it is time you were coming out again to see us. You better be visiting before Brother Eli has to go back to the army. The friends are well. Give my love to Brother. Write soon to your devoted sister,

      Hattie

86. March 21, 1863

 Private Azariah Denny, Company C, 21st Regiment N.C. Troops, letter to his father, Joel Denny, and family, Surry County, N.C. Source: Jackson, *Surry County Civil War Soldiers* (1983).

 For most of the winter, Azariah Denny and his regiment, the 21st North Carolina Troops, held a position along the Rappahannock River, conducted patrols and stood picket. Denny described a possible movement which was avoided and the high cost of food in the Fredericksburg area.

    March the 21st 1863
    Camp near Fedricksburg Va
Dear father,
 I now seat myself to drop you a few lines to inform you I am still in good health and good spirits and truly hope these few lines may come safe to hand and find you all well. It is cold here now. We had orders to cook up 2 days rations the other night and be ready to meet the yankes but they whiped them and we did not have to fight. Since that we have been on picket at the river. I stood in talking distance of the yankes but I did not speak to them but they are trading [fire] all the time. I sent you $25 by Captain Snow he said he would leave it at John Joneses. When you get it let me know. I will draw my wages in a few days that was my state bounty. We spend nearly our wages here and then don't get more things than I have to have. Every letter I pay the postage on costs me 25 cents paper 4 dollars a quire, pork is worth $1.25 cts. per pound and brandy is worth 1 dollar a spoonful or 25 dollars a quart. The boys here is all right that you are acquainted with. So I must bring my letter to a close by saying I still remain your
     Lazy boy
     "Az"

87. March 25, 1863

 Captain Stephen Whitaker, Company E, Walker's Battalion, Thomas Legion, letter to his parents, Cherokee County, North Carolina. Source: Stephen Whitaker Papers (36), Private Manuscripts Collection, North Carolina Division of Archives and History.

 Stephen Whitaker was one of Valley Town's most influential citizens. This farmer and businessman was born in 1814 and married Mary Bibgy Taylor, whose family was prominent among the Cherokee. During a time when the Cherokee were not allowed to own land in North Carolina, Whitaker helped the nation buy thousands of acres, which later became part of the Qualla Boundary. Stephen used this respect and influence to help him raise a company from Cherokee and Clay counties, and was appointed Captain on November 29, 1862.[23] Whitaker commanded a company in Walker's Battalion which was ordered to duty in staunchly Unionist east Tennessee.

    Knoxville Mar 25th 1863
Dear Father & Mother
 After a bisey day at this sity I write you a few lines. I left my company at Cold Creek last Friday all well except some slight sickness not worth note. I have bin to col. Thomas head quarters his legion is now under Gen. A. E. Jackson[24] and our boundary appears to be Western N. C. and Eastern Tenn. I am to remain at cold creek a while yet to search [for] deserters & to prevent catel from being driven from the state.

I was at the S[trawberry] Planes [Tennessee] 2 days but did not get to see David as he was out on a scout. I bought today 3 tombstones 2 for my litel children & 1 for mother. It is nearly five ft long & 10 inches wide. He is to put on it all the leters you sent & finish it off for $50 and is to furnish a footstone & deliver it at the deport of this sity. My 2 costs 24 dollars for very small size.

I understand Brother Silas Raised a company in Gilmore County [Tennessee] yet it is gon to severville [Sevierville, Tennessee] and I do not know the truth of it. I supose it is so. Father I may not git home again till the war is over & probly never. I want you to try and go to my house & git the date of birth of my litel childrens and the death & send it to me at cold creek so that I can have the tombstone leters made. I hope that you or someone else will see that them and mothers is put in there proper place.

It is the uncertainty of life that prompts me to ask this of you tho I hope to see it don myself. There is no war news of intrest except that Rus and Vance[25] are falling back from [illegible] burow.

Father write to me soon as I want to here from you and my friends. I would like to say that I have 120[26] men in my company. I have no trouble with them yet. My orders has never bin disobeyed and has not disobeyed one single one yet. I am tired and it is about nine oclock.

    Your son
    S. Whitaker

88. March 27, 1863

Captain Elisha Alexander Perkins, "The Davis Dragoons," Company F, 41st Regiment N.C. Troops (3rd N.C. Cavalry), letter to his brother, Robert Perkins, Morganton, Burke County, N.C. Source: Perkins Family Papers (3894), Southern Historical Collection, Wilson Library, University of North Carolina at Chapel Hill.

Transfers in the Confederate army were very difficult to obtain. Official channels began with the commanders, but final approval had to come through a bureaucracy similar to those of modern militaries. John Micheaux's request was either denied, or he chose not to pursue it any further. Perkins talked about providing his own rations (as officers were required to do) and one of the biggest worries among cavalrymen—the forage and health of their horses.

    Dover Road 8 miles from
    Kinston NC Mar 27

Dear Brother

I recd your letter a few days since I have been a little unwell for several days but am about well again. I think it was nothing but cold. We are on pickett nearly all the time and the weather has been cold and wet. We had sleet reain and snow for 35 hours a few days ago but it is clear and moderate weather now. I don't think we will have much more cold weather you say Jno Micheaux[27] wishes to be transferred to my company. The only way that I know of doing it is for him to write an application for a transfer and get his officers to approve it. It will then be sent here and I will approve it and then it will have to go to the secretary of war for his approval. That is the way that I transferred three of my men to infantry. I don't know whether they will transfer from infantry to cavalry or not. The application to be addressed to Maj. Darden AAG. He will ask to be transferred from Co (b) 11 NCT to Co (f) 41 regt NCT.

I want your horse, that is if mine should fall and he might under the treatment he is getting. We only get 8lbs of corn per day and some times two or three days at a time. We get none.

There is no corn in the country around here to buy. All we get comes by railroad and I don't know where it comes from. If they want to impress your horse tell them you are keeping him for me and I want you to do it. And I expect you had better keep some meat and flour for me too. We are drawing rations like the men. We get ⅓ lbs of bacon but we eat worse than that. Our mess bought over 100lbs some time since it cost us from 1¼ to 2 dollars per lb. We have enough to do us a while but I don't know where we can get any more. The company will not sell us any. I am writing on my knee and cant think of any news. I will try and write a longer letter next time. Give my love to sister Sue.

Your affectionate brother
Alex[28]

89. March 28, 1863

Corporal William H. Proffit, "The Wilkes Valley Guards," Company B, 1st Regiment N.C. State Troops, letter to his family, Wilkes County, North Carolina. Source: Proffit Family Papers (3408), Southern Historical Collection, Wilson Library, University of North Carolina at Chapel Hill.

The Proffit brothers were very close, and the death of one, Calvin, was very hard for the others to bear. Calvin's death was especially hard on Alfred, his twin brother. When a family member died, it seemed that only one person was appointed to report all of the particulars of the death. William concentrated on his brother's good name among fellow soldiers and his Christian faith as facts to console his family with. William, who was now serving as a corporal, had to be very concerned as well, as he had had several bouts with disease over the past month, despite his assurance at the end of the letter.

Camp of the 1st NC T
March 28th 1863
Dear Father, Mother, and Sister:

I drop you a few lines to give you the Sad news that brother Calvin is dead. He died about day break on the morning of the 25th inst. I suppose that the brain was affected which was the principle cause of his death. It is, indeed, an appauling thought to think of the death of one so dear, but sad as it is, we have some consolation to know that he remained usually pious while surrounded with all the vice and immorality of the camp, and instead of participating in this, devoted much time in reading the Scripture. Some of his companions expressed the thought that he was prepared to meet his God in peace. We have another consolation that he had won the confidence and esteem of his officers and fellow soldiers, and that every possible means was applied in burying him decently. A good coffin, clean clothes, etc were provided. Sad as the thought is, it is no worse than thousands have endured since the commencement of this unholy war. I hope you will all try to refrain as much as possible from unnecesary grief, as it is a thing of no avail.

I have sent the <u>Biblical Recorder</u> to Sis. It will come to Lewis Fork, PO. You will see in it an account of brother Calvin's death. You will find it under the head of Obituary. Be shure to find it and preserve the paper. A. J. and Alfred [his brothers Andrew J. and Alfred N. Proffit] were down to see me yesterday. They are as well as common. They will write you the full particulars of Calvin's death and burial as they were there soon after he died. They sent for me also, but I did not go, as I was unwell myself. Let me hear from you as often as you conviently can. Yours,

W. H. Proffit
PS My health is very good at present

90. March 31, 1863

Private Robert Gaston Freeman, Company A, 60th Regiment N.C. Troops, letter to his wife, Sarah, Henderson County, N.C. Source: Violet Marshbanks Cook in *Henderson County Heritage* (Winston-Salem: Hunter Publishing, 1985).

Robert Gaston Freeman was born in Rutherford, Tennessee, in 1836. This Tennessee native resided in Buncombe County with his wife, Sarah, before enlisting on May 7, 1862. Freeman was mustered in as a sergeant until he deserted in December 1862. Freeman returned to duty in February 1863, but was reduced in rank to private. Freeman wrote this letter to his wife from the 60th North Carolina's camp at Tullahoma.

> Tullahoma, Tennessee
> March 31, 1863
>
> My Ever Beloved Wife,
>
> Again I take my pen in hand to let you know that I am well, truly hoping that these lines will find you and my little babies and all the rest well. I have been looking everyday for a letter from you, but I fail to get one though 1 hope I will get one before long. There is one thing I want to mention before I forget it. I want you to be sure to send me a lock of your hair in the first letter you write for I want something to remember you by.
>
> There is strong talk of peace at this time here. I find that the most of our head men, Officers, think that Peace will be made in time for us to make a crop this spring, and they think that if Peace is not finally made that there will be an armistice of six months to let the men all go home at that time, and if this should be so, the men will be at home by next month, but I fear it will not be so, yet it may be, for everything is quiet all over the Confederate States. I hope that it may be so, for it would be a great satisfaction to me to get to come home and live with you for you are all my thoughts when I am away from you. It seems to me that if the war ever would end and let me come home and live with you that I would be as happy a man that ever lived on this earth, and I do pray fervently for that time to come, and I hope everyone prays for that. Anybody at home has no idea about camps and how disagreeable camplife is, The snow is six inches deep here now.
>
> Sarah I shall send you some yarn cloth home if I have a chance. I bought the shirt that you sent me for $1.50, and I want to send two shirts and a pair of slippers home if I have any chance at all while I am as near home and then write to you where they are so you can get them for I cannot wear them here on account of body lice. We have oceans of them here.
>
> Sarah, I want you to be sure that you send me a lock of your hair in the first letter that you write after you get this without fail. I did aim to get it before I left home, but I forgot it.
>
> I have nothing more of interest to write at present. The next letter that I write to you, I will write a little letter and put in it, and I don't want you to let it be seen by anybody at all. I have sent you four or five letters and have not got one yet but shall expect one from you every week, so no more. Only write soon for I want to hear from you for you are my whole heart's delight.
>
> Remember me.
>
> Your affectionate
> R.G. Freeman

91. April 1, 1863

Captain Asbury T. Rogers, Company A, 62nd Regiment N.C. Troops, letter to "Miss Mary A. L.," Haywood County.

Source: Private Collection, Mr. William J. Best, III, Asheville, N.C.

The North Carolina Militia offered many mountain citizens an exemption from the Conscription Act. Despite that exemption, several militia officers volunteered for service anyway. Though he was commissioned a lieutenant colonel in the 112th Militia (Haywood), and served under his brother, C. C., Asbury T. Rogers left his militia commission and enlisted on July 14, 1862, becoming the captain of Company A, 62nd Regiment N.C. Troops.[29] In April of 1863, the Federal threat in east Tennessee was diminished, but a substantial garrison was kept at Zollicoffer, Tennessee. In this correspondence with "Miss Mary A. L," Asbury described some religious activity in camp, prospects for future fighting, and assessed the war situation with a somewhat grim attitude. Rogers and his company performed faithful service until the regiment surrendered at Cumberland Gap on September 3, 1863. While imprisoned in Ohio, Asbury was promoted to major, but would never get a chance to perform the duties of this new office.

              Head Quarters
              Zollicoffer April 1st 1863
Miss Mary A. L.

I wrote before I left home and thought that I would have received an answer before this time. But I suppose that it has been misplaced as many things are done these times. I have been very anxious to hear from you for some time. I would have visited you before I left Haywood if I had not been ordered off some sooner than I expected. I received a note from you desiring me to come down to your Quarterly meeting which request I was sorry not to fulfill from several considerations. We have been at this front near a week and we have a cold time of rain, snow, sleet and hail. It is colder here than in N. Carolina, or I have got so that I cannot endure the cold.

We had fast day here the other day and preaching. A good many country people were out and among them many fine ladies. This is the greatest place for ladies that I have seen in East Tenn, and I believe they would all like to marry if they had a good opportunity, but whether they will get that or not I cannot tell. The citizens here say that Gen. Carter will attack us soon, but I do not think he will be over very soon, although we will keep a close watch out. If they do come we Conscripts will do the best we can.

I would like to know very well how you are getting along with your school, and if you still like the occupation. Let me know how all the girls on H are doing and whether they have got tired of the war or not. If not, tell them to rest contented a little longer. Let me know how G. W. McCracken[30] and his Octave is getting along. There is a great deal more fun at a party in Buncombe than laying in camp at Zollicoffer or any other place.

I do not hear of any fighting at this time, though several big fights are in expectation. If they have to fight, hope they will fight soon, so that we may soon know our doom. It is very uncertain whether the war closes in two years or not. If our arms are successful this spring the war may close in six months. If not, we may prepare for two years longer and against that time many will never see their homes nor families. There is a time when there will be peace, though we may be ruined and I hope to live to see the worst of evil, though it may not be very pleasant and there may be nothing worth living for. Both sections of the country will become bankrupt and insolvent. I will quit this subject and leave it for your secret meditation.

Write soon and let me know all the

good and bad news in your country. It is very cold today and I shall have to close by saying that I am still your absent but true friend.

A. T. Rogers,
62nd Regiment

92. April 26, 1863

Sergeant Lewis Warlick, Company B, 11th Regiment N.C. Troops, letter to Laura McGimsey, Pleasant Hill, Burke County, North Carolina. Source: Laura C. McGimsey Papers (2680), Southern Historical Collection, Wilson Library, University of North Carolina at Chapel Hill.

As the 11th North Carolina pulled away from Washington, N.C., the men were upset to be leaving the city, and eastern North Carolina in the hands of the enemy. Little did men like Warlick know that in two months, their unit would be marching into Pennsylvania and carrying the war to the enemy. In the following letter, Lewis talked about the end of the campaign, the death of his sister, and several other matters of military significance with his sweetheart.

Asbury T. Rogers, a Haywood County teacher, commanded Company A, 62nd North Carolina, until its surrender at Cumberland Gap. (William Best III and descendants of A. T. Rogers.)

Hed Qtrs. Pettigrews Brigade
Camp near Hookerton N. C.
April 26th 1863

My dearest Friend

We came to this place last Sunday from Washington via Greenville in two days and you may guess that we were somewhat fatigued. Remained here until Tuesday morning when we got marching orders. Fell in and marched back the road 9 miles towards Greenville—pitched camp and the next morning received marching orders for Kinston to report there that night but to our gratification the orders were countermanded when we reached here or before and here we have been ever since. We were all disappointed at leaving Washington in the hands of the enemy, when we went there we were confident that Washington would be ours with all its contents but not so from some cause or other the siege was abandoned, supposed to be from the fact that our battery at fort Hill below the town could not successfully blockade the river the enemies boats would pass on very dark nights without being discovered bringing in supplies and reinforcements. Some think that it was not Hills intention to take the place but to draw forces from Suffolk to weaken that point so as Longstreet could work out his plans successfully: my notion is that the former was Hills plan—to take the place. We busted six of our best guns at fort Hill and Rodmans farm, a few miles above the former.

I received two days since the sad intelligence of my sister,[31] sorry was I to hear it but God's will be done. Its a debt we all owe and have some day or other to pay. Our family has been distressed greatly for the last four years for in that time I have lost a mother, brother and two sisters. I do hope that there will not be another death in the family while the war continues as that gives sorrow and sadness enough to be borne; but we know not the day or the hour we have to bid adieus to this world. There may be more of the same family distant this life before the expiration of this horrible war. Surely (the war) has caused more trouble than anything that has happened in our beloved country since the Revolution. Alas! and when will it end?

Yesterday there was a detail of 50 men from the brigade sent to Randolph and Chatham to hunt up deserters. Reuben Branch[32] was detailed from our company They are offered fifty dollars and a furlough for every one they catch.

I am getting tired of this country because we have not drawn but one days rations of flour since we came to Greenville, corn bread all the time except on a march. Then sometimes hard bread which is but little better. I want wheat to get ripe soon and lots of it. But then we will get but little of it as there is but little raised in this part of the country and they want us to eat up the corn that is made here and ship the flour to other parts. I would give considerable now for some nice biskets and butter. And wouldnt object to having a little honey sprinkled over it such as they have at "Pleasant Hill".

Phifer Erwin has not left yet, he did not accept the appointment of Lt. In the 7th N. C.—is looking for a better one—Quarter Master of the 60th—hasn't got the appointment yet, but has been written to to know if he would accept it. David Moody[33] has been discharged. I understand a few days since that Reuben Hawks a member of our company died lately at the hospital—dont know the certainty of it.

Our tents have been sent to Wilson together with all heavy baggage, dont suppose we will get our tents any more. I must quit as I have to report at the guard house immediately for guard duty. Direct to this place
              Ever affectionately
              Lewis

93. May 9, 1863

Private Thornton Sexton, "The Ashe Beaureguard Riflemen," Company A, 37th Regiment N.C. Troops, letter to his parents, Pryor and Mariah Sexton, Ashe County, North Carolina. Source: Thornton Sexton Letters (4749), Manuscripts Department, Special Collections Library, Duke University.

Sexton survived the battles of Second Manassas, Sharpsburg, Fredericksburg, and Chancellorsville. At Chancellorsville the 37th North Carolina, of Lane's Brigade, advanced early on the morning of May 3, 1863, in a line of battle and carried the first line of enemy works. Thornton describes "bad looken times," with "trees and bushes being cut to peses with balls and grap shot." This probably refers to the time when the 37th's right flank was turned by enemy infantry and artillery, releasing a severe enfilade, and compelling the 37th Regiment to withdraw. Ten days later, thirty-two members of Company A deserted en masse, among them, Thornton and Marion Sexton.[34]

> May the 9 1863
> Dear father
> I take my pen in hand to let you no that I am well at presant hopen when thes few lines comes to hand may find you in joyin the same blessings. I can in form you that I have not had nothing to eat in two days an almoast starved. I want you to bring mee a box of pervisions if you can for times is hard. No news is com. I com threw the battle safe an was not hirt. Maryan was not hirt. It was bad looken times. The trees and bushes was cut all to peses with balls and grap shot. Right soon and let me no how times is at hom at this time.
> Dear mother I would like to be at hom if I cood. Well i never new what bad times was before in my life. Give all my friends my best respets that I can give them. I have not receved no money sence I was at home. I neede somthing to eat mity hard if I cood git it. Father if you can com er send mee and Mareyn a box please do.
> So i must close for this time. Right soon as you git this letter. I still remain loving son tel death Thornton Sexton to Mr. pryier sexton. My love a true respts to my father and mother.

94. May 15, 1863

Corporal Andrew J. Proffit, Company D, 18th Regiment N.C. Troops, letter to his father, William Proffit, Lewis Fork, Wilkes County, N.C. Source: Proffitt Family Papers (3408), Southern Historical Collection, Wilson Library, University of North Carolina at Chapel Hill.

Chancellorsville was both a great and horrible battle for all soldiers of Lane's North Carolina Brigade. On the third of May, the 18th along with the brigade conducted an advance. According to Proffit, the absence of the 28th Regiment on the 18th's right left Proffit and his regiment exposed to dangerous enfilade fire, despite their success in gaining the first line of breastworks. The 18th faced a counterattack and was forced to fall back. The survivors formed on the left and acted as skirmishers. Corporal Proffit, along with the regimental colors, was captured by members of the 7th New Jersey Volunteers.[35]

> Camp Lee Richmond va
> May the 15th 1863
> Mr. Wm. Proffit
> Dear Father,
> I take this kind opportunity of writing you a few lines which will inform you that I am again on the southern soil, well and doing finely. I am sorry to inform you that I unfortunately fell into the hands of the enemy on Sunday the 3rd inst. I will now try to tell you how it happened as we were on the march to the battlefield.
> I with another corporal were appointed to guard the flag, one of the most dangerous positions in battle. On Saturday night there fell a bomb in my company & exploded in 4 or 5 feet of me & wounded the flag bearer and five or six of my co taking off one mans leg & wounded my lieutenant. When the flag of my country fell to the earth I grabbed it with my own hands. My colonel told me to thrown down my gear and hold on to my flag which I did. That night the Yankees charged on us but we soon repulsed them. The next morning we made a charge on them &

routed them from their first breast works & proceeded to the second and was order to charge them which part of us did. I carried the flag to the breastworks. We routed a long line of them & held our position but the 28th NC Regt on our right failed to charge them. The enemy commenced fireing upon our lines and gave them a chance to retake their works again which gave us no chance to escape. I lay there with two lines of battle cross fireing at me at a short distance & three batteries throwing grape at me not more than 3 or 4 hundred yards distant. The first I knew the yanks were in five steps when two jumped over the breast works & grabbed the flag out of my hand & said to me fall in John ha ha ha. John fell in but did not like to do it.

They took us to washington and kept us about 13 days. They treated is with great respect, gave us plenty to eat. When they brought us from washington we came down the Potomac through Chesipeak bay by fortress monroe, then up the james river to city point near Petersburg where we landed. We came here to camp Lee Richmond last night. I do not know when we will be carried to our regiments but I suppose shortly. I am unable to say what became of A. N. & W. H. [his brothers Alfred N. and William H. Proffit]. A. N. give out the night before I was taken. We had had nothing to eat for a day or so & marched hard which made him sick & he was sent back to the rear. I think that nothing but fatigue & hunger was the matter. W. H. was in the fight some of his co is here as prisoners. They say that he was not hurt the last they saw of him & I hope he was not. My Col was killed & my Liuet Col was wounded & the great Gen. Jackson was mortally wounded by his own men & is now dead.[36]

Father I am getting use to all kinds of hard ships in warfare & though I say it my self I know nothing of cowardice & God forbid that I ever should. The lord has been very merciful to me & I fear I have not a heart to praise him as I ought. I want you & all my friends to remember me at a throne of grace. I will now close. Give my warmest love to mother, Sis and all my friends. Write soon & direct to Co. D, 18th Regt NCT, Richmond, VA. I remain yours with great respect.

J. Proffit

95. May 18, 1863

Captain Stephen Whitaker, Company E, Walker's Battalion, Thomas Legion, letter to parents, Cherokee County, North Carolina. Source: Stephen Whitaker Papers (36), Private Manuscripts Collection, North Carolina Division of Archives and History.

In May of 1863, Captain Whitaker and his company had not taken part in any pitched battle in east Tennessee. However, the Confederates defending the region were subject to unfriendly and hostile civilians as well as repeated Federal incursions, and frequent skirmishes. In this letter, Captain Whitaker discussed the battles of Jackson, Mississippi, and Chancellorsville, Virginia. Captain Whitaker was a staunch Confederate and refused to believe the "union lie" about Jackson.

Greenville Tenn
May 18th 1863

Dear Father and Mother

I write you a few lines. I am well but some what tired. I just back from Jones borrow at 3 oclock last night. I did not sleep any for 2 nights. My self and my company is giting along very well except some 3 or 4 sick. I got a leter from home to day which informed me that the Family was sick with the measles. I can not git to go home now but I think I will before long. I was sorry to here that you was ailing and I hope you will soon git beter.

Father the service is hard on me but I stand it as well as any of my men and had harder days before me. We are still under Gen. Jackson & I think we will be ordered back to the railroad. The news this morning is that the yankeys have taken Jackson Missisipi[37] but it is thought to be a union lie. We gained a grate victory at Fredersburg [Battle of Chancellorsville] v.a. and we take it that we got 40000 stands of arms & routed the yanks and drove them back across the river.

Father I herd from David yesterday. He is giting well fast as can go about and will soon be able to ride. Manuel Setson is here an will go on in a few days. We are soon looking for Eli Ingram badly. I had two men deserted the other day. They were caught and will be tride by a Gen. Court Martial. This policy will be adopted here after-all men absent without Leave that is arested & do not come in on there own will be tride. Without a lasting peace I do not want to return home, and nor would I want to do so while I am abel to do duty.

The yankeys cant whip us nor starve us out. Wheat crops is beter than usual & thar is a very large crop of corn planted. It looks promising We under stand that Gen. Prise [General Sterling Price (CSA)] has got an army in Massouri of 60000 men & provisions plenty.

Father I have not time to write more now. If you here from Joshuas boys please let me know and if some of them has bin killed at Fredersburg. Let me know how you and mother is giting along. I sent you some things by Mark which I hope you have got. I know all you want to write soon. I have not had a leter from you sence I left cold creek.

Your son as ever,
S. Whitaker

96. May 20, 1863

Private Lorraine W. Griffin, Company D, 16th Regiment N.C. Troops, letter to his family, Rutherford County, North Carolina. Source: G. W. Griffin Papers (153), Private Manuscripts Collection, North Carolina Division of Archives and History.

Lorraine Walker Griffin, the son of William and Elizabeth Griffin of Floyd's Creek, worked as a farmer in Rutherford County before volunteering for service on May 1, 1861. Griffin was admitted to a hospital in Culpeper, Virginia, on October 1, 1862,[38] with a gunshot wound to the hand. After the Battle of Chancellorsville, the Confederate Army was divided into three corps. With A. P. Hill promoted to corps command, the 16th belonged to Scales' Brigade as part of William Dorsey Pender's Division.

Camp near Fredricksburg [sic]
May 20/63

Deer farther and famely

I take my sete this morning to let you know I am well & hope this may come to hand and find you all well. I haveint heard from home since John Sutton[39] came back. I am looking for george every minite. I think he must be coming. I wood like to see him so I cood her from home. I am uneasy about home. Maby I will git a leter from home this eavning.

I havint much news to write to you. Every thing is quiet along the lines but I don't know how long it will be so. We was revewed yesterday by old Gen. Lee and Lieut General A. P. Hill. The hole division was in the field. You will her from it in a few days. Hill is promoted to lieutenant gen. He is in G. Jacksons place. He is a fine looking man.

They have run in lots of troops from NC for what I cant tell. We will cross the river which I expect we will be fore long. I hope not for I don't want to cross the river if we was too so many wood be killed in crossing the river and will cut us to pieces on the bridge. But if they say to go we will go and I think we will hafta stay her as long as we live. When you her about the battle at chancellorsvill whar we whip old fighting Jo and can whip him agin if he comes over the River any mor.

Farther you must write to me and write me all the news and report how you have got along about stilling for I can her and behave. I wood like to know all about it for I cant be satsifide till I her from you. Harris[40] cood not tell me any thing.

I will wait till the mail comes to send this. I if don't get a leter from home, I wrote this one and it makes 4 since the fight. The brigade mail boy was arested and confined for braking open leters. He is to be shot I reckon. He belongs to the 22 NC Reg. He stold lots of my mail. The Mail has come and I got a leter from Mary but none from home. I hope I will git one to read from you! I will close this time.

Your Absen sun till deth
L. W. Griffin

97. May 31, 1863

Second Lieutenant Harvey Y. Gash, Company E, 7th Battalion N.C. Cavalry, letter to his sister, Samantha, Henderson County, North Carolina. Source: Gash Family Letters (1541), Private Manuscripts Collection, North Carolina Division of Archives and History.

Harvey Gash was one of several Gash men from Henderson County to fight in the 7th Battalion, and later 65th North Carolina Troops. Harvey enlisted in Henderson County at age 23 on July 15, 1862, in Company D and was transferred to Spann's company, E of the same battalion, on October 1, 1862, where he served as a farrier in early 1863, and was promoted to second lieutenant on May 3, 1863. Harvey expressed his concern over his brother Martin, who was a member of the same company. At this time the 7th Battalion was posted along the Cumberland river performing picket duty, and would remain in the area until June 1863.[41]

Camp near Monticello
Kentucky May the 31/63
Dear Sister

As it is Sunday morning and we have no orders to move I concluded to answer your letter so that you might know where we are and how we are doing. I am well myself. Mart[42] is not well. He has not been well for two months and he gets no better and it is a bad chance to get any place to stay in this country and he cannot get a sick furlough now and if he could I do not know whether he could get home or not. I tried to get him sent home to Hardans but they would not let him go. The doctor cannot send a man to a private home unless he can tend to himself without help. There is no hospittal near.

All the rest of our relations are well that is here though some of our boys is very unwell at present. Penny Carr is pretty sick and some others. Well, Mant we had a pretty hard time a coming over here. We did not get anything to feed our horses on for three or four days, only grass and it is not very good some of the time, but we faired pretty well ourselves. We would kill a hog or sheep when we would need it and we found some in good order and we done well.

Well Mant we are in Kentucky and pretty close to the yankees. A courier came after us the other morning and we was a bout ten miles from Monticello and we had to double quick nearly all the way there. The report was that the yankees had crossed the Cumberland river but when we got there it was not so. Then we went back 6 or 7 miles. Then the next morning the news came again for us to go back that they were fighting and we went down there and heard all the way that they was fighting. They had been fighting a little and our men run them over the river again. We was not in the fight. One Georgia Regiment drove them back. I expected that we would have a general engagement but we did not. I would not be surprised if we did have a fight in a few days but we have got a pretty good force here. In the skirmish we lost no men but some wounded and our men killed some say 1 and some say 4. I do not know myself.

I must close. We have orders to move but I do not know where. I do not know whether this letter will get there or not. Write and direct to Knoxville Tenn and they will be forwarded on. You need not be uneasy I will write again soon if I have a chance and send it.

Yours truly,
H. Y. Gash

98. June 1, 1863

Private James W. Wright, "The Wilkes Volunteers," Company C, 26th Regiment N.C. Troops, letter to his wife, Fanny Wright, Wilkes County, North Carolina. Source: John Wright Papers (1594), Private Manuscripts Collection, North Carolina Division of Archives and History, Raleigh, N.C.

James W. Wright lived in Wilkes County, North Carolina, with his wife Fanny and son Charley. James enlisted into service in Pitt County, North Carolina, on March 20, 1863.[43] Wright joined the "Wilkes Volunteers," Company C, 26th North Carolina Troops. Pettigrew's Brigade, of which the 26th Regiment was a part, was stationed at Hamilton's Crossing, Virginia, until June 8, 1863, when it began its infamous march into Pennsylvania.

June 1st 1863
Dear Fanny

A few words to you. This leaves me in common health at this time. I have been right bad off. I am in the poorest you ever saw me. I was taken sick with a bad cold on the 9th of May and never saw a well day from that time to the present. I feel now like I will soon be a man in health again. Don't think hard of me for not writing to you about it for I know it would do no good and would cause you all to see trouble when you could do no good. I was not confined kept up all the time but could [not] move around much.

I have been to the Doctor twice and I feel like he has almost made a new man of me. I feel better this evening as I have for nearly a month. I feel like I have a little life about me and if I could see you and Charley I believe I could hold him in one arm and slap your jaws. Still you could get as mad as an old cricket.

Dear Fanny don't mind my jokes for I want to see you and Charley so bad I hardly know what to write. It would give me great pleasure and satisfaction to be with you. I don't know how I should do if I could be released from this war and know that I was going to spend the balance of my days with you and Charley and my dear old gray headed Parents[44] who have taken so much trouble to raise me. I know something about good raising and any body would to see and hear what I do every day of my life. I thank my God that he gave me such Parents.

O Fanny I cant tell you my feelings. I cant express them to you my dear creature who made me a good wife while I was with you and if I am so fortunate as to get home I think we can live together happy. Do the best you can and get on smooth and even take good care of my little boy and hug him for me. Ruben is well. He got a letter from Ed. He was well. Give my love to

your Pa an Ma. Tell them I want to see them. I remain
>Your loving husband
>James W. Wright to F. A. Wright

99. June 2, 1863

Mr. Joel Denny, Tom's Creek, Pilot Mountain, Surry County, N.C., letter to his son, Private Azariah Denny, Company C, 21st Regiment N.C. Troops. Source: Jackson, *Surry County in the Civil War* (1983).

In May of 1863, Private Denny was captured during the Battle of Second Fredericksburg, an action fought against Sedgewick's Union force remaining at Fredericksburg, while Hooker's Union Army was massed around Chancellorsville. Most of those captured were paroled within the month of May. For Private Denny, his term as a Union prisoner was short; however, upon returning he would begin an extensive stay in the hospital.

>Toms Creek Surry County
>June 2 1862

Dear Son,

I this morning seat myself to write you a few lines to let you know that we are all in common health at this time and hope that these lines may come safe to you and find you doing well. I was much afraid to hear that you was missing from your company after the battle. I feared that you was killed and lost among strangers but I received a letter from Mr. Whitlock[45] that informed me that you was alive and well for which letter I feal thankful to him who takes care of little boys in time of battle. I also received your letter stating your misfortune of being taken prisoner and that you was sick of Petersburg and I cant help but be uneasy about you for fear that you will get worse. Please to write as soon as you get this letter and let me know how you get along. I wrote a long letter to you a few days before the battle you never wrote wheter you got it or not. Your mother wants me to write for her—that her and the little girls is well as common and wants you to come home on your parole if you can and if you get any worse please to write to me as soon as possible and I will try to come after you. We are getting on tolerable well with our crop. Jonathan came home yesterday morning he is well as common and so is Betty and children.[46] What they will do with him for coming home I cant tell. Leaving the camps and coming home appears to be common these days. I have the bad news to write to you that Isaac Ashburn[47] was brout home ded yesterday and Wm Hill from 55th Regt. the day before. I hear that your Unkle Wm Key's boy is at home. Either on furlough as I cant tell. The times here is common everything high—and money plenty the country quiet at this time but I cant tell how long it will remain. There is some hopes of peace and I think the sooner the better—I think that we have had men enough killed and our national debt long enough for us to begin to reflect and inquire where this strife will end if only left to the sword. So far—well for the present write me a letter on the back side of this and tell me all the news you can and how you come to be captured. Try to be a good boy and do the best you can.
>to A. Denny Joel Denny

100. June 22, 1863

Todd R. Caldwell, Morganton, Burke County, North Carolina, letter to his son, John Caldwell, Company E, 33rd Regiment N.C. Troops. Source: Todd R. Caldwell Papers (382), Private Manuscripts Collection, North Carolina Division of Archives and History.

In 1863, Todd R. Caldwell was one of

Burke County's, and western North Carolina's, most prominent political leaders. Caldwell, the son of an Irish immigrant, first won recognition in 1840 as a criminal prosecutor after graduating from the University of North Carolina. In 1850, Caldwell, a very ardent Whig, served multiple terms in both the North Carolina House and Senate. With the onset of the war, Caldwell chose not to support secession. John Caldwell was Todd's only son to survive infancy. In the following letter, Todd gave appropriate advice to his son who has been appointed to serve as a Lieutenant in the Confederate Army.[48]

        Morganton, NC
        22nd June 1863

My Dear Son[49]

As no one has written to you since you left home I have concluded to write this afternoon, although I have nothing of interest to write about. We all miss you very much but hope that you are in good health and doing well. I was much pleased to hear that you had a good position in the army and I must sincerely wish my dear son that you will exert yourself to make yourself deserving of the post to which you have been assigned; strive to do your whole duty as well as those who in command over you as to those who are under your charge; treat your superiors with proper respect and those under you with kindness and consideration; make it your study to discharge all your duties faithfully and then you will merit and receive the approbation of all whom good opinion is worth having. Don't be tyrannical or overbearing toward your men. Be kind and obliging to every one no matter how low or humble his position may be, and if you get into battle be like a man and a true soldier. Be kind and merciful to your enemies if any should be placed in your power. It is a badge of true courage and of a gentlemanly Christian spirit to show mercy and kindness to your enemies and it may in the fortunes of war happen that you may need the friendship of those you are fighting against. Observe vigorously the golden rule, "to do unto others as you would have them do unto you." Oh what would I not give if this cruel and unnatural war was ended and you and your army and in honor return home to your friends. I pray to God that the day may soon come when peace will reign over our land once more forever. I know that our people are truly tired of this strife of bloodshed and I believe the same feelings predominate in the North and were it not for the wicked rulers of both sides, the whole matter could be speedily settled in a way perfectly honorable and satisfactory to a large majority of the people.

I have no news to write you except that old John Kincaid is very low and not expected to live. Two of Jo Brittain's children, one 16 & the other 6 years old, Molton & Joe died one day last week and were both buried in the same grave. Mr Jonas Erwin was stricken with paralysis on last Friday and is now threatened with apoplexy. I understand he is some better today but the doctor will not allow him to see any company. All are well at Cherry Field. Bob is still alive and about as he was when you left. I expect to go to Raleigh day after tomorrow to attend a meeting of the committee appointed to investigate the affairs of the railroad.

We had a letter a day or two ago from Mattie.[50] She is still in Hillsboro doing very well when she wrote. I have not commenced cutting my wheat yet, but will tomorrow or the next day. Johnny I suppose you know how anxious we feel about you and I therefore hope you will write home every opportunity at least once a week. I will send you some money by Jink Walton when he goes back to his company. Samuel Kirkland is here and says you ought not to think of buying a uniform coat until cool weather. Did you see your Cousin Alex Perkins[51] when you were in Petersburg? The last we heard from him he had not had his trial. Give my respects to Col. Avery[52] and tell him I heard from his folks today and all were well.

The bell has rung for supper and I have nothing more to write so I will bring my letter to a close. All send their love to you in which I most heartily join them.

Your affectionate father
Todd R. Caldwell

101. July 2, 1863

Colonel Isaac E. Avery, acting brigade commander, note to Major Hugh M. Tate, 6th Regiment N.C. Troops, Gettysburg, Pennsylvania. Source: Isaac E. Avery Papers (1190), Private Manuscripts Collection, North Carolina Division of Archives and History.

The 6th North Carolina spearheaded an attack on Cemetery Hill on July 2, 1863. Colonel Avery, commanding Hoke's Brigade positioned the regiment for the attack, under fire and over difficult terrain. These were the last written words of Colonel Isaac Erwin Avery of Burke County. Colonel Avery died a soldier's death. This soldier said so much with so few words.

Major—
Tell my Father I died with my face to the enemy.[53]
I E Avery

102. July 17, 1863

Major John T. Jones, 26th N.C. Troops, letter to his father, Caldwell County, N.C. Source: Edmund W. Jones Papers (3543), Southern Historical Collection, Wilson Library, University of North Carolina at Chapel Hill, N.C.

Isaac Erwin Avery, a Morganton bachelor, commanded a company of the Sixth North Carolina Troops. At Gettysburg Avery took command of his brigade in the absence of General Hoke. (North Carolina Division of Archives and History.)

The Confederate Army retreated back into Virginia after the defeat at Gettysburg. Federal cavalry offered chase to the Confederates, resulting in rear-guard clashes. The last such rear-guard action and the unofficial end of the Gettysburg campaign, was known as the Battle of "Falling Waters," on July 14, 1863. Key among the rear-guard defenders of Lee's army was the 26th North Carolina which had already suffered greatly at Gettysburg. Acting brigade commander John T. Jones described his command's combat and final disposition after the engagement at Falling Waters, Maryland, to his father.

Bunker Hill, Va
July 17, 1863

Dear Father,

I am again on this side of the Potomac. Again in the land of Dixie. We crossed last Tuesday. My Brigade was last to leave and the last to give the Yankees a round. They attacked us about two miles from the river, the cavalry dashing right among us and sabering several men; in the melee Gen Pettigrew was wounded and I am sorry to say there is little or no hope entertained of his recovery. The command then devolved on me and I am now in command of the brigade and have been since the battle of Gettysburg except a short time. I lost the last day about 250 men in the brigade, nearly all prisoners. Our brigade is in a bad fix. With no other field officers except myself and a very few company officers.[54] The last days fight was the funniest affair I have ever been in. We had traveled all night through the mud and about eight o'clock stopped on a hill in open ground. We stacked arms and lay down on the ground and were all soon asleep feeling secure as there was a force of cavalry between us and the enemy. I neglected to state that few of our guns were loaded and few that were would fire. I was aroused in about an hour and jumping up I saw the Yankee cavalry all among us cutting and sabering. The men jumped for their guns and then commenced a hand to hand fight as is seldom seen in this war. The men clutched their guns and knocked the Yankees off their horses. One man knocked one off with a fence rail and another killed a Yankee with an ax. We soon routed them or killed them as I saw only two of the whole number that made their escape. I was then informed that Gen Pettigrew was wounded and I was in command of the brigade. I have just received notice that the General is dead having breathed his last about 4½ this morning. The General was shot by a Yankee major at the same time that he shot at and wounded him. When the general fell the Yankee was riddled by our men. I then received orders to fall back gradually to the river which I did. After going about a hundred yards the

John Thomas Jones of Caldwell County rose to the rank of lieutenant colonel in the 26th N.C. Troops, and commanded Pettigrew's Brigade on the retreat from Gettysburg. (Society for the Preservation of the 26th N.C. Troops, Inc., Catawba, N.C.)

103. July 29, 1863

Captain Thomas W. Patton, Company C, 60th Regiment N.C. Troops, letter to his mother, Asheville, Buncombe County, N.C. Source: Patton Family Papers (1739), Southern Historical Collection, Wilson Library, University of North Carolina at Chapel Hill.

After the fallout from Murfreesboro, Captain Reynolds resigned as commander of Company C, and Thomas Patton was promoted to that vacant post on March 10, 1863.[56] In June of 1863, the 60th North Carolina was assigned to a force under journeyman General Joseph E. Johnston, sent to relieve the Vicksburg garrison. After receiving the news Vicksburg had fallen, Johnston's force fell back to Jackson, Mississippi's capital city.

John Chambers. "Lieut Chambers and I rode out yesterday evening to try and get our supper. We had to hunt a long time ... but succeeded at last." (North Carolina Division of Archives and History.)

Yankees again charged us but we turned and gave them a volley which sent them back. I fell back slowly in order to protect the troops on my left but after while I found they were gone and left me entirely unsupported. I then fell back as fast as I could but not before I was flanked in the left and several of my men taken. I have heard nothing from Wat since I left but I know Dr. Warren[55] will do all he can for him. How long we will stay here I can't tell. The fall of Vicksburg was a terrible blow to us. The mail is going out and I must stop. My love to all my friends.

Your aff son,
J. Jones

Camp 60 NC July 29th / 63
My Dear Mother

I received your letter of Friday the 17th inst this morning. I am very sorry that you are giving yourself so much troubles and anxiety about me, and I will begin to think that you are "of but little faith;" at all events your troubling yourself can do no possible good, and may do a great deal of harm by injuring your health on which so much depends. I have tried to write regularly and frequently and have seized on every opportunity for sending a letter home. As we all know that the mails are very irregular and uncertain, so you ought to decide whenever you fail to get a letter, that the fault is entirely with the mail and that you will get one by the next.

I think I will have a chance of sending this direct to Asheville, as Genl

Johnston issued an order the other day, that hereafter furloughs should be granted one man out of each twenty five so that each could stay at home two weeks, and also leave of absence should be granted to officers for the same length of time. Never, however, without leaving at least two com officers in each company. Lieut Davidson[57] will take the first turn in my company, as he has never been at home for nearly twelve months. I expect he will get off today or tomorrow. As I was the last one at home, I will have to take the last turn for a furlough and unless the order is countermanded before then (as I fear it will be) I hope I will get home about Christmas, but I rather think some chance will turn up before that time and you may be sure I will keep my eyes open and improve every one that offers. At all events, one advantage of being the last is that then I may take a little over my time as the others will not be so anxious for me to get back—as their furloughs will not depend on it.

A rumor was afloat among us last week that we would all be sent to Mobile, and I have reason to believe that orders were issued for our division to go there, but they were countermanded before we could make a start. I wish we could have gone, as any change would be an improvement over this country. We moved our camp yesterday about five miles further from the Rail Road and to a much better place where we can get tolerably good water. I think we will probably stay here for some time as the Yankees are reported to have left Jackson, and fallen back even as far as Big Black. I don't think we will return to Jackson, as it would do us no good. My impression is that Grant will ship his troops down the river and make his next effort on Mobile, in which event we will have to fall back either to that place or Demopolis. I do not at all like to see the seat of war moving near to Greensborough, and wish I could persuade my friends to leave there for some safer country as event the presence of so many soldiers would make any country int[ol]erable.

I have not heard from Nannie for some time. Her last letter, which I enclose, being dated the 8th. I am becoming very uneasy about her, as she wrote that little Isaac Beatty was very sick with Typhoid fever, and, as Mrs. Croon was away from home, she had to nurse him.

Col Hardy[58] has not returned yet, and I have no idea that he will for sometime, at least not before he goes home & back. I am quite sure I would get off, if I was in his place. Capt Coleman, Lieut Chambers[59] and I rode out yesterday evening to try and get our supper. We had to hunt a long time before we could find a house where we could get it, but succeeded at last and while we were waiting, dark came on and it commenced raining hard and under those circumstances, we were sure we could not find the way back to camp. So we made ourselves as comfortable as possible and staid all night, getting an excellent supper and a nice bed to sleep in which are things not very common with a soldier. We got back this morning about day-light.

This country is very poor and thinly settled but few of the people have provisions enough for their families, and so of course, it is a bad chance for a soldier to do any foraging. I am still acting Q M and will probably continue for some time as Capt Roberts is still absent sick. I have no objections as long as there is marching on hand. Tell Fannie I think she owes me a letter, but I will write to her, (and aunt C too) again soon. I wrote by Lieutenant Israel[60] to Brother James. I suppose of course you will see the letter. Countinue to direct as heretofore, as I know no name to give this place. Your letters will find me sometime or another. Love to all. Sam sends his respects.

Your Affec Son
Thomas W. Patton

104. August 2, 1863

Captain Stephen Whitaker, Company E, Walker's Battalion, Thomas Legion, letter to parents, Cherokee County, North Carolina. Source: Stephen Whitaker Papers (26), Private Manuscripts Collection, North Carolina Division of Archives and History.

Among the strategic points in east Tennessee were Carter's Depot, a small town along the Virginia and Tennessee railroad and the Holston river, and the three hundred-foot span over the Watauga river. Whitaker tells an interesting story about two Confederate lieutenants who were kidnapped and executed by bushwhackers. Whitaker also reacted to the fall of Vicksburg and arranged the transportation of the tombstones when couriers come through Cleveland, Tennessee, on their way to get salt.

Carters Depot
Aug 2nd 1863

Dear Father and Mother

I wrote you a few lines to let you know whar I am and what I am doing. I am very unwell at this time and have had a saver cold and it has turned to some thing like the Plauzy. I suffer very much to still on my feet. If I do not git any beter I am next to git to a house. Martial[61] is very sick tho not dangerous. Wetherman & Graham[62] is both on the mend. Walkers Batt is here. We are garden the Bridge over Wattoger & keeping out pickets. The bushwackers came in 4 miles of her a few nights ago to a Mr. Johnston & cawled out his sons both lieut in the army & told them that the yankeys had taken carter depot & was coming on them and for them to make ther escape. By this they got up and went out and was taken off by the cowardly reches & one of them was shot and the other one is probably murdered. The one that was found was buryed by my men yesterday. They was both fine young men one in the recruting service, the other at home on furlow. Thar has bin a force sent to NC to put down the bushwackers thar.

Father I wrote you from Knoxville a few days ago in relation to the toombstones. I thout then I might be sent to Charleston or back to Loudon. If I had I could have seen to giting the stones hauled up. They are shipt to Cleveland. You can git some one that is goin after salt to haul them. Doct. Washham will have salt thar in the space of a week. If you cant do this you can git 2 of my men & send after them.

David got her safe. He slept with me Friday night. His company is in Yancey Co NC. He is goin to report to gen jackson & report for orders for he cant git through the mountains to his company now for the bushwackers. The vixsburg Prisoners is giting home daly. They had a hard time. They do not blame Pemberton [General John C. Pemberton, CSA] for the surender & say that Gen Johnston [General Joseph E. Johnston, CSA] did all he could to releave him but was not able to do so. We lost 27000 Prisoners in the worst lick of the war, but we still have about 40000 yankey Prisoners after exchanging in for the vixsburg men. I got this information from an officer in the exchange department & now her with me.

Father I have paid Hays a det I have long owed him. Col Thomas is at Knoxville under orders. I do not know all the charges against him. The principal one is for disobedience of orders.[63] Thomas will be smart enough for them. Thar is grate pregatis against him. Col Walker is her. I beleave I have the good will of all the officers from Gen Jackson down. My own men is all very good to me. They will do any thing for me. I have not an inimey that I know of in the company, but not so in Cherokee County as I have bin lide about very much. All will come rite & the rite will be sustained. The young man that was supposed to be murdered has bin recvoered by a Union man & brought home to stay. This must be grate satisfaction to his father who thought he was killed. Father you will git tired of reading this long leter.

Green Woods boy had a leter come to camp the first chance. He can come by Rocky Point & to Knoxville or Strawberry Planes & then on the railroad to this place. Fther write to me and give me all the news. Direct your leters to Carters Depot Tenn Walkers Batt. Father give my respects to the friends & reserve afection for your self.
S. Whitaker

105. August 10, 1863

Private William H. Proffit, Company B, 1st Regiment N.C. State Troops, letter to his sister, Louisa, Wilkes County, North Carolina. Source: Proffit Family Papers (3408), Southern Historical Collection, Wilson Library, University of North Carolina at Chapel Hill.

On May 3, 1863, William H. Proffit, one of the first members of "The Wilkes Valley Guards," was promoted to sergeant. Proffit served as a sergeant, but was frequently on sick call, having not fully recovered from a previous illness. Proffit wrote his sister about spending leisure time in August of 1863, long after the Chancellorsville and Gettysburg campaigns. Proffit seems adamant and patriotic toward the southern cause. Six weeks later, Sergeant Proffit died of "febris typhoides" at Gordonsville, Virginia.[64] He was the second of the three Proffit brothers to die.

Camp of the 1st NC Troops
Near Orange Court House, Va.
Monday morning, August 10th 1863
My dear sister Louisa;

Another week has gone bye and I have not received a letter from you or any of my friends in Wilkes, neither have I heard a word concerning Andrew and Alfred [his brothers], consequently, I am becoming quit impatient, as well as uneasy, although I have no thought that it any fault of yours.

All has been quite since I wrote you last. We are enjoying most all the comforts of a quite camp, but how long we will be permitted to remain in camp is not known. The two great armies of the Potomac; I believe, are both quiet and at least temporarily stationary—the yankees in the vicinity of Culpepper C. H. and the Confederates at Orange C. H. The weather has been excessively hot for the past ten days, but as we have very little to do, we lie in the shade and pass the time as agreeably as possible. I have three or four books including my bible with which I spend a great part of my time. We have had three or four fine rains withing the past week—crops look remarkably well in this neighborhood, indeed, I do not see how they can be better. I understand the people of Wilkes are badly whipped and willing for our patriotic old State to return to the pretended Union, and claim Abraham Lincoln as their chief magistrate. I have also been told that the country was full of deserters and no effort is being made to arrest them, but that they are more highly respected than a soldier who is toiling and fighting to redeem their country from chains and Slavery. I would be glad to hope that such were not the case, but no ground for believing the reports are untrue.

I am not in favor of a termination of the war, until it terminates in the independence of the Confederate States. Our late reverses are not cause for submitting to our enemies, but should cause us to make the more determined and vigorous efforts to accomplish what we first began. And as regards to deserters, I would as soon hear of a christian friend of mine being shot through the brain or heart as to hear of him deserting the army and resorting to the rock houses of his native mountains.

My health is good. Tell Pa & Ma that I would be happy in seeing them and will get a furlough as soon as possible and visit them. When you write me give me all the information you can of A. J. & A. N. Your acquaintances in this company are well, those who are present. It is feared that John Estes is dead, although we have no certain account of it.

Affectionately your brother
W. H. Proffit

106. August 21, 1863

Sergeant William J. Smathers, Company C, Love's Regiment, Thomas Legion, letter to his father, G. F. Smathers, Haywood County. Source: Private Collection, Mr. William Best, Asheville, N.C.

Sergeant William Jasper Smathers, a Haywood County resident who enlisted on June 13, 1862,[65] was one of nine Smathers that fought in Captain Elisha Johnson's Company C of Love's Regiment, Thomas' Legion. The exact relation of all the Smathers is not known; however, it appears to be at least two sets of brothers. In 1863, Love's Regiment was consistently one of the poorest equipped and shod units that operated in East Tennessee. It goes without saying that Sergeant Smathers considered these hardships when he returned thanks for items from home and considered joining a cavalry company. Smathers reasserted his courage to his father and vowed never to desert unless "tims gits worse about sum thing to eat."

Fredom Tenn
Washington Co. Aug 21st /63
Mr. G. F. Smathers

Dear father I take my pen in hand to drop you a fiew lines which will in form you that I am well at the present time hoping theis fiew lines will cum safe to hand and find you and all the rest of the famley well and doing well. I received your leter yesterday and was glad to here from you but was truley sorey to here that you was sick. I hope that you will soon git well agin. You was rong in formed about me being cuming home at camp meeting. I hav giv my name to go with the cavelry and if I git in withe them I will be at home sum time this fall to git me a horse. Father I wold like to see you the best in the world but I recon it is out of the question un less you git able to cum out here. I got the nuse that you got the muney that I cent you by J. P. Justice. I got my pants and socks and unions that mother cent me. We are at a vary good place now but I dont no how long we will git to stay here tho we may git to stay here a long time yet.

You rote that never wanted me to run away like sum of them has dun. Rest contented about that. I do not expect to ever run away unless times gits worse about sum thing to eat. Be fore I will parrish I leav if they hang me for when my life is gon what will this world be worth to me. I had as soon be hung or shot as to starv to death. I wish

If you hav muney by you that you wold keep hit till I see Whitker. I git in the cavelry or not. If I do I will hav to borey sum to by me a horse. So I must close. Give my best respects to all my friends. Yours truley un till deathe. Tell Jane that I cold ent rite to her this time I had just started her old leter. Fare well father for this time.

Sgt. W. J. Smathers to
Mr. G. F. Smathers

107. September 1, 1863

Sergeant Lewis Warlick, Company B, 11th Regiment N.C. Troops, letter to Laura C. McGimsey, Pleasant Hill, Burke County. Source: Laura C. McGimsey Papers (2680-z), Southern Historical Collection, Wilson Library, University of North Carolina at Chapel Hill.

During the fall of 1863, Pettigrew's Brigade recuperated from its severe losses during the Gettysburg campaign. At the three day battle, the 11th Regiment reported fifty killed and one hundred and fifty-nine wounded. Also among the casualties were a large number of captured, including Sergeant Warlick and others from his command. Included in the Gettysburg campaign was the affair at Falling Waters, Maryland, in which the 11th suffered several casualties and lost additional men to the Yankees. After a stay at David's Island, New York, Warlick was transferred to City Point for exchange. Warlick wrote his sweetheart on September 1, 1863, from the safe confines of Petersburg, Virginia.[66]

> N. C. Hospital Petersburg, Va
> Sept. 1 1863
>
> My dearest Corrie
>
> How thankful I ought to be and how glad I am that I am again in Dixie. You know not the many times I have wished myself out of the enemy hands while a prisoner and that wish after a long while has been gratified. I arrived here Friday last from Davids Island N. Y. in company with six hundred and ninety paroled wounded prisoners. I would have written to you immediately after my arrival but learning the medical would not sit yesterday I concluded I would postpone writing until I learned whether or not I would get a furlough but the board failed to meet for some cases as others I will have to wait till Monday before I know whether or not I will succeed in getting one as the board does not meet again til then. I think it probable I will get one when the board meets as I was recommended to go before the board yesterday wish it had have met.
>
> I am improving but slowly cant walk but very little with my crutches, my face has healed up nicely. I have heard of several of our boys since my arrival who are in the hands of the yanks. Lt. Parks and Michaux are in jail in Baltimore.[67] Tom passing off as a private all the officers having been sent to Sandusky, Ohio.[68] I cant hear a thing from Harrison Parks I fear he was killed. Bob Carlton, S. Wakefield, Bob Hermessee, S. Brown and others are at Fort Delaware hope all are doing well.[69] Capt. Armfield is there also well. Havent heard a word from Tom Moore[70] other than he was severely wounded dont know what became of him. I was so glad to hear Port got home I heard that through Mrs. May and Elizabeth Ann Kincaid who are here with their sick husbands. They are improving. I was kindly treated while in the hands of the enemy but never do I want to fall into their hands again for I have such great hatred for them I dom care about seeing them only as dead, wounded, or prisoners on the battlefield.
>
> I wrote to you twice while at The Island, did you get them? if you did I guess you laughed to see how I addressed you, I will explain that for we were only aloud to send family letters. All were unsealed and read before they passed through the lines, therefore I developed you as a cousin. I know our friends and relations have suffered with grief without description since the fight at Gettysburg for so many thousand poor fellows were killed and wounded, never do I want to witness another such a sight if I had not got use to it my heart would sicken at the thought. Often since I have been wounded have I thought of you and wanted to be at home where I could hear from you and

see you occasionally. I wish that would be so. As ever
                                    Lewis

108. September 5, 1863

Captain Julius Gash, Company D, 65th Regiment N.C. Troops (6th N.C. Cavalry), letter to "Colonel." Source: Mary Gash Papers (59), Private Manuscripts Collection, North Carolina Division of Archives and History.

Nearly a year has passed since Jule's last letter. The 7th Battalion was merged to form the 6th Cavalry Regiment on August 3, 1863, and was assigned to a command in east Tennessee. At the engagement at Sweetwater, Tennessee, the 6th Cavalry was among troops commanded by Colonel Scott and General Buckner. After the described engagement, Buckner's force destroyed the bridge at Loudon and fell back to the small hamlet of Charleston on the Hiwasse River.[71] With baggage captured and surprise desertions, the situation looked pretty bleak for Jule's company and regiment. Jule voiced his contempt for deserters and inquired about land for sale at home, and valued the lost items.

                Charleston, Tenn
                Sept 5th 1863
Dear Col.

You will perceive from the heading of this note that we are moving slowly south. Since we left the gap at "Big Creek" we have been moving most of the time until the last three days. We have been quiet at this place. We moved huridly until we came to Loudon where we halted until the Yankees came in for us. The 2nd Inst that came to Loudon. Our boys were drawn up in line in the town where they were exposed to the shells of the enemy. The boys generally thought it a pretty hot place they were exposed a short time but long enough to kill one man dead of Gillespies Co[72] & wounded another of Dobsins. The man killed of Gillespies was by the name of Feagins from Polk County. When he fell from his horse it seemed to frighten our boys considerably & they were very anxious to change positions. About that time however, Col Scott ordered us away from that position. There came a considerable force above us and aimed to cut us off at Sweetwater which they came near, but we succeeded in making our escape.

There are a good many troops at this place moving about but I have no idea if they intend fighting any at this point. The infantry is all moving below. There will be a big two-horse fight somewhere in the country (but I know not when it will come off) upon which depends the fate of Tennessee and in fact has something to do with the fate of the Confederacy. I am strong in the faith that we are destined to be victorious in the pending battle.

The officers of our command played the Devil generally while they were at the Gap. Myself among the rest. We were a little fearful we could be gobbled up at the Gap & all sent our trunks to Knoxville for safe keeping and now the Yanks have possession & as a matter of course they are all "gone-up" for ninety. I had a uniform in mine worth Three Hundred ($300) Dollars besides all of my other clothing and a quantity of stationary—a Pistol worth $100—a watch worth $100 and various other articles of trifling value, but which I regret very much to loose. One thing was a young ladies miniature which I prized very highly. No use groaning after spoiled milk, I'll make it all back if I have good luck and enough of it

My company papers, receipts, muster rolls and all gave up. I don't care a D—n. My company has about gone up too! All deserted or at home without leave. Twenty-five men of our Regt started home about a week ago, but were nearly all apprehended! Two of my company among them. Gen. Buckner says he intends shooting every man of them, and I do hope to God he will. Beard's Battalion and ours have been consolidated and formed the 66th N.C. Regt.[73] Both battalions can make about two good companies. There are now from both battalions 35 men in arrest who Buckner says he is going to have shot. Since the big stampede two of my men have deserted. Dick Osteen who had just returned from home, and the last man I would thought of deserting and John C. Edney, who was a Liut in Balums Co.[74] You know him very well I guess. Dick was very much alarmed at Loudon. He told some of the boys that day if another Cannon ever got a chance at him it would be smart and sure enough that might he "took up his bed" and skedadled.

I have learned during this war that there is no confidence to be placed in white men. I'll swear men have deserted my company who I had the most implicit confidence in and men too who have been for near twelve months good soldiers as I thought was in the Confederate Army. I wish I could express the contempt I naturally cherish for a deserter, and men who will at this particular time desert. I do candidly think ought to be shot. I think it is nothing more than what they justly merits. Why! Confound a man who is void enough of principal to desert his country in so perilous a time as now. Should all things work together for good and I live to see this difficulty adjusted. There is a day when I'll get revenge from deserters, mark it. You are probably tired of this subject and so am I for when I think of deserters I get so mad it bothers me to keep from saying Cuss words.

I learned from some source that Mrs. Allisons lands on Boilton were for Sale. Three Hundred (300) acres for sixteen hundred ($1600) Dollars. If so I think it must be a bargain. I wish you would try and learn something about the fact of the matter. You can ascertain from Geo. Orr, but you need not let him know that I wish to know anything about it. If so, please examine the lands and if you think it is a bargain make the trade for me. You can sell Gold enough to pay for it. It will not take much. I suppose it is worth $10 there. I could readily get $20 if I had it here. The Yanks are so near if you succeed please see that the titles are all right. If it fails to work, [don't] say anything about the matter. Elisha Allison has been armaying me ever since I commenced writing, about giving you his best respects, now take them will you. I think of nothing else. Please inform me if you ever got your Two Hundred $200 Dollars back. I sent by some body I don't recollect who. I remain

Truly Yours
Jule

Address Charleston, Tenn. 66th N. C. Regt. Cav Pegrams Brig.

109. September 21, 1863

Captain Thomas W. Patton, Company C, 60th Regiment N.C. Troops, letter to his mother, Asheville, Buncombe County, N.C. Source: Patton Family Papers (1739), Southern Historical Collection, Wilson Library, University of North Carolina at Chapel Hill.

The Battle of Chickamauga redeemed the reputation of the 60th North Carolina Troops. Since the expedition to Mississippi, the 60th North Carolina was serving in Stovall's Brigade of Breckinridge's Division of Hardee's Corps. On September 20, 1863, Hardee's Corps, under the command of General D. H. Hill, advanced against Federal forces under General George H. Thomas. The first attack was beaten back with relative ease by the Federals. During the first attack the 60th advanced into Kelly's Field and were confronted by the

Lieutenant Colonel John Ray's arm was hurt severely at Chickamauga. Ray resigned his commission in December after a painful convalescence at home in Buncombe County. (North Carolina Division of Archives and History.)

2nd Minnesota. The men of the 60th took cover in the tree line opposite the field and went prone. The exchange got the best of the Minnesotans and the 60th fought well until being forced to retreat when the Stovall's command began to fall back. By the time Stovall made a second assault about dark, Thomas' Federals were beginning to retreat. The 60th North Carolina advanced and drove steadily until halted near the Chattanooga Road. Chickamauga proved to be a great victory for the officers and men of the 60th, restoring their reputation, for a while.

               Battle Field September 21
               1863
My Dear Mother,
   I have been in a hotly contested battle and thanks to our Heavenly Father, have escaped unhurt. For God's sake I would rather be still Quarter Master but was relieved and ordered on duty a day or two or ago. I have escaped thus far and I hope I will eventually, so please rest quietly and I will write to you as often as possible. Our Brigade made two noble charges on yesterday. In the first we were repulsed by superior numbers. We rested a while and just at dark, charged again and drove the enemy from their position and held the field. The old 60th acted bravely—loss heavy in wounded, not many killed. Among the former, Col Ray, Liut Davidson, of my company—Lt. White, Lt. Reynolds, Lt. Huff[75] and two men of my company killed. Col. Ray, I hear expects to start home immediately & will take this. I do not know whether he will be engaged again or not, but am sure that the same kind of providence which watched over me yesterday will do so again. I have many exciting & interesting incidents to tell you, or to write at a more leisure moment. The Yankees, as far as I can judge are getting decidedly the worst part of it. We now hold the Chattanooga Road which has been the point of contention for two days past. Genl Polk I think is safe. Genl Helm of our Division killed. Gen. Adams of the same, wounded & a prisoner. I have not heard as yet any particulars as to our loss or that of the enemy. Lieut. Davidson is only slightly wounded in the leg. Lt. White had a leg amputated & Lieut. Reynolds right hand amputated. Yesterday will furnish material for many interesting conversations of these days & I assure you will not soon be forgotten. I would telegraph you but we are not near any town & so have no means of telegraphing or writing except occasionally by hand.
   I now have to close as the messenger who carries this to Col Ray is leaving. No sign of Yankees as yet today & it is

now near noon, perhaps we will not have any more fighting. Love to all.
    Your Affec Son
    T W Patton

110. September 28, 1863

First Lieutenant J. L. Henry, "The Buncombe Rangers," Company G, 1st N.C. Cavalry Regiment (9th Regiment N.C. State Troops), letter of resignation to General Samuel Cooper, CSAG, Richmond, with attached letter from Governor Zebulon B. Vance. Source: J. L. Henry Papers (587), Private Manuscripts Collection, North Carolina Division of Archives and History, Raleigh, N.C.

With the request of Governor Vance, Lieutenant Henry, a Buncombe County resident, accepts the commission as a commander of N.C. Home Guard cavalry in the North Carolina mountains. Henry commanded a company under Major John Woodfin's Battalion, which was later redesignated the 7th North Carolina Cavalry in the late stages of the war.[76]

    1st No Ca Cavalry
    Bakers Brigade
    28th Sept 1863
Gen S Cooper, Adj Genl:

Having been appointed captain of a cavalry for Home Defense I respectively tender my resignation as 1st Lieutenant, Company "G" 1st Regt N C Cavalry. Amended see Govr Vance's letter.
    I am very Respectfully
    Yr ob Sevt.
    J. L. Henry

    Executive Department
    Raleigh, NC Sept 24 1863
    Capt. J. L. Henry
Dear Sir—

I have appointed you to the command of a cavalry company in the mountains, where is nearly complete for the state defence. His occupation of East Tennessee has opened all western N C to destructive raiders of the enemy and I am raising troops and the army as fast as possible for their defence.

Please reply promptly, if you can get your resignation accepted, as I have no competent man in that country to command cavalry except Maj. Woodfin, who commands the Home Guards.
    Respectfully Yours,
    Z. B. Vance

111. October 8, 1863

Private William T. Tippet, Company B, 39th Regiment N.C. Troops, letter to Captain Alfred W. Bell. Source: Alfred W. Bell Papers (417), Manuscripts Department, Special Collections Library, Duke University.

In the fall of 1863, Captain Alfred Bell left his command and returned home to Macon County. During this time, the 39th North Carolina left Mississippi and fought in the Battle of Chickamauga on September 19–20, 1863. The 39th, as part of McNair's Brigade, charged to the support of Gregg's South Carolinians, and drove the enemy about three-quarters of a mile. The regiment held an exposed position and when faced with dwindling ammunition, retired to a position with the rest of their brigade. The next morning, the 39th North Carolina fought as part of Longstreet's command. The regiment repulsed an attack at 9:30 A.M. and began to drive the enemy with the rest of the left wing. During the fighting, General McNair was wounded and Colonel Coleman assumed command of the brigade, ordering the 39th across Dyer's field to charge a battery. After eight Yankee pieces fell and were secured by Coleman's men, the command was called on yet again. The 39th North Carolina, along with Coleman's Brigade, charged in support of Fulton's Brigade, crossed a hill, and after a fierce fight, drove the enemy in front of them on horseshoe

Macon County's Corporal James T. Winstead (left) of Company I and Third Lieutenant William Holbrook of Company B were both wounded in action at Chickamauga. (North Carolina Division of Archives and History.)

ridge. Of the 247 men of the 39th present for duty, over one hundred were killed or wounded.[77]

                Camp Bruen Meridian Miss
                Oct 8 1863
Dear Capt
    I recd your leter by Lt. Anderson and was glad to hear from you but by your leter & anderson I learn you to be in rether a panful condition. I am sorry it is so for I know they are a great many thingss going on in Macon that are very disagreeable with you and man of your pluck. It must be miserable that you have no beter a way of helping your self than you doo. I think if you was with Co B you would be obeyed mutch beter than you are in Macon, no doubt you would be mutch beter pleased your self. I hardly know what to think about our Hoam folkes turning our to Derleckting and incouraging dissertion from all acounts thay are but very trew Petreotical citizens in Macon who I thought would of helt to the South unlike the last hav lost all faith & say some hoam quick & let evr thing go to a Union man & I belive it is right. You spok for men disserting that you was not thinking of. I was surprised so very mutch for I cant tell you I doant think thay was a loyal Soaldier among them.
    Co B was in the fight and did hur duty. All fought like herows but Mason Jos Meton, E. Talout was cut prety bad.[78] This poor felow hardly got to fire a gun untile his branes was shot out. Serg West[79] came verry right being captured too or three times again. He will go before in Spite of the Devil. Capt we done a great deal harder fight-

ing at Chickamauga than Murfeesboro [*sic*]. Jo Mason reached camp and appears like he will make a great deal beter soaldier than Peter did. The Co is small but beter men doant walk than the old part of co B. John Lov, John Henry,[80] poor felows was severly wound but I am in hops both will git well. Thay was both doing thar duty but I cant prase one man than another. All don well, but Al Grag run lik the very Devil from the Start.

Capt, I hopt you will soon be relieved and will have the plasur of meeting your company. We will be glad to see you at any time but if you had a force sufician to rout and rile them D D Loring I would rather you would stay for I know you would delight in Doing so. Excus my short and bad leter. Wright soon and often to your sincer friend.

W T Tippett

112. October 8, 1863

Private Andrew J. Proffit Company D, 18th Regiment N.C. Troops, letter to his father, William Proffit, Wilkes County. Source: Proffit Family Letters (3408), Southern Historical Collection, Wilson Library, University of North Carolina at Chapel Hill.

Far from the battlefield of Chickamauga, Private Andrew Jackson Proffit was recovering from a very serious fever in a Gordonsville hospital. Proffit was captured along with the regimental colors of the 18th North Carolina at Chancellorsville, Virginia. Apparently, Proffit contracted the fever shortly after his exchange and return to the army. Proffit made a full recovery and would be reported present through the winter and spring of the upcoming year.

Near Gordonsville Va
Oct the 8th 1863

Mr. Wm Proffit

Dear father this note is to inform you that I am with my regiment enjoying a

Colonel David Coleman of the 39th assumed command of McNair's Brigade at Chickamauga, leading it to great success on September 20. (North Carolina Division of Archives and History.)

reasonable portion of health. I have been absent three months sick with the fever. I was at a private house & treated very kindly. The fever fell in my feet & legs so that I could not walk far nor get off of my bed for sometime. I was not out of the house for seven weeks and no one who saw me thought that there was any chance for me to live but the God who rules & governs all things saw fit in his tender mercies to raise me up again for which I shall ever feel greatful.

I have no news of interest to write at this time. We have been cooking three days rations to day in order for a march but to what place I am unable to say as news is scarce & my hand is quite nervous. I will soon close. A. N. [his brother Alfred N. Proffit] is quite stout & looks finely. You will please write me as soon as this comes to hand and give me all the news how you are getting along & how your crop is about to turn out. Give my love to Mother, Sis & all my friends. I will close by sub scribing my self yours with great respect &c.

    A. J. Proffit
Co D, 18th reg NCT, Lains Brig, Wilcox's division, Richmond Va

113. October 8, 1863

Private Phillip Walsh, Company F, 37th Regiment N.C. Troops, letter to his parents, Wilkes County. Source: Proffit Family Letters (3408), Southern Historical Collection, Wilson Library, University of North Carolina at Chapel Hill.

This letter from Phillip Walsh was written on the same paper as the preceeding correspondence from Andrew Proffit. The mother of the Proffit brothers was Mary Walsh. The Walsh, Proffit, and Miller families seem to have had a very strong relationship. Phillip Walsh, who was a veteran of all the campaigns of the 37th Regiment,[81] and a fellow soldier in Lane's Brigade, wrote on the same day regarding the movements of the unit.

  Hd Qtrs Co F 37 NC Troops
  In camp near Liberty Mills Va
  Oct 8th 1863
Dear Father an Mother

I wonce more seate my self to drope you a few lines wich will in forme you that I am well an not forgetting to hope this will fine you all well an doing well. I hant got any good nuse to rite at this time. I will say to you that we have orders to cook three days rations an be ready to march. We are cooking them to day. I dont know whar we will go but it is thought that we will advance on the yankes an I think we will by all accounts. I wood muche rather not go. It is sead that troops ar moving now an I recond it is so for I see the artilery going to wards the river. It is [no] telling what this move will determine. It may be for our Good an it may be for our worse. I cant say but I hope it will be for our Good. A. J. and A. N. Proffit is here an ar both well an sends you all their love an best respects. I recd a letter from W. L. Welch an Elisebeth an I answer it the next day but I dont know weather thay have got it or not. I hope it wont be long untell this war will come to a end so I can come home. I want you all to rite to me an give me all the nuse you can. I will close. Phillip Walsh to Thomas Walsh

114. October 18, 1863

Captain George W. F. Harper, Company H, 58th Regiment N.C. Troops, diary entry. Source: Harper Diaries, G. W. F. Harper Papers (313), Southern Historical Collection, Wilson Library, University of North Carolina at Chapel Hill.

George W. F. Harper was born in 1834 to James Harper of Lenoir. In his younger life, George attended Davidson College and graduated in 1856. Shortly after, George returned home to be a merchant. He married Ella Rankin in 1859, and the two would have two children together. On May 10, 1862, Harper enlisted into service and was appointed first lieutenant on August 19, 1862. Harper became commander of Company H on April 25, 1863, with his promotion to captain.[82] Harper voiced his opinion on religion and God's role in ending the war. The victory described here his unknown, as the last major battles in the east were Gettysburg and Bristoe Station, both of which were defeats.

 Oct. Sun 18—Mud and rain from S. W. Short rations by reason of high water. Not well. Communion season at home. When shall we be permitted to praise God beneath our roof again and to meet with the people of the Lord in his house on earth. May he in mercy hear and answer the prayers that may be offered up to Him this day for the spread of the Gospel and for Peace. Adjutant Perry came. Heard of Lee's victory

115. October 24, 1863

Captain Virgil S. Lusk, Company A, 5th Battalion N.C. Cavarly, Prisoner of War—Johnson's Island, Ohio, letter to Daniel Carpenter, Esq. Source: Virgil S. Lusk Papers (717), Private Manuscripts Collection, North Carolina Division of Archives and History, Raleigh, N.C. (Excerpted.)

Virgil Lusk, a young attorney from Marshall, Madison County, commanded Company A after Captain Baird's promotion to major. Lusk volunteered for service on May 20, 1862, and was appointed second lieutenant; he was promoted to captain on December 24, 1862. As a squadron and company commander, Lusk would "go into disputed territory and challenge the Federal outpost." This series of daring raids came to an end in Jackson County, Kentucky, when Lusk and nearly three-fourths of his company were captured on August 3, 1863. Lusk was incarcerated in Johnson's Island Prison with other Confederate officers and remained there until the end of the war. All of Lusk's letters are written from prison, [83] and this one describes Lusk's situation and an interesting story about courtesy to a captured soldier.

Virgil S. Lusk worked as an attorney in pro-Unionist Madison County before the war. Lusk was captured in Kentucky in 1863. (North Carolina Division of Archives and History.)

Johnstons Island, Ohio
October 24, 1863

Dan Carpenter, Esq.
Dear Friend:

Your favor of the 15th came safe to hand on the 21st inst containing $5.00, the receipt whereof is hereby acknowledge and at the same time you will allow me the pleasure of retiring herewith the sincere thanks of a grateful heart. I am delighted to think that I have one friend in the United States that (if they do not sympathize with me politically) sympathize with my sufferings as a prisoner of War. Philanthropy is Philanthropy under any and all circumstances, and it matters not, whether I differ in politics with others it is not magnanity in them to heal me with contempt or cruelty. It is a pleasure to me to know that I have acted during this war, in such a manner that I am not ashamed to meet my enemy on any occasion. Federal prisoners have frequently fallen into my hands since the war commenced, and I am willing for them to say what kind of treatment they have received at my hands. I do not blush to meet and recognize them, but on the contrary, it is a relief to meet with them, while they on their part, are found to do me the justice, to say, that I have always treated them with all the kindness in my power. Many instances I could enumerate, but all this would be uninteresting to you. One instance I cannot forbare mentioning—Last Spring it happened that a union soldier fell into my hands. He was an artilerist from the State of Ohio and because of his helpless condition, and knowing that a man South without money, owing to our fine governmental accommodations, I gave him Fifty Dollars. It so happened that he was not detained long in the South. After I was captured and brought to Camp Chase, in Ohio, I met and recognized the same man. He asked me if I wanted anything. I remarked to him that I was in the same situation he was, the last time I saw him. He said he would assist and wait for his money which was some distance off, but before he returned I was hurried off for this place. So I have not heard from my friend since. I have the misfortune to have very few friends living within the federal lines, you may therefore imagine the assistance I receive is very small. I have been here ever since the last of July, during which time I have not had "a red." The remittance you sent me being the first. The government furnishes us with substantial diet, but nothing else. This, those substantial and necessary to sustain life, is enough, and, in the course of time, grown very monotonous, and a person who has been used to having all that a healthy appetite could crave, feels the affect.

There are those here who, judging from there outward appearance, and the circumstances surrounding them, scarcely realize the fact that they are prisoners. They seem to enjoy themselves as though they were in the midst of fashionable society and surrounded with their friends, enhailing the air of freedom. I must say that there are men here, as prisoners, who do really enjoy themselves better than they did when at home and in liberty, but for my unworthy self, I see but some enjoyment, nor do I anticipate a change until I am released from imprisonment, be that event long or short. Those who are not tried a life in imprisonment know but little of the feelings of a prisoner. Did you ever imagine yourself in a Prison? Deprived of your liberty? Cut-off from all social relations with those so dear to your heart? Surrounded by an enemy on all sides? No prospect of being liberated soon, and last, but not least of all, no person or friend to whom you can look for sympathy or assistance? If so, your feelings, I dare to say, was not pleasant, but the imagination can in no respect be equal to experiencing the reality. Accustomed as I have always been, to want for nothing that money could procure, never having a whim that was not satisfied, my liberty not being restrained from my earliest recollection, you will readily imagine how I cam cramped within the present occasion.

I received a letter from Aunt Eliza at the same time I received yours. Tell her if you please that I have seen the two Gash Boys. They have both been sick. Thomas is about well, the other Lt. Gash, I think has pneumonia fever.[84] He is in the same mess with me. I will see as far as I am able that he is well cared for. I hope we will have peace soon, but I look upon it as a hope without a foundation, for I see no prospects for a settlement of our national difficulties. I wish I could see a prospect, and that peace could be made and our once happy nation, once more at rest, and lasting in the sunshine of peace and quiet. Our trouble is indeed great. Our nationality is gone. We have no security for our person or our posterity, but all, all is rout and confusion. Though rich today we may be poor tomorrow, though free at noon, night my force is in prison. Oh peace, peace, when will she return?

        Yours truly
        Virgil S. Lusk

116. October 27, 1863

Private John W. Reese, Company F, 60th Regiment N.C. Troops, letter to his wife, Christena, Buncombe County, North Carolina. Source: John W. Reese Papers (4417), Manuscripts Department, Special Collections Library, Duke University. (Excerpted.)

In June 1863, Reese was once again struck down with disease. Private Reese stayed in various camps and hospitals throughout the end of October 1863. In this letter Reese wrote his wife Christena about problems at home, the death of an uncle, and affairs back on his farm. With her husband gone, Christena, like many wives, had to take over John's responsibilities on the farm.

        Oct the 27 1863
Dear wife

With pleasure I tak my pen in hand to let you no that I am well hoping these fue lines may find you and the children all well an dooing well. I recived your kind letter the 22 of the this month. I was powerful glad to her from you but was sorey to hear that things was as tha air in old Buncomb but I was not mutch disbelived. I am in hopes that they Rayes propurtiy will not be con fisc cated for this will onley ad fuel to the fiar. Lying and stelling and all ther mean ness that can be thout of.

I am in the Convlesting Campes. I hav bin hear ever sence the 5 of October but I shal start to my regiment next monday. I was sorey to hear that unkel Jo was ded but he has paid that grate det up. He was pre paird for that grate throne. He is bettur off to day than we who is left in the midst of this un holy war.

Tena I rote to you that I was cuming home in this month but I hav not cum plide with my worde. I hope you will not think hard of me. Tena I want to git what tha air owing mee. Tha air owing a bout sixty dollars and I want you and my children to hav it yes and I expect to bring it to you in the bargin. Because I hav not cum plied with my word you need not think I will all ways doo so. I hav rote to you this makes fiv letturs sence I left home I hav got onley one in all. Tena I want you to rite to mee as soon as you git this lettur and let mee no the times thair and if the malisha is still at the camp ground yet or not and if thair is any talk of the yankeys a goin to cum up thair or not. David wagner tells mee that walter cook is gon to the feds. I want you to rite if you got that hay or not. I under stand that you had frost up thair a bout the mid dle of September. Rite or not and how you managed your fodder and if that man braut that leather or not. The each and lice keeps me rite bis sey. Tena I want you to git enuf of wheat if you can to sow then ground an the far cide of the branch if you can find the wheat to sell anywhair.

117. November 13, 1863

Private Thornton Sexton, "The Ashe Beaureguard Riflemen," Company A, 37th Regiment N.C. Troops, letter to his parents, Pryor and Mariah Sexton, Ashe County, North Carolina. Source: Thornton Sexton Letters (4749), Manuscripts

Department, Special Collections Library, Duke University.

The majority of the May 19th deserters returned to their command in Company A on September 1, 1863. Thornton wrote his parents from what would become the Army of Northern Virginia's winter camp and talked about the men in his mess and advised his cousin Joseph Sexton to return to the army as soon as he can. Sexton requested items from home such as shirts and molasses.

          Camp Near Orrange Court House
          November the 13th /63
Dear father mother brother and sister

I once more embrace the present opportunity of writing you a few lines that I am in tolerably good health at this time truly and forever hoping these few lines may reach you in due time and find you all well and doing well. I can in form you I have nothing interesting to write at this time, only we are hear in camp near orrang court house in the same old camp but I cant tell you how long we will stay hear for we have our orders to cook two days rations but we dont no where we will go yet. Some think we will go to Fredericksburg but i dont know. We git enough to eat at this time. I can in form you i was in a fight last Sunday but come through safe. There was not but one killed in our regiment and all the rest of our Ashe boys is well. Calvin Childers and John Black and George Blackburn[85] is in my mess and i want you to tell Jo Sexton[86] that he had better come back as quick as he can for he is reported absent without leave and when he comes i want you to send me all you can to eat and i will sadisfy him when he comes. I expect we will have a bully of a fight hear before long. Levi griffon[87] is going to start to Abingdon in the morning. I will send the letter by by him. They have got the officers under arrest out there. Capt Pacily and the rest of the officers we was under at the Saltworks and Liut Norwood and Liut Griffon[88] is going to git our money for us. I want you to rite if you no anything of Marvin or not and if you do and can give him any word tell him to come back hear as quick as he can and tell him not to come under guard for if he does he will be shot and if he will come rite on he will come clear for Robert Mecarmick[89] has come and has come hear and is out of the guard house. Tell Jo to fetch me some unions, a couple cheese and some molasses some butter and a hat if you can git it and if you cant send it now i want you to git some wool and get Miller to make me one and send it to me. So rite soon and often for no more at present only remain your affectionate son until Death.

          Thornton Sexton
To Pryor Sexton and family

118. November 14, 1863

Colonel William H. Thomas, Thomas Legion, letter and orders to Colonel William C. Walker, Cavalry Battalion, Thomas Legion, Murphy, Cherokee County. Source: Stephen Whitaker Papers (39), Private Manuscripts Collection, North Carolina Division of Archives and History.

The Thomas Legion was a substantial force indeed; however, the full weight of the Legion was never brought to bear upon the enemy. Instead, the Legion functioned in its four components for most of the war; Love's Regiment (infantry), Thomas' Indian Battalion (2–4 companies), Walker's Battalion (cavalry) and Levi's Battery (artillery). These orders, written to a convalescing Lieutenant Colonel Walker, specified the point for a rendezvous of troops from different components of the Legion.

          Nov 14, 1863
Col William C. Walker[90]
Dear Sir

I received your note per J S Berry.

I enclose herewith a copy of Brig Genl Vance's letter, from which you will percieve that it was contemplated that you should for the present remain in Cherokee, collect in your troops and report to me and I to Brig Genl Vance. Looking however to a forward movement and a reunion of the Legion, about ten days ago the portion of it under Lt Col Jas R. Love[91] was at Greenville and as the enemy has but little or no force at the strawbery Plains, it is quite probable that our troops will be there in a few days.

If in your opinion any of the troops under your immediate command now in cherokee [are] neccesary for the restoration of law and order and the defence of the good citizens, retain them and use them for what purposes. But the Indian company, I and Smith and Mattey will come on with out delay to Rocky Point. I expect to be there myself in a few days. I presume from what J S Berry tells me that you are not able for active service. The home guards of cherokee co … thrown in with your troops will for the time be subject to your order.

As you have sent on a few of the troops, they can fall in with the Indian company in Chero or Rocky Point. I have no doubt but that a passage will be open to their companies in a few days. And it is quite probable that the militia will be able to maintain order in cherokee as soon as our army gets full. Send of a portion of your men who are no longer needed in Cherokee county. You and they can come on and join the remainder of the troops with me at Rocky Point of some other place. Brig Genl Vance will move down French Broad and he recently made a move down that river and brought out a quantity of hogs etc.

Your obt servt
Wm H Thomas[92]
Col T L.

119. November 18, 1863

Private Azariah Denny, Company C, 21st Regiment N.C. Troops, letter to his father, Joel Denny, and family, Surry County, N.C. Source: Jackson, *Surry County Soldiers in the Civil War* (1983).

By November 18, Azariah Denny reported that he was recovering nicely from his illness. In his letter, Denny asked for clothing and shoes. In the spring of 1864, Denny participated in the 21st North Carolina's movements in eastern North Carolina and fought against Butler's force at Bermuda Hundred. Denny was killed in action on June 6, 1864, at Cold Harbor, Virginia.[93]

General Hospital No. 1
Richmond VA
Nov. 18 1863

Dear father,

It is with pleasure I now seat myself to rite you a few lines to let you now that I am yet alive though I am not very well. You rote now what ales me. I think it is the effect of the measles. I dont see that I get any better. I am hardly as well as I have bin though I can walk about where I please I go to the [commissary] and eat. I have drawn my money. I have got 32 dollars. You must not think that I was troubled with you in the least because I got no letters. I know you rote but I did not get them. It will not do me any good for you to come after me. if he is going to give me a furlough he will do it anyhow. I think in the course of a week or two if I don't change in my health I will get one. They give a good many here. If you are going to come to see me and have got any coat and shoes you had as well bring them though it might be that I would draw some sometime though there is a good many barefoot & bare backed here. If I had a good coat I could sell it for 20 dollars, a good pair of shoes will bring 15 dollars. I am somewhat stumped about Jonathan for I got a letter dated the 10th of Nov. It stated that him, Gid and James[94] was at home but from the way you rite it seems like you now nothing about him. When I herd that they was all at home I thought they had run but I expect that my news was feeble. I am surprised that Wm. Key is doing so. I think that I done the best way that a boy could do though I have seen a hard 'time but I had rather go through with the same again than to lie in the woods. H. Marion is still with me. As for as small pox is concerned I dont think there is any danger. You must tell the neighbors that I wish them all good luck and am sorry for all that has to leave home for there is no fun in that. If you bring them shoes please bring me one good strong pair of socks and if I dont get to go home I will have plenty for the winter so I must close by saying I still remain your son until death.

          To Joel Denny A.
          Denny & Nancy
          Denny rite son

120. November 20, 1863

Private Calvin Leach, "The Wilkes Valley Guards," Company B, 1st Regiment N.C. State Troops, letter to his mother, Montgomery County, N.C. Source: The Letters of Calvin Leach, Calvin Leach Papers (1875-z), Southern Historical Collection, University of North Carolina at Chapel Hill.

After the Battle of Antietam, Calvin Leach continued to serve as one of the best soldiers in Company B. In November 1863, the First N.C. Troops belonged to the brigade of Gen. George "Maryland" Steuart, along with two Virginia regiments under Edward Johnson's Division of the Second Corps. Calvin wrote about getting ready to go on picket, and the arrival of two new recruits from Trap Hill, a community in western Wilkes County.

          Frid Nov 20th 1863
          Culpeper C. House, Va
Dear and afection Mother

I take my pen in hand to write you a few lines having neglecting it longer than I expected, but we have [been] moving about lately and I did not have time to do it. I am happy to tell you I am tolerably well at this time and have been improving slowly since I came to camp. I am very anxious to hear from home as I have not heard from home since I left. I wrote Lydia the 10th was the last time I wrote I wrote and I hope some of you have written to me before now.

We have been on picket since I wrote before. Last Thursday we left camp and moved down to Raccoon Ford where our Brigade relieved another one on picket. Friday we remained in reserve. Sat also in reserve. That night it rained till 12 oclock and I wraped my blanket round me and stood by the fire until it quit. In the morning about sunup we heard the firing of guns down on the line. We got up and went down the river to see what it was. It was the Yankee sharpshooters that got in some houses on the opposite sides of the river fireing at our men. Our men brought up their Artillery in position and began to shelling the house and made them leave in an awful hurry with our men taking one prisoner.

This evening we went on the front line of pickets. I walked the post from 2 to 4 in the night watching for Yankees. On the 16th our Brigade was relieved from our picket duty and we marched out and took up camp where we have been working on the breastworks ever since. I think we will be able to stand the Yankees in a fight if they come on us in the works. Gen Lee has lost so many men he is now going to adopt the plan of fighting behind breastworks. Our army is all right and smart heartened.

All the boys are generally well. McClean and Robinson[95] have been sick but are better. We have 2 new recruits from us from the Trap Hill country. We have been drawing enough to eat lately. We drawed Irish potatoes and I had a splendid breakfast this morning. If I have some of my honey and butter yet. I have done my own washing since I came back. I do not believe I have an enemy in the company. They all seem like brothers to me and they will do anything to accommodate me.

I hope that you will continue in prayer for me that I may continue to discharge my duties as a Christian soldier while I am permitted to live in this unfriendly world of sorrow. I try to raise my weak and feable petitions in behalf of you all that if we meet no more on earth we may have a happy meeting in heaven of bliss where parting will be no more.

Your affectionate son,
Calvin

Calvin Leach, Co. B, 1st NC Infantry, Steuarts Brig, Johnstons division, Richmond

121. November 26, 1863

Private Samuel E. Love, "The Henderson Blue," Company G, 56th Regiment N.C. Troops, letter to father, Henderson County, North Carolina. Source: Matt Love Papers (3276), Manuscripts Department, Special Collections Library, Duke University.

Samuel E. Love of the Henderson Blues was reported present from April 12, 1862. In November 1863, Samuel was assigned to a detail, along with others from the regular army, that assisted the Wilkes County home guard and militia in an attempt to control the deserter situation in western North Carolina.[96] It is possible that the deserter killed in Wilkes County was a soldier in Company A, 37th N.C. Troops.

Rockes Spring Church
Wilkes County
Nov. the 26th 1863

Dear Father

I seat my self to pen you a few lines to let you no that I am well at this time hoping this may find you all well. The Toreys havent got me yet. I havent anything new to write to you at this time. We killd one man yesterday. He was in the wader and started to run. He was shot three times in the head. His name was Blackburn. There was four of them in a gang. We got them all. We still git a few of them.

I wish I could git home this fall but I dont no when I will git to go home. I want you all to write to me as soon as this comes to hand. We are seeing a fine time hear. Thare is a grate deal of difernce in this and the armey. I hope that we will all git to go to Ashville some time soon. Write to me soon. So I will close. No more only I remain yore obedient Son till death.

S. E. Love

122. November 26, 1863

Captain George W. F. Harper, Company H, 58th Regiment N.C. Troops, diary entry. Source: Harper Diaries, G. W. F. Harper Papers (313), Southern Historical Collection, Wilson Library, University of North Carolina at Chapel Hill.

The Battle of Chattanooga resulted from Bragg's attempt to lay siege to the Union garrison at that Tennessee town after the Confederate victory at Chickamauga. The Union received reinforcements and more able commanders such as Grant and Sherman, who decided to attack Bragg and lift the siege. Reynolds' Brigade, of which the 58th N.C. Troops was a part, put up a brave resistance, and fell back in good order. However, the same cannot be said for most of Bragg's army that day, including the 60th North Carolina. The

Confederate defeat at Chattanooga paved the way for the resulting Atlanta campaign, and gave the Confederate Army of Tennessee a new commander, Gen. Joseph E. Johnston.

> Tues 24—Heavy Clouds and some rain. At breastworks. Fighting going on all day on Lookout Mountain. Night eclipse of moon and night clear. Wed 25. In the breastworks at foot of Missionary Ridge. Pickett driven into breastworks. PM evacuated breastworks and fell back to the top of the ridge. The enemy at the same time charged the heights. Our line broken in two places and fell back. Reformed at near foot of ridge and checked pursuit. Thur 26. Clear, cool Pleasant am—hard frost. Retreat began at Chickamauga depot at 5 am. Came to Ringgold and camped near Catoosa Station. Tired and very sleepy having slept little for three nights.

123. December 10, 1863

Private Thornton Sexton, "The Ashe Beuareguard Riflemen," Company A, 37th Regiment N.C. Troops, letter to his parents, Pryor and Mariah Sexton, Ashe County, North Carolina. Source: T. Sexton Letters (4749), Manuscripts Department, Special Collections Library, Duke University.

By the middle of December, the 37th North Carolina had been in winter quarters for some time. Sexton believed that the unit would be moving west in the near future, perhaps the spring of the following year, to the Shenandoah Valley. While a force would move to the Shenandoah in June 1864, Hill's Corps, of which Lane's Brigade was a part, remained firmly around Richmond. Sexton also admitted that Calvin Childers wrote his letters.

> Camp near Orrange CH
> Dec. the 10th 1863
> Dear father mother brother and sisters
> I embrace the present opportunity of writing you a few lines that i am well at this time truly and forever hoping this may find you all well and doing well. I received your very kind letter bearing date of Nov the 28th which gave me great Sadisfaction to hear from you and to hear you was well. I have nothing interesting to write at present more than we are hear in our old camp yet but I dont now how long we will stay hear all winter I hope. So I want you to come as quick as you can. You stated in your letter you received three letters from me. I think you will git some more letters from me.
> Calvin Childers he writes all of my letters. He writes them when I want to tell his folks he is well, fat and saucy. There is no news interesting to rite at the present. There is no talk of any fighting hear at this time. I think the fighting will be in the west. John Black and G. W. Blackburn is well at this time. We expect to move to the west. Our wagon trains is ordered to stay herar on account of us having to move to the west. I can in form you I need some things but I recon i can make out without them. I need some pants and a hat is all i need at the present and i want some apples cheese and all you can send.
> Tell Hiram and David[97] I hant forgoten them yet and i hope they hant me. Tell them I would be glad to see them and be at home with them this winter but there is no chance for it now but I hope this war will soon end so we can be together once more. So you must rite soon and often and fail not in so doing and give me all of the news in ashe. So no more at present only remain your affectionate son until death.
> Thornton Sexton to Pryor Sexton
> Mariah Sexton
> PS Calvin Childers sends his best wishes to you.

124. December 14, 1863

Captain John L. Swain, Company B, 17th Regiment N.C. Troops (2nd Organization), diary entry. John L. Swain Diary, John L. Swain Papers (3074), Southern Historical Collection, Wilson Library, University of North Carolina at Chapel Hill.

Captain John L. Swain, a Buncombe County farmer and lay leader in the Methodist Church, led an unlikely command of eastern North Carolina men. Exactly how and why Swain received his commission to lead men from Martin County is still unknown; however, Captain Swain was commissioned on March 10, 1862, and was reported present in official records until November 27, 1864.[98] The reference to the "Old British Camp" demonstrated the connection some soldiers felt to their revolutionary predecessors.

> December 14 1863. On picket on the coast from Whitesville to Stump Sound. I hold HD Quarters at new Topsail inlet on Topsail Sound and sent a detachment of 15 men to Hollow Shelter 13 miles in the country to Old British Camp. There is a portion of Lord Cornwallis Troops held winterquarters in 1777 or 8, and the sign is yet visible. Our army was employed first in erecting huts (when not engaged in Picket duty) also in getting Oysters with which the waters abound. These were had in great profusion and the Boys sold many.

1864

We have a close time here at this time. Tha have cut our rashions down to a qarter of a pound of bacon and one pound of flower and evry thirde day we dont get that. We drew to day one spoonful of shooger and not so much coffee and no bacon. We have close living.

—Private Jesse Miller, Wilkes County, Company K, 53rd Regiment North Carolina Troops, Outside Orange Court House, Virginia, January 3, 1864.

Our boys have been bushwhacked. Some one of our company was killed, a man from Polk county by the name of Tom Peterson. He was a good soldier and a brave man and he was shot through the breast and killed instantly.

—Second Lieutenant Harvey Y. Gash, Company D, 6th Regiment North Carolina Cavalry, Camp Devault, Tennessee, February 8, 1864.

I found the regamant in fine helth as fur now. I cant giv mutch reliable tho I am hear in a line of battle whair tha hav bin fiting for sum time. I got to the Regamant last sunday eaving in a allful thicket. I lay down and went to sleep and a bout a leven oclock I was wakend by that powerful noyes of canonading.

—Private John R. Reese, Company F, 60th Regiment North Carolina Troops, Baldon County, Northwest Georgia, May 31, 1864.

I thought Tim would be very proud of the axe as it is one of the best I ever cut with. I reckon it went safe. I sent my old drawers and a tick which I reckon you can find a use for it. So you see that I am quite stingey for most of the soldiers are throwing out all their old clothes, but I send them as presents to my wife & I imagine that she is glad to get such pieces.

—*Captain Alfred Bell, Company B, 39th Regiment North Carolina Troops, Atlanta, Georgia, June 30, 1864.*

We are sorry to hear of the Tories cutting up so in that county and hope they will quiet down some time soon. There is some little talk of ours disbursing this winter. If we do Woe to all the Bushwhackers and diserters in Watauga. We would like to be back there this winter to take Big belgian and drink that old brandy that you are saving for us.

—*Private George F. Adams, "The Watauga Rangers," Company D, 1st Regiment North Carolina Cavalry, November 16, 1864.*

125. January 1, 1864

Private William N. Whitaker, "The Cane Creek Rifles," Company H, 25th Regiment N.C. Troops, diary entry. Source: William N. Whitaker Papers (1034), Private Manuscripts Collection, North Carolina Division of Archives and History.

William Whitaker, a Buncombe County farmer, volunteered for service at the age of 21 on June 15, 1861. Whitaker served with the 25th North Carolina until he was captured at Five Forks, Virginia, on April 1, 1865.[1] In this entry in his brief diary, Whitaker mentions key distances between towns. Before the war, such places were all but foreign to most mountain residents. Perhaps Whitaker's attention to the distances demonstrated a soldier's awareness and more possibly, the isolation felt in a post so distant from home.

Januarey the 1 1864
We ar still at Weldon the distence from Weldon to Elizabeth City is 100 and 14 miles to Franklin 42 miles. The distance from Weldon to Petersburg is 97 miles and from Weldon to Raleigh 96 miles. From Weldon to Golesboro 67 miles from Charlotte to Columbia S. C. 100 and 10 miles from Columbia to Greenvill 100 43 miles from Charlotte to Raleigh 100 and 76 miles from Golesboro to Wilmington 80 miles.

126. January 3, 1864

Private Jesse Miller, Company K, 53rd Regiment N.C. Troops, letter to William and Mary Proffit, Wilkes County. Source: Proffit Family Papers (3408), Southern Historical Collection, Wilson Library, University of North Carolina at Chapel Hill.

Before the war, Jesse and his wife Elizabeth Miller raised their five daughters in the Reddie's River area of Wilkes County. Miller frequently had dealings with his cousins, the Proffits. On March 15, 1862, Jesse Miller volunteered for service at the age of thirty-eight.² On January 3, Private Miller sat down and wrote his aunt and uncle about the privations, sickness, and short rations which prevailed in the winter camp of the 53rd North Carolina Troops.

> Camp of the 53 Reg.
> 8 miles North East
> of Orange C H, Va
> January 3rd 1864
>
> Mr Wm and Mary Proffit
>   Dear Father and Mother I with grate pleasure drop you a short note wich will in form you that I am in tolerable helth owing to hardships and privations of camp life. I do grately hope when these lines comes to hand you and famely may be in Joying good helth.
>   I have no news for to communicate wich would inter rest you. I have no war news at presant times & all is still in this vicinity at presant & we have just got up some of our huts. I got mine done the first of this instant all to the done shelter. I had not laid in a house nor under a tent for eight months. We have just taken the wether as it came and you can give a gess how we have fard and the wether is powerful cold here at this time and we are scarce of blankets but if we can get to stay here in our huts I think we can do verry well.
>   We have a grate manny that is sick in our briggade and some ar dieing. John Wodey died at Orange the 15 of December.³ Harrison Brown was sent off to the horse pittle yester Day. Barnet Owens was sent this morning.⁴ Boath was verry sick men. I have no thout that Owens will live. We have bin so exposed I feer that we shal have a grate Deal of sickness. Orders came round last nite to furlow one man for evry twenty men in camp that some of them will be coming home constantly.
>   We have a close time here at this time. Tha have cut our rashions down to a qarter of a pound of bacon and one pound of flower and evry thirde day we dont get that. We drew to day one spoonful of shooger and not so much coffee and no bacon. We have close living.
>   I have bin looking for a letter from you for some time. I wrote you a letter just as soon as I herd W. H.⁵ was ded but has failed to receave an anser yet & when these lines you receave please respond to me. So I will close by acknowleding my self as ever,
>   Jesse Miller

127. January 13, 1864

Major William W. Stringfield, Love's Regiment, Thomas' North Carolina Legion, diary entry. Diary of William W. Stringfield, W. W. Stringfield Papers (109), Private Manuscripts Collection, North Carolina Division of Archives and History.

William Stringfield, as major of Love's Regiment, was perhaps the most respected and loved member of the Thomas Legion. Before his commission on September 27, 1862, Stringfield attended Strawberry Plains College (co-founded by his father), served in the 1st Tennessee Cavalry, and functioned as an enrolling and Provost officer.⁶ In his first featured diary entry, William recorded gifts he received from a couple of lady admirers.

> Bristol, TN January 13th 1864
>   Came here by 3pm & am at Uncle King's where I am always welcome & treated to as can be by my good aunt and uncle. The Zollicoffer Bridge is completed and the cars will go to Carters to day. I rec'd as a present from Miss Lizzie Rhea—a splendid waist coat at 2 this morning. Many thanks. I hope she may be wooed and won by a worthy man and gallant soldier of the South. I must not fail to record here in kind acknoweldgments to my particular friend Miss Mollie T. at Carters for two splendid pairs of socks. Knit by her own

Though a Tennesseean by birth, William W. Stringfield became one of the most devoted and faithful Confederate officers of the Thomas Legion. (North Carolina Division of Archives and History.)

hand and presented to me at her house. Such presents are calculated to make a bachelor such as I, one of necessity, inclined to give up the dreams of single blessedness.

128. January 23, 1864

Captain Thomas W. Patton, Company C, 60th Regiment N.C. Troops, letter to his mother, Asheville, Buncombe County, N.C. Source: Patton Family Papers (1739), Southern Historical Collection, Wilson Library, University of North Carolina at Chapel Hill.

After a busy fall campaign featuring battles at Chickamauga and Chattanooga, the 60th N.C. Troops, as well as most of Johnston's Army of Tennessee, went into winter quarters in northwest Georgia. Johnston assumed command of the Army of Tennessee, after Bragg's defeat and rout at Chattanooga and subsequent resignation from his post as commanding general. Patton wrote his mother about his new commander and what kind of rules the general wanted to enforce. Patton also talked about Captain Jesse R. S. Gilliand's arrival and what purpose Captain Gilliand would serve in the regiment.

Dalton Georgia
January 23 1864
My Dear Mother
 I will favor you with this as I expect Nannie will be on the road here before this gets home. I will be looking for her now every day, but if she should not have started before this reaches you, I think she had better post-pone her journey until she can take it under more favorable circumstances. Cousin Rose Clayton reached here this morning and reports that she had to travel in a wagon to Greenville. How I did wish that Nannie could have accompanied her, but with my contradictory dispatches and letters I do not suppose she could start before next Monday or Wednesday night if then. Our stay here seems to be very uncertain at least it is considered so by some. I however, hope that we will be allowed to remain quiet for some time to come, but rumors are a float that we will be moved to the front to take the place of Cleborn's Division at Tunnel Hill and again that we will soon be sent to Virginia. As I said

R. B. Vance (seated with arms crossed) at Fort Delaware. General Vance and his staff were captured by the 15th Pennsylvania Cavalry in East Tennessee. (Vance Papers, Southern Historical Collection, U.N.C.)

before I do not think that these rumors are well founded, but they would at all events make me very uneasy if Nannie were here, and it would be awfull after she had taken such a trip for us to be moved so that we could not be together. I have engaged a room for her at the house of Mrs. Alston, but it is at a very inconvienient distance from camp. Cousin Rose is now staying there, and Mrs. Hardy has been until quite lately but has now moved out to a house quite near to camp. She is quite sick and has been for several days past. I do not know what is the matter. Captain Robert was certainly expecting his wife to come along with Cousin Rose, and of

Asheville resident Robert A. Coleman served on General Vance's staff as the department's quartermaster. (North Carolina Division of Archives and History.)

course, was very glad to get Nannies letter of Sunday last. You and Fannie and Aunt Charlotte seemed determined to leave all the letter writing to Nannie. I have only received one letter from you and none at all from the other two. Nannie seems to be indefatigable and expresses herself in every letter as being very happily situated and particularly speaks of your kindness to her, for which of course I am most grateful. I was most happy to hear from your letter that she was making herself agreeable to all of you.

I do not know what fate is in store for me now. As soon as Capt Gililands[7] commission arrives I suppose I will be reported supernumerary again and will get off on some duty again. If Brother James will attend to the matter about which I wrote him in my letter from Kingston, it may have some good effect the next time I send up my papers. But such fortune as being ordered to Asheville seems to be too good ever to fall to my lot. I believe I wrote you that Genl Hardee had gone off to be married. He has not yet returned, but has the handsomest house in Dalton fixed up in elegant style for the reception of his bride and his daugthers, so much for being a general. Frank Pattons health seems to be very delicate indeed. He suffers constantly with diarrhea and looks must miserably indeed. He has been on a court martial and staying up in town for some time past. He has applied for a furlough for sixty days but I do not think he will get it. The surgeon would not give him a strong enough certificate. A man has to be almost dead before he can get a furlough on Surgeon's Certificate.

Courts martial seem to be the order of the day now. One poor fellow is soon to be shot for desertion and one of our Regiment was sentenced to have one side of his head shaved and marched with a barrell over his shoulders, through the Brigade, each day for ten days with the drum and fife playing the rogue's march behind him. Don't you think this is severe punishment? He has just passed my tent. This is the fifth day of his punishment.

I have nothing to do, but suppose I will be stuck on some kind of duty soon. I have been working very hard this morning in cutting a load of wood for Sunday, but the weather has been so beautifull for several days past that we have no need of fires except cooking. I do not like Genl Johnstons course much thus far. He has issued a very rediculous order trying to make every things very strict and in accordance with Army Regulation. He even goes so far as to appoint the hours for eating breakfast, dinner, & Supper, which seems rather farci[c]al when you reflect that the poor soldiers do not get more rations for all day than are sufficient for one good meal.

I don not know what company Nannie can get if you decide for her to come. There are several officers partially expect her with them—but if she has not started by the time this gets home, I think she had better post-pone coming indefintely as it is getting on into spring and it will not be very long till we may expect the opening of an active Spring campaign. What do the substitute men about Asheville think of the recent law of congress? Capt Gilliland is anxious to know if his cousin Preston Patton will go into service now. Capt G is a great acquisition to the Regiment and an extremely clever, hard working man. I am particularly pleased with him. Good-bye for the present. Love to all

Your Affec Son
T W Patton

PS What a bad piece of business that war for Genl Vance to let himself be captured. I saw the news first in the Atlanta paper, and seems to be confirmed by Bob Clayton, who is direct from Buncombe, so I suppose it is true. I hope my friend Bob Coleman was not ... home at the time.[8]

129. January 26, 1864

Corporal James W. Wright, Company C, 26th Regiment N.C. Troops, letter to his wife, Fanny Wright, Wilkes County, North Carolina. Source: John Wright Papers (1594), Private Manuscripts Collection, North Carolina Division of Archives and History, Raleigh, N.C.

After James' last featured letter, he survived the battles of Gettysburg and Bristoe Station unharmed, and was promoted to corporal on January 1, 1864.[9] In this letter from winter camp, James reports on some friends and fellow company members, as well as sending various items home by different soldiers.

> Camp near Orange C. H.
> Jany 26th 1864
>
> Dear Fanny
>
> It is with the greatest pleasure I again drop you a few lines informing you that I am in common health and truly hoping this short letter will reach you in due time and find you and Charley both well and hearty and in fine spirits. I have nothing of interest to write at present only we are all enjoying the times as well as we can. Rufus is tolerable well. I saw Ed the other day. He passed here on his way to North Carolina. He told me that Hokes whole Brigade was on their way there. He looks very well. I think that Rufus will get to go home before long and it may be that I will get to come too. If I do I shall certainly leave in haste to go see you all again. I am very anxious to see you though if I got a furlough it will only be 18 days and it will be a good while before I can get one. It may be in April or May or not at all. If I get one you will know it for I shall certainly start for old Wilkes.
>
> I received a few lines from you by A. Cain[10] last night. I was glad to hear from home again but you did not state in your letter whether you got one from me or not that I sent by him nor whether you got the little budget of old clothes I sent by him. I would not have sent them home but I did not want to throw them away knowing they would be of some use at home also I have never learnt whether you got those needles I sent by Ambrose Mullis. I sent two dozen. You said in your last letter that you wanted to send me some things by George Parker. I would be glad of a few things but if you cant send them handy you need not put yourself to any trouble.
>
> I can make out somehow. I have sent four caps by Josiah Millsap.[11] He left here for Wilkes on the night of the 24th. He said he would leave them at John Brothertons he lives close by there. He will get home about the last of this month. I stacked them together and put them in a little sack that I made and wrote your name on a piece of paper and sewed it on the sack. There will be some passing to Brotherton, or you can get some body to bring them to you some of Chapels[12] family will be passing and if you get them you can take one or two of them for Charley and sell the rest for corn or something you need. If you sell them you ought to get a bushel or corn a piece for them. They cost a soldier two dollars a piece in his monthly wages. You can do as you please with them. If you get them I would like to know it. I have nothing more at present.
>
> Write soon. I remain your affectionate husband. Give my love to your Pa and family.
>
> James W. Wright
> to F. A. Wright

130. February 1, 1864

Corporal James W. Wright, Company C, 26th Regiment N.C. Troops, letter to

This sketch accompanied Private James W. Wright's description of the military execution in his brigade. (North Carolina Division of Archives and History.)

his parents and wife, Fanny Wright, Wilkes County, North Carolina. Source: John Wright Papers (1594), Private Manuscripts Collection, North Carolina Division of Archives and History, Raleigh, N.C.

Unfortunately, military executions were a common facet of life in the army in 1864. In the next letter, Corporal Wright describes the scene at such an execution. His description is typical. The brigade was formed in a hollow square around the condemned. The ten man squads used to execute each of the two deserters, who were tied down, seemed more than adequate. Such shows of force were meant to deter desertions from the army. Wright was so interested or disgusted that he included a sketch of the scene.

Camp near Orange C.H.
Feby 1st 1864
Dear Parents and Fanny

I again drop you a few lines to let you know that I am yet in the land of the living tolerable well. I have a bad cold that pesters me right smart. Hoping this finds you all well and hearty and doing well.

I have witnessed a scene that I never want to again. I saw two men shot today they belonged to the 52nd Regt. I have drawn a scale of the Brigade and how it was formed. Each regiment is numbered the way it was formed. After the command to fire was given one of the prisoners hallowed a few times. The guard was ordered to fire a second time and a third before he was killed. The other was fired at twice. The guard was about five paces from the prisoners. After they were dead the whole Brigade was marched by where the lay and were tied to the stakes. It was an awful sight. A terror to all deserters or those who ought to be. I do not ever think I will ever bring such a disgrace on my family and relations. It is true camp life is a hard one, but to die the death of a deserter is a worse one.

I have but little news to write. The yankees have made moves on our lines and captured about 30 of our men near Rapidan river above Rappahannock Station. We will go on picket the 2nd inst. The whole brigade will go. I will write again in a few days. I have not heard from home since [Anderson] Cain came back to his Regt. Write often and soon,

I remain your son and husband
James W. Wright.

131. February 8, 1864

Private Thornton Sexton, Company A, 37th Regiment N.C. Troops, letter to his parents, Pryor and Mariah Sexton, Ashe County, North Carolina. Source: Thornton Sexton Letters (4749), Manuscripts Department, Special Collections Library, Duke University.

This was the first letter written in Thornton's own hand, although he had some help in writing it. The original letters of February 8 and December 10, bear distinct spelling and handwriting differences. Thornton described the sentence of punishment given to his brother and Calvin Testerman for desertion. Also, he informed his mother that his messmate and friend Calvin Childers may have lied to his mother in order to receive more provisions. Thornton served through the spring of 1864 and fought at the Wilderness and Spotsylvania before being wounded in action at Turkey Hill, Virginia, on June 2, 1864. Thornton Sexton died of his wounds on June 5, while his brother Marion deserted again, after his sentence of hard labor was over.[13]

Camp near orange CH Va
Feb the 8th 1864
Dear parence

It is with pleasure that i am one more time blest with the opertunity of riting to you. I am well at presant and hoping these lines will find you all well and doing well. I have some nuse to rite. The yankeys has bin trying to come a cross the river but they dident git a cross. They had a nice little skirmish yester day but we drove them back and took one peace of artilery from them and kild severil yankeys. We had a tolerable hard march last nite. They are looking for a Big fite in NC that is all the nuse I have to rite.

Well I will tell you a bout Marien. Him and Calvin Testerman[14] is sent to richmond for 12 months and a tolerable hard punishment on them. They are to do hard laber and ware a ball and chain. Well mother you said in your leter that Calvin Childers had rote to his mother that he dident git the things that she sent to him. I will tell you [he] got every thing that was sent to him and if he rote that he rote a lie and a damd on at that and if you dont beleve me rite to george Blackmon and Jurry and they will tell you the same. So I will wind up with the hope that in a reasonable time I may here from you.

Thornton Sexton
to Prier Sexton

A few lines to Nancy
Dear sister

After respects to yo I can say that I am well and harty hoping these lines reach you in due time and find you well and doing well. I was sorry to here that father was sick. I hope the next time I here from you that all will be well. I will tell you I have bin faring tolerable well sence you left. We dont git mutch to eat now. We had a tolerable hard march yester day but we are back in camp to day. So no more only I still promise my self your Brother Thornton sexton to Nancy Welch

132. February 8, 1864

Second Lieutenant Harvey Y. Gash, Company D, 65th Regiment N.C. Troops (6th N.C. Cavalry), letter to his father, Henderson County, North Carolina. Source: Gash Family Letters (1541), Private Manuscripts Collection, North Carolina Division of Archives and History.

After the victory at Chattanooga, Tennessee, Maj. Gen. US Grant sent two army corps under Gen. William T. Sherman to relieve Burnside's garrison at Knoxville, under threat by a division under James Longstreet. After his failed assault, Longstreet withdrew and utilized the 6th N.C. Cavalry as a rear guard and reconnaissance gathering unit throughout the winter of 1863–1864. Gash worried about the situation in the west where the Confederacy had been cut in two since the fall of Vicksburg. Also, Gash included a description of a combat with bushwhackers.

> Camp Davault
> 65 Regiment NC
> Feb the 8th 1864

Dear Sister

I take the present opportunity of writing you a few lines to let you know that I am in the land of Bersheby. We have been out on dress parade. All of the companies was out and the artilery. This is Sunday and a bugle has sounded for that perpose. A man named Harris is a going to preach. He is appointed to preach for the regiment and he is a bad chance for a preacher, but Folk appointed him. He is one horse preacher from Macon County, N. Carolina. Our battalion has been changed to a regiment the 65 regiment NC Cavalry. We was ordered to Kentucky last week but the order was countermanded and I don't know how long we will stay here but I expect we will stay in this state some time. It is uncertain we may be ordered any time to leave.

A good many of the men want to go to Kentucky and some wants to go to Texas and some want to stay here and some want to go home and I believe the majority is in favor of going home. Some of our officers has held up that peace is going to be made. General Price has gone on to Richmond as a mediator for the north western states. He told Captain Folsom that the north western states was coming south if they could get free navigation of the Missippi River. They say that they was not fighting for the Union and they are sending troops to Kentucky to help them out. But if the South cannot get more help or more territory I believe we will starve to death before another year rolls around. But if those states come over I think the war will end before long. We hear that the Blockade is raised at Charleston SC and it will take 60 days to blockade it again.

Our boys have been bushwhacked. Some one of our company was killed, a man from Polk county by the name of Tom Peterson. He was a good soldier and a brave man and he was shot through the breast and killed instantly. Perry L. Suford[15] had his canteen shot through and his comfort cut on the back of his neck and another one from the other side cut his coat. He says one came nearer his face than any of the rest. Perry is a brave boy and several others had their clothes cut.

Col. Folk gave our men and Gillespies the praise I suppose that he said our men was the bravest in the battalion though they thought our men shot three or four of the bushwhackers and hung two and left them there.

Bob Loftis was a Capt of the bushwhackers.

I must close. We are all tolerably well. I left Milton [his brother Martin Milton Gash], he is not well. J. H. Crawford is not well he has the Measles. Direct your letter to Haynesville Tenn in Care of Capt S. J. Spann 65 regt NC Troops. If brother Lee[16] comes home tell him to come to see us. Yours as ever,

H. Y. Gash

133. February 12, 1864

Captain John L. Swain, Company B, 17th Regiment N.C. Troops (2nd Organization), diary entry. John L. Swain Diary, John L. Swain Papers (3074), Southern Historical Collection, Wilson Library, University of North Carolina at Chapel Hill.

In the late winter and early summer, Confederate forces mounted another attempt to liberate parts of eastern North Carolina, specifically the cities of Kinston, Washington, and most importantly, New Bern. The following entry detailed the assembly of a force under Gen. James G. Martin, former adjutant general, who now commanded a brigade composed of the 17th, 42nd and 50th North Carolina Troops. The patriotic, motivational speech relied on a little embellishment, as General Lee never came to New Bern.

I rec'd orders to collect my foarces at Virginia Creek at 10 a.m. after being relieved. 1 p.m. relief arrives and also another courier with orders to collect all my foarces at the road and await the arrival of Troops tomorrow at 9 a.m. With no couriers and my comd at 4 different posts embracing a distance of 16 miles it was impossible to collect all so I moved to the road and awaited the arrival. In due time the 17th & 42nd Regts N.C.V. arrived Capt Parris and Ellis of the former arrived with a 6 gun Va light battery & the latter with a 4 gun NC battery of light artillery and Capt Jackson and a Major of a Bat. Of 2 cos of Cavalry joined us. This augmented about 2000. We moved on Newport Barracks, an intermediate port between Beaufort & Newberne 8 miles from the former near a village called Shepherdsville directly on the railroad leading from Beaufort to Newberne.

The roads were heavy but our march was rapid in the morning of our approach Genl. Martin rode past our lines, halted in front of it and says "Soldiers, you hear the Guns of Genl Lee. He has come to take Newberne and he has sent you down here to take this camp and cart off supplies and he expects you will do it." "We will, we will" cried Lt. Col. Lamb[17]

134. February 25, 1864

Captain Alfred Bell, Company B, 39th Regiment N.C. Troops, letter to his wife, Mary Bell, Franklin, Macon County, N.C. Source: Alfred Bell Papers (417), Manuscripts Department, Special Collections Library, Duke University.

In February of 1864, the 39th North Carolina was posted in Alabama to guard against further Federal incursions from the Vicksburg garrison. While the main Confederate force was concentrated at Mobile, the actual target of the Federal raiders was Meridian, Mississippi. In this letter, Bell referred to a failed raid into western North Carolina, the value of Confederate securities, and a possible appointment as a mail contractor.

Camp Dog River 6 miles
South West of Mobile, Ala
Feby 25th 1864

My Dear wife

As Jessey Bird[18] of my company starts home in the morning on furlough & it being time for me to wright you againe

I proceed to do so. I am very anxious to hear from home. I see in the Mobile papers a few days ago that the yanks had made a raid into Macon, but Thomas' indians bushwhacked so that they turned back 20 miles below Franklin capturing Capt T. P. Siler but he made his escape.[19] Last eavning our Adjt came from home in NC & says Swepson told him that Franklin was burned down. I hope it is not true. This makes us very uneasy & we all are very anxious to hear from home.

As for war news I have but little. The Yankees that ran us out of Miss is now running back to Vicksburg & I hardly think we will fight here yet for a while. I now hear the cannon at Forts Morgan & Powell some 25 miles below this place. They have been shelling ever since we have been here & for the last few days very heavy. It is said that those forts are very strong and impregnable.

We all are ordered to Mobile today on general review. I hate the trip to walk 12 miles just for a general to see us & then blistered feet is the result. We are fairing pretty well. Rations are rather short but I am in hear no complaint or grumbling. My boys are all up. No body sick, 2 or 3 complaining of belly ache— too many sweet potatoes.

I would send you 8 or 10 hundred dollars. Le the old ishue has to be funded by the first April or it loses 33 cent on the dollar. So I will post pone drawing untill I can get the new ishue which will be in Aprill I reckon.[20] I will send you my watch as it don't run to do any good & it would cost 20 or 25 to have it cleaned here. I send your pen stock but I keep your pen. The stock wont hold the pen good. There is a pen in my tool drove. It was too limber for me but probably you can wright with it. I send your snuff box also that I think you will like as it will be so handy to convey in the packet.

As for our furloughs I think they probably will come. It maybe some time before it may be in a few days. Jess Birds furlough was sent up only 3 days before the Col's was & his got back yesterday, so ours may come soon. If the Yanks have not been in Franklin I should like to be there with Co B & we would make some of them bite the ground.

Should my bid for the mail contract be accepted you must have it certified by the PM & county court clerk. That is a copy & send it to me, but I hope I will be thare soon so I can attend to it myself. If I aint too tired this eavning I will write some more. If I can think of anything elce to wright. As for your family operations you must be the judge & do as you think best.

I wrote Jo the other day. Your cos Joe Gray is here. I see him every day. He is camped in a few steps of my tent. He wants a transfer to my co so he can visit you. He enquired of you & your father & family. I think he is a clever fellow. I will close. My love to all. Kiss my babes often for me & believe me your ever devoted & true husband untill death.

Good bye
Alfred W. Bell

135. March 8, 1864

Private Thomas L. Gash, Company D, 65th Regiment N.C. Troops (6th N.C. Cavalry), letter to cousin, Pauline Carpenter. Source: Mary Gash Papers (59), Private Manuscripts Collection, North Carolina Division of Archives and History.

Thomas was born in 1841 to Leander and Adeline Gash of Hendersonville. Thomas left his father's mercantile business and was reported as living with and working for Mr. Jesse Siler, a prominent businessman in Macon County, and a relative of the Gashes. Thomas returned to

Hendersonville and volunteered on July 15, 1862, to serve in the 7th Battalion, N.C. Cavalry. Thomas was captured in Monticello, Kentucky, in June 1863 and confined at Point Lookout, Maryland. In June of 1864, Thomas's cousin and Lieutenant Harvey Gash, arrived at the same prison. Thomas survived the war, and was listed as a farmer in Brevard, Transylvania County, in 1870.[21]

> Prisoners Camp
> Pt. Lookout, Md
> March 8th 1864
>
> Mrs. Dan Carpenter
> Dear Cousin
>
> Your very kind and interesting letter of the 1st inst came to hand to day. I was truly glad to hear from you and to hear that you were all well. But sorry to hear that you had never received my letters. I wrote two letters to Cousin Dan and one to Lou last Nov and never received any answers to them till Mr. Dooley recd a note of inquiry from you. I then wrote you again but have not received any answer to it yet. I should have wrote again before now but I neglected it. I have got three letters from home since I have been here. Things were all well the last account. H. C. Osborne[22] is here and well. He has got two letters from Mollie lately one dated 20 of Feb and your relations were all well. Henry O and me are both out of money and kneed a little very badly.
>
> Could you send us a check on Baltimore or New York for a small amount $5 or $10 a piece will be enough. We also kneed a suit of clothes a piece. I don't care how coarse the clothes are so they are warm. We need shirts and pants worst. I think the money will be apt to come safe most of the prisoners get their letters & money. H. C. Osborne sends his kindest regards to you. Direct to me at the above camp, Co. B, 8th Division. Henry O is in Co D, 8th Div. My kindest regards for all the relations. I will write soon again.
> As ever
> T. L. Gash

136. March 12, 1864

Captain George W. F. Harper, Company H, 58th Regiment N.C. Troops, diary entry. Source: Harper Diaries, G. W. F. Harper Papers (313), Southern Historical Collection, Wilson Library, University of North Carolina at Chapel Hill.

After February 28, the Army of Tennessee went into camp north of Dalton, Georgia. The men enjoyed this time of rest, and even had the famous snowball fight on March 22, 1864.[23] Harper was absent on duty, then returned to the front, checked on a friend and subordinate, and distributed cloth for the officers. In a few short weeks, this restful period would erupt into the Atlanta campaign.

> Thur 10. A.M. Cloudy and Rain P.M. clear and warm. Augusta 5 a.m. Sent on boxes by Sgt Thompson and others and stopped until next train. Dr. W. H. Tutt—photographed by Tucker and Perkins. Left package with Dr. Tutt to send home. Night train at 7 p.m. for Atlanta. Fri 11. Clear, Windy, Cool, Pleasant. Atlanta 9 a.m. overtook my part in Atlanta. Brown and Hope. Visited hospitals to find Lt. Page[24] and heard of his death on the 9th. Write A. Page and board cars at 7 p.m. for Dalton. Sat 12. Clear, warm, pleasant. Dalton at daylight and camp soon afterwards. Settled off bounties and distributed officers cloth. Rev. Wood. I recd letters from E, L, R. Wrote E by Miller of Watauga.

137. March 16, 1864

Sergeant James W. Love, Company A, 25th Regiment N.C. Troops, letter to his sister, Elizabeth J. Love, Henderson County, North Carolina. Source: Matt Love Papers (3276), Special Collections Library, Duke University.

James was promoted to sergeant on August 25, 1862, and was reported present throughout 1863 and 1864. In March of 1864, the 25th was involved an active campaign in an attempt to liberate occupied territory in North Carolina. Prior to that campaign, Ransom's Brigade advanced upon the port facilities at Norfolk and engaged Union colored troops.[25]

>Camp of the 25 Reg NC Troops
>March 16th 1864
>
>Dear Sister I take the pleasure of dropping you a few lines to let you know that I am well at this time truly hoping these few lines may safely reach and find you all well. I received your kind letter by Robert yesterday. Erwin brought on and one by mail so I will answer them both at once. Erwin and Robert is well and all the Smiths are well. I was sorry to find you was so out of heart. You must cheer up. You might want your tricks close. You thought I was joking last spring when I told you about the Boys steeling the sweetning out of a giner cake tho it is so. We are in our old Camp at newbern. Erwin got here on the 4th. He sed george was coming soon. I will tell you about the nigrs.
>
>Well we first went down to norfolk va or we went in 10 miles of it and took some prisner but they was white men and we got lots of Bacon on our salt and then we went to Sufflok and there we routed the negros. We killed some of them and they killed 2 men of ours—1 24th the other 49th. They was some of them negros got in a house and they shot till the last. They sat the house on fire and they staid in till they burnt up 5 of them.
>
>We had the hardest kind of marching for 17 days but we are resting. You said you want to see me and all at home. You cant want it worse than I do as Ring is just ready to start. I close I will write soon and you must. So nothing more at this time.
>
>From your brother
>J. W. Love

138. March 18, 1864

Private Calvin Leach, "The Wilkes Valley Guards," Company B, 1st Regiment N.C. State Troops, letter to his sister, Louisa, Wilkes County, N.C. Source: The Letters of Calvin Leach, Calvin Leach Papers (1875-z), Southern Historical Collection, University of North Carolina at Chapel Hill.

Calvin Leach wrote to his sister Louisa Leach about the life in camp. He talked about a windy day out on picket, life in his winter cabin, cooking with a canteen half, and rations. Leach remarked that his mess gear was very handy and that he intended to keep it through the summer if he should live. Private Calvin Leach was killed in action in the vicinity of Spotsylvania Court House, Virginia, on May 30, 1864,[26] weeks before the first day of summer.

>Camp 1st N.C. Infantry
>Friday March 18th 64
>
>Louisa afectionate sister,
>
>I take my pen in hand to write you a few lines for I know if you could write you would be sure to write me a letter. I am well at this time wishing these few lines may reach you and find you all well.
>
>I have nothing of any importance to write but I will write something maybe it would be interesting to you. Last Sunday a cold windy day and our brig was on picket and the soldiers as they would pass by they would have the wind blow off their hats and they had nothing else to do but pick up their hats. Their would be a few haw haws over it and all

would be all right. Finally on Monday the 4th Brig (Louisianans) came to relieve us and about 2 oclock we started back to camp and the closer to camp we got the faster the men walked. And when I got almost to camp I stumped my toe and fell down but I had nothing else to do but get up and go on.

We got to camp and since then I have been enjoying the good of my cabin ever since. It has been tolerably cool weather lately and it seemed right pleasant to be in a cabin. The next day after I got to camp I washed my clothes. I washed them with the soap you sent me from home, that ought to last me all summer.

The more coffee and sugar that we draw does me a great deal of good but I do not know how long we will draw it. I have me a boiler I carry with me on the march to make coffee in. I also carry me a little friar made out of a half a canteen which I carry to fry my meat in. I have my knife & spoon up yet and expect to carry them through the summer if I should live. If you have a chance you might send me a piece of ham.

Rufus Jones[27] got off home. He took my blanket but did not take my vest. I do not know where he will leave it he will probably leave it at Statesville. You recollect my writing about John Estes.[28] I rec'd a letter from him written with his left hand. He is now going to school at home and I recon enjoying himself as well as could be expected with his arm off. I am as ever

Your brother
Calvin

139. March 24, 1864

Private William H. Horton, Company I, 58th Regiment N.C. Troops, letter to his sister, Mary A. Council, Watauga County, North Carolina. Source: Mary A. Council Papers (1259), Special Collections Library, Duke University.

Shortly before the Battle of Chickamauga, William and his friend Elbert Davis (mentioned below) were detailed from the 58th to serve as teamsters for the army's wagon trains. William would serve in this capacity through November 1864. William offered general comments on receiving letters and being away from the 58th Regiment. The engagement he reported is in question; however, due to the description, it may be the Battle of Rocky Face Ridge on February 25, 1864, and the subsequent flanking attempt by units of George H. Thomas's Federal infantry at Crow Valley. Confederates in Reynolds' Brigade and Clayton's Brigade repulsed three Union attacks.[29]

Camps near Calhoun
March the 24 1864

Dear Sister

It is with the gratist of love and pleasure that I seat my self to rite you a few lines in answer to your kind letter that I received a few minutes ago and I was truly glad to hear from you and to hear that you was well. I got a letter from you and one from Rip & Carrie & J. S. Councill. They was all rote on the 20 of february. They was rite smart while on the road but I was glad to get them for that was the first time that I heard from my dear Carrie since I left home.

Dear sister I havent any news worth riting to you. Everything is still a long our lines as far as I now. We are away from the Army and we dont hear anything hear. We are about twenty miles below dalton. Me and Elbirt Davis. We are driving wagons in the general Army Supply train. It has bin near a month since I saw any of our Regt but they rite us every now and then. We have some very bad wether hear for the time of year. I think it rained as hard last nite as I ever heard it rain in my life. It has snowed two snows in this month.

Dear sister as to what I rote about the Rebbles a fighting at tunnel hill they neadent to dispute my word for I dident rite that. I saw it for I wasent there but they was lots of men that told us that it was surtin shure for they said that they had seen the wounded men a going to the horse pital and they told them that they got hirt. Well Polly you can tell them that they can dispute my word as mutch as they please so they dont dispute it to my fase. I think if every body was clear of riting lyes and telling lyes as I am I dont think that they would bee half as many told. Anuff about that.

Well Polly I want you and my dear Carrie to rite to me every day or two for I want to hear from her and you and little Jo every day. Give my best love and respects to Carrie and to all of my friends and tell them to rite me. Give my respects to Clary and tell her if she likes to kiss just to go over and kiss Beckey Walkers ASS. You must rite soon and often. No more only I remain your brother til death.

From W. H. Horton
to M. A. Councill

140. March 25, 1864

Captain Virgil S. Lusk, Company A, 5th Battalion N.C. Cavalry, prisoner of war—Johnson's Island, Ohio, letter to cousin, Pauline Carpenter. Source: Virgil S. Lusk Papers (717), Private Manuscripts Collection, North Carolina Division of Archives and History

By the date of this letter, Lusk had been confined for about nine months. Virgil wrote often to his cousin Pauline, the wife of Daniel Carpenter, about the letters he had and had not received. Lusk also told Cousin Pauline Carpenter about his attempts to write poetry, which helped him to pass the time and break the monotony of prison life.

Johnsons Island, Ohio
March 25, 1864

Cousin Pauline:

Your kind favor of the 11th instant has been received and always glad to receive a letter from any person, as our correspondence is the only thing that seems to break the monotony of prison life, but the pleasure derived from your letter came from another soul, but it was not only from a kind and sympathetic friend, but the supposition that you have ceased to favor me with your interesting letters was truly dispelled. I had given it up that you and your noble husband had forgotten me, or that something seriously had befallen you. I am very sorry that I did not receive Mr. Carpenters letter of which you speak, though it is not uncommon to lose letters here, they have such round about way to go before they are delivered to us. After this if you do not receive an answers to your letters immediately you may thereby know that all is not well—for I answer all letters immediately on reception.

I am sorry indeed, to hear that your Ma has been ill, but since its been her misfortune to be sick, I am glad to hear that she's better and hope that she is restored. Prison life is as much as usual, no important changes. You see by the news of the day they are exchanging prisoners on a small scale—three or four lots of seven hundred or a thousand and at intervals of a week have already been exchanged—almost as good as no exchange at all, agreeable to that mode of exchange. I will be in prison yet for many a day and weeks before it comes my turn.

I received a letter a few days previous from Mrs. Mollie all the information it gave me was that grandfather's family and family relations were all well. I am very fond of music, and under any other circumstances than the present, I would gladly accept your invitation to the entertainment. I have just turned into an author and have just finished writing a poem, "Tis Midnight Hours." Unless I am sent away from here very soon I intend writing a story or novel, "the Shautorn Bride." Tis all I can do to read, write, and think, and as I have no books worth reading, and as thinking without action is pure pastime, I fall back upon my imaginary facultıes like Byron[30] of old. Respects to all, and please write soon.

Your cousin,
Virgil S. Lusk

141. April 2, 1864

Private Alfred N. Proffit, Company D, 18th Regiment N.C. Troops, letter to sister, Rachel L. Proffit, Wilkes County, N.C. Source: Proffit Family Letters (3408), Southern Historical Collection, University of North Carolina at Chapel Hill.

Alfred and Andrew Proffit had survived a year and a half of the war. Both brothers were camped along with their regiment on the southern side of the Rappahannock River, awaiting the advance of the Union army. Andrew talks about his difficulty in receiving letters, the weather, rations, and a visit by Governor Vance. Also mentioned is the 53rd North Carolina, a regiment which had a large complement of Wilkes County men in company K. For the Proffit brothers, some of the hardest fighting of the war lay just ahead.

April 2nd 1864
Camp of 18th NCT
R. L. Proffit
Beloved cister,

I again attempt to write you not in anser to a letter from you for I have not had any inteligence from home cince I left onley what I heard through other letters I have wrote home. All so A. J. [his brother Andrew J. Proffit] has don the same. If you have not got them you should have written us any how. I expected to git some letters when J. E. Luther came back but I failed to do so and I have all most sworn off even wrieting home any more if I knew you had not started me a letter. Yet I would bind to my oath but as I have a better opinion of you I will try you a little longer and see if you think any thing of me. I dont think that you have mutch right to think anything of me but still if you dont I think you could write me a while any how. I think this will do on this subject so I will stop these remarkes etc.

Cis I will now give you a sketch of the times. I can in form you that we have the most rain and snow I ever saw. It is raining and snowing now the wind blowin etc. As for rations, it is like Pap sayes we draw only what we by and make it do. I guess we make the wilde onions git up and git. We fish a goode part of our time that is a vary good traid, mutch like where you live. We jeneraly have fisherman's luck, a wet ass, and a hungry gut.

Governor Vance is in our Brigade. He was to speak yesterday. The weather would not admit it then today is worse than yesterday and I dont know when he will speak.

I have no news from the 53rd as late as 27th March. The boys are all quite stout and harty. I saw P. W. & J. E. L. with others of your acquaintances yesterday. They are in good health. My self with A. J. are vary stout and harty. I trust you, father and mother and the rest of my friends are well in good health etc. etc. Write me as soon as you git this. Give me a long and interesting letter. Let it contain the important news from home and Wilkes. Give me the account of our privat affairs etc. As I have no news to write I will soon close. I remain your

Affectionat brother untill death
A. N. Proffit[31]

142. April 24, 1864

Private George W. Love, "The Henderson Blues," Company G, 56th Regiment N.C. Troops, letter to his sister, Elizabeth J. Love, Henderson County, North Carolina. Source: Matt Love Papers (3276), Special Collections Library, Duke University.

George was another of the Love brothers who served in the 56th North Carolina Troops. George enlisted on February 29, 1864, at the age of eighteen. Love participated in the Confederate victory at Plymouth, North Carolina, which he reported on in the letter, and was hospitalized in early 1865. Love was captured at Ft. Stedman, Virginia, on March 25, 1865, and was confined at Point Lookout, Maryland, until June 28, 1865, when he was released after taking the Oath of Allegiance.[32]

> Camp near plimouth N C
> April the 24 1864
>
> Dear sister it is with pleasure I seat miself to inform you that I am well. We left Weldon the 14. We got down hear a Sunday and commenced the fight and Monday and Tuesday & Wednesday morning we marched into plimouth. They was 2 from our Co killed dead. The feala was Ark Kinsey and Thomas Nobling and seven wounded.[33] One or two was very bad. R. C. has not come back. S. E. was gone with lieut Lane[34] with some prisoners to Carickville South Carolina. The have not got back. There is no fun in fiting. Shure we captured about 24 hundred prisoners and about 5 hundred wagons. 3 hundered of them was soldiers. There was 10 in our regiment killed dead and 67 wounded. I must close. The male is going out soon. If I could see you.
>
> From your brother G. W. Love

143. April 25, 1864

Captain Wesley N. Freeman, Company C, 25th Regiment N.C. Troops, letter to Joseph L. Cathey, Forks of Pigeon, Haywood County, North Carolina. Source: Joseph L. Cathey Papers (214), Private Manuscript Collection, North Carolina Division of Archives and History.

Captain Freeman, a prominent Haywood County merchant prior to the war and a father of three, had gained valuable experience leading his company through the Battle of Sharpsburg and action in eastern North Carolina. Freeman also served as acting regimental adjutant from August 21, 1861, to August 20, 1862.[35] By April of 1864, Captain Freeman's experience prepared him to make a run for the state House of Commons for the next term. In this letter to one of Haywood County's most respected citizens, Joseph L. Cathey, Freeman sought Cathey's endorsement and help in announcing his political agenda at the upcoming session of court.

> Camp 25th N.C.T.
> Near Weldon
> April 25th 1864
>
> Col. J. Cathey
> My Dear Sir
>
> Two years since my friends used my name as a candidate for a seat in the House of Commons and being encouraged by the very flattering vote cast for me at that time and yielding to the express wishes of many, both in and out of the army, I have announced my name as a candidate to represent the people of Haywood in the Commons of North Carolina. At the time this announcement was made, I expected to be able to meet our citizens at the many sessions of our court, and then make public the announcement and give them my views on the war, the principle subject which now claims the attention of every one. Owing to the very active and exciting campaign on our coast which our Brigade at this time are participating [in], I fear that it will be impossible for me to obtain a leave for my command.

I will therefore presume upon your friendship as far as to ask you to announce (at the session of the court referred to) my name as a candidate for the office spoken of. I will state briefly that I am in favor of a vigorous prosecution of the war, believing that on the success of our arms depends our future nation's safety. That a peace that would prove lasting or beneficial must be conquered, that terms should be proposed by our adversary, and not by us as our proposals are still on record and are unsuccessful by them.

I am in favor of a hearty and cordial support of the present administration. I am in favor of the reelection of Gov. Vance to the position he now fills with honor to himself and to the State. I am opposed to the calling of a convention, and the agitation of any such question at this time regarding such a course as disastrous in the extreme [to] our cause and could not possibly result in any good.

As to any matters of State policy that might arise for consideration I should endeavor to the extent of my ability to represent and reflect the interest of my constituents. I am not aware of any competitors that I may have, or who they may be and have made this request of you not with my view to find any one to my support, but simply to have it publicly proclaimed that I was a candidate.

I am very respectfully,
Your obdt Servt
Wesley N. Freeman

144. April 26, 1864

Lieutenant Colonel John T. Jones, 26th Regiment N.C. Troops, letter to his father, Edmund Jones, Patterson, Caldwell County, N.C. Source: Edmund Jones Papers (3543), Southern Historical Collection, Wilson Library, University of North Carolina at Chapel Hill. (Excerpted.)

After Bristoe Station, the winter of 1863–1864 was a quiet one for men of the 26th North Carolina. While picketing and details were being conducted, the regiment was without a sustained engagement until May of 1864. At the Battle of the Wilderness, Colonel Jones led his men into battle and was mortally wounded on May 5–6, 1864. When Surgeon Gaither told Jones that his wounds were mortal, Jones remarked, "It must not be. I was born to accomplish more good than I have done." John Thomas Jones died in the service of his country ten days after he sat to write this letter.[36]

Camp ____hall
April 26th/64

Dear Father.

I have just received your letter by Holden and was very much surprised to hear that you had not had but one letter from me since my return. I have written at least five letters if not more. I sent you photographs in two which I hope you have gotten.

I hardly know what to think of our friends movements in this quarter. It is generally thought here now that Grant has received no material reinforcements. Whether under the circumstances or not, he will advance somewhere soon. It may be on the Peninsula only to hold us here. I had a long conversation with Gen Lee, a day or two ago since. He is in the highest of spirits and seems to think our prospects here never been so in Virginia. He says other movements of importance are on foot in North Carolina. I hope they may succeed. If we are only successful this campaign I believe will find us all at home. We should certainly advance soon if Grant does not. We have sent all of our tents and waggons to the rear and are ready to march or a remain until Longstreet's command has not arrived down towards Fredericksburg and a greater part of the cavalry has. The Burnside expedition is the one we have most to fear from. I think it is intending to advance by the Peninsula and will more with a rapidity when it starts. I hope we will be ready for him. Our Army certainly was never in so fine a condition and they feel confident of our success. I think you need not fear that we will be able to hold out on account of provisions. You people do not know how little your son lived upon. I find a splendid dinner today of corn bread and a slice of pork. Yesterday I had only bread. I got the books you sent me by Lt. Sudderth,[37] they suit me very well. You spoke to me in your last letter on the subject of religion. I can tell you this much, I often think seriously of such things and think I would be confirmed if an opportunity should happen. I thought of speaking to Annie on the subject when I was at home but had no chance.

I am glad that Judge Reed spent a few days with you. I think such company helps you from being lonely and I fear you will grow rather [?]. Do you not think there is danger of it. I am surprised that you have not found some excuse to visit Greensboro. We have just seen a short piece of Gov'r Vance's speech at Fayetteville and I must say a great many of his friends in the army are not pleased by its tone. They think he is rather backing down. What do you think of it?

Did you see that letter of mine in the Enquirer to Col Burgwyn? I was surprised at this being published as I never had any idea he would. He wrote to me saying he intended writing a piece to defend Pettigrew's brigade and asking me to give him a short sketch of the 3rd Days fight at Gettysburg which I did thinking he just wanted a few points from which to write his article. It was written in a great hurry just as we got back to Culpepper and then once one or two slight misunderstandings. My love to aunt and her children.

Your aff son
JT Jones

145. April 26, 1864

Major William W. Stringfield, Love's Regiment, Thomas' North Carolina Legion, diary entry. Diary of William W. Stringfield, W. W. Stringfield Papers (109), Private Manuscripts Collection, North Carolina Division of Archives and History.

The action at Carter's Depot was fought between Love's Regiment, Thomas Legion and a contingent of about two thousand Federals.[38] The battle was extremely hot for men under Stringfield's command who were very close to the enemy at several points during the battle, having to fight from structure to structure against the advancing Federals.

> Carter's Depot, TN April the 26th 1864
> Yesterday and today are noted ones for the people and place. The Yankees came and attacked us 700 strong yesterday morning about 11am—the 3rd Ind. And 9th Michigan cavalry. Their first demonstration was at Devault's Ford below here. The river being too deep to ford they returned to this point and pitched into us. They were handsomely repulsed at all points. I had some narrow risks but a Kind Providence shielded me through all. Our loss 5 capt 1 killed. Theirs 3 captured 3 killed & 17 wounded. One reports their loss at 19 killed and 27 wounded besides several drowned at the Ford. Our men all did their duty well.[39] The fight lasted till dark last evening afterward the enemy retired to Jonesboro. I was ordered by Gen. Jackson to follow them which I did to Johnson's Depot. I was pleased that they had finally left. So much for standing one's ground and fighting when the occasion presents like this.

146. April 30, 1864

Private Albert W. Blair, "The Watauga Rangers," Company D, 1st N.C.

Cavalry Regiment (9th N.C. State Troops), letter to parents, John and Abigail Blair, Deal's Mill, Caldwell County, North Carolina. Source: Blair Letters (1206), Private Manuscripts Collection, North Carolina Division of Archives and History.

Albert Blair was the youngest of John and Abigail Blair's sons who entered service. Albert enlisted in nearby Watauga County on March 10, 1864, and was reported present through the spring campaigns of 1864. On June 22, 1864, the 1st N.C. Cavalry was part of a command that attacked a Federal raiding party, composed of two cavalry divisions under Generals Wilson and Kautz, which attempted to cut rail communications on the Petersburg & Weldon and Southside & Danville railroads. In the pursuit, Albert W. Blair was killed in action.[40]

> Camp near milford Depot Va
> April 30th /64
> Dear father and mother
> This eavning I seat myself to drop you a few lines to inform you how we are giting a long & that we are going to leav hear in the morning. We are going up on the rapdan on picket & I dont supose we will come back to our winter quaters any more. We are all well & is fine. Spevity got a leter from uncle Frank to day. He is well. They hav moved from there winter quaters a mile. Frank says tat they are especting a fight at all most any time so are we.
> I ansured your leter of the 17th inst whitch is all the leters I have received from home. Yet I will have to cut my leter short but I will rite again as soon as I can. My horse has mend ill since I left home. I got plenty to eat myself and plenty for my hors. I rote to you to send me a short coat but you need not do it fur I will draw one before long. I am riting the soiled side of the paper but I supose you can ceep up with it. I want you all to do the best you can & rite to me offen as you can & I will do the same. I will close for the presant.
>
> > Yours truly til death
> > M. Blair to Mr. John
> > Blair and A. V. Blair
>
> To Back your leter to Richmond
> First N C Cav. Company D
> In cear of capt Blair[41]
> Army of northern V A
> Excuse dirty paper

147. May 1, 1864

Private John W. Reese, Company F, 60th Regiment N.C. Troops, letter to his wife, Christena, Buncombe County, North Carolina. Source: John W. Reese Papers, Manuscripts Department, Special Collections Library, Duke University. (Excerpted.)

Reese was reported present through the Chattanooga campaign and was listed with his company until he was once again struck with sickness in February 1864. The Confederate Army of Tennessee had a new commander—Joseph E. Johnston—who instituted widespread change and increased discipline throughout the Army of Tennessee. These veterans generally accepted these changes and would face a renewed offensive by Sherman's Yankees within two weeks; however, Private Reese's thoughts were of home, far away from the battlefields of northern Georgia.

> Atlanta ga May 1 1864
> Dear wife
> With grate pleasure I tak the opportunity of droping you a few lines in answer to your vary kind letter that came to hand yesterday. It found mee well as common. My leg is still vary stif yet and pains mee sum but I sit a side my crutches this morning. I hope and trust thes few lines may find you and the children all well. You dont no how proud I was to git your letter. I was as proud as a little girl with red shoos on

but sorey to hear that pap was ded. I did want to see him one time more in this life, but deth is a bound in the land. He has paid the det that we all hav to pay. You did not state what was the matter with him and whair he died at and if he sed anything in regard of meeting his God. Tell lucey that I can simphey thise with hur in regard of hur brother. I take it to be hur name and stabey tell them both a gane in peace if tha will but try I wood like to say more but for want of paper.

Tena you did not say whither this was the first letter you had rote sence I hav bin hear or not. Pleas number them all as you rite them this is the forth one that I hav rote to you. Tena I want to see you and the children the worst I ever did in my life. May the God of heaven hav mercy and proteck you and keep you and what good news it wood be to mee to hear that you was a changed woman. Tena this is my harts prair. Every day I pray that it be answered in peace. I want you to rite to mee as soon as you git this and rite lots of it and let mee no how your cowes and your lings is dooing and if you hav got my gun at home. If you hav I want you to git hur at home and keep hur oiled in cide. Tell Mar garett that she need nt cum after mee when the yankees cums for I intent to cum then. Tell your mother howdy for mee. Tell hur that I git a good cup of coffey onse a while and I think of hur while drinking it. Tell all of my friends howdy and to rite to mee. Tell mar garett to send me sum tobacco fur I hav got to smoking reglear. Tena I hav saw lots and learnt a good deel. Tena if I was at home I wood git vary fleshey a gane. My chin begins to hang with fat and cheacks vary fair and red and my lipps needs kissing powerful bad. Tell John to feed yard well so he can tree sqirles and Rupert to rais lots of chickens and mar garett the big fite will soon be off.

I will rite a gane this week. Tena be shore to rite onst a week to mee. Fair well for a few days when the ling gets rite hav me cum.

John W. Reese to C. V. Reese

148. May 15, 1864

Captain George W. F. Harper, Company H, 58th Regiment N.C. Troops, diary entry. Source: Harper Diaries, G. W. F. Harper Papers (313), Southern Historical Collection, Wilson Library, University of North Carolina at Chapel Hill.

On May 15, 1864, Union and Confederate forces engaged each other at Resaca, Georgia. This battle was the first major encounter that the 58th N.C. Troops would have with "Uncle Billy's Army." Overall the 58th fought well, moving under fire to an advanced position and holding it after Stewart's division on their right had been driven back by troops under Union generals Butterfield and Williams.

Sat 14. Clear, Pleas. Army in line of battle on the hills about two miles from Resaca. Reynolds Brigade held in reserve. Several men wounded by shells and stray balls from sharp shooters. Fighting at various points along the line. P.M. Stevensons Division on our right, center moved out of breastworks and charged the enemy who ran for dear life. Magnificent charge. Advanced our lines over a mile and halted after dark. Occupied the ground until after midnight when we withdrew to our original position. Sun 15. Clear, Pleas. A. M. Brigade in line in front of breastworks about two P. M. advanced to support other brigades who were holding advanced works from the repeated charges of the enemy. Relived Brown's Brigade in the trenches and repulsed several charges of the enemy. About 6 p.m. Stewart's Division on our right charged the enemy and the 58th now ordered to cooperate on their left flank. Moved over the breastworks, under heavy fire and formed and advanced on the enemy, our lines not connecting with Stewart (who by the way was repulsed about or before this time.) We were compelled to withdraw to the entrenchments. In this charge received a flesh wound through the calf of the left leg. Hobbled back to surgeon; no ambulance being at hand. Wound dressed and was sent on foot to the Division hospital which I reached after dark without difficulty about two miles southeast of Resaca on R. R. Refreshed with drink of spirits and lay down on my blanket on ground to rest. Slept until nearly daylight when a train wasat hand to carry off the wounded. Have been under fire many times today. Thank God I have suffered no worse. Casualties in Co H. 58th NC—Wounded Pvts. A. J. Bolick and Saml McLeod (shoulder severely) Capt G W. F. Harper, Cpl. W. L. Crisp (hand), W. F. Bumgarner (Shoulder, by shell)

Captain George W. Finley Harper survived his wound at Resaca and was given permission to return home until his wound was healed. (North Carolina Division of Archives and History.)

149. May 19, 1864

Captain Stephen Whitaker, Company E, Walker's Battalion, Thomas Legion, letter to parents, Cherokee County, North Carolina. Source: Stephen Whitaker Papers (36), Private Manuscripts Collection, North Carolina Division of archives and History.

Saltville, Virginia, was one of the most strategic villages in southwestern Virginia. It was vital for its rail link, but more importantly it was the single largest supplier of salt in the south. With key areas of the southern coast under Union occupation, this inland salt depot had to (was able to) supply the entire upper South. There were several battles in and around the area. The forces defending the region were small battalions of infantry and cavalry, with artillery support. Whitaker believed that the war was over in Tennessee, and both armies had moved to Richmond. He could not have been more wrong; however, it is a good example of rumor and speculation in one of the war's lesser-known theatres.

Saltville May 19th 1864
James Whitaker Sen.
Dear Father
I take this time to write you a few lines. I have writen you often since I left

home but I doubt whether you have received them. The mail is so uncertain. I am well as usuual & so is the company. We left Carters Depot on the 7th inst to meet a yankey Raid on this place. We got her on the 8th and lay in line of battle for 3 days. The yankeys turned ther force around and attacted Dublin. Our forces met them thar. They had a suver fight. The yankeys drove our forces back & burnt the Depot & the Bridge over the Little River & done some damage to the railroad & telegraph wire but they was afterward driven off. We lost some 250 men killed, wounded & Prisoners. The yankeys lost more in killed and more in Prisoners 120 of them is her now. They had 10,000 men. We did not have one third as many. We her that Gen Brecanrige[42] has captured thar trane of wagons and part of the men. The news from Richmond is of the best kind tho you will her well about it before this reaches you. The news from the west is also good. If half we her is corect the war will soon be at an end. We also her that Gen Johnson has whipt Thomas at Chattanooga and that both armeys has gon to Richmond. It seames that it is the intention of both forces to decide the contest thar.

Father we are all confident of gaining our independence before long as we hope this sumer will wind up the war. Father we are at this time cut off from all the world except part of Tenn. The railroad is cut east of her. We cant her from home. We thout when Charlie Truit got back we could her from our friends but he, it seames, is not coming back this time. His time has bin out for a month & now he cant git her if he wanted to.

Saltville is 9 miles from the R.R. with a branch R.R. leading to it. You have no idea how much salt could be made her tho the workers is nerly all idel now. Thar is a large store of salt her if I could git it home I could git as much as I pleased but thar is no chance of giting in shipt away. The Northern works is idel & so is the govt works. It is uncertain how long we will sty her. We will very likely go to Richmond or we may go back to Tenn. I herd yesterday that Gen Forrests cavalery was at Cleaveland Tenn. If it is so, one could go thar & see whether the tombstones is thar or not. I fear they are lost or split. I would rather than five time the cost they would have bin got home and put up, but it cant be helpt now.

I have nothing else of intrist to write. Lieut Ingram is well. Green woods is well & makes a good soldier. Tell Litel Jim we would like to see him her if he was well enough. Tell him we whipt the yankes at Carter the worst kind. The boys done ther duty as usuual. We only had 3 wounded, one since dide. The yankes lost near fifity killed & wounded. This is the last time they have ventured so far from Knoxville.

A Tennessean by the name of Rown will take this leter to N.C. whar he will mail it or he may take it to you. You can send it to my wife as I have not time to write more to night & he is going to start soon in the morning. This will give her the news. If you write direct to Saltville Va be sure to name the Battalion, Legion & Briggade. If you do this leter will follo us wharever we go.

Your son
S. Whitaker

150. May 19, 1864

Private Azariah Denny, Company C, 21st Regiment N.C. Troops, letter to his father, Joel Denny, and family, Pilot Mountain, Surry County, N.C. Source: Jackson, *Surry County in the Civil War* (1983).

The North Carolina campaign of 1864 was a victorious one for the 21st North Carolina Troops, though it was decidedly cut short in its ultimate success with the forces of Ransom and Hoke being ordered to Bermuda Hundred to fend off advances made by Union general Benjamin Butler. Private Denny informed his father about the Battle of Bermuda Hundred on May 16, 1864, and the continuous shelling of Confederate positions by Union gunboats. "Bob Lee's" fighting referred to the bitter combat at the Wilderness and Spotsylvania Court House, Virginia, going on at the same time as Bermuda Hundred.

> Camp of the 21st Regt NC Troops
> Near Drewerys [sic] Bluff
> May the 19th 1864
>
> My dear Parents
>
> I again seat myself to drop you a few lines to let you no that I am still alive & in moderate health though not so well as the tooth ache & many biles but I am still on duty. We have had very hard times usual. I have the last 13 days. We have bin in line of battle & still remain, the 16th we was in a desperate fight. I was in 5 or 6 different charges. I was struck under the arm by a ball. It did not hurt me. Our company did not lose a man killed nor wounded. I dont think there is any danger of fighting much more here at the present. We have run them back under cover of there gun boats & have fortified our selves so there is not very much danger they can shell us from the boats. They threw a good many hundred pounders over us yesterday but to range then over the river banks. They generally go very high over us. I could write you a very interesting letter if I felt like riting. Bob Lee has bin fighting the hardest he ever did in Northern Va & has succeeded well when I feel more like riting I will rite more. There was none of your acquaintance hurt in this fight. Direct your letters to richmond, Va Co. C 21st Regt. Hokes Old Brigade. So no more
>
> A. Denny[43]

151. May 19, 1864

Second Lieutenant Lewis Warlick, Company B, 11th Regiment N.C. Troops, letter to Laura McGimsey, Pleasant Hill, Burke County, North Carolina. Source: Laura C. McGimsey Papers (2680), Southern Historical Collection, Wilson Library, University of North Carolina at Chapel Hill.

Grant's renewed offensive at Spotsylvania Court House resulted in one of the most fierce battles of the entire war on May 12, 1864, and spurred continued activity throughout the following week. While a sergeant, Lewis was wounded and captured at Gettysburg. After confinement at David's Isle, New York, Lewis was exchanged and returned to service. He was promoted to second lieutenant on February 15, 1864, but sadly, his promotion followed the death of his brother, Portland Warlick, who held the post previously.

> Spotsylvania C. H. Va.,
> May 19th 1864
>
> My dearest Corrie,
>
> As there is an opportunity or soon will be of sending a letter I will write to you again. I wrote two or three days since but being aware that you will be very anxious to hear from me frequently during these fighting times I will endeavor to write as often as an opportunity affords.
>
> We had a mail to-day, the first in nearly two weeks, none from you. Our command has not been engaged since I last wrote but expecting every night and day to be attacked; the enemies line of battle is in full view, about a thousand yards in our front but I think it very probable he will never attack us in our strong position, if he should he will be repulsed as heretofore. We were under a terrible shelling yesterday for two hours with very little damage. Ewell repulsed the enemy yesterday three times making great slaughter in his (the enemy) ranks.

To-day so far everything is quiet the skirmishers dont even fire at each other but seem to be quite friendly, meet each other and exchange papers and have a talk over the times; one came and met Capt Brown of the 44th[44] and after having a chat he, the Yankee, told Brown that Lee had destroyed half their army; there has no doubt been an awful slaughter in their ranks as, men who have fought over many bloody fields in Va. Say they never saw dead Yankees lie so thick on the ground as they do in front of the works where they charged. Their dead lie unburied from the Wilderness, well I wish they could all the time have such victories I consider when an army is driven back leaving their dead and wounded both in the field and hospitals that they have been badly whiped, dont you? That is the kind of a victory they gained at the Wilderness for I was there and know it to be so, we remained on the field till Sunday evening of the 8th and not an enemy could be found in front by our scouts.

We have to mourn the loss of many good officers and soldiers since the fight began. From all quarters we have good news, every where our arms have been victorious. Butler driven back Grant checked, Steele captured with his command and many other places we have been successful for which we ought to give God the praise. In my last I wrote to you of the death of brother Logan I also wrote to his wife. Bill McGimsey had an attack of cramp yesterday is nearly well today. Aus P. has been a little unwell but improving. Pink and I are very well.[45] I am very thankful that we have come out through so many dangers as well as we have, nothing but the hand of an Allwise providence has protected us thus far, for which we ought to be very humble and give him all the praise for his goodness. My wound is not well but does not hurt me. I saw Sam Tate when we were coming down here—haven't seen or heard from him since. We have had a hard time since we left camp, have been marching, lying in line of battle and fighting all the time, are now in the works not allowed to leave any distance as Grant is a sly fellow and has to be watched closely. Grant is twice as badly whiped now as was Burnside or Hooker but he is so determined he will not acknowledge it, but I think before he gets through with Lee he will have to own up.

I haven't had any clean cloths since I le[f]t camps the wagons are in the rear and we can not leave to go where they are to get our cloths, all the officers are in the same fix, so you may well suppose we are somewhat dirty. Give my love to uncle John, Puss and Sue. Do you get your papers?

Your devoted Lewis

152. May 26, 1864

Captain Virgil S. Lusk, Company A, 5th Battalion N.C. Cavalry, prisoner of war—Johnson's Island, Ohio, letter to Daniel Carpenter, Esq. Source: Virgil S. Lusk Papers (717), Private Manuscripts Collection, North Carolina Division of Archives and History.

With the domestic situation in the South deteriorating, Daniel Carpenter was forced to place more emphasis on his position as a civil official instead of corresponding with Lusk. Lusk understood this and politely replied that Pauline's correspondence was adequate. Lusk also described the way in which Daniel's $50 gift (October 24, 1863) was spent in helping more than one officer.

Johnson Island Ohio May 26, 1864

Cousin Dan
My Dear Sir:

I guess you are pressed for time, but I feel it my duty to you, and if you should find it an intrusion upon your time to answer me, I ask of you, my dear friend, not to spend time which might be otherwise more profitably spent in seeing of your own interests. Leave our correspondence to Cousin Pauline, that will do, she writes a very nice letter, highly interesting and very commendable. I suppose you have business enough to attend to that consumes all of your time. I understand how matters stand in Mo—"Rout pig or die." Everybody must look to their own business as there is no one to look for them and so it is reasonable to suppose that men of business have something else to do, instead of writing social letters.

It is of something else that I write—to give an account of my stewardship is the chief object of this communication. Your charitable donation has been spent as follows: 200 lbs of flour for $10, 3 gallons of molasses $5, 5Lbs butter $3, 10 lbs of dried fruit $2 50—Coffin subscription $2. It gives me pleasure to inform those Christian philanthropists that they have made comfortable even in the jaws of death, many [a] poor and helpless man. God will reward them. I spent one dollar of the donation to have an aching tooth extracted. I took the neuralgia in the face, suffering, almost death, I am nearly well now. I have 50 cts left. I will keep it until some poor fellow dies, when it will be given to assist in purchasing a coffin, in which [to] consign his lifeless clay to a final resting place.

The health of the prison is much improved since last winter. The most of the sick are sent to Point Lookout some time since. I do not know whether they have been exchanged or not. Two of my messmates have died since I wrote you last. Some of the prisoners are going blind. Capt. Neill is losing his sight. I have not heard from home since the occupation of Cty M by the Union army—respects to all.

Yours truly,
Virgil S. Lusk

153. May 29, 1864

Private Robert C. Love, "The Henderson Blues," Company G, 56th Regiment N.C. Troops, letter to his sister, Elizabeth J. Love, with note from S. A. Phillips to a cousin, Henderson County, North Carolina. Source: Matt Love Papers (3276), Manuscripts Department, Special Collections Library, Duke University.

Robert Columbus Love was born in Henderson County on May 20, 1844 and worked as a farmer before enlisting on April 12, 1862. At the age of nineteen, Robert was wounded in the head at Drewry's Bluff, Virginia, on the 16th of May, 1864,[46] a couple of weeks before Love wrote this letter. Robert talked about several casualties in the recent action as well as his desire to get some "Salet," a mixture of loose greens that came in season during the summer. Also enclosed is a note from Stephen A. Phillips, also of Company G, 56th North Carolina.

In the trenches on or
Near James River V. a.
May the 29th 1864

Dear Sister

I received your kinde letter a day or two ago and I was glad to hear from you and to hear that you was all well. I have not got much new to write to you only we are all well. Times are quiet this morning along the lines but I don't know how long it will remain so for we are only about two hundred yards from the yankees. We have not been in a fight sence Friday was a week ago. We had enuff time though that day. We lost 95 men killed and wounded out of our Regt that Day, There were four of our Company wounded. Sam Smith[47] was wounded very Bad but I heard yesterday that he was getting better, and mending fast of his wound. I can not tell anything about when we will fight again. We may fight before knight and we may not fight in a month. I saw Westley this morning and he was well. Mathew is gone to weldon. He will be back this eavning. Erve and George[48] is well. Erve says he has not had a letter from you all sence he left home. I can tell you we have a tiresome time of it a laying in the old ditches and can get nothing to eat, only bread and meat. We cant get out to get us no Salet. I would like to get to come home and eat a few messes of Salet. I have some milk to drink. I would like to see you all very much. I hope that this campaign will end the war. I will close hopeing to hear from you soon.

       Your affectionate Brother
       R. C. Love

  Co. G, 56th Regt
  NC Troops,
  Ransomes Brigade,
  Petersburg V.A.
  Camp near Drury's Bluff Va
Dear Cousin

I drop you a few lines to inform you that I have not forgot you. This leaves me well and harty truly hopeing this will reach you in due time and find you well and in high spirits. All is quiet along our lines today although we are looking for a general engagement here evry day. We have got good fortifications all along our lines. The yanks keep throwing their 200 pound shells over us once and a while. We have been digging the earthworks evry day since I have been here. I think we will desire this fight here in the cors of two week. I hope we will drive the yanks back. I will close. Write soon as you get this and give me all of the news.

       Yours truly
       S. A. Phillips[49]

154. May 31, 1864

Private John W. Reese, Company F, 60th Regiment N.C. Troops, letter to his wife, Christena, Buncombe County, North Carolina. Source: John W. Reese Papers (4417), Manuscripts Department, Special Collections Library, Duke University.

On May 31, 1864, John Reese was reported present with his company, perhaps hoping that his sickness had run its course. The 60th had been involved in battles at Resaca and Dalton, Georgia, in the month of May. Reese joined the 60th in a line of battle north of Marietta, Georgia. He described the skirmishing along the Confederate lines. Reese was possibly assigned as a blacksmith or teamster, working with a friend.

Two months later, Reese lost his continuing battle with disease on August 1, 1864, when he died in a Forsyth, Georgia, hospital.[50]

      Baldon Country Georgia
      may the 31 1864
Dear wife

With pleasure I am pur mitted to drop you a fue lins to let you no that I hav got to my regamant. I am still suf fering sum with my ankel. I had to walk ten or twelve mils after I got off the cars and that did not doo mee any good. Tena I hop and trust thes fue lins may find you and the children all well. I found the regamant in fine helth as fur now. I cant giv mutch reliable tho I am hear in a line of battle whair tha hav bin fiting for sum time. I got to the Regamant last sunday eaving in a allful thicket. I lay down and went to sleep and a bout a leven oclock I was wakend by that powerful noyes of canonading. We had to fall in and march out to a old field and thari we lay tell day brak. Then we mooved a long the line a bout two mils whair wee ar yet. Thair was no fiting last nit bardley but tha air dooing a little this morning. The canons is roring. How this thing will end I cant say not noing but we ar a bout 12 miles from maretter. The fit commenct at dalton sixty mils from maretter. We hav lost a heep of men an kild a heep of yankeys and hear we go all dont no a thing a bout hard times and de struct tion of propirty. If you cood see the corne fields and wheat fields that is ful of stock and all is de stroid. Thats the truth. No one escaps the hors of this thing whair we go. We hav lost but vary fue out of this Regamant. Tha giv mee a gun to tote but this morning colonel weaver had it turnid over so I hav no gun to tote. I am helping Elic wagner[51] at tend to the horses at my old trad a gane.

Tena dont be uneasy a bout mee I can say to you that I recieved your lettur yesterday. Tena you dont no how glad I was to hear from you. It was rote the 22 of may. I was sorey to hear that Peter Ball was gon. I am in hopes he will find women a plenty in the country whair he has gon. Tena I must cum to a clos. I will rite in a few days a gane and mor of it. The arme is fed vary well. We git a half pound of bacon pur day and plenty of bred. Tena if my leg dont git well by the time this fite comes off I will git a fur low and cum home. O how glad John would be. Tena colonel weaver told mee that you was a pattern for all others to go by in trying to liv. I am glad to hear this but new you wood doo your best. May gods blessings be with you and my sweet ones. I rote this in a hury. Go over the bad ritin. Direct your letturs as you did the last.

J. W. Reese
to C. V. Reese

Buncombe County's James Thomas Weaver started the war as a minor lieutenant, but rose to the lieutenant colonelcy of the 60th North Carolina. (Library of Congress.)

155. June 1, 1864

Private Lorraine W. Griffin, Company D, 16th Regiment N.C. Troops, letter to his family, Rutherford County, North Carolina. Source: G. W. Griffin Papers (153), Private Manuscripts Collection, North Carolina Division of Archives and History.

The 16th North Carolina had been engaged for some time fighting against Grant's offensive. Griffin describes the massive frontal assaults as hard fighting and even believes that the Union soldiers must be drunken to fight in such a fashion. Griffin survived the Union onslaught and was promoted to sergeant on October 1, 1864. Sergeant Griffin remained with his company until Appomattox Court House.

> Camp in 8 miles of Richmond
> Dear Farther & family
> This morning a fords me the pleasur of writing you a few lines to let you know I am a livin yet and as well as common tho mity wored by fighting and times is very scary her. Fighting is going on her yet we ar in our ditches and the have to keep out of the way of the bulets. They fly thick at times. We had to fall back last knight and bild more Breastworks. I cant write for I am so sleepy. You must over look my bad writing. I will try to do better when this fight is over if I live thro. I am al most redy to give up. I live in hopes my last brother is gon and it may be my time next tho I live on time more but I got a heap to go thro before this fight is over. This is the 28th day since we comenced and I haven bin out of musket range. Oh if I cood git out of this fight but there is no chance of it. The yankes has not got to Richmond yet but I am a fraid for the place for they fight mity hard her. They ar all Drunke when they charge our lines and wont cear for nothing. They kiled our men and they was lots of men that go to them but I will keep out of ther hands as long as I can. The compeny is all her. Only what I wrote to you before. Eli is ded or is a prisoner. I cant tell which.[52]
> I will close for this time hopeing to her from you soon as I havint herd since Harrill[53] came. I wood love to her from home at this time. Give my love to all of my people. Tell them to write to me.
> I remain your loving sun till deth
> L W. Griffin
> PS George[54] died from his wound. I don't know how he was wounded for I cant her from nobody knows. I hope you have heard all about it by this time.

156. June 5, 1864

Major William W. Stringfield, Love's Regiment, Thomas' North Carolina Legion, diary entry. Diary of William W. Stringfield, W. W. Stringfield Papers (109), Private Manuscripts Collection, North Carolina Division of Archives and History.

The reassignment of Love's Regiment placed the unit under the Valley division of John C. Breckinridge and the brigade of William "Grumble" Jones. The Battle of New Hope is also known as Piedmont, Virginia, and was fought against Union troops under David Hunter prior to the arrival of Jubal Early's Second Corps from the Army of Northern Virginia.

> June 5th Battle of New Hope[55]
> General W. E. Jones commanded our army and placed us before the Enemy who attacked vigorously at 9 am. We repulsed every assault gloriously until 3pm when our right wing held by the 60th Virginia Regiment gave way and threw the whole line into confusion – giving the field to the enemy. My men did well.[56] Our loss will reach 100 killed and 250 wounded and 455 prisoners. The enemy's loss is very great in killed and wounded. We lost no wagons or artillery. The loss in my Regiment is 15 killed, 24 wounded, 21 missing.

157. June 5, 1864

Captain Virgil S. Lusk, Company A, 5th Battalion N.C. Cavalry, prisoner of war—Johnson's Island, Ohio, letter to cousin, Pauline Carpenter. Source: Virgil S. Lusk Papers (717), Private Manuscripts Collection, North Carolina Division of Archives and History

After a year in confinement, Lusk still

maintained his correspondence with cousin Pauline Carpenter. In this letter, the Madison County prisoner instructs his cousin to shorten her letters to only one page as letters longer than that are declared contraband and not delivered. Lusk also talked about getting an image made and requested the all-important prison commodity—tobacco.

     Johnson's Island Ohio,
     June 5th 1864
Dear Cousin Pauline:
 Fatality, I think is the most practical and plausible theory of religion! The mere fact of our having an existance on earth is prima facia evidence that our exsistance here is for a certain purpose, which is pre-arranged by the fore knowledge of our omniscent God, which it is impossible for mortals as we are to await. I am only fulfilling my mission on Johnson's Island. This being the case it becomes me to submit quietly to whatever may occur, however hard it seems. I received an envelope from you yesterday evening, the letter having been pronounced contraband in consequence of length, and taken out. I was very sorry that I did not get the letter and I today am vexed. I would only be telling a simple truth. Here after when you write to me you must confine your letters to one page, and be cautious what you say if you wish me to get them. This looks hard, but I suppose its fair. As they say, "All's Fair in War." This is only the beginning of trouble. The skys are darkening hour by hour and ere long the blast will burst in all the fury of its rage. I can only watch and wait. I having nothing more to write you. It is true, nevertheless, that we have rumors of war, and other rumors all, however by the "Grape Vine Telegraph" signifying without foundation or untraceable to any foundation, that our rations are to be curtailed, if so, good bye, I'm off to the other side of Jordan.

 I send you a photograph such a thing as it is, but it is the best I can do. It was taken by a pencil artist, a prisoner, and photographed in Sandusky. You are not surprised then that it is bad work—very bad considering the circumstances I hope you will excuse it. You cannot recognize me as being the individual of several years ago. Will you send me yours and Cousin Dan's? No news from home. If you know of any person sending any expresses to Johnsons Island please remember me with smoking tobacco. It is both meat and drink, otherwise don't put yourself to any trouble for me. Give my respects to all "whom it may concern."
 As ever your Cousin
     Virgil S. Lusk

158. June 8, 1864

 Colonel Joseph L. Cathey, Forks of Pigeon, Haywood County, N.C., letter to Capt. Lyons. Source: Joseph L. Cathey Papers (214), Private Manuscript Collection, North Carolina Division of Archives and History.

 Joseph L. Cathey (1803–1875) was one of Haywood County's most prominent citizens. Cathey, with no formal education, became a successful businessman and despite no desire to enter politics, served as a delegate to the state constitutional convention in 1835 and as a state senator prior to the war. During the war, Cathey, a secessionist, served as one of the county's executives. In this brief correspondence, Cathey was to supervise the formation of a junior reserve company; however, it appears that the situation was less organized than it should have been.[57]

     Forks of Pigeon N.C.
     June 8th 1864
Capt. Lyons
 Sir, you will recolect that I was at Waynesville on the 1st day of this

month at an appointment you had for the 17 years old boys to form a company, but as there was 19 present you appointed Tuesday the 7th as another day for organizing the company on the 7th. I sent my son Thomas H. and he was told the organization was made on the 6th with 27 present. Now as the representative of my minor son I asked you how many would have to be present to form a company and elect officers and you answered me that 40 was the smallest number that could.

I respectfully ask you to inform me how it is that the organization was made before the day appointed and with so small a number present?

Your ob't serv't
J. Cathey

159. June 11, 1864

Sergeant William J. Smathers, Company C, Love's Regiment, Thomas Legion, letter to his parents, Haywood County. Source: Private Collection, Mr. William Best, Asheville, N.C.

While a company of new reserves had completed its formation in Waynesville, a veteran company in Love's Regiment was prepared to advance up the valley as part of General Jubal Early's offensive in the summer of 1864.[58] Sergeant Smathers reflected on the recent Battle of Piedmont (also called New Hope) on June 5 and listed its casualties. Smathers seemed either excited or terrified at the prospect of fighting again against what he perceived to be a full strength enemy corps.

Camp near Fishersville Verginia
June the 11 1864
Dear father and mother
I take my pensil in hand to drop you a fiew lines which will inform you that I am well truley hoping theis fiew lines will cum safe to hom and find you all well. I received a letter from you dated April the 1. I wold hav rote before now but I hav not had the chance. I can inform you that I hav bin in two fites one at Carter and one in the valley of Verginia. And it was a hard fite. We got in at six oclk in morn and fought untill two then we was bound to retreat. Hit is a offee cene. The Yankey loss was sed to be sice [six] hundred. J. H. Smathers is well. J. D. Smathers is well. I will give you a list of the kild and wounded of our company. V. H. Williams & J. W. Bugg kild and Lieutenant Smathers & Lieutenant Chavre E. D. Sharp wounded John Red Sleeve missen. We dont no whiter kild or capchered.[59]

We are now behind our brest works looking for a norther fite. We has bnin in line of batle for two days. The numbers we are contending withe is twenty three thousand and they will fite if you call cuming close anuff to club guns over each others heds anything! I wold like to see all of you again but I recon their is no chance yet a while. Tell Merion to cum back and help us whip them out so we can all cum hom. I must close. Write soon

Yours truely untill death,
Sgt. W. J. Smathers

160. June 18, 1864

Sergeant Martin M. Gash, Company D, 65th Regiment N.C. Troops (6th N.C. Cavalry), letter to his sister, Henderson County, North Carolina. Source: Gash Family Letters (1541), Private Manuscripts Collection, North Carolina Division of Archives and History.

After extensive movement in east Tennessee during Longstreet's failed campaign against Knoxville, the 65th North Carolina (6th Cavalry) was transferred to eastern North Carolina. Sergeant Gash volunteered along with his brother Harvey and served as a private in Company D, 7th Battalion, and as a sergeant in Company E, when the 5th and 7th battalions were merged. Sergeant Gash was captured at Jackson's Mill, Kinston, on June 22, only four days after this letter. Gash was confined at Point Lookout, Maryland, until July 31, 1864, when he died of dysentery.[60]

    Camp Wise fork near Kinston
    June the 18 1864

Dear Sister

We arrived here last night a little after dark and found the boys all well and in good spirits. We are on picket about five miles below kinston all quiet here at present. This is a pretty level country. Crops look fine and corn is about waist high. We are camped in a nice pine grove with a very good tent to stay in and a fly for a kitchen. The boys were all glad to receive their little packages from home. The horses all look well and are in good fit for service. The latest news from virginia is that the yankees had taken the outer works at petersburg and was shelling the city. I do not know what will be the result. The boys are split up on the governors election. Holden[61] will get a good share. Doc Jones will get a good vote here if he runs. We got the boxes along without much trouble and dident have anything to pay on them. I will close as I have nothing of interest to write. Write soon.
    Yours
    M. M. Gash

PS I want you to send me the Standard that has vice presidents Stephens[62] speech in it.

161. June 30, 1864

Captain Alfred Bell, Company B, 39th Regiment N.C. Troops, letter to his wife, Mary Bell, Franklin, Macon County, N.C. Source: Alfred Bell Papers (417), Manuscripts Department, Special Collections Library, Duke University. (Partial letter.)

In June of 1864, Captain Bell and the 39th North Carolina were holding their position in the fortifications encircling Atlanta. Since his last letter, Bell had traveled to Alabama and back to Georgia, had been arrested for neglect of duty—a charge which was never prosecuted—had fought with his regiment at Dalton, Georgia, and had helped defeat the Union forces three days before at the Battle of Kennesaw Mountain.

    Camp 2 miles from Atlanta ga
    June 30th 1864

My Dear wife,

It is with continued pleasure that I again seat myself to write to one who is so dear to me. Your kind and loving letter of the 17th came to hand the 27th and I assure you that it was red with pleasant delight. I was so glad to hear that you & babies friends generally was well & that you was getting along so well and you have felt quite easy about affairs at home. I am very glad that the carpet bag & contents got home safe and so quick. I think Alex Baldwin is a very clever man. I am glad that they are so proud of their shoes. I could have got 2 pair like those but I thought such as those would be too heavy for Polly. You did not say whether they fit or not. I guest at the size & I thought Polly's size from what you wrote me was about my size but I suppose they fit pretty well or you would have said something about it. I thought Tim would be very proud of the axe as it is one of the best I ever cut with. I reckon it went safe. I sent my old drawers and a tick which I reckon you can find a use for it. So you see that I am quite stingey for most of the soldiers are throwing out all their old clothes, but I send them as presents to my wife & I imagine that she is glad to get such pieces out from her old boy. I did not send the key as I had but one fit or I made it fit my other carpet bag and I knew that you had one at home that fit the one that I sent.

As for news I have been in battle of much importance ever since there has been some heavy fighting at this point in the last few days. The yanks have charged our lines at severil places at different times & have been slaughtered powerful killed hundreds and fell in heaps and were repulsed with terrible loss compared to us. We have taken a good many prisoners. Report came last night that Morgan[63] is in their rear with 10 thousand men and captured 25 thousand yanks. I hope it is so, but I fear it not. If true, Mr. Sherman and his horde will have to fight a desperate battle to come to Atlanta for provisions or beet a hasty retreat for the rear.

Our boys have been fighting some as Harm Penland[64] wrote me a few days ago that Jeff martin[65] of my co was wounded in the knee. I do hope this thing will be ended soon. The weather has been very hot for several days. This morning it is raining a little which will cool the air.

162. July 11, 1864

Major William W. Stringfield, Love's Regiment, Thomas' North Carolina Legion, diary entry. Diary of William W. Stringfield, W. W. Stringfield Papers (109), Private Manuscripts Collection, North Carolina Division of Archives and History.

Love's Regiment remained in the Shenandoah after Piedmont and was assigned to Early's Second Corps. The regiment advanced through the Valley and on to Frederick, Maryland, even camping in Sharpsburg, Maryland, on the campaign. Stringfield, who was ill and with the wagons, made an interesting observations about what would happen if Washington were to be taken.

July the 11 1864

Monday Evening. In front of Washington City DC! See the unfinished dome of the Capitol. I am still very unwell and remain with the wagons which are one mile in advance of my division which is guarding the rear. Gen. Early has demanded the surrender of the city which he can take by considerable loss of life. The enemy are driven back to their inside works. The mansion of Post Master Genl. Blair is burnt. Our army is very anxious to enter Washington city. I fear for the people if they ever do enter there. So much misery has been brought on our people by the vile miscreants living there that they could not be restrained. If the proper ones were the only sufferers I would say turn them loose upon the city. It always will be a bone of contention among us any way. I am very weak and not able for duty but must travel.

163. July 25, 1864

Eliza Murphy Walton, Creekside, Burke County, N.C., letter to her son, John "Jock" Walton, Company F, 41st Regiment N.C. Troops (3rd Cavalry). Source: Thomas George Walton Papers (748), Southern Historical Collection, University of North Carolina at Chapel Hill. (Excerpted.)

On June 28, 1864, one of most daring raids in the history of North Carolina brought warfare to the doorsteps of Morganton. Col. George W. Kirk, a well-known mountain partisan, launched a raid whose main objective was Salisbury. Sneaking into North Carolina across the Tennessee line, Kirk and his raiders rode all night and came across Camp Vance outside Morganton on the morning of June 28, 1864. The Union raiders soundly defeated the camp's garrison of conscripts and began their return to Tennessee. On the way they were pursued by Colonel William W. Avery, whose Morganton Home Guard skirmished with the raiders at Winding

Stairs. After a brief assault the Home Guard was defeated, and Kirk returned to Tennessee unmolested by further pursuers.[66]

Creek Side July 25
My dear Jock
The second letter from you since you left Petersburg was received the 10 day of May. We was so glad to hear you were well also one from Jink he is safe tho he does not mention his health. I suppose it is good he had not been so fortunate as you in his first accounts of the raid as he heard our place was destroyed. You have not received Mary's letter written directly to you after your Aunt Louretta's death. I hope you have before this as it gave you all the particulars. She seemed very gratified at your being so thoughtful of her and seeming so anxious about her. She was only rational at very short intervals for two days before she died. It was one of the saddest events of my life, only three sisters and one of them gone.
Eliza is at Mr. Erwins & will spend the summer with them. She looks very badly. W. W. Avery died of the wounds he received two days after he made a will and left Alphonso his Esecutor, who is here now and intends on resigning. Uncle Molton did not make a will and his family are troubled about getting someone to attend to his business. Lizzie is in great distress.[67] Mr. Houke was also wounded in the raid very badly. I hope we will not suffer again as there is a Reg and 2 companies of cavelry here now and your father is appointed Col of the Home Guard.[68] The Reg is from the adjoining counties. The Cavelry companies pursued a band of deserters and Yankees and captured 27 of them and brought them back a couple of days ago.
Your aunt Mary has been very sick with the measles her recovering was thought doubtful for a few days. Mr. Caldwell also has them badly. Maggie is

George Washington Kirk, Commander of the 2nd N.C. Mounted Infantry. (United States Army Military History Institute, Carlisle, Pa.)

William Waightsill Avery of the Morganton Home Guard was killed in pursuit of Kirk's raiders. (William W. Avery Papers, Southern Historical Collection, U.N.C.)

letter he was going to Richmond on a pleasure trip. They are very near it now and said all the Officers had been nearby and they wanted to get away from the Yanks a while. Willie Avery's wound is very painful and he is very much reduced in flesh. I did not think you had much to spare when you left home. How do you look? How are your boots holding out? I suppose you got a supply.

Lola and Mary are going to town and will send a letter to you and ink to put in the office. I hope you will soon be at some place where you can write regularly and get letters from home. Hugh and Herbert are as bad as every. They are out all the time in the sun. Do write again soon. I will make May write you soon before she leaves home. Your devoted mother,

E. M. Walton

Have your daugerotype taken before you write again.

still at home & will remain a week longer. Miss Lounders is with her. Ella Erwin will return with them. Frank Craig and Tom McEntire were here at the time of the raid and gave all the assistance in their power. Frank has been sick ever since. Dr. Pearson was wounded in the knee and will be a long time recovering. Old Chandler Foster of the one in Capt. P- Company was killed.

We have had a very long dry spell, our gardens and fields are all suffering for rain very much. We have had a splendid crops of black berries. I am glad to get milk and butter now. I know you enjoy it so much. Jink said in his

164. August 3, 1864

Major William W. Stringfield, Love's Regiment, Thomas' North Carolina Legion, diary entry. Source: Diary of William W. Stringfield, W. W. Stringfield Papers (109), Private Manuscripts Collection, North Carolina Division of Archives and History.

August saw the return of Jubal Early's Valley army to a defensive posture in the upper Shenandoah Valley. In this entry, the intelligent Stringfield discussed the current moral and spiritual state of the men around him. He also reported that his brother, Chaplain James Stringfield, 1st Tennessee Cavalry, had preached a sermon to the Legion.

Tuesday August 3/64
Army remains in Status quo waiting

for the approach of the enemy who seem inclined to meet us since the rout at Kernstown. Brother James preached for our command at 8 am today. At 10 Maj. Bell, formerly of Gen. Steuart's staff preached to our brigade. At night the chaplain of the 36 Va preached in the village. The clergy seem to be a little aroused. I am glad of it, for oh the wickedness in camp. I am making a poor effort to do right but it is a struggle against a swift opposing current. May heaven protect and sustain me and return me uncorrupted to those I love. A good letter from "my girl." All right.

165. August 18, 1864

Captain Alfred Bell, Company B, 39th Regiment N.C. Troops, letter to his wife, Mary Bell, Franklin, Macon County, N.C. Source: Alfred Bell Papers (417), Manuscripts Department, Special Collections Library, Duke University.

The 39th North Carolina rendered good service throughout the defense of Atlanta; however, it appeared that Captain Bell was never a participant in any of the major battles or skirmishes. Bell, perhaps stemming from his disputes with his regimental commander, often served as a provost officer, which explains his earlier absence from his command. However, Bell was among his men in the fortifications by this time. The number of officers who wished to resign is interesting, but it was not uncommon at this stage in the war, and Bell made it a point to talk about the low morale of the men during a prolonged siege.

Atlanta Ga Aug 18th /64
My Dear Wife
Yours of the 25th came to hand the 11th and found me well & in the ditches with the boys. I was on a visit to see them and I found them generally well, but a good deal of grumbling & dissatisfaction—rations rather short and so much duty to do that they are worn out. The yanks breast works are in plain view here & a constant shelling which keeps the boys close to their breast works. The pickets fight all the time. Its one continual roar of small arms in plain view of both breast works.

Our regt has escaped remarkably well lately. None killed since I wrote you last, 3 or 4 have been wounded. Collins (Eli's son) & Nichols (David's son) of Co I.[69] Collin's middle finger left hand was amputated. Nichols right side by a piece of shell and some others who you are not acquainted with. I started out yesterday morning to see the boys and the shelling was so heavy that I came back. I think thare was 40 or 50 struck within 100 yds of me & I thought some came near hiting me and learning the regt was going out on picket last night I came back to the cooking train where I stay badly scared as for war news. I have but little. Wheeler is certainly gone to the rear of Sherman & reports say tore up 20 miles of R Road. If so, Sherman will have to fight or retreat. If he charges our works he is whiped. He must do something soon for his supplies for he cant get them from the country. Both armies are well fortified here. The yankees shell Atlanta both day and night. They bomb a house nearly evry day or night & occasionaly kill some they have killed several women & children. Still that dont make them leave town. I feel sorry for them I think they ought to take their children & git out of harms way & the reach of shells.

Well I have an apology to make you. This is the first letter I have written since I left Griffin over 2 weeks ago. The cause of my not writing you last week was the yanks had cut the R Road & stoped communications for a few days & then I thought I would wait until I visited the Regt. The day I rec'd your letter I wrote out my resignation which was excepted by the Col. I asked for leave of absence which was not granted, so I waited until I could hear from the later paper hoping that I could git to go home but Coleman disaproved it & so did all the others. I suppose it will be 30 days before I hear from my resignation which has to go to Richmond. I tendered it unconditionally and immediately. I said nothing to my boys about it as they told me they heard I was going to resign & if I did they swore they would go too. I told Lt. Anderson about it & he hated it very much but said he could not blaime me. The boys all know it now & I fear as soon as they git their pay which I learn will be in a few days, many will go home. Woodberry Owens left for home a few nights ago 12 or 14 of the Jackson co has gone home. If this seage last much longer I fear half of our armey will leave but I have hope that Sherman will have to retreat soon & we may yet drive them back. Capt Dyche and Lt. Whitaker[70] have tendered their resignation & asked for a leave of absence. Their resignations were excepted but they have not heard whether leave is granted or not. Capt Hughes & others say they are going to resign. John Reid is trying for a furlough but has not heard from anyone yet. I got a letter from Joe a few days ago dated July 18th. He was well their & near Petersburg. I also got one from Samey dated July 29th.[71] He was in Richmond in the quarter masters dept & said he heard that Joe was about to loose one of his eyes. I have not received your letter giving me the particulars of Anns death in that this is the only one I have recd lately except the one Anderson brought me & I supposed what you said was that Ann died on your birth day. Will Woodfin also told me of her death.

I will go out to the regt in a day or two or I may strike out to git off soon.

The yanks are shelling very heavy this evning. It is a continual fire a general engagement could not be much heavier. I hope to be with my two wives soon to receive the good things presents they have in store for me. The clothing I dont need at present so bad but the sleeping with my wife I am very needy. I hope the time is close when I can git both clothing & the sweet kisses & pleasant bed mate.

Kiss my sweat babes often for me. My love to all. I ever remain your devoted husband. Write often

Alfred

166. September 1, 1864

Private Alfred N. Proffit, Company D, 18th Regiment N.C. Troops, letter to his sister, Rachel, and cousin, Sarah Walsh, Wilkes County. Source: Proffit Family Papers (3408), Southern Historical Collection, Wilson Library, University of North Carolina at Chapel Hill.

The relatively quiet lines in front of Alfred Proffit's regiment at Petersburg were a contrast to the heavy fighting he was involved in during the month of May. Proffit received a very painful wound at the Battle of the Wilderness when a minnie-ball actually lodged in his sinus cavity. Fortunately, Alfred survived the war despite this wound and returned home to Wilkes County. Andrew married Sarah McNeill after his return and the two raised ten children at their Lewis Fork home. Andrew often suffered from severe headaches until one day a violent sneeze expelled the minnie-ball from his sinus cavity. After being relieved of that pain, Andrew lived out the rest of his life until his death on August 3, 1929.[72]

Petersburg v.a.
September 1 1864
R. L. Proffit & S. R. Walsh
Esteemed sister and cousin yours of the 22nd is at hand and it did not fail

to interest me vary mutch to learn that you war all well. I am glad to hear from those fine revivals in Wilkes & also your fine crops—wheat, turnips, corn etc. I should love to be thare to help you eat some vegitables as they are so dear here. I can hardly buy them.

I will give you the prices of a few artickels: Appls from 2 to 5 dollars per dozen. Peaches and the same for onions $3 per quart. Water mellons from 3 to 10 dollars a peace. Butter $15 per labs. Small loves of bread $2 a cake. Milck $4 per quart and other things according. I am glad to hear of your good prospect for potatoes for I just paid one dollar for four little things. I give you some account of our fight on the 20th inst so I will no more about it.

We are now in our breast works two miles south west of Petersburg. Thare are no yankees in our front nearer than one mile and a half but the picket duty is hard as our brigade is vary small. We are drawing vary good rations. We all have as mutch bread and meat as we want. Old strong bacon but we got some beef today.

Sarah inform me in your next of Unkle Andrew and Ant Mary and all the family of the brig and what Regts do thay belong, the health of cousin Piley's health etc. In form me how you like to live in Wilkes & what the prospect for Marages is. Write me soon and excuse me for my imposition by asking so many questions. I hope you will excuse

This image of Alfred Newton Proffit was taken shortly after his enlistment. He would be the only one of four brothers to survive the war. (Mrs. Ruth Proffit Gregory, Wilkesboro, N.C.)

me for not recollecting your name when you first wrote to me. Tell davy I should be proud to see her for I could tell her some rich jokes. We have lots of fun along the lines.

Sis and Sarah give my love and best wishes to all of my friends and consider your selves two of them. I am vary glad that you formed the resolution to give me a letter once a week for I have looked in vain many a long day. Dont break your intention. Sis I send Julyan Miller a [illegible]. Tell the rest I have run out but if I have the chance I would make them all one. Give her it as soon as you can if it is two small tell her to give it to one of the rest and I will make her another. These lines leaves me in the best of health hopeing thay may find you the same.

Yours as ever,
A. N. Proffit

167. September 2, 1864

Corporal James W. Wright, "The Wilkes Volunteers," Company C, 26th Regiment N.C. Troops, letter to his wife, Fanny Wright, Wilkes County, North Carolina. Source: John Wright Papers (1594), Private Manuscripts Collection, North Carolina Division of Archives and History.

The following is the last selected letter from Corporal James W. Wright. The 26th North Carolina, and the rest of Hill's third corps, were stationed in the trenches around Petersburg, Virginia, in the fall of 1864. In this letter, Wright talks about his first sergeant, Samuel Pryor, making out the rolls for his company, his recent clothing and ration issues, and his hopes of seeing his family again. Almost two months later, James was captured at Burgess Mill, Virginia, on October 27, 1864. James was confined at Point Lookout, Maryland, until he died of chronic diarrhea on January 31, 1865.[73]

Petersburg Va
Sept 2nd 1864

Dear Fanny

Your letter of the 25 August came to hand today. It found me well. I was very glad to hear from you again. I was looking for a letter for August to bring me a letter from you. The mail is much behind. Sergt Pryor[74] was ordered to go to another company to get the rolls made out. I thought I could do it myself. I went to work and made out a return of them and then went to the Maj commanding the Regt and asked him if it was done right. He said it was the Quartermaster said so too it was the first time any one tried to make them out. Our company is very small. Around 26 have tried for a furlough and the second time none yet.

You wrote in your letter that you wanted to send me a shirt and a pair of socks. I do not need the shirt as I have enough. The socks you may send some time this fall. I want need them yet I will want a pair by cool weather.

We draw clothing plenty of clothing at this time and rations enough. We are doing very well in that respect. We need rest and above all we want peace so we can all get home to our loved ones and be free men again. It would be the most pleasing thing to us to hear that peace was made that could be told. But when that will be who can tell. Yet I hope to get through all safe and sound by the help of an Almighty God who has protected me through all these campaigns to whom I feel very thankful for his mercy and hope he will yet spare me to get home to you all again. When I think of what I have passed through I am almost lost in meditation to think how many has fallen on my right and left and in front and rear and yet I am spared.

I feel like the prayers my people in my behalf have been answered and I hope they will yet be answered. Dear Fanny look to God for protection and he will not forsake you. He is able to feed you with the bread of life. Teach Charley to be a good boy and be firm with him in your commands. I must come to a close. Give my love to your Pa and family.

I remain your loving husband,
James W. Wright

168. September 8, 1864

Second Lieutenant Harvey Y. Gash, Company D, 65th Regiment N.C. Troops

(6th N.C. Cavalry), Morris Island, South Carolina, letter to his father, Alfred, Henderson County, North Carolina. Source: Gash Family Letters (1541), Private Manuscripts Collection, North Carolina Division of Archives and History.

On June 22, 1864, Lieutenant Gash and the majority of Company D were captured at Jackson's Mill, Kinston, North Carolina. Harvey was confined to Old Capital Prison, Washington, D.C., Ft. Delaware, Delaware, Hilton Head, South Carolina, and Ft. Pulaski, Georgia, and was finally placed at Fort Delaware, Delaware, until June 17, 1865, when he was paroled and released after taking the Oath of Allegiance. Harvey was one of the "Immortal Six-Hundred" officers who were sent to Ft. Pulaski and Morris Island to act as human shields for the Union Army.[75]

After being captured at Kinston in June 1864, both Colonel George N. Folk (pictured above) and Harvey Gash were imprisoned on Morris Island, part of the "Immortal Six-Hundred." (North Carolina Division of Archives and History.)

Morris Island S. C.
Sept the 8th 1864

My Dear Father

I now attempt to write you a few lines that you may know that I am still in the land of the living. I arrived here last night. I have been on the Boat 18 days since I left Fort Delaware. I thought we would be exchanged soon as we arrived, but no exchange was agreed upon yet. I still hope the day is not far distant.

I received a letter from Tom Gash[76] the day before I left Fort Delaware with the sad news in it that Brother Martin was dead. He died the 31 day of July 1864. He, J. H. Crawford, & M. A. Young[77] was taken out to be sent to some other prison, Almiry New York I expect.

Martin was sick and sent back to the hospital and died in a short time. I hope he is gone to a better world where wars and prisons is not known. Tom was well and all the Boys that was captured with me. I have not heard a word from home since I was captured. I don't expect you have heard from me since I was captured. I hope to soon be released and return home again. John Lain is here & well. Folk is good that was captured with me. Uncle Lee ought to send Tom some money. A prisoner stands a bad chance without money. I have tried it. I am going to write to Jule[78] to send me some but I hope I will not stay here long.

Write soon. Direct to Morris Island, H. Y. Gash, Lt Prisoner of War S. C. by Flag of Truce. I hope this will find you all well. Give my kindest regards to all my friends.

H. Y. Gash.

169. September 20, 1864

Major William W. Stringfield, Love's Regiment, Thomas' North Carolina Legion, diary entry. Diary of William W. Stringfield, W. W. Stringfield Papers (109), Private Manuscripts Collection, North Carolina Division of Archives and History.

The Battle of Third Winchester on September 19, 1864, was a substantial defeat for Confederate forces. After the defeat the Confederates retreated to Strasburg where they drew a defensive line and reformed. The legion carried in approximately 160 men, of which they lost 75, along with several experienced company officers.

> Winchester fight
> Tuesday the 20th—Strasburg
> Yesterday our force was defeated in a general fight with the enemy. My division lost two thirds of its total number. The Legion lost 75. Lieutenants Welch and Ashely are killed. Captain MaKinney and Capt Singleton, Lts. Young, Jule and George are all captured. There was a stampede of wagons at night. We travelled all night. The troops are now in line at the breastworks.[79]

170. October 18, 1864

Private William H. Horton, Company I, 58th Regiment N.C. Troops, letter to his sister, Mary A. Council, Watauga County, North Carolina. Source: Mary A. Council Papers (1259), Special Collections Library, Duke University.

William Horton's duties with the supply wagons had protected him from the vicious battles of the Atlanta Campaign, and may have possibly saved his life. After the fall of Atlanta in September 1864, Gen. John Bell Hood, commander of the Army of Tennessee, intended to strike back into northern Georgia and Alabama, and retake a large portion of Tennessee. Sherman, knowing he had a large garrison at Nashville under the capable General Thomas, began his destructive "March to the Sea" with the only other real Confederate force marching the opposite way, and into the jaws of the Army of the Ohio.

> Camps near Jacksonville Alabama
> Oct the 18th 1864
> Dear Sister
> It is with love and pleasure that I seat myself this morning to rite you a few lines which will inform you that I am well and harty at this time and truly hope when these few lines comes to your hands that they may find you all in good health for good health is the only sadisfaction that I see these days.
> Well sister I havent any newse worth riting to you but I will rite a few lines to you any how. The health of the Regt is tolerable good as far as I now. I havent seen the Regt in 8 or 10 days. The last newse we got from them the Report was that our army was at dalton Ga but I dont rite it for the truth for we hear so many lies that we dont now when anything that we hear. We have bin on a march about three weeks. We travel two or three days and then we stop and rest a day or two. The newse has bin all the time that we was on our road to Tennessee but we have bin hear for four days with the waggon train and they is some talk now of us a putting up winter quarters hear and staying hear til Spring but I dont know whether it is so or not.

The most of the waggon train is hear but the Army I dont now where it is. We hear so may tails about it that I cant rite anything about it for I dont now anything. Ther newse is hear that the yankees is in Atlanta yet and our men has got all of the railroad above Atlanta up to dalton but I dont now whether it is so or not. I dont beleave anything that I hear and only beleave half of that.

I see this cruel war commenced with lies and it will end with lies if it ever ends and I am in hopes that it will end before long. I want to go home to live with my dutch gal for I am a getting mity tired of living the way we haft to live hear. We only fair tolerable hear for something to eat. We only draw beef and corn meal. We got anuff meat but the beef that we get for one day rations only makes one small mess but I am with the waggon train and we can buy sweet potatos and get some pump kins and we can buy flour and we can sorter make out to live but it is a hard life. I hope and trust to god that I may live threw this war and go home to live with my dear dutch gal again.

Well Polly if we take up winter quarters hear I want you to make my dear Carrie and Rip come and bring

Lieutenant Robert T. Conley of Company F, Love's Regiment, survived the 1864 campaign and commanded sharpshooters until May 1865. (North Carolina Division of Archives and History.)

me some clothes. If Carrie wants to come I want her to come. Polly give my best love and respects to Carrie and tell her to rite to me. Give my respects to all of my friends. I will haft to quit this time. You must rite soon and often. Direct your letter to Co I 58 NC Regt Browns Brigad Stevensons Division Lees Corps Blue mountain Alabama Army of Tennessee. I have got the cart before the horse but you can tell him no more. I

remain you Brother til deth.
From W. H. Horton
to M. A. Councill

171. November 2, 1864

Private Job R. Redmond, Company I, 65th Regiment N.C. Troops (6th N.C. Cavalry), letter to his family, Leicester, Buncombe County, N.C. Source: Military Collection, North Carolina Division of Archives and History.

In 1860, Job Redmond worked as a farmer in Buncombe County. On May 14, 1862, the 29-year-old Redmond left his wife Malinda, and his three children, James, William, and Cissy, and joined Captain Allen's Cavalry, Company A, 5th Battalion. In August of 1863, Jobe's company was transferred to the 6th N.C. Cavalry Regiment. Shortly after being transferred, Redmond deserted at Cameron, Tennessee. On April 30, 1864, Redmond was reported in arrest. He remained in arrest until his execution.[80]

Kinston N C
November the 2 1864
My Deir Wife and children

I seate my self this morning with a troub beld harte and a de strest mind to try to rite a few lines to let you no that I hierd my sentens red yesterday and hit was very Bad. I am very sory to let you no all read dy I hafte to bee shot the 9 of this month. I am sory to in form you that I hav but 7 dayes to live but I hope and trust in god when tha hav slane my body that god will take my sole to este whier I will meete my little babe that is gon be fore. My dier wife I think I could die better sadesfide if I could see you and the children one more time on erth and talk with you but my time is so short I donte exspect to ever see you and my dier little children eny more on erth.

I can in form you that I receved 2 letters from yo yesterday witch I red with plesur witch you giv me some sadesfaction to heir that you was all well and doing well. I receved the close that you sent to me by lt smith. I exspect tha will be my bearying close. I receved a canteen of brandy also but am in too mutch troub ble to drink. My dier wife I wante you to come to see mee if you can git abner brooks to come with you if can my dayes may be per longed. My dier wife if I see you no more on erth donte grieve for mee nether lamente nor morne mee. I hope I shal with my Jesus bee while you ar left a lone. I pray that god will be with you and helpe you rase your children up in the noledge of the truth and the lorde and savior Jesus christe.

A woird to my children witch is nir my harte in nature seem to bind. James I wonte you to bee a good boy and obey your mother and keepe out of Bad company. You must bee a smarte boys and obey your mother. Also sissy you muste bee a smarte little girl and bee good to the babey and call to Jobey. I hope that god will bee with you all so far well children you cante see your papy no more on erth.

My dier wife thes times has ben sweet. I have spent with you but now I muste depart from you and never more return but let this not griv your harte. I pray that the lorde will bee with you and helpe you out in all your troubles and trile hier bee low. So far well dier wife.

J. R. Redmond condem to Die

172. November 16, 1864

Corporal George F. Adams, "The Watauga Rangers," Company D, 1st Regiment N.C. Cavalry (9th N.C. State Troops), letter to his parents, Sugar Grove, Watauga County, North Carolina. Source:

Alfred Adams Papers (19), Special Collections, Perkins Library, Duke University.

By November of 1864, George has survived some of the most grueling campaigns of the 1st Cavalry. George was concerned about the bushwhackers, Tories, and deserters back home in Watauga, and with the election of Abraham Lincoln. Adams would be promoted to Sergeant in December and was reported present until he was wounded and captured at Chamberlain's Run, Virginia, on March 31, 1865. George F. Adams died in a Washington, D.C., hospital on April 22, 1865,[81] almost four hundred and fifty miles away from home.

> Camp of 1st N.C. Cavalry
> Nov the 16th 1864

Dear Pa & Ma

In answer to your very interesting letter of October 30th we send you this scribble. I can say to you that we are in fine health & spirits hoping this will find you well and doing well. We have nothing of note that would interest you as every thing quiet, in the way of fighting. Nothing a doing at all. Abe is certainly elected President of the United States again and I suppose that we are doomed to another four years war. God forbid. I hardly know what will be the result from his reelection. Everything is quiet. If it was not for this camp life we would hardly know that their was war going on. Rations starve but we make out but I cannot tell how long it will be that we can get enough to eat. We are sorry to hear of the Tories cutting up so in that county and hope they will quiet down some time soon. There is some little talk of ours disbursing this winter. If we do Woe to all the Bushwhackers and deserters in Watauga. We would like to be back there this winter to take Big belgian and drink that old brandy that you are saving for us. I think if we was to come back we ought to have a little of it anyway as we have struck this year pretty well. Don't you think so? Will save it a little longer. We will be back afterwhile if we live. Give our love to sister Sallie. Tell her to write to us. I am surprised that you spoke of McCormick in your last letter. It was the first time we have known you to write but what you said something about Mc. He thinks that you have forgot him. Tell Silas McBride and family that we have not forgot them and that we will write to them soon. We have a nice little mess now. Only three of us GF Adams, DC Davis[82] and BC McBride. Our eating costs about three dollars a day besides what we draw. I will close for the present. Write soon and often. We remain your two soldier boys

> Alfred Adams G F Adams
> Elizabeth Adams B C. McBride[83]

173. November 30, 1864

Private William H. Horton, "The Watauga Boys," Company D, 58th Regiment N.C. Troops, letter to his sister, Mary A. Council, Watauga County, North Carolina. Source: Mary A. Council Papers (1259), Special Collections Library, Duke University.

Private Horton was last reported present in the official records in November 1864. His final disposition in the army, or any further service, was unreported. His wife Caroline and his sister Mary remained at home while William continued his duty with the army supply wagons facing short rations of meat and sweet potatoes. Horton also talked about the aggravation in supervising the "georgia negroes" and the trouble with body lice.

> Camped at Eutaw Green County
> November the 30 1864

Dear Sister

It is with love and pleasure that I seat myself this morning to rite you a few lines which will inform you that I am well and harty at this time and I truly hope when these few lines come to your hand that they may find you all in good health. Good health is all the sadisfaction that I see these days. Dear sister I havent anything to rite to you that is interesting but I thought I would rite a few lines to you to let you now where I am and what I am a doing. I am at Eutaw Ala. I am waiting to get a drove of mules to take to the Army. We are about two hundred miles from the army. We brought about four hundred old condemmed mules down here and they swap them for good mules and pay the difference.

Well Polly I can tell you that we only fair tolerable hear in this war. We only get one pound of meat for four days and that is tolerable large rations but I have lived tolerable well for the last five weeks since I left the Army for I have lived on Sweet potatos but I am about out of them now. I will have to start buying potatoes. Dear sister I am sorry to tell you that I am out of money and clothes and tobacco and friends. I will do the best I can. I hant got but one old pair of ragged britches and one old ragged shirt but I hope and trust to god that they is a day coming when poor privates will be as free as big rich officers. This cruel war is a rich mans war and a poor mans fight.

Dear Sister I dont have very mutch to do but the fool Georgia negroes that we have with us and the body lise is a nuff to aggrevate any man to death but I will try to stand them the best I can. Well my dear sister I dont think that I will stay in this cruel war more than forty years longer now. I want you and my dear Carrie to rite to me for I hant heard from none of my friends in six months. The last letter that I got from Carry was rote the 22 of May. You dont now how bad I want to see my dear Carrie. Oh if I only could see you all you dont now how glad I would be. When I had to come down hear I was in hopes that I would haft to stay hear all winter so you and my wife could come to see me but I haft to go back to the army just as soon as we can get a drove of mules to take back with us.

Well Polly I want you to tell my dear Carrie where I am and what I am doing. I sent a letter to Carrie the 28th of this month but I dont now whether she will get it or not. Give my best love and respects to all of my friends and save a portion for yourself. Give my best love and respects to my dear Carrie and to rite soon and often. Direct your letters to the Regt & the Army of Tennessee. No more only I remain your brother til death.

From W. H. Horton
to M. A. Councill

174. December 1, 1864

Private William Cathey, Company A, Love's Regiment, Thomas' Legion,[84] letter to father, Joseph L. Cathey, Forks of Pigeon, Haywood County, North Carolina. Source: Joseph L. Cathey Papers (214), Private Manuscript Collection, North Carolina Division of Archives and History.

In the winter of 1864-1865, the mountains of Western North Carolina were subject to numerous raids by outlaws, bushwhackers, and regular Federal troops. Protecting the counties of Cherokee, Jackson, Clay, and Macon fell to young Major William W. Stringfield. In this letter private Cathey, of Stringfield's command, wrote his father about a government tannery, and the capture of seventeen Yankees by forces under Stringfield.

Opposite: (From left) William, Benjamin, and Francis Cathey of Jackson County fought in the early campaigns in western Virginia as members of Company A, 16th N.C. Troops. (North Carolina division of Archives and History.)

Qualla Town N C
Decr. 1st /64

Dear Father

I recd you kind letter by Jas. E. I was glad to hear from you. You will let F. B. Evans have [line illegible] you wrote. You will please attend to it for me. Take this note or arrange it as you think best & I will be satisfied. I have not seen Will Lames sence I recd your letter. My mule would not suit him as he wants a riding horse. If he has not bought a horse he will come by and see yours as he goes to Rutherford. He is going there to put up a tannery for the Government. He is said to be a first-rate tanner & a man that can be relied upon. Col. Thomas[85] has not returned yet wrote he would be here in a few days. Maj. Stringfield[86] has gone to Cherokee County. We caught 17 yanks & one deserter the other day. They have been sent to Asheville. I will close. Give my love to all. I am well.

Your son,
Wm. Cathey

175. December 29, 1864

Captain George W. F. Harper, Company H, 58th Regiment N.C. Troops, diary entry. Source: Harper Diaries, G. W. F. Harper Papers (313), Southern Historical Collection, Wilson Library, University of North Carolina at Chapel Hill.

Fortunately for men of the 58th North Carolina, the unit was not part of Confederate general John B. Hood's disastrous campaign into central Tennessee. While the Army of Tennessee was, for all practical purposes, being destroyed at Franklin and Nashville, the 58th North Carolina was guarding prisoners being transported westward and keeping an eye out for Federal movements in Mississippi.

Wed 28—Clear, cool, pleas. Train to Tupelo, thence marched on R. R. to Chawla Creek 6 miles north of Okolona and camped. Good supper and haversacks filled at Townsends. Dark walk to camp over R. R. trestles sore feet. Horses in the rear. Thur 29—Cloudy, Cold, Windy. P.M. Clear. Ground frozen hard. Rations of pork and sweet potatoes. March at 8 a.m., called at Capt Rowes' Mrs. H and family. Okolona 11 a.m. Same R. R. track torn up and a number of trestles burned. Enemy reported at Egypt (7 miles) moving west.

1865

There seems to be a good deal of despondency felt among the people out here about the final issue of the war. Many of them have given up all hope. I am not by any means among this number but still feel confident that yet all will be well.

>—Mr. Thomas W. Patton, Lowdens County, Alabama, to his mother, January 6, 1865.

Sherman is playing the Devil generally seemingly unmolested. I still think he will get himself thrashed before he gets much farther into our country. Chester S.C. was his HdQrtrs when last heard from. Charleston evacuated and Wilmington "gave up."

>—Captain Julius Gash, Company D, 6th Regiment North Carolina Cavalry, Kinston, North Carolina, February 24, 1865.

Muddy road and tiresome walk. Threw up breastworks and waited for advance of the enemy who failed to make his appearance. Noon marched to within 6 or 7 miles of Smithfield and camped after dark. Road exceedingly wet and muddy. Tiresome and disagreeable march. Peach trees in bloom.

>—Major George W. F. Harper, 58th Regiment North Carolina Troops, March 22, 1865.

There is a dark cloud hanging over our country and every passing breeze comes laiden with the din of war, devastation, and death. The sun in his course at midday is frequently shut out by a dense column of smoke, from consuming wealth but it is useless to attempt to discribe what has no word to discribe. It is perfectly horrible but orders have come and I must stop here.

—*Captain John L. Swain, Company B, 17th Regiment North Carolina Troops, April 16, 1865.*

176. January 1, 1865

Captain Virgil S. Lusk, Company A, 5th Battalion N.C. Cavalry, prisoner of war—Johnson's Island, Ohio, letter to cousin, Pauline Carpenter. Source: Virgil S. Lusk Papers (717), Private Manuscripts Collection, North Carolina Division of Archives and History.

With the start of a new year, Virgil Lusk continued to write letters to his cousin Pauline Carpenter and seemed to be growing even more dissatisfied with prison life. Faced with recent health problems, Lusk was left with no other options but to continue to endure his lot. In June 1865, Captain Lusk was released from his two-year-long imprisonment, and within a short time, returned to his home in Marshall.[1]

Johnson's Island, Ohio Janry 1, 1865

My Dear Cousin:

Your kind letter of the 22d ult was received on the 30th, was very glad indeed to hear from you, as it had been a long time since I had had the pleasure. The last letter I had from Mo was from "Sister Lace." Tell her I received it today perfectly well and answered it immediately. I waited long and anxiously for an answer and had argued myself into the belief that she had forgotten me; but it is without reluctance that I am convinced that I was in the wrong. You scold me, Cousin Pauline, for not writing to you oftener. Pau, I don't think you ought to do that, for I always answer every letter immediately on reception, and if you don't get them I cant help it. Though I confess, that in the uncertainty of the times, true friends should not stamp out those small points, such as waiting on an answer from our friends to the letters we write them, and at this point, I plead guilty, beg your pardon and promising to do better in the future, and awarding the credit to you of being better than I. If you see anything of Price tell him to stay out of Mo, for to him I attribute the interruption in our correspondence. Your presumption concerning Capt Neill is incorrect, his is neither dead or sick. I have not heard from him since the 30th of September. They were all well then. I have been sick nearly all Summer. I have been suffering for the last 10 days with Palputations of the Heart. I never had the disease before, and hope I'll be well again soon, thought I am suffering at times, intensely.

When you write to Uncle James, tell him where I am and request him, to write to me. You can tell him as much as I know respecting his relations. Though I may hear something from home, soon, as I think we will have a Flag of Truce before long, if so, I will write you immediately that you might give him any information I may receive. It may be that he will be sent here, as Price's operations in Mo has already reinforced Johnson's Island to a considerable extent. This prison life is killing me, the great wonder is that I have lived as long as I have under the circumstances. If it was practable, I could tell you things that would chill you with horror, the blood of Nero.[2] Give my love to "Dan" and your Ma. When I come to my sense I'll write you a sensible letter.

As ever
Virgil S. Lusk

177. January 6, 1865

Thomas W. Patton, letter to his mother, Harriet Kerr Patton, Asheville, Buncombe County, N.C. Source: Patton Family Papers (1739), Southern Historical Collection, Wilson Library, University of North Carolina at Chapel Hill.

After leading company C, Captain Patton resigned his commission on August 8, 1864, in order to take care of family and personal matters back at home. In January of 1865, Patton returned to the plantation in Alabama where he visited in February of 1862. The end of slavery and the slaughter of a prize hog seemed to be the most important items on this former officer's mind.

Lowndes County Ala
Jany 6 1865

My Dear Mother

My negro boy Tom Weaver got me to write the accompanying edifying epistle to his old friends & fellow servants. It is a good production being his own dictation. I promised Susan to write to you particularly for her giving her best love etc and begging that you will try and communicate with her folks at Mr. Robinson's & let them know that she is well & doing well. She has a fine baby, a girl. All of the negroes here seem to be better contented than I ever found them before. They make no complaints at all to me. They are all well shod from shoes made by one of them, leather being tanned on the place. Altogether I think they are the happiest I have met with since the war having nothing in the world to trouble them.

It is the opinion out here that our "peculiar institution" is forever dead and I am inclined to that opinion myself. If such is the case I am sure the negroes are most to be pitied. Mr. Fagg offers to take a hundred dollars in gold for every one he has—so certain is he that they are lost to us forever as slaves.

There seems to be a good deal of despondency felt among the people out here about the final issue of the war. Many of them have given up all hope. I am not by any means among this number but still feel confident that yet all will be well. I have never yet had so trying a time about not knowing from home & just at a time that I am most anxious to hear. I still have strong hopes of seeing you all this winter—so keep in good spirits at home. Our big hog was killed the other day, but did not weigh as much as I expected, 900lbs gross & 806lbs net. I remain

Your Affec Son
Thos W. Patton

178. January 6, 1865

Thomas Weaver, body servant to Thomas W. Patton, letter to his friends, Buncombe County, N.C. Source: Patton Family Papers (1789), Southern Historical Collection, Wilson Library, University of North Carolina at Chapel Hill. (Written down by T. W. Patton.)

This is a letter of either a free black or a slave of Thomas W. Patton. Patton referred to him as "my boy Tom Weaver" in a previous letter; however, his identity is in question just as is that of Sam Capps.

Capps worked as a body servant for Captain Patton; however, it was not mentioned in records whether Capps was free or a slave. The identities of those mentioned are unknown, perhaps fellow slaves, and it is possible that the Sam mentioned here is Sam Capps.

>Lowndes County Ala
>Jany 6 1865
>
>My Dear Friends
>
>It has been so long a time since I have heard any thing of you that I avail myself of this opportunity to drop you a few lines to let you know that I am well & doing as well as could be expected these times. I wish very much I could see you all once more. I have had a tolerably good time Christmas with Sam, who has been here for a week past. Tell Aunt Rhodie he is well and also his sister Lucy. Give my best respects to Aunt Rhodie & her family also especially to Solomon. Tell Mat & Mauson I wish them both much joy in their estate, as I understand they have become married men. Tell Aunt Eliza I have not forgotten her yet & hope she will keep me in remembrence. Give my respects especially to Sam Morrison & Abram and tell them I am very anxious to see them. You must tell howdie to all my old friends and tell them I hope some of these days to see them all once more & spend some more happy Christmas in their company. Tell Spencer his two sons are well and doing ditto & are very anxious to see him again. Remember especially to my old friend Minor. Tell him not to forget me. Love my best love to your wife Sallie and also Sandy & Evelina. I remember you all with much affection. It is my fortune to be far away from you but I will never drop you from my memory & time in hope that we may all meet each other again some of these days. I hope none of you will forget your old friend.
>
>Tom Weaver

179. January 11, 1865

Private James W. Parleir, Company G, 54th Regiment N.C. State Troops, letter to his brother, Noah B. Parleir, Pore's Knob, Wilkes County, North Carolina. Source: Box 85, Folder 28, Military Collection, North Carolina Division of Archives and History.

James W. Parleir was one of the eleven children of Jonathan and Rebecca Shin Parleir of the Pore's Knob community of Wilkes County. Parleir, a husband and father, was conscripted in Wilkes County on November 1, 1863, and captured only days later at Rappahannock Station, Virginia, on November 7. James was confined at Point Lookout National Prison, Maryland, until March of 1864 when he was paroled and transferred to City Point, Virginia, for exchange. Parleir was exchanged on March 30, 1864. After returning to service, Parleir was reported absent without leave in September–October 1864.[3] Apparently, James returned after this last record and was wounded in some unspecified action. In the following letter, James informed his brother Noah about a procedure by which a ball was extracted from his hand while in the hospital.

>Jan the 11 1865
>Camp near Petersburg, Va
>
>Dear Brother
>
>It is threw the kind hand of Providence I am bless with the opportunity of droping you a few lines to let you no that I am well as comon Truly hoping this note will find you all well and hearty. N. B.[4] I want to see you all very bad and I can inform you that I recived your very kind letter dated the 5 which gave me much satisfaction to hear from you all. You must excuse me for not riting to you sooner for I have bin at the hospitle part of the tim and had a ball cut out of my hand. It was lodged against the bones in the back of my hand. It nearly made me twist my tale

when the doctors was cuting it out but it is nearly healed up. I can scarely rite that is all I can do. I think this cussed ware will end soon and in the way I have thought all the time. N. B. the tims is hard here and I want you to send me a nother ham bone. Please help Phoebe[5] to fickes me a nother for I don't get half Enough to eat. Rit soon & often.

Yours,
J. W. Parleir[6] to N. B. Parleir

180. January 27, 1865

Second Lieutenant Lewis Warlick, Company B, 11th Regiment N.C. Troops, letter to Laura McGimsey, Pleasant Hill, Burke County, North Carolina. Source: Laura C. McGimsey Papers (2680), Southern Historical Collection, Wilson Library, University of North Carolina at Chapel Hill.

In January of 1865, Lewis and his company were posted in the trenches outside Petersburg, Virginia. From the chimney corner of his winter cabin, Lewis' thoughts were obviously turned toward home and to Cornelia. In this letter, Lewis talks about Sergeant Galloway's absence and his desire and attempts to get a furlough. Lewis survived the war, but died shortly thereafter. His sweetheart, Laura Cornelia McGimsey, married William Avery,[7] instead of the man she courted for four years.

Near Petersburg
Jan 27th 1865

My dear Corrie,

Knowing you are always anxious to hear from me I have concluded to pen you a few lines today although it is remarkably cold and has been for several days, it seems that we are not to have any more pleasant weather soon. I have been jamed close up in the chimney corner for 3 or 4 days and calculate to hold my position as long as I can until detailed to go on picket again or some other duty.

Galloway[8] hasn't made his appearance yet and from what I hear from the crowded state of the roads, I give him till the first of next week to arrive—hope how soon he may come as I think in all probability he will bring me something good to eat. I went to Capt. Kerr Comdg. Regt. Last Monday and asked him if he would forward a furlough for me, he replied, no as Genl. MacRae had ordered him not to forward any more until those who were absent should report. I fear it will be some time before I will be able to get a furlough as nearly every officer in the regiment are waiting for the absentees to return so they can send up furloughs. I fear they will get in ahead of me, but I have studied out another plan, it is this. I'm going to Genl. MacRae and tell him I have some unsettled business at home that requires my immediate attention and I wish to have a furlough forwarded. It may be that he will forward mine instead of some others, if he should believe my statement. I do hope and trust that I will get home soon for I'm as anxious to see you. My health has improved but little since I last wrote—not sick enough for the surgeon to recommend me to the board for furlough and barely able to do duty.

Sometimes I wish I would just get sick enough to get a furlough but it may be wicked for me to wish that.

Everything is very quiet—no news afloat except camp rumors of every kind. Write often to your devoted

Lewis

181. January 31, 1865

Captain Alfred Bell, Company B, 39th Regiment N.C. Troops, letter to his wife, Mary Bell, Franklin, Macon County, N.C.

Source: Alfred Bell Papers (417), Manuscripts Department, Special Collections Library, Duke University.

In the first month of 1865, the Confederate Army of Tennessee was reeling from a disastrous campaign, culminating in the debacle at Nashville in December 1864. Bell was left as provost officer and was not involved in any major action. After the defeat, the three corps of the Army were scattered across Mississippi, Alabama, and Georgia, far way from the advancing army of William T. Sherman.

> Meridian Jan 31st 1865
>
> My Dear wife
>
> I again seat my self after a long silence to write again. I wrote you last from Corinth but I doubt whether you got it as Mr. Sherman cut communication from you & this section of the country.
>
> Well I reckon you have heard all about the Tenn campaign. I was not in that run. I was stoped at Corinth & was put on provost guard there during the campaign & when the armey fell back I was put in charge of prisoners & have been marching ever since for one month & came here day before yesterday tired down & wore out. I passed within a few miles of our regt at Tupelo, but was too tired to go see the boys. They sent me 2 letters from you dated 17 & 24 Nov which I assure you was gladly read as I had not recd any from you since Reid came & I have not saw him yet. I suppose I will git to see the boys soon as they are coming here as reports say that Stewart's corps is going to remain here. Lee's and Cheatam's to geo [Georgia]. The cars is covered with them goin to geo. Thare is a good many being furloughed. I dont know who out of my company. I for one shall resign as soon as the company arrives. If they will accept my resignation.
>
> I cant give you all the particulars of the casualties. My co has lost one—a recruit for Raleigh. Kill Morgan lost his left arm & was left. Marve Solomon— wounded and left in the hands of the enemy. Both are doing well. Bill Corbin was wounded by cannon ball on the back. Wash Thomas was wounded there too & was slight & will be able for service soon. Poke Rusill was shot through the thigh. All was doin well and was at Corinth when I left able to walk. Thomas Coleman & John Hall (Rob's son) was captured. Bob Hall also was wounded but I did not see him though the boys say he came out & was doin well.[9]
>
> I am sorry you have become dissatisfied with you Negroes.[10] I reckon your Rena & Dr. had better be back. I am also very sorry you have became dissatisfied with your farm. Well we will go to Texas as soon as the war closes. The people here have peace made now & an Armistice & everything else but war. So I dont know how it will turn out but the papers are full of peace news. I hope it is so but I have little confidence yet. I will send you some money first chance. I draw a months pay. I also have some yankee money I will send you. Do the best you can & dont give up. Tell Pa if he has the money I wish he would pay that Bill Siler debt for me.
>
> I am so nervous & tired & have rumatism that I cannot wright so well. You will have to excuse this as I am sitting by a pine tree wrighten in my knee. I will wright again in a few days. Kiss my sweat babies often for me. Love to all & believe me ever a devoted & true husband.
>
> I remain love, your own
> Alfred
>
> Direct to Meridian as I supposed we will stop here. I shall remain here unless the comdg leaves. I turned the prisoners over yesterday.

182. February 15, 1865

Captain Alfred Bell, Company B, 39th Regiment N.C. Troops, letter to his wife, Mary Bell, Franklin, Macon County, N.C. Source: Alfred Bell Papers (417), Manuscripts Department, Special Collections Library, Duke University.

The 39th, along with its fellow Tar Heels, the 29th North Carolina, of Ector's Brigade, formed the Mobile garrison and held that port city until the fall of Spanish Fort in April 1865. In March, Bell's resignation went through. Bell, however, remained with his regiment, as acting surgeon, relying on his abilities as a druggist, until the end of the war.[11]

> Mobile Ala
> Feby 15 1865
>
> My Dear Wife
> As John Vanhook[12] & others of my co start home in the morning I thought I would drop you a few lines as my letter by Sid Slagle[13] was short. I was too nervous to wright much of a letter yet altho I am not suffering from rhumatism so bad. I took & salts both today & its not operating much as I have had headache & my bowels hurt me for several days. So I thought I would help it by then purging my self.
>
> I have no war news to wright. We are all laying quitely in camp and are doing light dutey & get plenty of rations. I have not been on duty since I came to the comd. Capt Hughes[14] is in comd of the regt. He wanted me to take comd but I declined in his favor. So I recon he will be the Maj. He is a very clever fellow as the regt had no doctor he gave me the place to act as phsician. So its quite a pleasure position as thare is but little sickness in the Regt now.
>
> I sent by Sid Slagle 200 dollars, a gold pen & silver stock which I hope will go safe. I know it will. If he goes safe so you will see that I am not a spend thrift for I only drew 130 & sent you 200. I have 60 left to spend besides I have 30 in Yankee money which I could have sold at 12 for one. Don't you think our money is nearly plaid out?
>
> Well, I sent up my resignation on the

Paschal Hughes, a young officer, functioned as commander of the 39th for several months in 1864-1865. (North Carolina Division of Archives and History.)

6th inst. It was excepted by Coleman and Cockrell who comds the Div so I reckon it is all right. I also asked for leave of absence for 30 days. It was not granted so I reckon I shall have to wait for my promise to return from Richmond which generally takes a month but may take longer now Sherman has the road cut. I also hear that the armey is to organize this spring and give the officers 60 days to select their comds that is the oper [?]. I think it right & I don't care how soon it takes place.

Well, I am very anxious to hear from you & the babies. The last was dated the 29 Dec. It seams like it has been a year but I must endure in these war times but I would not if it was any other times but we must gain & endure & hope for peace & better times. It is thought we will draw money soon. I hope we will. I will try & settle with Jeff & not get so behind with him. I wish if Pa has they money he would pay the Bill Siler debt for me as it is due & I want it paid.

I was sorey to hear of the deaths in Old Macon. John Reids mother & old uncle John Hall but that is what we are bound for to die & we cannot avoid death. I am glad that the girls still want to marrey & do so on every occasion. One of my boys Jos Fulcher to write McConnells daughter & Jeff McConnell to Jos 3 daughters. Well, I reckon it right but if I was a single man I should not marrey untill the war was ended.

Mollie please excuse me for my shortness for I ashure you it is not because I don't want to wright but I am so nervous that it is a task beside it straining to me trying to study my [?] Wright me to Mobile Ectors Brig Frenchs Div as the corps is all gone to geo [Georgia]. None are here but French's Divison so leave off the Stewarts Corps. My love to all. I send you a news paper to read. I close. Kiss my babies for me. I ever remain
Your true loving
Alfred

183. February 24, 1865

Captain Julius Gash, Company D, 65th Regiment N.C. Troops (6th N.C. Cavalry), letter to his uncle, Henderson County, North Carolina. Source: Mary Gash Papers (59), Private Manuscripts Collection, North Carolina Division of Archives and History.

With the fall of Wilmington and Charleston, the army of William T. Sherman was closing in on the Confederate forces in North Carolina. Gash returned thanks for a letter he received from Daniel Carpenter and voiced his bleak outlook for the war's future prospects. After the war, Jule returned home; however, life in North Carolina could not satisfy him, and the veteran cavalryman moved to Texas where he remained for the rest of his life.[15]

Hd Qrtrs 6th N.C.Cavalry
24th February 1865

Dear Uncle

Your note enclosing a letter from Carpenter was thankfully received a few days ago. I was much pleased to hear from him as it had been so long since I had heard Dan give me fits about my sweet heart, according to his views. I will have to let him make the selection for me. I am very sorry Theodore and Thad will not get home while Old Price was in Mo. It would have been such a gratification to his mother could he have been permitted to visit home. You think the scales are very heavy over my eyes, they may be, but I cant see the hole yet. I may some day.

Sherman is playing the Devil generally seemingly unmolested. I still think he will get himself thrashed before he gets much farther into our country.

Chester S.C. was his HdQrtrs when last heard from. Charleston evacuated and Wilmington "gave up." We are daily expecting the Yanks on us here, and come they will very soon for their object will be to cooperate with the force at Wilmington and Sherman. I would be very much surprised if we [don't] get cut off down here if things do not change soon. Some time since we were all very much sated with the idea of an early peace, but after the return of the Commissioners, that was dead as a hammer. What the result may be yet remains to be seen. I am in very much hopes we will gain our independence.

I am not at all despondent notwithstanding there hangs a Dark Cloud over our horizon at this time. You did right in keeping the stamps. You might have kept them all as I had some. I hope you will not need any more to write to them as they are Exchanging all Prisoners. Give my love to Aus & family.

    Truly Yours
    Jule

184. February 26, 1865

Captain Lawson Harrill, Company I, 56th Regiment N.C. Troops, letter to Mrs. Griffin, Rutherford County, North Carolina. Source: G. W. Griffin Papers (153), Private Manuscripts Collection, North Carolina Division of Archives and History.

Captain Lawson Harrill served as an officer in the 56th Regiment from May 1, 1861. This Rutherford County physician was later promoted to first lieutenant and transferred to Company N, 16th North Carolina from Company D on April 7, 1862. Company N was assigned to the 56th Regiment as Company I on June 19, 1862, and Harrill became its captain.[16] In the following missive, Lawson attempts to justify his actions at Ware Bottom Church, Virginia, on May 20, 1864, and to assure one of George Griffin's four sisters that he did all he could.

Petersburg Va
Feby 26th 1865
Miss Griffin, My Friend

I received your letter two days ago making an inquiry about your brother George.[17] I can only say that he, with several others from my company were all killed or wounded near the same spot. I saw him when he fell. I also saw my only brother fall about the same time but I could not assist either.

I was not a little surprised at you for thinking I could have carried him off the field when I left brother Amos[18] lying by him and could not keep either without being captured myself. The yankees were charging us at the time and soon passed them where they lay. In a few minutes we drove them back till our wounded were in between the lines and Amos then, although mortally wounded, crawled on his hands and knees to our lines and was carried to the rear where he died. Don't you think it is reasonable to say that if I could have carried any one off the field I would not have left a brother there to fall into the hands of the enemy? And do you think it at all reasonable to say I could have saved a friend when I could not save a brother? Your brother was a particular friend of mine and there was no one except my brothers who are always first—that I would have favored sooner.

I think there is no doubt about his death. His wound through the bowels was mortal no doubt. I hope you will not longer think I could have performed an impossibility.

    Your friend
    L. Harrill

185. March 8, 1865

Private Edward Jones, "The Davis Dragoons," Company F, 41st Regiment N.C. Troops (3rd Cavalry), letter to his father, Edmund Jones, Clover Hill, Happy Valley, Caldwell County, N.C. Source:

Edmund Jones Papers (3543), Southern Historical Collection, Wilson Library, University of North Carolina at Chapel Hill.

Late war volunteers were few and far between for the Confederacy in 1865. Private Edward "Coot" Jones was one such volunteer. Despite losing two of his older brothers in the war, fifteen-year-old Edward volunteered sometime shortly before writing this letter.[19]

> In Camp at Stoney Creek Va
> March 8th
>
> Dear Father.
>
> I reached here all right yesterday evening & was forthwith received into the company & fortunate for me that I got here when I did for only one more man could get in the quota being filled. I can not write you a long letter as we are preparing to march to Dinwiddie C. H. I suppose we will be gone ten of twelve days before we return. I have found several old acquaintances since I came. The Regiment numbers 950 men but only five hundred present for duty (most the others being at home on detail). The Army I am sorry to say is deserting very badly. It is by far more general in infantry than in cavalry. Our Regiment, I am glad to say, has had but two. The third is a splendid regiment. We are drawing very good rations & the men are well satisfied. Father you must not be uneasy if you are several weeks together without a letter. The movements of cavalry are so uncertain. You must excuse this letter. I am writing on an inverted bread hay. It is inspection time. Write soon.
>
> Your Aff. Son
> E. Jones

186. March 14, 1865

Private Edward Jones, "The Davis Dragoons," Company F, 41st Regiment N.C. Troops (3rd Cavalry), letter to his father, Edmund Jones, Patterson, Caldwell County, N.C. Source: Edmund Jones Papers (3543), Southern Historical Collection, Wilson Library, University of North Carolina at Chapel Hill.

Edward Jones remained optimistic the week after his first letter and describes a false alarm and the good condition of the regiment in clothing and equipment. Jones survived the war and returned to Caldwell County where he and his wife raised four children: Eugenia, Augustus, Edmund, and Sarah. At the age of 22, Jones was elected to the General Assembly and served during the years 1870–1874 and 1879–1880. In 1898, Jones became a captain of Company C, 2nd US Volunteers and fought in the Spanish-American War.[20]

> March 14th Camp of 3rd N.C.
> Cavalry near Dinwiddie CH
>
> Dear father,
>
> We moved up here about a week ago from our old camp at Stoney Creek. We & the fifth Regiment are on picket now. The third is on reserve. We had a grand alarm Sunday morning early. They blowed us up an hour before day & had us in line of battle. The entire army of infantry, artillery & cavalry were in line. It proved to be the enemy sending some troops back to City Point to supply the place of some out from there to reinforce Scofield in NC.[21] I have seen several men from Petersburg who say that our hope there are faring [?] & have stopped deserting which I think is probable true for I know that we are faring very well. We get a third of a pound of meat a day & one pound of flour & sometimes one and a half. The men too are all well clothed. I have not seen a man barefooted since I came out. They all have good shoes.
>
> I like my company & officers as well as any I could have. Captain Perkins is a splendid old fellow & Lieut Bennet[22] is well as the rest of our Lieuts is a nice

fellow. The general impression is that we will have pretty hot work here soon as the roads get good enough.

Have the Bushwhackers committed any more depredations lately up there? I feel very anxious about you all up there. I do hope the quiet happy Valley will not be disturbed by them. Are they making any headway stopping them? You must keep me posted on the news there & I will do so far as is in my power to do the same here.

In your next letter please send me a few envelopes & some stamps as I have neither & the first chance you get send me some hard soap & a couple of cotton shirts. I forgot to mention in my last letter that Mr. Fries made me a present of a hat. I could not help myself so I had to take it & I still have that five dollars in specie.

I think I shall like the army first rate. The regiment is filling up rapidly now. I think in two months it will number 800. My paper is out so I must stop. My love to all in the Valley. Direct to E. Jones Co F, 3rd NC Cavalry, Barringer's Brig, W. H. F. Lee's Div, Army Northern Va.

    Your aff son
    E. Jones

187. March 15, 1865

Private Andrew J. Proffit, Company D, 18th Regiment N.C. Troops, letter to his father, William Proffit, Wilkes County. Source: Proffit Family Papers (3408), Southern Historical Collection, Wilson Library, University of North Carolina at Chapel Hill.

At Spotsylvania, in May of 1864, Lane's Brigade participated in some of the fiercest fighting on the eastern side of the famous "Mule Shoe." One of the soldiers captured at that battle was Andrew J. Proffit. Proffit was imprisoned once again, this time at Elmira, New York. Andrew was paroled and transferred on February 20, 1865, and was transferred to James River, Virginia, for exchange. After being exchanged prior to February 28, Proffit was admitted to a Richmond hospital. Proffit died "in the service of the Confederacy" on March 27, 1865, leaving Alfred Newton Proffit the only son of four to survive.[23]

    Rich Mond VA
    March 15th 1865
Dear father

I drop you a short note which will in form you that I am in Howard's grove hospittle. My health is quite bad though I do not think I am danger ous for I am improveing. I can get a furlough to come home. If I was able to come though I do not know when that will be. I have been sick so long ever since the middle of Nov. I can walk about the ward & set up a little. I hope to be at home in a few weeks. Tell mother that I shall want some fine beer & a great many nice little things to eat such as eggs pickles &tc. If there is any brandy in the country I want you to try to procure me a little as I am quite weak. I will close. Please write as soon as this comes to hand & direct thus to Gen Hospittle Howards Grove Second Division Ward "F," Rich Mond va.

    Yours Truly
    J. Proffit

188. March 22, 1865

Captain George W. F. Harper, Company H, 58th Regiment N.C. Troops, diary entry. Source: Harper Diaries, G. W. F. Harper Papers (313), Southern Historical Collection, Wilson Library, University of North Carolina at Chapel Hill.

The Battle of Bentonville was the last attempt by the Army of Tennessee and Department of North Carolina to oppose the advance of Sherman's forces, March 19–21, 1865. The initial attacks on Sherman's isolated wing proved successful with the rout of some XX Corps units. The success of the Army of Tennessee was unable to be followed up as their attack began to stall, and no progress was made against Morgan's Federal division on the left. With this defeat, Captain Harper and his command retreated westward with the Army of Tennessee. In the midst of all these events, Harper still noticed the peach trees.[24]

> Sun 19—clear, warm, pleas. Battle of Bentonville. Moved into line of battle 3 miles S. of B. at 10 a.m. Skirmish line soon afterwards driven in. Charged the enemy's works at 2 p.m. and carried 3 lines and broke the 4th but not supported and flanked out of last line. Enemy then charged in the open woods without defense and were repulsed. Obstinate fight until after dark without further change in disposition. Some artillery and prisoners captured. Firing ceased at 8 p.m. At 12 p.m. retired to the position we occupied that morning. 3 killed and 23 wounded in the Reg't. Mon 20—Clear, Pleas. 58th in front line breastworks with Petters Brig. Skirmishing in front and fighting going on on our left. Not well. Lt. L. W. G. returned. Tues 21—Rain, Cool, Same as yesterday. Not well. Wed 22—Clear, windy, pleas. Evacuated position at 2 a.m. and retired. Crossed 2nd creek north of Bentonville and bivouaced. Muddy road and tiresome walk. Threw up breastworks and waited for advance of the enemy who failed to make his appearance. Noon marched to within 6 or 7 miles of Smithfield and camped after dark. Road exceedingly wet and muddy. Tiresome and disagreeable march. Peach trees in bloom.

189. April 1, 1865

Unknown soldier, Company A, 2nd North Carolina Mounted Infantry (US), letter to Elizabeth J. Love, Henderson County. Source: Matthew N. Love Papers, Manuscripts Department, Special Collections Library, Duke University.

The identity of the author of this April fool's note is somewhat in question. Service records suggest that the soldier might have been Private Henry P. Evans, a Unionist who served in Company F, not A, of the 2nd North Carolina Mounted Infantry.[25] Included in this April fool is a marriage proposal, and, depending on the situation, some tongue-in-cheek humor.

> Asheville North Carolina
> April the 1st 1865
>
> Miss E J Love
>
> As to day is the first of April you know it is common for some one to play a prank on some young Girl or mother and I thought I would write you a note and let you known that their was some one a going to give you a April fool but you may look out for it for it is a coming as sertain as you ar 17 years old. I was a going to ask you one question but I believe that my heart will fail I think if I stay in this war much longer. I will get courreg a nuf to pass the question as they call it. I hav to take a Chaw O tobacco then I think I can do it. I believe my heart will fail yet if you will a gree and marry me. I would be the happyest man in the world although I am in this war and I never saw you but I recieved a discreptive list of you the other day and the discriptions suited me and I thought now was my time. I am a man about 30 years of age and that may brake it up. I am a good war man and I under stood that you was and I think that we will make a verry nice match for I would not have a Girl if she was not for her country. Well I will close hoping to hear from you soon. Adress H. P. E. Asheville, Co A, 2nd Battalion,
>
> Yours,
> APRIL FOOL

190. April 16, 1865

Captain John L. Swain, Company B, 17th Regiment N.C. Troops (2nd Organization), letter to Julius, Buncombe County, North Carolina. Source: John L. Swain Papers (3074), Southern Historical Collection, Wilson Library, University of North Carolina at Chapel Hill.

With the defeat at Bentonville, the Confederate army was all but through and streaming westward. Captain Swain received a letter from his brother Julius, who had sworn to volunteer, even at this late stage in the war. This letter demonstrates Swain's concern for the life of his brother, and shows a Confederate officer who has come to grips with the impending defeat of the Confederate army.

> Camp near Smithfield NC
> Monday April 16th 1865
> Dear Juilus
> Your favor of some time ago came to hand in good time expressing a determination to enter the field of strife if Gen. S occupied Goldsboro. He has done so and I may gather from that, that you are either in or expecting shortly to be in the army. Now as one who has fully tried it and whose heart is in the cause, and who sadly feels the necessity of more men yet for your Ma and Sisters sake I would advise you that you remain with them as long as you can. The laws of the land now give no room for the display of patriotism and even if it did, patriotism is not rewarded.
> There is a dark cloud hanging over our country and every passing breeze comes laiden with the din of war, devastation, and death. The sun in his course at midday is frequently shut out by a dense column of smoke, from consuming wealth but it is useless to attempt to discribe what has no word to discribe. It is perfectly horrible but orders have come and I must stop here. Let me hear from you soon. Give my best regards to all your dear family and trust in a gracious Providence.
> J. L. Swain[26]

North Carolina Union troops, such as Hugh Hamilton's 2nd North Carolina, occupied Asheville after the surrender. (United States Army Military History Institute, Carlisle, Pa.)

Appendix 1: Distribution of Letters, Diary Entries, by County and Author (166 Letters, 22 Diary Entries, 2 Miscellaneous)

Distribution of entries

County	Number of Entries	Author
Alleghany	0	None
Ashe	6	Thornton Sexton, Marion Sexton
Buncombe	31	William Brown, Robert Vance, Zebulon Vance, Thomas Patton, John W. Reese, R. G. Freeman, Joseph Henry, John L. Swain, William Whitaker, Job Redmond, Tom Weaver
Burke	22	Lewis Warlick, Clark M. Avery, Laura C. McGimsey, I. Whisenhunt, John Walton, Isaac E. Avery, E. A. Perkins, Todd Caldwell, Eliza Walton
Caldwell	16	John T. Jones, Walter Jones, Robert Blair, George W.F. Harper, Edward Jones
Cherokee	4	Stephen Whitaker
Clay	0	None
Haywood	13	Roland Osborne, G. Cunningham, Asbury Rogers, W. W. Stringfield Wesley Freeman, Joseph Cathey, William J. Smathers
Henderson	14	C. P. Gash, John H. Kinzey, James Love, Matt Love,

Appendix 1. Distribution of Entries by County and Author

County	Number of Documents	Author
		Harvey Gash, Samuel Love, George W. Love, Robert Love, Martin Gash, Union soldier (?)
Jackson	3	William Thomas, William Cathey
McDowell	1	Rev. Robert Abernethy
Macon	10	Mary Bell, David W. Siler, Alfred Bell, William Tippett, Thomas Gash
Madison	5	Virgil Lusk
Mitchell	0	None
Polk	1	Anonymous
Rutherford	4	Tolivar Davis, Lorraine W. Griffin, Lawson Harrill
Surry	8	James H. Baker, Azariah Denny, Joel Denny
Transylvania	6	Addie Patton, John Phillips, Juilus Gash, Harriet Gash
Watauga	9	Jordan Council, William Horton, George Adams, Phillip Shull
Wilkes	30	Calvin Leach, James B. Gordon, William Proffit, Alfred Proffit, Andrew Proffit, Calvin Proffit James Wright, Phillip Walsh, Jesse Miller, James Parleir
Yancey	2	James R. Neill, John W. McElroy

Appendix 2.
Units with at Least Four Companies from the Mountains

UNITS WITH ALL COMPANIES FROM THE MOUNTAINS

    6th Regiment N.C. Cavalry (65th N.C. Troops
    7th Regiment N.C. Cavalry (69th N.C. Troops)
    16th Regiment N.C. Troops (6th N.C. Volunteers)
    25th Regiment N.C. Troops
    29th Regiment N.C. Troops
    39th Regiment N.C. Troops
    58th Regiment N.C. Troops
    60th Regiment N.C. Troops
    62nd Regiment N.C. Troops
    64th Regiment N.C. Troops
    Love's Regiment (Infantry), Thomas' Legion
    5th Battalion N.C. Cavalry
    7th Battalion N.C. Cavalry
    Indian (Cherokee) Battalion, Thomas' Legion
    Walker's (Cavalry) Battalion, Thomas' Legion
    2nd Regiment N.C. Mounted Infantry (US)
    3rd Regiment N.C. Mounted Infantry (US)

UNITS WITH AT LEAST FOUR COMPANIES FROM THE MOUNTAINS

    1st Regiment N.C. Cavalry (9th N.C. Troops)
    22nd Regiment N.C. Troops (12th N.C. Volunteers)
    26th Regiment N.C. Troops
    34th Regiment N.C. Troops
    37th Regiment N.C. Troops

Appendix 3. Companies Organized in Mountain Counties[1]

ALLEGHANY COUNTY

Company F, 22nd N.C. Troops (the "Allegheny True Blues")
Company K, 37th N.C. Troops (the "Allegheny Tigers")
Company D, 70th N.C. Troops (Jr Res) (part)
96th Militia Regiment

ASHE COUNTY

Company A, 9th N.C. Troops (1st Cavalry)
Company A, 26th N.C. Troops (the "Jeff Davis Mountain Rifles")
Company A, 34th N.C. Troops (the "Laurel Springs Guard")
Company A, 37th N.C. Troops (the "Ashe Beaureguard Riflemen")
Company L, 58th N.C. Troops
Company M, 58th N.C. Troops (part)
Company D, 70th N.C. Troops (Jr Res) (part)
66th Battalion Home Guard
97th Militia Regiment

BUNCOMBE COUNTY

Company E, 1st N.C. Volunteers (the "Buncombe Rifles")
Company G, 9th N.C. Troops (1st Cavalry) (the "Buncombe Rangers")
Company F, 14th N.C. Troops (the "Rough and Ready Guards")
Company F, 16th N.C. Troops
Company H, 25th N.C. Troops (the "Cane Creek Rifles")
Company I, 25th N.C. Troops (the "Pisgah Guards")
Company K, 25th N.C. Troops (the "Black Mountain Guards")
Company C, 29th N.C. Troops (the "Bold Mountain Tigers")
Company H, 29th N.C. Troops (the "Buncombe Lifeguards")
Company D, 39th N.C. Troops (the "Highland Grays")
Company A, 60th N.C. Troops (the "Buncombe Light Artillery")
Company C, 60th N.C. Troops
Company E, 60th N.C. Troops (the "Buncombe Farmers")
Company F, 60th N.C. Troops
Company K, 60th N.C. Troops
Company B, 69th N.C. Troops (7th N.C. Cavalry)
Company C, 69th N.C. Troops (7th N.C. Cavalry)
Company F, 69th N.C. Troops (7th N.C. Cavalry)
Company I, 69th N.C. Troops (7th N.C. Cavalry)

Appendix 3. Companies Organized in Mountain Counties

Company K, 69th N.C. Troops (7th N.C. Cavalry)
Company A, 70th N.C. Troops (Jr Res)
42nd Battalion Home Guard
108th Militia Regiment
109th Militia Regiment

BURKE COUNTY

Company G, 1st N.C. Volunteers (the "Burke Rifles")
Company D, 6th N.C. Troops
Company E, 6th N.C. Troops
Company D, 11th N.C. Troops
Company E, 16th N.C. Troops (the "Burke Tigers")
Company K, 35th N.C. Troops (part) ("Burke & Catawba Sampsons")
Company F, 41st N.C. Troops (the "Davis Dragoons")
8th Regiment Home Guard
100th Militia Regiment
101st Militia Regiment

CALDWELL COUNTY

Company A, 22nd N.C. Troops (the "Caldwell Rough & Ready Boys")
Company F, 26th N.C. Troops (the "Hibriten Guards")
Company I, 26th N.C. Troops (the "Caldwell Guards")
Company E, 58th N.C. Troops
Company H, 58th N.C. Troops
19th Battalion Home Guard
95th Militia Regiment

CHEROKEE COUNTY

Company A, 19th N.C. Troops (2nd Cavalry) (the "Cherokee Rangers")
Company D, 25th N.C. Troops ("George's Guards")
Company A, 29th N.C. Troops (the "Cherokee Guards")
Company A, 39th N.C. Troops
Company C, 39th N.C. Troops
Company F, 39th N.C. Troops
Company G, 39th N.C. Troops
Company H, 39th N.C. Troops
Indian Battalion (4), Thomas' Legion

Company H, Love's Regt., Thomas' Legion
Company I, Love's Regt., Thomas' Legion
Company A, Walker's Bttn., Thomas' Legion
Company B, Walker's Bttn., Thomas' Legion
Company E, Walker's Bttn., Thomas' Legion (part)
Company H, Walker's Bttn., Thomas' Legion
47th Battalion Home Guard
115th Militia Regiment

CLAY COUNTY

Company G, 25th N.C. Troops (part) (the "Highland Guards")
Company E, 39th N.C. Troops
Company B, 62nd N.C. Troops
Company E, Walker's Bttn., Thomas' Legion (part)
116th Militia Regiment

HAYWOOD COUNTY

Company C, 25th N.C. Troops (the "Haywood Invincibles")
Company F, 25th N.C. Troops (the "Haywood Highlanders")
Company E, 29th N.C. Troops (the "Haywood Fireshooters")
Company A, 62nd N.C. Troops
Company C, 62nd N.C. Troops
Company I, 62nd N.C. Troops
Company E, 69th N.C. Troops (7th Cavalry)
Company C, 70th N.C. Troops (Jr Res) (Part)
Company C, Love's Regt., Thomas' Legion
Company E, Love's Regt., Thomas' Legion
38th Battalion Home Guard
112th Militia Regiment

HENDERSON COUNTY

Company I, 16th N.C. Troops
Company A, 25th N.C. Troops (the "Edney Greys")
Company G, 35th N.C. Troops (the "Henderson Rifles")
Company D, 60th N.C. Troops (the "Henderson Rangers")
Company G, 69th N.C. Troops (7th Cavalry)
Company C, 70th N.C. Troops (Jr Res) (part)
41st Battalion Home Guard
106th Militia Regiment

Appendix 3. Companies Organized in Mountain Counties

JACKSON COUNTY

Company B, 25th N.C. Troops (the "Jackson Guards")
Company F, 29th N.C. Troops (the "Jackson Avengers")
Company K, 39th N.C. Troops (the "Jackson Rangers")
Company G, 62nd N.C. Troops
Company H, 62nd N.C. Troops
Company F, Love's Regt., Thomas' Legion (part) ("Conley's Sharpshooters")
Company G, Love's Regt., Thomas' Legion
113th Militia Regiment

MCDOWELL COUNTY

Company E, 6th N.C. Troops (part)
Company B, 22nd N.C. Troops (the "McDowell Rifles")
Company K, 22nd N.C. Troops (the "McDowell Boys")
Company B, 35th N.C. Troops (the "Marion Men")
Company F, 58th N.C. Troops (the "McDowell Rangers")
Company A, 70th N.C. Troops (Jr Res) (part)
58th Battalion Home Guard
102nd Militia Regiment

MACON COUNTY

Company K, 9th N.C. Troops (1st Cavalry) (the "Nantahala Rangers")
Company H, 16th N.C. Troops
Company G, 25th N.C. Troops (part) (the "Highland Guards")
Company B, 39th N.C. Troops
Company I, 39th N.C. Troops
Company D, 62nd N.C. Troops
Company A, 65th N.C. Troops (6th Cavalry)
Company B, 65th N.C. Troops (6th Cavalry)
Company C, 65th N.C. Troops (6th Cavalry)
Company G, 65th N.C. Troops (6th Cavalry)
Company F, Love's Regt., Thomas' Legion (part) ("Conley's Sharpshooters")
114th Militia Regiment

MADISON COUNTY

Company H, 2nd Battalion N.C. Troops (the "Madison Guards")
Company B, 16th N.C. Troops
Company D, 29th N.C. Troops
Company B, 60th N.C. Troops
Company I, 60th N.C. Troops (the "French Broad Guards")
Company A, 64th N.C. Troops
Company C, 64th N.C. Troops
Company D, 64th N.C. Troops
Company E, 64th N.C. Troops
Company F, 64th N.C. Troops
Company G, 64th N.C. Troops
Company L, 64th N.C. Troops
Company M, 64th N.C. Troops
Company D, 69th N.C. Troops (7th Cavalry)
110th Militia Regiment

MITCHELL COUNTY

Company E, 6th N.C. Troops (part)
Company I, 29th N.C. Troops
Company A, 58th N.C. Troops (the "Mitchell Rangers")
Company B, 58th N.C. Troops
Company K, 58th N.C. Troops
99th Militia Regiment

POLK COUNTY

Company K, 16th N.C. Troops
Company I, 54th N.C. Troops (the "Tryon Guards")
Company G, 60th N.C. Troops
Company C, 70th N.C. Troops (Jr Res) (part)
28th Battalion Home Guard
105th Militia Regiment

RUTHERFORD COUNTY

Company D, 16th N.C. Troops
Company G, 16th N.C. Troops
Company B, 34th N.C. Troops (the "Sandy Run Yellow Jackets")
Company C, 34th N.C. Troops (the "Rutherford Rebels")
Company I, 34th N.C. Troops (the "Rutherford Band")

Appendix 3. Companies Organized in Mountain Counties

Company G, 50th N.C. Troops (the "Rutherford Farmers")
Company I, 50th N.C. Troops (the "Rutherford Rebels")
Company K, 50th N.C. Troops (the "Green River Rifles")
Company F, 62nd N.C. Troops
Company B, 70th N.C. Troops (Jr Res) (Part)
69th Battalion Home Guard
103rd Militia Regiment
104th Militia Regiment

Surry County

Company B, 2nd Battalion N.C. Troops
Company A, 2nd N.C. Troops
Company C, 21st N.C. Troops
Company H, 21st N.C. Troops
Company I, 21st N.C. Troops
Company A, 28th N.C. Troops (the "Surry Regulators")
Company E, 53rd N.C. Troops (the "Farmer Boys")
Company H, 54th N.C. Troops (part)
21st Battalion Home Guard
73rd Militia Regiment
74th Militia Regiment

Transylvania County

Company E, 25th N.C. Troops (the "Transylvania Volunteers")
Company E, 62nd N.C. Troops
Company K, 62nd N.C. Troops
Company D, 65th N.C. Troops (6th Cavalry)
Company A, 69th N.C. Troops (7th Cavalry)
Company H, 69th N.C. Troops (7th Cavalry
107th Militia Regiment

Watauga County

Company D, 9th N.C. Troops (1st Cavalry) (the "Watauga Rangers")
Company B, 37th N.C. Troops (the "Watauga Marksmen")
Company E, 37th N.C. Troops (the "Watauga Minutemen")
Company D, 58th N.C. Troops (the "Watauga Boys")
Company I, 58th N.C. Troops
Company M, 58th N.C. Troops (part)
11th Battalion Home Guard
98th Militia Regiment

Wilkes County

Company B, 1st N.C. Troops (the "Wilkes Valley Guards")
Company C, 26th N.C. Troops (the "Wilkes Volunteers"
Company D, 33rd N.C. Troops (the "Wilkes Regulators")
Company F, 37th N.C. Troops (the "Western Carolina Stars")
Company K, 42nd N.C. Troops (part)
Company F, 52nd N.C. Troops (the "Wilkes Greys")
Company K, 53rd N.C. Troops (the "Wilkes Rangers")
Company E, 54th N.C. Troops (the "Higland Guards")
Company G, 54th N.C. Troops (the "Wilkes Guards")
Company B, 55th N.C. Troops
Company D, 70th N.C. Troops (Jr Res) (part)
68th Battalion Home Guard
92nd Militia Regiment
93rd Militia Regiment

Yancey County

Company C, 16th N.C. Troops
Company B, 29th N.C. Troops
Company G, 29th N.C. Troops
Company K, 29th N.C. Troops
Company C, 58th N.C. Troops (the "Yancey Boys")
72nd Battalion Home Guard
111th Militia Regiment

Appendix 4: List of Employees at Asheville Armory

This list of operatives was found among the papers of Governor Zebulon Baird Vance. The roster was dated November 13, 1862, and contained a list of the all male operatives and their assignments at the armory, in order to ensure their exemption from the Conscription Act. This list does not include the ages of the men; however, the vast majority fell under the age of twenty-eight.[2]

Name	Occupation
A. W. King	Act'g Master Armorer
Z. L. Clayton	Military. Storekeeper
A. M. Kitzmiller	Clerk
E. Clayton	Carpenter Foreman
W. D. Riley	Filer Foreman
W. D. Copeland	Barrels Foreman
J. Hildebrand, Jr	Machinery Foreman
Joseph Reed	Smiths Foreman
George W. Whitson	Stocking Foreman
A. D. Ashe	Stoker
Erwin Boone	Smith
James Begg	Machinist
W. F. Baird	Machinist
M. C. Benson	Filer
H. M. Bright	Carpenter
C. S. Bechtler	Capt of Guard

Appendix 4. List of Employees at Asheville Armory

Name	Occupation
George Britt	Collier
Robert A. Ballew	Barrel Borer
X Brank	Pattern maker
W. A. J. Barnett	Polisher
John Ballew	Filer
A. Bechtler	Filer
M. G. Buckner	Filer
W. F. Brank	Wood Chopper
C. B. Brank	Getting lumber
L. Creasman	Teamster
J. A. Clark	Guard
Alsey Cordell	Wood Hauler
J. J. Dirigler	Guard
E. Ensley	Smith
David Foard	Asst. Founder
Herman Frants	Rifler
H. N. Francis	Filer
S. C. Fradey	Polisher
W. Gillespie	Filer
George Goodlake	Hauling charcoal
A. M. Gibson	Asst Smith
Hamilton	Getting lumber
A. E. M. Howard	Machinists
James Hurdner	Filer
R. Holesclaw	Filer
J. Hildebrand, Sr	Barrel turner
Joseph Henley	Smith
A. W. Hopper	Asst Smith
S. T. Hopper	Smith
D. H. Hamilton	Getting lumber
G. M. Jetton	Filer
Noah Jacobs	Pattern maker
W. M. Justus	Filer
W. D. Justus, Jr	Filer
L. M. Jordan	Smith
Archibald Kitzmiller	Machinist
Jennings Kitzmiller	Barrel Corer
G. S. Kirby	Armcaler
Hugh Keman	Hauling wood
J. M. Lang	Grinder

Appendix 4. List of Employees at Asheville Armory

Name	Occupation
L. H. Lick	Smith
J. W. Linfield	Filer
J. M. Ledford	Carpenter
L. T. Miller	Smith
J. F. Miller	Shoptender
Pink Miller	Shoptender
Thomas Miller	Barrel Corer
R. R. Maxwell	Barrel Corer
C. R. McIntuff	Smith
William Martin	Machinist
J. E. Mabers	Machinist
John Matthew	Guard
C. C. Matthews	Wood Chopper
J. J. A. Moore	Asst Smith
John Rowe	Smith
H. Reichart	Stocker 40
James T. Reed	Filer
Abner Rhodes	Stocker
H. N. Reid	Machinist
E. D. Ramsey	Machinist
C. C. Rush	Machinist
W. R. Reed	Filer
J. A. Reed	Miller/ Driller
H. C. Roberts	Asst Smith
S. M. Reed	Filer
W. Rudisill	Filer
W. R. Ragland	Founder
C. W. Rilet	Miller. Driller
J. L. Rice	Hauling charcoal
J. T. Sorrel	Guard
Carl Seidel	Shoptender
B. F. Staggs	Filer
G. W. Staggs	Miller/ Driller
C. Stradley	Miller/ Driller
Frost Snow	Stocker
E. W. Stubbs	Machinist
S. U. Swanson	Smith
J. D. Smith	Asst Smith
T. W. Swan	Asst Smith
Thomas Stradley	Wood chopper

Appendix 4. List of Employees at Asheville Armory

Name	Occupation
J. L. Swanson	Smith
Riley Sercey	Teamster
W. E. Smith	Hauling Firewood
Richard Tranthern	Smith
N. H. Woods	Smith
G. B. Wing	Tool maker
J. L. Wilkie	Tool maker
A. Westmoreland	Furnace Man
J. Westmoreland	Shoptender
N. E. Walker	Asst Smith

Appendix 5: Letter Writers and Diarists Herein Who Died in Service

Colonel Isaac E. Avery, Burke County
Private James H. Baker, Surry County
Private Azariah Denny, Surry County
Brigadier General James B. Gordon, Wilkes County
Private William D. Horton, Watauga County
Lieutenant Colonel John T. Jones, Caldwell County
Private Walter L. Jones, Caldwell County
Private John H. Kimzey, Henderson County
Private Calvin Leach, Wilkes County
Private Roland C. Osborne, Haywood County
Private Andrew J. Proffit, Wilkes County
Private Calvin L. Proffit, Wilkes County
Private William H. Proffit, Wilkes County
Private Job Redmond, Buncombe County
Private John W. Reese, Buncombe County
Sergeant William J. Smathers, Haywood County
Second Lieutenant Lewis Warlick, Burke County

Appendix 6: A Poem Composed by Private Harvey Davis

The following poem was composed in rhymed couplets by Private Davis of the Watauga Rangers, Company D, First North Carolina Cavalry on February 16, 1864, with the help of J. C. Critcher.

On the 16th day of February Commenced our march both long & dreary.
On the night of the first days travel, We encamped near Mitchel in a muddy level.
We groomed our horses, baked our bread, Broke off pine brush and made our bed.
Ere 10 oclock were all asleep, But the lonely sentinel who watch did keep.
When on our beds down first we lay, The stars shown bright and brilliantly.
But ere that we had closed our eyes A dismal cloud obscured the skies.
When near midnight we did awake, The snow came pitting flake by flake,
Which caused each head to cover As in Infant days by a fond Mother.
Ere the gray gleams in the East did peep, The snow was nearly shoe top deep.
When the bugle did us awake, And bid us from our slumbers break.
Off to the fence, to get some rails, The loss of which the widow bewails.
We built our fires, cooked our repast, And still the snow was falling fast.
Near 10 oclock the Genl. did sound. And when the Officers tents pulled down
(Whitaker, Boykin &.Gains, they had tents),'" Then on our weary Journey bent
Oer broken road & rotten land. Near 10 oclock crossed the Rapidann.
That eve the secrets of our soul did unravel As we through muddy lanes did travel.
And ere from our stupor arouse, We had arrived at Orange Court House.
Then through long lanes and at the end, turned into the woods the night to spend.
And to the fence we quick applied, Built up fires and soon were dried.
With our feet snow scraped away, Spread our blankets and down we lay.
By this time the weather had changed, from falling snow to drizzling rains.
By next morn we all were wet, and the rain was thickly falling yet.

Notes

1861

1. Vance would go on to be captain of Company D, 4th N.C. Volunteers, colonel of the 26th N.C. Troops, and Governor of North Carolina. William Caleb Brown served as assistant quartermaster of the 14th N.C. Troops, and would have been appointed to serve with the Vance administration, if he had not died of disease in Richmond on July 6, 1862. Samuel met the same fate as William, dying months earlier in February 1862 at Smithfield, Virginia. John E. Brown would go on to become one of New Zealand's most prominent citizens and legislators. Louis Manarin and Weymouth T. Jordan, *North Carolina Troops 1861-1865: A Roster* (Raleigh: N.C. Division of Archives and History, 1966–), 5: 386, 394, 444-446. Hereafter cited as "Manarin and Jordan, *N.C. Troops*." Summary, William J. Brown Papers, Southern Historical Collection. Greg Mast, *State Troops and Volunteers: A Photographic Record of North Carolina's Civil War Soldiers* (Raleigh: N.C. Division of Archives and History, 1996), 85. Hereafter cited as "Mast, *State Troops and Volunteers.*"

2. Manarin and Jordan, *N.C. Troops*, 3:40. A previous transcription of these letters was completed by Mike and Carolyn Lawing of Durham, N.C. It was also featured in various issues of the *Burke County Genealogical Society Journal*. Hereafter cited as "Lawing, *Warlick Civil War Letters.*"

3. Private G. W. Anthony volunteered at Morganton on April 18, 1861. He was mustered out of service in November 1861. Manarin and Jordan, *N.C. Troops*, 3:36

4. More than likely, these are the sisters of Portland and Lewis Warlick. Editorial note from Lawing, *Warlick Civil War Letters*, 3.

5. Captain Clarke Moulton Avery, commander of Company G at this time. Avery was a son of the prominent Avery family of Morganton, and would later go on to serve as a colonel in the 33rd North Carolina Troops.

6. Robert B. Vance would become and officer as well. In the summer of 1861, Vance recruited his own company, the "Buncombe Life Guards" which became part of the 29th North Carolina Troops. Vance was promoted to colonel of the 29th North Carolina, and after the Battle of Murfreesboro, served as acting brigade commander. Vance was appointed to head the Department of Western North Carolina in early 1862 and discharged this duty until January 1864, when he was captured in east Tennessee. Frontis Johnston, ed., *The Papers of Zebulon B. Vance* (Raleigh: North Carolina Division of Archives and History, 1964), xx–xxi, 2, 66–68. Hereafter cited as "Johnston, *Zeb Vance Papers.*"

7. The companies reported here under their captains eventually formed the core of the 16th North Carolina Troops; Robert G. A. Love's (Henderson) company—Company L; John Peek's (Madison) company—Company B; Shipp's (Henderson) company—Company I;

John S. McElroy's (Yancey) company—Company C. Johnston, Vance Letters, 102–103; Manarin and Jordan, *N.C. Troops*, 6: 50–75.

8. William John Brown. Refer to William J. Brown, letter to John E. Brown, April 26, 1861.

9. Information from author's personal research and from Isaac T. Avery, Jr., "Clark Moutlon Avery," in *Burke County Heritage* (Winston-Salem: Hunter Publishing, 1985), 79; Isaac T. Avery, Jr., "Clark Moulton Avery," in William S. Powell, ed., *Dictionary of North Carolina Biography*, Six Volumes (Chapel Hill: U.N.C. Press, 1979), 1:67–68, hereafter cited as "Powell, *N.C. Biographical Dictionary*"; Manarin and Jordan, *N.C. Troops*, 3:36; and Edward H. Phifer, "Saga of a Burke County Family," *North Carolina Historical Review*, 39 (1962).

10. Refers to Colonel Daniel Harvery Hill of the 1st Regiment N.C. Volunteers. Colonel Hill was an officer during the Mexican War, a professor at Washington College in Lexington, Virginia, and at Davidson College in Mecklenburg County, N.C., as well as the founder of the North Carolina Military Institute in Charlotte.

11. The Gash-Patton-Osborne family is mentioned several times in this work. Adeline Gash Patton (September 30, 1831–July 13, 1899) married Eli Patton sometime prior to 1860. Addie survived the war and lived out her life in Boyd township of Transylvania County, North Carolina, and was buried at Davidson River Presbyterian Church. *Notes on Gash Family*.

12. On June 29, 1861, seventy-nine men volunteered for service at Waynesville. After recruiting more troops through August 1861, this group of men became known as the "Haywood Highlanders" and served under the command of Captain Thomas Isaac Lenoir. Among these troops was Addie's brother, Roland C. Osborne. Manarin and Jordan, *N.C. Troops*, 7: 414.

13. Julius Gash, Company E, 7th Battalion, N.C. Cavalry.

14. The return of settlers to their ancestral homes was not uncommon. Another example of this was Davidson County farmer Henry Shoaf, who would return to his home in Pennsylvania for six months every two years. Other examples includes the McAfees of Cleveland County, moving between North Carolina and Texas.

15. Manarin and Jordan, *N.C. Troops*, 3:161; and Federal Census of Wilkes County: 1860.

16. Colonel Montford S. Stokes commanded the 1st North Carolina State Troops.

17. Paul Branch, "James Byron Gordon," in Powell, *N.C. Biographical Dictionary*, 2:318–319; and Manarin and Jordan, *N.C. Troops*, 2:8.

18. Hamilton "Allen" Brown succeeded James B. Gordon in command of the "Wilkes Valley Guards." Brown led company B through 1861 and commanded the company in action during the Seven Days Battles around Richmond. On July 8, 1862, Brown was promoted to lieutenant colonel and served in that role until wounded in action at Payne's Farm, Virginia, on November 27, 1863. After a brief recovery, Brown was promoted to colonel in December 1863, and commanded the regiment until he was captured at Fort Stedman, Virginia, on March 25, 1865. After the war Brown married Amelia Gwyn and the couple moved to Columbia, Tennessee. Sarah Holeman, "Hamilton Allen Brown," in Powell, *N.C. Biographical Dictionary*, 1:246; and Manarin and Jordan, *N.C. Troops*, 3:141, 155.

19. Colonel Robert Ransom of Warren County, N.C., who served as a commander in United States Cavalry before resigning at the onset of the war. Manarin and Jordan, *N.C. Troops*, 2:7.

20. Walter Jones served in Company A, 22nd North Carolina until February 24, 1863, when he was transferred to Company I, 26th N.C. Troops. Jones was wounded and captured at Gettysburg, Pennsylvania, on July 1–3, 1863. He died shortly thereafter. Manarin and Jordan, *N.C. Troops*, 7:19, 579. Family information from Federal Census of Caldwell County: 1860.

21. General Theophilus Hunter Holmes, a native of Sampson County, was a West Point graduate and a major in the 8th United States Infantry during the Mexican War. With the outbreak of the Civil War, Holmes was commissioned a brigadier general on June 5, 1861, and major general on October 7, 1861. Holmes commanded a brigade at Manassas, and a division through the Peninsula Campaign. After June 1862, Holmes served as a commander in Arkansas, and helped organize the N.C. Junior and Senior Reserves. Holmes died in 1880 and is buried in Fayetteville, North Carolina. Ezra

Warner, *Generals in Gray* (Baton Rouge: LSU Press, 1956), 141.

22. Colonel Charles C. Tew, 2nd North Carolina and Colonel Montford S. Stokes, 1st North Carolina.

23. Nickname for Edmund Jones, Walter's younger brother.

24. John Thomas Jones was the second son of Edmund and Sophia Jones, and two years older than his brother Walter who was currently serving in the 12th North Carolina Volunteers. Manarin and Jordan, *N.C. Troops*, 3:22, 7:563; and Federal Census of Caldwell County: 1860.

25. The field officers of the 26th North Carolina Troops included Colonel Zebulon Baird Vance, an Asheville lawyer and United States Congressman, who had previously served as a company commander in the 4th N.C. Volunteers. Lieutenant Colonel Henry King Burgwyn graduated from the University of North Carolina in 1859, and soon thereafter entered the Virginia Military Institute. With the outbreak of the war, Burgywn was recommended for a commission by his professor, Thomas Jackson, for a commission in the artillery. Burgwyn, not even twenty years of age, was assigned to duty as a drillmaster, and was later elected colonel. Major Abner Bynum Carmichael of Wilkes County was elected on August 27, 1861. Carmichael served as major until he was wounded in the mouth and neck at New Bern on March 14, 1862, and died shortly after. Manarin and Jordan, *N.C. Troops*, 7:463; and George Underwood, *History of the 26th Regiment N.C. Troops* (Raleigh: Edwards & Broughton, 1900), 103–104.

26. Third Lieutenant Milton Blair would be promoted to second lieutenant on September 1, 1862, and then first lieutenant on September 27, 1862. Blair was reported present until wounded at Wilderness, Virginia, and was then reported absent until he returned on July 1, 1864. He was present after this brief absence until he was paroled at Appomattox Court House, Virginia, on April 9, 1865. Manarin and Jordan, *N.C. Troops*, 7:573.

27. Sidney E. Conley died at Camp Fayetteville near Yorktown, Virginia, on October 10, 1861. Manarin and Jordan, *N.C. Troops*, 3: 675 (Addenda).

28. Federal Census of Wilkes County: 1860; and Manarin and Jordan, *N.C. Troops*, 3:163.

29. Corporal Thomas C. Land, Company B, 1st North Carolina State Troops. Manarin and Jordan, *N.C. Troops*, 3:160.

30. All acquaintances of the Proffit family serving in Company B, 1st North Carolina State Troops, Manarin and Jordan, *N.C. Troops*, 3:157, 163, 165–166.

31. Johnston, *Zeb Vance Papers*, I–XXIX; John G. Barrett, "Zebulon Baird Vance," in Powell, *N.C. Biographical Dictionary*, 6:85–87; and Manarin and Jordan, *N.C. Troops*, 7:463.

32. Edward W. Herndon was Vance's brother-in-law and served as a private in Vance's first company. Herndon was promoted to first lieutenant on September 20, 1861, and was appointed assistant quartermaster of the 29th N.C. Troops, and later served on the staff of another brother-in-law, General Robert B. Vance, commanding the Western North Carolina District. Afterwards, Herndon served as a quartermaster in Lane's brigade for a brief time before becoming a probate judge in Buncombe County. Manarin and Jordan, *N.C. Troops*, 5:445; Johnston, *Zeb Vance Papers*, 118.

33. Manarin and Jordan, *N.C. Troops*, 3:280; Federal Census of Surry County: 1860; and Hester B. Jackson, *Surry County Soldiers in the Civil War* (Dobson, N.C.: Surry County Historical Society, 1992), 13. Hereafter cited as "Jackson, *Surry County Soldiers*."

34. Manarin and Jordan, *N.C. Troops*, 6:5–6, 82.

35. Lieutenant Colonel Robert Gustavus Adolphus Love, from Henderson County, was elected Lt. Colonel on July 13, 1861. Love served as lieutenant colonel until he was defeated for re-election on April 26, 1862. Love later served as colonel of the 62nd North Carolina Troops. Love's report of the movement of the 16th was correct, as Lee abandoned his operations in western Virginia and the 16th was transferred to the Manassas Garrison, and was placed in a brigade under South Carolina's Wade Hampton. Manarin and Jordan, *N.C. Troops*, 6: 2–3.

36. Manarin and Jordan, *N.C. Troops*, 6:350, 414; and James E. Woolley, *Early Marriages of Haywood County 1808–1870* (by the author, 1979).

37. The 1st N.C. Cavalry was engaged in a

scouting mission on November 26, 1861, and encountered a similar number of Federal cavalry in the vicinity of Vienna, Virginia. After a brief fight, the 1st Cavalry drove their enemy back to camp. Manarin and Jordan, *N.C. Troops,* 2:1.

38. Both Mary and Alfred were originally from Macon County. Before the war, Alfred operated a dental practice in Rome, Georgia. The 1860 census lists them in Franklin, owning $3,090 in personal property; those same records reveal that the couple owned no slaves in 1860, but purchased 3 afterwards. Federal Census of Macon County: 1860.

39. Blair was promoted to corporal in January of 1863 and was wounded in action at Gettysburg, Pennsylvania, on July 1, 1863. After recovering from his wounds, Corporal Blair was present with the 26th North Carolina during the Battle of Bristoe Station, Virginia, on October 14, 1863, where he was wounded a second time. Blair was taken from the field and sent to a Gordonsville, Virginia, hospital where he died of his wounds on October 21, 1863. Manarin and Jordan, *N.C. Troops,* 7:575. Biographical information from Federal Census of Caldwell County: 1850.

40. Private John A. Teague, a 23-year-old carpenter from Wilkes County, who survived his illness and was reported present throughout the war, surrendering at Appomattox Court House, Virginia, on April 9, 1865. Manarin and Jordan, *N.C. Troops,* 7:587.

41. Private Clinton Lee. Lee volunteered on July 26, 1861, at the age of forty. Lee would be discharged by reason of "being overage," on May 13, 1862, under provisions of the Conscript Act of 1862. Manarin and Jordan, *N.C. Troops,* 7:582.

1862

1. Corporal Thomas Land and Musician Thomas C. Miller, Company B, 1st North Carolina Troops. Manarin and Jordan, *N.C. Troops,* 3:160–161.

2. Refers to Captain Mark D. Armfield, a Bruke County resident, and an officer under Avery in the 1st N.C. Volunteers. Armfield may have been a source of the prejudice against Avery. Apparently, Armfield was sent to Burke County for the purpose of raising a company for the 33rd N.C. Troops. Armfield, however, raised a company of his own, out of re-enlistees from the Burke Rifles and new recruits, which was assigned to the 11th North Carolina, a regiment in which Armfield became a colonel. Manarin and Jordan, *N.C. Troops,* 3: 27.

3. Major William Gaston Lewis served as a first lieutenant in Company A, 1st N.C. Volunteers. He was promoted to the position of major in the 33rd N.C. Troops on January 17, 1862. At the Battle of New Bern, N.C., Lewis "distinguished himself" in a manner which earned him respect and a promotion to lieutenant colonel in the 43rd North Carolina on April 25, 1862. Manarin and Jordan, *N.C. Troops,* 9:118.

4. Manarin and Jordan, *N.C. Troops,* 9:488; and Federal Census of Watauga County: 1860.

5. Mess size usually ranged from four to as many as twelve. Private Council's mess was composed of the following privates: William R. Danner, David A. Cook, Jonathan Cook, Jackson V. Benfield, Joseph L. Benfield, William Bryant, Jesse Brown, Jordan D. Council, and Charles H. Davis. With the exception of those two who are unidentified, six members of the ten member mess would not return from the war. Manarin and Jordan, *N.C. Troops,* 9:486–489.

6. The Pattons of Asheville were one of the county's most prominent families, along with the Browns, Vances, McDowells and Woodfins. The 1860 census reveals that James W. Patton, Thomas's father, owned almost a quarter of a million dollars in real and personal estate. This included a thriving business in Asheville, as well as a plantation worked by as many as 78 slaves. Federal Census of Buncombe County: 1850, 1860; and Foster Sadley, *A History of Buncombe County, N.C.* (1930), 633, 672–675, 815. Thomas W. Patton volunteered for service on April 24, 1861, at age 20. Manarin and Jordan, *N.C. Troops,* 3:25

7. Thomas's cousin John E. Patton. It is unknown to which unit Mr. Fagg belonged, though his name appears several times. A man by the name of Fagg served as a lieutenant in Company H, 58th North Carolina; however, the unit was not formed until July of 1862. Manarin and Jordan, *N.C. Troops,* 14: 375.

8. Manarin and Jordan, *N.C. Troops*, 9:482; and Federal Census of Ashe County: 1850, 1860.

9. Susanna Sexton, the daughter of William and Sarah Sexton, a cousin to Thornton. Federal Census of Ashe County: 1860

10. In reference to the naval battle fought between the blockading squadron and the CSS *Virginia* in the Suffolk and Hampton Roads, Virginia, vicinity. The battle occurred on March 8, 1862, and ended in the historic encounter between the *Virginia* and its Union conterpart, the *Monitor*. Prior to that encounter, the CSS *Virginia* had had great successes against Federal ships such as the *Congress*, *Minnesota*, and others which were run aground. Of all of the traditional wooden vessels, the *Cumberland* earned special respect from Lieutenant J. T. Wood, as "no ship ever fought more gallantly." Robert Underwood Johnson and Clarence C. Buel, eds., *Battles and Leaders of the Civil War*, four volumes (New York: Century, 1883), 1:688–693, 701. Hereafter cited as "Johnson and Buell, *Battles and Leaders*."

11. Manarin and Jordan, *N.C. Troops*, 7: 402.

12. First Lieutenant Joshua Garren, Company G, 35th N.C. Troops. Garren volunteered on October 5, 1861, and was appointed second lieutenant. He was promoted to first lieutenant on December 25, 1861, and was reported absent on recruiting service when he died at Kinston on April 15, 1862. Manarin and Jordan, *N.C. Troops*, 9:420.

13. Refers to some of James' brothers, Robert Columbus Love and Samuel Ervin Love, who would fight in the "Henderson Blues," a company in the 56th Regiment N.C. Troops.

14. Refers to the Second Regiment N.C. Cavalry

15. William Barbour, 37th N.C. Troops, studied at Peter S. Ney's academy and graduated from St. James College in Hagerstown, Maryland. He was admitted to the bar in Wilkes County in 1859 and practiced law with James Gordon in Wilkesboro, N.C. On September 24, 1861, Barbour volunteered for service as an officer and was promoted to lieutenant colonel on November 20, 1861. Barbour was actually a lieutenant colonel at the time of this letter. Johnson J. Hayes, *Land of Wilkes* (1962), 156–157. Hereafter cited as "Hayes, *Land of Wilkes*"; and Manarin and Jordan, *N.C. Troops*, 9:468.

16. Charles J. Hickerson, captain of Company F, 37th N.C. Troops, also a native of Wilkesboro, Wilkes County, North Carolina. Manarin and Jordan, *N.C. Troops*, 9:537.

17. Manarin and Jordan, *N.C. Troops*, 6:102; and Federal Census of Haywood County: 1850, 1860.

18. Three sons of George and Polly Cunningham served in Company L, 16th North Carolina. George, the author of this letter, would be wounded in action at Seven Pines on May 31, 1862. He died of his wounds in Richmond, Virginia, on July 12, 1862. John, who volunteered on the same day as George, died of disease on August 2, 1862. Joseph, who volunteered at age 21 on March 15, 1862, survived through the summer campaigns and was transferred to Company E, Thomas Legion Infantry on September 5, 1862. Manarin and Jordan, *N.C. Troops*, 6:102.

19. Joseph C. Council served as a private in Company B, 37th Regiment N.C. Troops until October 18, 1863, when he was transferred to the 6th N.C. Cavalry (65th Regiment N.C. Troops) and was appointed third lieutenant. Council was reported present through October 1864, and was officially paroled at Selma, Alabama on June 8, 1863. Manarin and Jordan, *N.C. Troops*, 2:38, 470, 492.

20. Colonel Charles C. Lee.

21. Jordan Council served along with the 37th N.C. Troops at the upcoming battles of Second Manassas, Sharpsburg, Fredericksburg and Chancellorsville before being reported absent without leave July–December 1863. Jordan returned sometime in early 1864 and was captured at either Wilderness or Spotsylvania Court House, Virginia, May 6–12, 1864. Jordan was confined at Elmira, New York, via Point Lookout, Maryland, until November 17, 1864, when he died of "pleuropneumonia." Manarin and Jordan, *N.C. Troops*, 9:488.

22. Private Whisenhunt was discharged on July 16, 1862, by reason of being over age. Whisenhunt later re-enlisted in the same company on September 4, 1863, in Virginia. He was reported present through October of 1864. Manarin and Jordan, *N.C. Troops*, 2:227.

23. Manarin and Jordan, *N.C. Troops*, 3: 40;

Joseph Walton, "Thomas G. Walton," in *Burke County Heritage* (Winston-Salem: Hunter Publishing, 1981), 453; and Edward Phifer, *Burke: The History of a North Carolina County* (Morganton: by the author, 1977), 182, 323–325.

24. Refers to Captain Thomas G. Walton and Sergeant James T. Walton of Company F, 41st N.C. Troops (3rd Cavalry). Captain Walton was later defeated for re-election by Alexander Perkins. Manarin and Jordan, *N.C. Troops*: 2:221–227.

25. John later enlisted in Company F, 3rd Cavalry even though his father and brother had both left by August 1862. John served as a private until October 28, 1863, when he was appointed as a cadet. Walton later enlisted in Company B, 11th N.C. Troops on March 22, 1864, with the rank of second lieutenant. Walton was reported present through February 1865. Manarin and Jordan, *N.C. Troops*, 2:227, 4:282.

26. Manarin and Jordan, *N.C. Troops*, 6:414.

27. After this letter, Love led his company through the Seven Days Campaign where he was wounded in action at Malvern Hill, Virginia. Love recovered from his wound prior to being wounded a second time at Fredericksburg, Virginia, in December 1862. After a two month rest, Matthew returned to his command and led the company until he was promoted to major on November 5, 1864, and to lieutenant colonel on January 1, 1865. Love survived the war and was paroled at Appomattox Court House on April 9, 1865. Manarin and Jordan, *N.C. Troops*, 7:357, 359.

28. Refers to the "Henderson Rifles," Company G, 35th N.C. Troops, which was raised by Henderson County native Joseph P. Jordan on October 5, 1861. The company passed to Lieutenant Walter M. Bryan upon Jordan's death on April 22, 1862. Captain Jordan died of typhoid fever at Raleigh, North Carolina. Manarin and Jordan, *N.C. Troops*, 9:419.

29. Privates Columbus H., Francis A., and Robert J. Stepp. Unfortunately all of Mrs. Stepp's sons in the 25th died during service. Columbus and Francis died of disease in the summer of 1862 and Robert was killed while listed as a deserter on February 2, 1864. Manarin and Jordan, *N.C. Troops*, 7:365.

30. Colonel Henry Middleton Rutledge, a native of South Carolina, succeed to regimental command after the promotion of Thomas L. Clingman to brigadier general on May 17, 1862. Manarin and Jordan, *N.C. Troops*, 7:357.

31. Manarin and Jordan, *N.C. Troops*, 5:21.

32. Refers to Colonel Collet Leventhorpe, commander of the 11th Regiment N.C. Troops.

33. Captain Mark D. Armfield previously served as a lieutenant in the 1st N.C. Volunteers. He was appointed Captain on December 10, 1861. Armfield was captured at Gettysburg, Pennsylvania, July 3–4, 1863. Captain Armfield died in prison on December 3, 1863, of "general debility." Manarin and Jordan, *N.C. Troops*, 5:20.

34. Private Alfred Walsh, Corporal Thomas Land, Sergeant Daniel Carlton, and Private Thomas W. Welch. Thomas Welch survived the Seven Days without injury. Land and Carlton were both wounded at Malvern Hill, Virginia, while Alfred was killed in action during the same battle on July 1, 1862. Manarin and Jordan, *N.C. Troops*, 3: 160–168.

35. The Sixteenth North Carolina played a significant role in Pender's Brigade at Frayser's Farm. According to one officer of the regiment: "We stormed the same with the bayonet. Just at this came Federal re-inforcments in overwhelming numbers.... As we stood against odds of four to one. [After hearing fire from the north] we closed up and raised the yell for we knew it was Jackson and that re-inforcements were at hand. The struggle continued till about sunset, we holding the center...." Benjamin Cathey, "Sixteenth Regiment," in Clark, *N.C. Regiments*, 1:754–759.

36. Privates Miles L. Killian and Samuel M. King volunteered in Henderson County in the summer of 1861. Both soldiers were reported killed in action. Manarin and Jordan, *N.C. Troops*, 6:87.

37. First Sergeant Thomas Brittain. After the Seven Days, sergeant Brittan would be wounded twice and promoted to second lieutenant. Manarin and Jordan, *N.C. Troops*, 6:83.

38. Colonel Charles C. Lee, commander of the 37th North Carolina Troops, was mortally wounded at the Battle of Mechanicsville on June 26, 1862. Octavious Wiggins, "Thirty-Seventh Regiment," in Clark, *N.C. Regiments*, 2:655.

39. Private Porter Welch of Company A died of dysentery on June 27, 1862. Manarin and Jordan, *N.C. Troops*, 9:484.

40. Captain William Hartsog resigned as commander of Company A after the campaign on July 15, 1862. Hartsog returned to Ashe County where he died of disease at home on June 18, 1863. Manarin and Jordan, *N.C. Troops*, 9:471.

41. Manarin and Jordan, *N.C. Troops*, 14: 520; and William S. Powell, ed., *The North Carolina Gazetteer* (Chapel Hill: U.N.C. Press, 1962), 376. Hereafter cited as "Powell, *N.C. Gazetteer.*"

42. For more information on the fate of Roland Osborne, refer to Roland Osborne to Addie Gash, 18 May 1862.

43. Private Henry Holden, Company I, 26th North Carolina Troops. Manarin and Jordan, *N.C. Troops*, 7:580.

44. Denny had two brothers who were also conscripted into service, Carey Bird (Company I, 21st N.C. Troops) and Gabriel (Company E, 53rd N.C. Troops). Manarin and Jordan, *N.C. Troops*, 6:557; and Hester Jackson, *Surry County Civil War Soldiers* (np:1986), 54. Hereafter cited as "Jackson, *Surry County Soldiers.*"

45. All of those mentioned were conscripts from Surry County who were taken into service about the same time as Azariah Denny. Benjamin F. Kidd, William C. Banner, W. T. Lewis, J.W. Creed, Jonathan Creed, and Daniel McGee were assigned to Company C while William Ashburn and Lewis Patterson were assigned to Company H, with David Johnstone being sent to Company I. No record of Tyre Clasby was found. Manarin and Jordan, *N.C. Troops*, 6:556–7, 560, 601.

46. Captain Andrew P. Shore was mustered in as a corporal when company H was formed on June 5, 1861. Shore was elected Captain on April 27, 1862, and served as company commander until he was killed in a skirmish at Hazel River, Virginia, on August 22, 1862. Manarin and Jordan, *N.C. Troops*, 6:600.

47. Jonathan Flinchum was married to Elizabeth Denny, Azariah's sister. Later, Jonathan would serve as a private in Company B, 2nd North Carolina Infantry Battalion. Jackson, *Surry County Soldiers*, 64.

48. Logan T. Whitlock was elected second lieutenant on May 20, 1861, and was promoted to first lieutenant on May 25, 1862. Whitlock was wounded in action at Cross Keys, Virginia, on June 8, 1862. After acting as captain and enduring two long hospitalizations, Whitlock was promoted to captain sometime prior to March 1865. Whitlock was captured at Saylor's Creek, Virginia and was confined at Johnson's Island, Ohio, until he was released on June 20, 1865, after taking the Oath of Allegiance. Manarin and Jordan, *N.C. Troops*, 6:555.

49. The diary of Harvey Davis was deposited in the Archival Collections at Catawba College in Salisbury, North Carolina. Francis Dedmond contributed the transcription of the diary and a postwar manuscript.

50. Thomas's cousin William Franklin Patton enlisted on July 8, 1862. Frank was reported absent sick November 1862–February 1863. Frank would later die of pneumonia outside of Tunnel Hill, Georgia, on June 28, 1863. Manarin and Jordan, *N.C. Troops*, 14:529.

51. Tolivar Davis was one of the largest landowners in Rutherford County. His holdings included several water-powered mills which provided the Cathey Creek area with lumber and ground wheat and corn. Davis represented Rutherford County in the House of Commons in 1844. Davis' staunch secessionist views were reinforced when he provided three of his sons to the service of the Confederate Army. Griffin, *Old Tryon and Rutherford*, 228–229. Johnston, *Zebulon B. Vance Letters*, 173.

52. General Samuel Garland, a native of Virginia, commanded a brigade consisting of the 5th, 12th, 13th, 20th, and 23rd North Carolina Troops. The brigade numbering only about 1,000 men was overwhelmed by superior federal numbers in their front and both flanks. After Garland was mortally wounded, the 12th North Carolina broke and the rest of Garland's brigade followed shortly thereafter. Johnson and Beul, *Battles and Leaders*, 2:563–565; and Walter Montgomery, "Twelfth Regiment," in Clark, *N.C. Regiments*, 1:626–627.

53. John M. Priest, *Antietam: The Soldier's Battle* (Oxford: Oxford University Press, 1989), 78–83.

54. Captain Thomas S. Bouchelle, a Wilkes County farmer, was promoted to captain on July 8, 1862. Bouchelle was wounded through

the mouth as described by Leach and was detailed to act as an enrolling officer for the Ninth Congressional District after he was taken off active duty on August 22, 1863. Captain Bouchelle was officially retired to the Invalid Corps on February 24, 1865. Manarin and Jordan, *N.C. Troops*, 3:165.

55. Second Lieutenant Joseph W. Peden. According to hospitalization records, he was wounded in the thigh. He was retired to the Invalid Corps in February of 1865 after being permanently disabled from his wound suffered at Sharpsburg. Manarin and Jordan, *N.C. Troops*, 3:165.

56. Roswell Sabine Ripley, an Ohio native, but married into Charleston society, commanded an infantry brigade under D. H. Hill composed of the 1st and 3rd North Carolina and 4th and 44th Georgia Infantry in September of 1862. Ezra J. Warner, *Generals in Gray* (Baton Rouge: LSU, 1953), 257.

57. Manarin and Jordan, *N.C. Troops*, 14:557; and Federal Census of Buncombe County: 1860.

58. Company I, 60th North Carolina was formed from men from several other of the Buncombe companies. Goodson Roberts, previously a second lieutenant in Company F, was elected captain on September 13, 1862. Manarin and Jordan, *N.C. Troops*, 14:523.

59. James Mitchell Stevens served as captain of Company F until August 1, 1863, when he was appointed surgeon and transferred to the regimental staff. Manarin and Jordan, *N.C. Troops*, 14:551.

60. The lesser-known Battle of Boetler's Ford was a near rout of Union forces which had crossed the Potomac in pursuit of retreating Confederates. Troops under A. P. Hill outflanked the enemy on both flanks and drove straight toward the river. Johnson and Buel, *Battles and Leaders*, 2:672.

61. Private Andrew W. Duncan was conscripted along with the Proffit brothers. Duncan was wounded at Sharpsburg, Maryland, and never returned to duty. Manarin and Jordan, *N.C. Troops*, 6:347.

62. All of the men were among the Wilkes County conscripts who served in the 18th North Carolina Troops.

63. William C. Proffit, Company G, 18th N.C. Troops, was also one of the Wilkes conscripts. His relation to the other Proffits is unknown. However, Proffit enlisted on the 14th of August in Iredell County. William died of pneumonia in a Mt. Jackson, Virginia, hospital on November 11, 1862. Manarin and Jordan, *N.C. Troops*, 6:387.

64. James E. Hannon, Columbus County, letter to Gov. Zebulon B. Vance, September 25, 1862. Governor's Papers (Vance), North Carolina Division of Archives and History.

65. Johnson L. Ward served as the first colonel of the 105th Militia (1861 Organization), when it was commissioned on December 21, 1861. Stephen Bradley, *North Carolina Confederate Militia Officers' Roster* (Virginia Beach: by the author, 1989). Hereafter cited as "Bradley, *Militia Officers' Roster*."

66. According to records, Robert Lyles was commissioned colonel of the Militia on August 28, 1862. Lyles' exact service is marked with discrepancies, including a statement that he died on August 10, 1862, nearly six weeks before this letter was written. Bradley, *Militia Officers' Roster*.

67. John W. Hampton was one of Polk County's founders and a justice of the county court. Griffin, *Old Tryon and Rutherford Counties*, 217, 232, 236.

68. Manarin and Jordan, *N.C. Troops*, 4:267, 317.

69. Dr. Pleasant A. Holt was appointed surgeon of the 6th North Carolina after serving as assistant surgeon of the 2nd N.C. Volunteers on August 6, 1861. On August 23, 1862, Holt was promoted and transferred to Brigadier General William D. Pender's staff. Manarin and Jordan, *N.C. Troops*, 4:269.

70. C. A. Henderson resided in Rowan County prior to volunteering at age 26 on May 16, 1861. Henderson resigned in December of 1862 due to "ill health." Manarin and Jordan, *N.C. Troops*, 4:268.

71. Sergeant Isaac A. Erwin of Company E. Erwin volunteered in Mecklenburg County on May 28, 1861. Erwin was mortally wounded at Sharpsburg, Maryland, on September 17, 1862. Manarin and Jordan, *N.C. Troops*, 4:321.

72. Manarin and Jordan, *N.C. Troops*, 14:391.

73. Amos Howell resided in Ashe or Watauga County and enlisted on July 24, 1862.

Howell was transferred to Company D, 5th Battalion, N.C. Cavalry on the same date. Howell may have carried this letter. Manarin and Jordan, *N.C. Troops*, 14: 391.

74. First Lieutenant James Mitchell Ray was elected lieutenant on May 16, 1862, and was promoted to captain on August 1, 1862. Captain Ray would later go on to serve as lieutenant colonel of the 60th Regiment. Manarin and Jordan, *N.C. Troops*, 14:551.

75. Private Andrew Jackson Martin enlisted on May 16, 1862, and was reported absent sick November 1862–February 1863. Martin returned to duty in April 1863 and was reported present until wounded in action on August 5, 1864. Manarin and Jordan, *N.C. Troops*, 14:555.

76. Denny's brother Gabriel, a private in the 53rd North Carolina. Gabriel Denny volunteered on April 17, 1862, and was reported present until listed as sick on February 1, 1863. Apparently Gabriel was given an unrecorded furlough and was to be brought back on a specific date, prior to being discharged on February 1, 1863. Jackson, Hester, *Surry County Soldiers*, 54–55.

77. That conscription act provided that that those falling between the ages of thirty-five and forty-five would be the last called up for service, only if all those younger were called first, or met a qualifying exemption. *Official Records*, Ser 4, 2:160. To make the labor shortage worse, Macon County had only a population of six thousand residents while five hundred nineteen were slaves. The county's economy depended on small farms and those families were the first to be hit with conscription and the loss of not only a loved relative, but a valuable breadwinner. Federal Census of Macon County: 1860

78. Colonel George N. Folk was in command of the 7th Battalion N.C. Cavalry.

79. James married Helen prior to 1859, when Edwin, their son, was born. James worked as a carpenter in the Burnsville area before enlisting in service. In addition to serving on the staff of the 29th Regiment N.C. Troops, Neill often functioned as the quartermaster on the staff of Robert Vance. Federal Census of Yancey County: 1850, 1860; Manarin and Jordan, *N.C. Troops*, 8:236, 309; and Stephen Bradley, ed., *North Carolina Militia and Home Guard Records*, 1:293.

80. Third Lieutenant David L. Brevard, Company C, 60th North Carolina was elected on July 8, 1862, and resigned on November 23, 1862, due to poor health. Manarin and Jordan, *N.C. Troops*, 14:523.

81. Sam Capps is listed as a Negro servant to Thomas W. Patton. However, Capps was not identified as a slave or a free black at the time of this letter. Manarin and Jordan, *N.C. Troops*, 14:526.

82. Colonel Joseph A. McDowell was elected captain of Company B on July 8, 1862, and to lieutenant colonel on August 1, 1862. On October 1, 1862, McDowell was elected full colonel in command of the regiment. Manarin and Jordan, *N.C. Troops*, 14: 502.

83. Edwin M. Clayton, a Buncombe County student, served in Company E, 1st N.C. Volunteers; he was appointed adjutant of the 60th North Carolina by Lt. Colonel McDowell on August 1, 1862. Clayton served in this capacity until April 1863, when he was promoted and assigned to command Company K of the regiment. Manarin and Jordan, *N.C. Troops*, 14: 502.

84. Abernethy, a native of Lincoln County, worked as a Methodist minister and teacher before being appointed a tax collector in McDowell County and later a quartermaster during the war. After the war, Abernethy became President of Rutherford College and was an outspoken advocate of the temperance movement. Johnston, *Zebulon B. Vance Letters*, 304.

85. Calvin was reported present until he died of brain fever at Camp Gregg, Virginia, on May 25, 1863. Manarin and Jordan, *N.C. Troops*, 5:362.

86. Privates William West and Smith Cox were both Wilkes County farmers before being conscripted into service at the same time as Calvin. West would be wounded in action at Chancellorsville, Virginia, on May 3, 1863, and would die of his wounds on May 21, 1863. Cox was wounded in action at Spotsylvania Court Hose, Virginia, on May 20, 1864, dying a week later. Manarin and Jordan, *N.C. Troops*, 5:358–360.

87. John Duval, a sergeant in Company B, 11th N.C. Troops, was captured at Gettysburg in July 1863. No records exist for this soldier

after October 1863. Manarin and Jordan, *N.C. Troops*, 5:24.

88. Refers to the 4th North Carolina Cavalry Regiment (59th N.C. Troops), under the command of Colonel Dennis Dozier Ferebee.

89. Thomas was born on February 5, 1805, in Haywood County, North Carolina. Tragically, the young Thomas never met his father, Richard, who drowned a few months before Thomas' birth. While receiving no formal or higher education, Thomas' reputation was as a businessman and a representative of the Cherokee people. Thomas' exact relationship with the eastern Cherokee was summarized by scholar Mattie Russell in 1956: "To Colonel William H. Thomas the East Cherokee of today owe their existence as a people and for a half a century he was as intimately connected with their history as was John Ross with that of the main Cherokee Nation." Thomas, at the onset of the war, lost a bid to gain a seat in the Confederate Congress, and returned home to raise a unit to defend the vast territory of the mountains which he admitted was "larger than England or France" and was the key to the Confederate war effort. Thomas expressed his points very tactfully to Governors Clark and Vance, as well as to President Davis; however, all existing miltary authorities believed that East Tennessee and western North Carolina was a minor theatre of operations. Vernon Crow, *A Storm in the Mountains*, Cherokee, N.C.: Museum of the Cherokee Indian, 1985), 3–13; Mattie Russell, "William H. Thomas: White Chief of the Cherokees" (unpublished Ph.D. diss., Duke University, 1956), 309–336.

90. McElory's service did not end with the militia. On September 26, 1863, the First Brigade of Home Guard was established in order to maintain lawful control in the mountain counties, as well as enforcing conscription and defending the region against geurilla and Federal incursions. McElroy was promoted to brigadier general and was given command of the First Brigade which included men from Henderson, Buncombe, Madison, Yancey, Watauga, Mitchell, Burke, McDowell, Rutherford, Polk, and Transylvania counties. Overall, in a report from the adjutant general's office, dated the same day, this brigade was composed of twenty-one to twenty-five understrength companies. McElroy's duties were not to be coveted—only one hundred modern arms were kept in an arsenal in Morganton. Numerous requests for uniforms, provisions, and arms, were basically ignored. Adding to the problem, McElroy's brigade (which actually had the strength of a full regiment) had to patrol an area which stretched one hundred fifteen miles, to say nothing of the actual square mileage. Federal Census of Yancey County: 1860; and Bradley, *North Carolina Militia and Home Guard*, 1:6, 2:63, 3:6, 16, 21.

91. Manarin and Jordan, *N.C. Troops*, 2:544.

92. Captain Carter W. Gillespie, commander of Company D, 7th Battalion N.C. Cavalry, who commanded another contingent of Henderson County men. Manarin and Jordan, *N.C. Troops*, 2:536.

93. Colonel George N. Folk, a attorney from Boone, Watauga County, North Carolina, raised Company D, 1st North Carolina Cavalry. In the summer of 1862, he was given authority to raise the 7th Cavalry Battalion, of which Jule Gash served as an officer. Colonel Folk held the rank of lieutenant colonel at this time, and was promoted to colonel when the 5th and 7th battalions merged to form the 6th N.C. Cavalry Regiment on August 3, 1863. Folk was captured at Kinston on June 22, 1864. During his incarceration, he was one of six hundred officers used as "human shields" outside Charleston, South Carolina, by the Union authorities. Folk was paroled and exchanged at Charleston on December 15, 1864, after the resolution of the crisis and returned to his command until he was paroled at Salisbury, North Carolina, on May 26, 1865. Kimberly Berger and Richard Howe, "George N. Folk," in Powell, *N.C. Biographical Dictionary*, 2:216; Manarin and Jordan, *N.C. Troops*, 2:36, 457, 516; Muriel Josyln, *Immortal Captives* (Shippensburg, PA: White Mane, 1996), 300.

94. Captain John J. Spann originally raised company E, 7th Battalion N.C. Cavalry in Hendersonville on July 15, 1862, after previously serving as a soldier in the 16th Regiment N.C. Troops. Manarin and Jordan, *N.C. Troops*, 2:544.

95. William J. Parker volunteered for service at Hendersonville, N.C., on July 15, 1862. He served as a private until he died of pneumonia

at Camp Roansneck around November 24, 1862. Manarin and Jordan, *N.C. Troops*, 2:542.

96. Private Baxter Hadden, Company D, Corporal William Montgomery Hood, Company D, Private John P. Orr, Company E, and Corporal Wesley M. Sinard of Company D. Of these men afflicted by the measles, only one, Wesley Sinard, died of the disease on December 1, 1862, without Jule's knowledge when he wrote this letter. Manarin and Jordan, *N.C. Troops*, 2: 539–542.

97. Manarin and Jordan, *N.C. Troops*, 2:40; and Federal Census of Watauga County: 1860.

98. Bazilla C. McBride enlisted at age 35 on May 11, 1861, and was appointed sergeant. McBride was captured at Willis Church, Virginia, on June 29, 1862. After a brief period as a prisoner, McBride was promoted to quartermaster sergeant on August 5, 1862, and served until December 1, 1863, when he was reduced in ranks to sergeant. Manarin and Jordan, *N.C. Troops*, 2:41.

99. Manarin and Jordan, N.C. Troops, 9:534; and Federal Census of Watauga County: 1860.

100. Sergeant James M. Farthing volunteered for service on September 18, 1861, and was mustered in as a corporal. Farthing was captured at Hanover Court House, Virginia, and was exchanged shortly thereafter. Farthing was "shot in the head" at the Battle of Fredericksburg on December 13, 1862. Private Nathaniel Shull was born in Johnson County, Tennessee; he volunteered for service in Watauga County on September 18, 1861. Shull was captured at Hanover Court House, Virginia, on May 28, 1862, and was exchanged shortly thereafter. At the Battle of Fredericksburg, he was "shot in the breast and killed." Manarin and Jordan, *N.C. Troops*, 9:528, 534.

101. Private William Franklin Parris, Company F, 60th N.C. Troops was reported absent on furlough December 20–31, 1863. Parris was issued a medical furlough, having suffered from Palsy for as long as he had been in service. Manarin and Jordan, *N.C. Troops*, 15:556.

102. Private William Littrell, Company F, 60th N.C. Troops, was executed on December 26, 1862, at Murfreesboro, Tennessee. He was the brother of Thomas Littrell of the same company. Manarin and Jordan, *N.C. Troops*, 14:555.

103. Refers to William Augustus Patton who was appointed quartermaster on August 1, 1862. "Gus" was frequently absent until he resigned on February 24, 1863, with "atrophoy of the heart." William died at Asheville on April 5, 1863. Manarin and Jordan, *N.C. Troops*, 14:502.

104. Private Thomas Newton Stevens, Company E, 60th N.C. Troops, was on duty as a teamster, and apparently foiled an attempted desertion. Manarin and Jordan, *N.C. Troops*, 14:558.

105. Brigadier General William Preston was a Harvard law graduate, a colonel in the Mexican War, and Buchanan's Minister to Spain in 1858, before being assigned to the staff of his brother-in-law, A. S. Johnston, with the rank of colonel. Preston served as brigade commander until he was appointed Confederate Minister to Mexico in 1864. Warner, *Generals in Gray*, 246.

1863

1. Manarin and Jordan, *N.C. Troops*, 2: 221–222; and Dr. Jean C. Ervin, "Perkins Family," in *Burke County Heritage* (Winston-Salem, Hunter Publishing, 1981), 350.

2. Private John M. Bristol, Company F, 41st N.C. Troops was discharged on March 22, 1862, by reason of "disease of the lungs unfitting him of duty." Manarin and Jordan, *N.C. Troops*, 2:222.

3. Clarke Moulton Avery, commander of the 33rd North Carolina Troops.

4. McElrath and McKesson are both familiar surnames for Burke County soldiers; however, the identities of these could not be confirmed. McElrath may refer to Private Robert J., a soldier in Company F. Manarin and Jordan, *N.C. Troops*, 2:225.

5. Lieutenant Patton was absent on duty as a quartermaster at this time. The poor conduct of those companies caused three captains to be court-martialed (Charles Fletcher was the only one removed), and two others, A. B. Duckett, Company B, and F S. H. Reynolds, Company C, resigned rather than facing charges. The regiment's commander, William W. McDowell, was absolved of immediate guilt, but was eased out, resigning in March 1863, of

"hemorrhoids." In all, eighteen officers including all the unit's field officers, were removed or had resigned by May of 1863. Manarin and Jordan, N.C. Troops, 14:432–433; and Alexander Stevenson, The Battle of Stones' River Near Murfreesboro TN: December 30, 1862 to January 3, 1863 (Boston: Osgood & Company, 1884), 116.

6. Refers to Privates Francis Marion Parham and William Pritchett, Company F, 60th Regiment N.C. Troops. Parham was actually captured at Murfreesboro and sent to a hospital in St. Louis, Missouri, where he died on January 24, 1863, of "typhoid fever." Pritchett was presumed killed in action. Manarin and Jordan, N.C. Troops, 14:556.

7. No record of a "Halen" or Haley Frisby was found. This could possibly refer to either Abner, Leander, or Solomon Frisby who were listed in Company F, 60th North Carolina Troops. Manarin and Jordan, N.C. Troops, 14:552.

8. Manarin and Jordan, N.C. Troops, 5:362.

9. Manarin and Jordan, N.C. Troops, 10:104–106. This seems to be the only official record of the 39th's role in the Battle of Murfreesboro. After the death or disabling of all field officers, Captain Bell took command of the regiment. Theodore Davidson, "Thirty-Ninth Regiment," in Clark, N.C. Regiments, 2:711.

10. Refers to Captain James G. Crawford, a former sheriff of Macon County, who was in command of Company I, 39th North Carolina. Manarin and Jordan, N.C. Troops, 10:172.

11. Private Washington Thomas, a 21-year-old volunteer from Macon County; Private Wilburn F. Roane, a 20-year-old farmer who was wounded in the left thigh and was later discharged in March 1863; and Private William A. Thompson who enlisted on December 1, 1862. After being wounded at Chickamauga, Thompson deserted and helped Union prisoners escape through western North Carolina. Manarin and Jordan, N.C. Troops, 10:127–128.

12. Colonel David Coleman, an attorney from Buncombe County, was appointed colonel when the regiment was organized on May 19, 1862. Coleman was wounded in the leg at Murfreesboro, Tennessee. Coleman displayed "surpassing gallantry in the field" and "unsurpassed heroism at Murfreesboro." Coleman went back to Asheville to recuperate and returned to the 39th North Carolina prior to May 1, 1863. Manarin and Jordan, N.C. Troops, 10:109.

13. This should possibly be the 16th Tennessee. The 39th acted in conjunction with the 16th Tennessee and official reports from that unit mention the role and compliment the performance of the 39th North Carolina.

14. Lieutenant Colonel Hugh Harvey Davidson, who previously commanded Company C of the regiment. Davidson actually had his resignation on medical reasons approved; however, word did not reach him, and he helped lead his regiment in battle. He was wounded shortly after the battle began. Davidson, for his perfomance in combat, was nominated for the Badge of Distinction. He was remarked as "a man of great strength of mind and firmness of character and had the faculty of inspiring confidence and affection beyond that of most men." Manarin and Jordan, N.C. Troops, 10:109–110.

15. Privates J. Wood Owens, Elisha McConnell, Kimzey Gudger, Will Roane, John Guy, and Jesse Gregory. Gudger and Guy would die of their wounds in Federal hospitals, while Jesse Gregory had to have his left arm amputated. Manarin and Jordan, N.C. Troops, 10:123–129.

16. Lieutenant John W. Rhea, a 47 year old who was killed in action, and First Sergeant John Whitaker who was shot in the head. Manarin and Jordan, N.C. Troops, 10:158.

17. First Lieutenant William T. Anderson, a 29-year-old Macon County man volunteered on October 19, 1861, and was reported present until he was wounded in both the shoulder and the groin during the Battle of Murfreesboro. Despite Anderson's wounds, Bell makes no mention of his leaving his post. Anderson's service record indicates he was nominated for the Badge of Distinction for gallantry at Murfreesboro. Manarin and Jordan, N.C. Troops, 10:120.

18. Brigaider Evander M. Law. In December 1862, his brigade consisted of the 4th and 44th Alabama Infantry, and the 6th, 54th, and 57th North Carolina Troops.

19. Alphonso C. Avery served as a first lieutenant in the 6th North Carolina before being promoted inspector general (major) and transferred on December 24, 1862, to serve on the

staff of Major General Daniel H. Hill. Manarin and Jordan, *N.C. Troops*, 4:317.

20. Manarin and Jordan, *N.C. Troops*, 3: 262, 280.

21. After the war, Davis returned home to his family in Watauga County, and, in 1868, he married Mary A. Hodge of Boone. Harvey and Mary would have one daughter, Ida, and three boys, appropriately named William H. F. Lee Davis (1868), Jefferson W. Davis (1870), and Wade Hampton Davis (1875). Sadly, Mary Hodge Davis died in childbirth with her last son. Davis worked as a farmer and lived the remainder of his life with his daughter, Ida, and her husband Millard Norris in the Grassy Creek area. Harvey Davis died on December 29, 1932, and was buried at Old Mount Pleasant Cemetery on Big Hill. Dedmond, *Diary of Harvey Davis*, 368.

22. This references the letter of January 10, 1863.

23. Wilma W. Millsaps, "Cpt Stephen Whitaker," in *Cherokee County Heritage* (Winston-Salem: Hunter Publishing, 1995), 493–494; Crow, *Storm in the Mountains*, 216.

24. Much to the dismay of Colonel Thomas, who wanted his legion to function as a defense force for western North Carolina, the unit was placed under the command of Gen. Alfred E. Jackson.

25. Refers to Brigadier General Robert B. Vance, an Asheville attorney, and former commander of the 29th North Carolina Troops.

26. A compiled roster in *Storm in the Mountains*, reveals that over one hundred-forty men served under Whitaker's command at different times in company E; the count of 120 is accurate for the early spring of 1863. Crow, *Storm in the Moutains*, 216–219.

27. At the time of this letter Micheaux was serving as a sergeant in Company B, 11th N.C. Troops. He was later promoted to first sergeant of the company. Manarin and Jordan, *N.C. Troops* 5: 27.

28. Alex survived the war and was paroled at Morganton, N.C., on May 15, 1865. After the war, he and his brother still maintained a close relationship, running a family farm together, and even marrying sisters. Alex married Julianna Gordon, and to this union was born four daughters: Mary, Emma, Susan, and Lizzie W. After Alex's death on August 16, 1897, Bob and some of the "Perkins Girls" continued on with the farm and even took in sick and old animals and took care of them. Manarin and Jordan, *N.C. Troops*, 2:221–222; Dr. Jean C. Ervin, "Perkins Family," in *Burke County Heritage* (Winston-Salem, Hunter Publishing, 1981), 350.

29. Rogers and his company performed faithful service until the regiment, as a part of General Frazier's command, with a few exceptions, surrendered to the Union forces at Cumberland Gap in September 1863. While imprisoned in Ohio, Asbury was promoted to major, but would never get a chance to perform the duties of this new office. After spending almost two years in prison, Asbury returned home to Crabtree in Haywood County. The health and behavior of the respected captain seemed to break down quickly, and some in the community feared him because of his mental state. Captain Asbury Rogers died in 1888. His wife, Lourena, would live until 1934. William Best II, letter to author, April 1, 2002; Bradley, *N.C. Militia Officers' Roster*, 296; and John W. Moore, *A Roster of North Carolina Troops in the War Between the States 1861–1865*, four volumes (Raleigh: Edwards & Broughton, 1883), 3:717. Hereafter cited as "Moore, *Roster*."

30. This might be in reference to George W. McCracken, a Haywood County man who served as a major in the 112th Regiment of Miltia. McCracken was commissioned on March 1, 1862, the same day as Lieutenant Colonel Asbury T. Rogers and Colonel Charles C. Rogers. Bradley, *N.C. Militia Officers' Roster*, 296.

31. Mary Ann Warlick died in 1863. Lawing, *Notes on Transcription*, 91.

32. Private Reuben Branch, from Burke County, enlisted on January 15, 1862, and was reported present through April 2, 1865, when he was captured at Petersburg, Virginia. No mention of his duty in Randolph and Chatam counties was found among his service records. Manarin and Jordan, *N.C. Troops*, 5:23.

33. David Moody was a 46-year-old volunteer from Burke County. Moody deserted on May 15, 1862, and was returned to service in August of that year. He was discharged on April 10, 1863, by reason of old age, among other ailments. Manarin and Jordan, *N.C. Troops*, 5:27.

34. The 37th Regiment suffered greatly during their withdraw at Chancellorsville, suffering thirty-four killed in action and nearly one hundred sixty wounded. General description of action taken from Col. William Barbour's official report, Official Records, s1, 25:923–924; and Octavious Wiggins, "Thirty-Seventh Regiment," in Clark, N.C. Regiments (1901); and Manarin and Jordan, N.C. Troops, 9:465.

35. Report of Lieutenant Colonel Forney George, Official Records, qtd. in Manarin and Jordan, N.C. Troops, 6:304–305.

36. Refers to Colonel T. J. Purdie, who was killed when a bullet went through his forehead, Lieutenant Colonel Forney George who, despite his wound, rallied the men of the 18th, and Lieutenant General Thomas "Stonewall" Jackson.

37. Jackson, Mississippi, fell to Union forces on May 14, 1863, and was a key step to the successful siege of Vicksburg. Ronald Mosocco, *The Chronological Tracking of the American Civil War Per the Official Records* (Williamsburg, Va: James River, 1993), 140.

38. Manarin and Jordan, N.C. Troops, 6:41; and Federal Census of Rutherford County: 1850, 1860.

39. Private John M. Sutton, a Rutherford County farmer who volunteered at age 24 on May 29, 1861. He was promoted to corporal sometime in 1862-1863, but was reduced in rank on August 13, 1863. Sutton fought until he was paroled at Appomattox Court House, Virginia, on April 9, 1865. Manarin and Jordan, N.C. Troops, 6:45.

40. Either Newton or George Harris, both reported present at the time of this letter. Manarin and Jordan, N.C. Troops, 6:42.

41. Manarin and Jordan, N.C. Troops, 2: 544; and Federal Census of Henderson County: 1850, 1860.

42. Martin M. Gash. For further information, consult entry for June 18, 1864.

43. Manarin and Jordan, N.C. Troops, 7:506.

44. John and Mary Wright. Federal Census of Wilkes County, North Carolina: 1850, 1860.

45. First Lieutenant Logan T. Whitlock. Refer to Azariah Denny to Joel Denny, 4 September 1862.

46. Jonathan Flinchum, Company B, 2nd Battalion N.C. Infantry, and his wife Elizabeth "Betty" Flinchum of Surry County. Refer to Azariah Denny to Joel Denny, 4 September 1862.

47. Private Issac Ashburn, Company B, 2nd N.C. Battalion, enlisted on September 1, 1862 and died in Raleigh, N.C. on May 29, 1863. Jackson, Hester, *Surry County Civil War Soldiers*, 6.

48. "Todd Caldwell," in Powell, *N.C. Biographical Dictionary*, 1:305.

49. John Caldwell was appointed second lieutenant in Company E, 33rd North Carolina Troops on May 3, 1863. John was killed two months later on July 3, 1863, at Gettysburg, Pennsylvania. Manarin and Jordan, N.C. Troops, 9:172.

50. Mattie Caldwell, sister of John and daughter of Todd R. Caldwell.

51. Captain Alexander Perkins.

52. Colonel Clark Moulton Avery, commander of the 33rd North Carolina.

53. This note passed to Major Hugh Tate, who informed Isaac Thomas Avery of his son's death. Avery was wounded in the neck and called for paper and pencil prior to lapsing into unconsciousness. After his death the next day, his black servant, Elijah, attempted to return his body to North Carolina. Upon reaching Williamsport, a band of Georgia troops were so offended by the odor, that they threatened to throw the coffin in the Potomac. The servant defended Avery's remains with a fence rail and held off the disrespectful Georgians until North Carolina troops arrived to bury the slain Colonel at Williamsport. Manarin and Jordan, N.C. Troops, 4:267; Powell, *N.C. Biographical Dictionary*, 1: 69–70; and Edward W. Phifer, "Saga of a Burke County family," *North Carolina Historical Review*, 39: 326–332.

54. Major Jones was the only field officer left in Pettigrew's Brigade. The 26th Regiment alone suffered 86 killed, 502 wounded, and 120 missing during the three day battle. Johnson and Buell, *Battles and Leaders*, 3:439. Jones was struck by a shell on July 1, 1863, while the regiment advanced on Gettysburg, and on the 3rd, he was "knocked down and stunned" but refused to leave the field. As a result of his courage, Jones was promoted to lieutenant colonel. His promotion was dated July 3, 1863. Manarin and Jordan, N.C. Troops, 7:463.

55. Wat Jones, Brother of Major John T.

Jones, and Doctor Edward Warren. Federal Census of Caldwell County: 1850.

56. Manarin and Jordan, *N.C. Troops*, 14:523.

57. Third Lieutenant Samuel L. Davidson, Company C, 60th North Carolina Troops. After receiving this furlough, Davidson would be wounded at three different times during the war. Manarin and Jordan, *N.C. Troops*, 14:523.

58. Colonel Washington Morris Hardy, a former company commander, was promoted to major on March 1, 1863, and then to lieutenant colonel on June 10 of that same year. In August of 1864, Colonel Hardy left this regiment. No further records. Manarin and Jordan, *N.C. Troops*, 14:502.

59. Captain R. L. Coleman served as assistant commissary of subsistence, before his position was eliminated by the Confederate Congress. He later served on the staff of General Robert B. Vance. Second Lieutenant James R. Chambers of Company E, 60th North Carolina. Manarin and Jordan, *N.C. Troops*, 14:503, 516.

60. First Lieutenant Pleasant Isreal, a Buncombe County student, was sent home at this time as part of a detail to gather recruits. Isreal was discharged from service on October 10, 1863. Manarin and Jordan, *N.C. Troops*, 14:505.

61. Private George W. Mashall of Clay County, N.C., enlisted September 25, 1862. Crown, *Storm in the Mountains*, 218.

62. Privates Henry H. Weathermon and Levi S. Graham from Cherokee County, who served in Whtiaker's Company of Walker's Battalion. Crow, *Storm in the Mountains*, 217, 219.

63. The charges against Thomas were for several accounts relating to conduct unbecoming and disobeying orders. These charges stemmed from Thomas giving contradictory orders to members of Love's Regiment without Jackson's knowledge. Thomas was found guilty despite his popularity. In November of 1863, Thomas went to Richmond to meet with Davis to resolve the situation; however, Davis upheld the ruling of the court-martial. Thomas remained the symbolic head of the legion, though his actual field command was over, except for command of the Cherokee Battalion in 1865. Crow, *Storm in the Mountains*, 271.

64. William Proffit died on October 23, 1863, in a Gordonsville hospital. Manarin and Jordan, *N.C. Troops*, 3:163.

65. Moore, *Roster*, 4:157.

66. Manarin and Jordan, *N.C. Troops*, 3:23.

67. After being captured at Gettysburg, First Lieutenant Thomas B. Parks and First Sergeant John Micheaux were taken to Fort McHenry, Baltimore, Maryland then imprisoned at Point Lookout. Manarin and Jordan, *N.C. Troops*, 3: 22, 27.

68. Officers and enlisted men were treated very differently when it came to prison accommodations. The officers were separated from the men and transported to a special prison at Johnson's Island near Sandusky, Ohio. A large contingent of officers was also held at Fort Delaware, Delaware.

69. Private Harrison Parks was reported "supposed killed" at Gettysburg. All other men mentioned here are part of Armfield's company. Bob Hermessee refers to Sergeant Robert J. Hennessa, a 21-year-old volunteer who was captured on the first day of Gettysburg. Manarin and Jordan, *N.C. Troops*, 3: 23, 26–28.

70. Private Thomas B. Moore survived his wound and his confinement. After being exchanged, Moore soldiered with the 11th N.C. Troops until he was killed in action near New Market, Virginia, on July 30, 1864. Manarin and Jordan, *N.C. Troops*, 3:27–28.

71. Manarin and Jordan, *N.C. Troops*, 2:454.

72. Carter Gillespie was captured on June 9, 1863, and was confined at Champ Chase, Ohio, and Johnson's Island, Ohio. While that officer was not in command, Jule still refers to the company as "Gillespie's." On September 9, 1863, four days after this letter was written, Captain Gillespie died of fever at Johnson's Island, Ohio. Manarin and Jordan, *N.C. Troops*, 2:470.

73. Actually the designation was the 65th Regiment.

74. Private Richard S. Osteen who served as a bugler after being transferred to Company D, 65th N.C. Troops (6th N.C. Cavalry) on August 3, 1863, and was present or accounted for through August 1864. Private John C. Edney, who may have been serving as an acting lieutenant deserted on September 2, 1863. Manarin and Jordan, *N.C. Troops*, 2:477, 480.

75. Colonel Ray was appointed lieutenant colonel in June of 1863. He was wounded in the

right arm at Chickamauga, a wound which caused a compound fracture. Ray resigned on December 23, 1863, after a convalescence at home in Buncombe County. Lieutenant Samuel W. Davidson, Company C, was wounded in the left knee. Second Lieutenant Robert L. White, Company F, First Lieutenant John H. Reynolds, Company C (and son of General A. C. Reynolds), and Second Lieutenant Leonard C. Huff, Company H, who was wounded in the right leg. James B. Ray, "Sixtieth Regiment," in Clark, *N.C. Regiments*, 3: 487–491; and Manarin and Jordan, *N.C. Troops*, 14:502, 523, 551, 564.

76. Manarin and Jordan, *N.C. Troops*, 2:61.

77. During the two day battle the 39th North Carolina charged three separate times and fought to the point where they nearly exhausted ammunition twice. After capturing the battery on September 20, the regiment was authorized to paint another cross-cannon insignia on its regimental colors. For a full report of the Battle of Chickamauga, and the 39th North Carolina's involvement, refer to Coleman's Report, *Official Records*, 30: 499–500; and Theodore Davidson, "Thirty-Ninth Regiment," in Clark's *N.C. Regiments*, 3:712–719.

78. Privates Peter C. Mason and Joseph Melton of Company B where wounded in action at Chickamauga, Georgia, September 19–20, 1863, while Ephraim Tallent was reported wounded with a serious skull fracture as a result of wounds received. Manarin and Jordan, *N.C. Troops*, 10:124–127.

79. William West, the company's first sergeant, was already nominated for the Badge of Distinction for his gallant conduct at Murfreesboro, and served meritoriously at Chickamauga. On October 13, 1862, West was rewarded with a promotion to third lieutenant. West served as an officer in Company B until he was killed in action at Kennesaw Mountain, Georgia, on June 18, 1864. Manarin and Jordan, *N.C. Troops*, 10: 124.

80. Tennessee native John Love would go on to make a full recovery. Private John Henry died from his wounds on September 30, 1863. Manarin and Jordan, *N.C. Troops*, 10:123–124.

81. Phillip Walsh volunteered for service in Wilkes County on September 24, 1861, at the age of twenty-four. Walsh was promoted corporal in March–October 1862 and was wounded in the finger at Ox Hill, Virginia, on September 1, 1862. After a rest, Walsh returned to duty by November of 1862 and was reduced in rank due to an unspecified reason in March of 1863. Private Walsh continued his service and received a promotion to sergeant on January 1, 1864. Within a week of the war's end, Walsh was captured at Petersburg and was confined at Point Lookout, Maryland, until June 22, 1865, when he was released after taking the Oath of Allegiance. Manarin and Jordan, *N.C. Troops*, 9:550.

82. Manarin and Jordan, *N.C. Troops*, 14: 374–375; and biographical information from Daniel Hill, *North Carolina*,Vol. 5, in Clement Evans, ed., *Confederate Military History* (Confederate Publishing Co, 1899), 531–532.

83. From Manly W. Wellman, *The Kingdom of Madison: A Southern Mountain Fastness and Its People* (Chapel Hill: U.N.C. Press, 1973), 82, hereafter cited as "Wellman, *Kingdom of Madison*"; and Manarin and Jordan, *N.C. Troops*, 2:337, 505.

84. Refers to Thomas L. Gash and Martin M. Gash, both of the 7th Cavalry Battalion and both captured.

85. Calvin Childers initially provided a substitute to fight in his place, but re-enlisted in company A in November of 1863. On December 14, 1863, Childers was promoted to corporal and served with that rank until killed in action at Spotsylvania Court House, Virginia, May 12, 1864. John Black enlisted in Iredell County on August 15, 1862. He was wounded in action at Chancellorsville and promoted to sergeant on December 14, 1863. On February 1, 1865, Black was promoted to first sergeant and survived the war, being paroled at Appomattox Court House, Virginia, on April 9, 1865. George W. Blackburn deserted along with Thornton and returned on September 1, 1863. Blackburn was wounded in action at Reams Station, Virginia, on August 25, 1864, and was placed on light duty until the end of the war. Manarin and Jordan, *N.C. Troops*, 9:473.

86. Joseph Sexton was Thornton's cousin who deserted on September 1, 1863, and returned in March 1864. Jo would be captured at Petersburg in July 1864 and imprisoned at Elmira, New York. Joseph died of disease at

Elmira on January 15, 1865. Manarin and Jordan, *N.C. Troops*, 9:473.

87. Levi W. Griffin, volunteered for service at 19 on May 19, 1862. He too would desert on May 19, 1863, and return that September. Levi was captured at Petersburg on April 2, 1865, and was confined at Point Lookout, Maryland, until June 6, 1865, when he was released after taking the Oath of Allegiance. Manarin and Jordan, *N.C. Troops*, 9:476.

88. The identity of the other officers is unknown; however, Norwood may refer to First Lieutenant Thomas L. Norwood of Company A. Manarin and Jordan, *N.C. Troops*, 9:472.

89. Private Robert B. McCormick, who returned to service on November 8, 1863, after serving time in the guard house for desertion. Manarin and Jordan, *N.C. Troops*, 9:478.

90. William C. Walker was placed in charge of the southwesternmost part of North Carolina. He was murdered in his home by bushwhackers on January 3, 1864. His loss was a personal one to Colonel Thomas, who had a force of twenty Cherokee who functioned as his personal bodyguard. *Charlotte Western Democrat*, 26 January 1864; and Crow, *Storm in the Mountains*, 55–56.

91. Lieutenant Colonel James R. Love resided in Jackson County, North Carolina. Before the war, Love was a North Carolina representative and prominent figure in mountain politics. Love was appointed to command the white infantry companies of the Legion, which were known as "Love's Regiment." The regiment performed service in eastern Tenesee and fought in the Shenandoah campaigns at Piedmont, Third Winchester, and Cedar Creek. In 1868, Love re-entered politics and was later elected to the state Senate. Colonel Love's daughter would marry William W. Stringfield. James R. Love died on November 10, 1885. Crow, *Storm in the Mountains*, 142.

92. After surviving a court-martial and constant bickering with his superiors, such as John B. Palmer, the war proved to be devastating to "Little Will." Thomas returned to his home in Jackson County, where, in 1867, his health collapsed. In even worse shape were his finances which had been devoted to the maintenance of the Legion and providing for the Cherokee people. Thomas' situation was exacerbated by the death of his wife in 1877. The three Thomas children went to live with William and Maria Stringfield, and Thomas himself would spend the next fifteen years in and out of various hospitals. On May 10, 1893, Thomas died an impoverished, depressed man at the Morganton State Hospital. Despite this rather dark end, Thomas is still revered by the Cherokee for his leadership and tenacity in fighting for the cause of his adoptive people. Crow, *Storm in the Mountains*, 142.

93. Jackson, *Surry County Soldiers*, 54.

94. Refers to Second N.C. Battalion privates Jonathan, Gideon, and James Flinchum, all brothers-in-law to Azariah Denny. Jonathan was court-martialed on December 1, 1864. Gideon Flinchum died of unreported causes on November 1, 1863, and James G. Flinchum was reported absent sick from April 1863. Jackson, *Surry County Soldiers*, 63.

95. David McClean, a 42 year old from Wilkes County. McClean would later be wounded at the Wilderness on May 5, 1864, and John Robinson, age 44, who would recover from his illness only to be wounded seven days after this letter at Payne's Farm, Virginia. Manarin and Jordan, *N.C. Troops*, 3:161, 163.

96. Manarin and Jordan, *N.C. Troops*, 13:666.

97. Hiram and David Sexton, the two younger brothers of Thornton and Marion Sexton. Federal Census of Ashe County: 1850.

98. Manarin and Jordan, *N.C. Troops*, 6:237; and *Archival Descriptor*, Swain Papers, Southern Historical Collection, Wilson Library, University of North Carolina at Chapel Hill.

1864

1. Whitaker was confined at Hart's Island, New York, until June 18, 1865, when he was released after taking the Oath of Allegiance. Manarin and Jordan, *N.C. Troops*, 7:435.

2. Private Miller was reported present until wounded in the left hip and captured in the Confederate defeat at Winchester, September 19, 1864. Miller was hospitalized at Baltimore, Maryland, and then taken to Point Lookout. Miller remained at Point Lookout until June 3, 1865, when he was released after taking the

Oath of Allegiance. *Wilkes County Heritage* (Charlotte: Delmar Publishing, 1990), 362; Federal Census of Wilkes County: 1860; and Manarin and Jordan, *N.C. Troops*, 13: 166.

3. Private Jonathan R. Woody died of disease on December 15, 1864, just as Miller reported. Manarin and Jordan, *N.C. Troops*, 13: 169.

4. Private Barnet Owens died the next day after being sent to the hospital. The 21-year-old soldier died of disease on January 4, 1864. Manarin and Jordan, *N.C. Troops*, 13:167.

5. William H. Proffit, deceased, formerly of Company B, 1st Regiment N.C. Troops.

6. William Stringfield also ran for election to the Tennessee legislature in 1861. Ironically, this 24 year old ran on the "Union Party ticket." When the state left the Union, Stringfield withdrew his candidacy. Stringfield was born in Strawberry Plains, Tennessee, and lived there until his twenty-fifth birthday. He is included in this volume due to his post-war allegiance to North Carolina. After the war, Stringfield was "exiled" from Tennessee and was welcomed with open arms in Haywood County, North Carolina. The remainder of his life was devoted to service to Confederate veterans, the Love family, the Cherokee people and western North Carolina in the North Carolina legislature. Crow, *Storm in the Mountains*, 142–143.

7. Captain Jesse R. S. Gilliand, a Buncombe County native, was previously commissioned a captain, and served in Company A, 4th Tennessee Infantry Regiment. He was appointed captain on November 17, 1863, and placed in command of Company D. Gilliand was regarded as an excellent officer and led his company throughout the Atlanta campaign. According to records, one night while sleeping, Gilliand was shot in the heel which produced a very serious wound. The wound was so severe, he was immediately issued a furlough and returned to Asheville. Captain Gilliand died due to his wounds shortly after arriving back home in Asheville. Manarin and Jordan, *N.C. Troops*, 14:531.

8. General Robert B. Vance, commanding the Department of Western North Carolina, was captured on January 14, 1864, and imprisoned at Fort Delaware, Delaware, until he was paroled and exchanged on March 10, 1865. "Bob Coleman" refers to Patton's friend Captain Robert L. Coleman, former assistant commissary of the 60th N.C. Troops, who also served on the staff of General Vance. Warner, *Generals in Gray*, 314.

9. Manarin and Jordan, *N.C. Troops*, 7:506.

10. Refers to Corporal Anderson Cain, Company F, 52nd North Carolina. Cain was born in Orange County, but resided in Wilkes County. Cain was wounded in the right leg at Jones Farm, Virginia, on October 1, 1864, a wound that required the amputation of his right leg. Cain was furloughed for sixty days on November 29, 1864. Manarin and Jordan, *N.C. Troops*, 12:468.

11. Private Josiah Millsap, who volunteered at age 25 on June 12, 1861. Millsap was captured at Falling Waters, Maryland, on July 14, 1863. After a brief confinement at Point Lookout, Millsap was exchanged on August 24, 1863, and promoted to corporal March–June 1864. Millsap lost his battle with disease in a Richmond hospital where he died on July 20–21, 1864. Manarin and Jordan, *N.C. Troops*, 7:500.

12. The family of deceased sergeant Franklin T. Chappel, who died of wounds received at the Battle of Gettysburg. Manarin and Jordan, *N.C. Troops*, 7:496.

13. Manarin and Jordan, *N.C. Troops*, 9:482.

14. Official records indicate that Sexton and Testerman were sentenced to "12 months hard labor." Calvin Testerman, an Ashe County farmer, volunteered for service on May 1, 1862. At nineteen, Calvin deserted on May 19, 1863, along with thirty-six fellow soldiers in company A, and returned on September 1, 1863. He was sentenced by a general court-martial and was returned to duty on December 1, 1864. Calvin soldiered throughout the rest of the war, being captured at Petersburg, Virginia, on April 2, 1865. He was confined at Point Lookout, Maryland, until June 20, 1865, when released after taking the Oath of Allegiance. Manarin and Jordan, *N.C. Troops*, 9:482–483.

15. Sergeant Perry S. Shuford enlisted in Henderson County on July 15, 1862. He was appointed sergeant on September 1, 1862, and served in Company E, 7th Battalion until transferred to the 6th N.C. Cavalry Regiment on August 3, 1863. Shuford was reported present or accounted for through October 1864. Manarin and Jordan, *N.C. Troops*, 2:476.

16. Leander Gash. Federal Census of Henderson County: 1850.

17. Lt. Colonel John C. Lamb, a Martin County merchant who served as commander of Company F, 17th N.C. Troops (1st Organization), and upon the second organization, served as commander of Company C, then was promoted to major on May 16, 1862. Lamb was promoted to lieutenant colonel on May 27, 1864. Lamb was wounded sometime during the Bermuda Hundred or Drewry's Bluff campaign and was admitted to a Petersburg hospital with a gunshot wound on June 17, 1864. Manarin and Jordan, *N.C. Troops*, 6:204.

18. Private Jesse R. Bird, a 21-year-old farmer, volunteered for service on October 19, 1861. Bird was present or accounted for through March 20, 1864. He was listed as "probably killed in action." Manarin and Jordan, *N.C. Troops*, 10:122.

19. This refers to a raid made by Major Nathan Paine and 250 members of the First Wisconsin Cavalry. The detachment was quickly discovered when it entered Macon County and was defeated by Thomas' Cherokee Battalion. Paine was able to capture several Confederates prior his defeat at the hands of Thomas. The most notable, Captain Siler, escaped from the disorganized detachment. William R. Trotter, *Bushwhackers! The Civil War in North Carolina: The Mountains* (Winston-Salem: Blair, 1988), 108–109.

20. Captain Bell was very financially savvy; however, some officers believed that he was too savvy and drew up charges of speculation against him in 1864. Bell was able to prove his innocence in both cases. Manarin and Jordan, *N.C. Troops*, 10: 120.

21. Manarin and Jordan, *N.C. Troops*, 2: 476, 538, 546; Federal Census of Henderson County: 1850; Federal Census of Macon County: 1860; Federal Census of Transylvania County: 1870.

22. Private Henry Osborne enlisted on July 15, 1862, as a private in Company E, 7th Battalion, N.C. Cavalry. He was captured at Monticello, Kentucky, on June 6, 1863, and was confined at Johnson's Island, Ohio, via Camp Chase until June November 15, 1864, when he was paroled and exchanged at Venus Point, Savannah River, Georgia. Manarin and Jordan, *N.C. Troops*, 2: 480, 549.

23. Manarin and Jordan, *N.C. Troops*, 14: 235–236.

24. Lieutenant Lafayette A. Page was a Caldwell County farmer before enlisting on May 13, 1862. He was promoted to first sergeant prior to March 1, 1863, and was promoted to second lieutenant shortly after. Page was wounded at Rocky Face Ridge, Georgia, on February 25, 1864, and died of his wounds in an Atlanta hospital on March 9, 1864. Manarin and Jordan, *N.C. Troops*, 14:375.

25. Love continued to serve as a sergeant until he was captured at Petersburg, Virginia, on April 2, 1865. James was confined at Point Lookout, Maryland, until June 25, 1865, when he was released after taking the Oath of Allegiance. Manarin and Jordan, *N.C. Troops*, 7: 401.

26. Manarin and Jordan, *N.C. Troops*, 3:161.

27. Private William Rufus Jones, a Wilkes County farmer who volunteered on May 31, 1861, at the age of 22. Manarin and Jordan, *N.C. Troops*, 3:160.

28. Private John Estes of Caldwell County volunteered for service in Wilkes County on July 1, 1861. Estes was wounded in action at the Battle of Chancellorsville in May 1863 and was discharged from service on December 12, 1863. Given Leach's comments, Estes had lost his right arm. Manarin and Jordan, *N.C. Troops*, 3:158.

29. Elbert Davis' service record appears in Manarin and Jordan, *N.C. Troops*, 14:389. The description of action at Rocky Face Ridge, Georgia, in the vicinity of Tunnel Hill was taken from Manarin and Jordan, *N.C. Troops*, 14:233–234.

30. Romantic Poet George Gordon Lord Byron.

31. Alfred Newton Proffit was wounded in the forehead at the Wilderness, May 6, 1864, and returned to duty that July. Alfred was reported present through February 1865. After the war he returned to Wilkes County were he married Sarah McNeill Proffit. The two rasied ten children. Manarin and Jordan, *N.C. Troops*, 6:352; and Ruth Gregory, "Alfred N. Proffit," in *Wilkes County Heritage* (Winston-Salem: Hunter Publishing), 415.

32. Manarin and Jordan, *N.C. Troops*, 13: 665.

33. Private Ozark D. Kinney and Thomas W. Noblin. Manarin and Jordan, N.C. Troops, 13:664, 667.

34. Private Robert Columbus Love and Samuel Ervin Love. Lane: First Lieutenant Benjamin D. Lane. Manarin and Jordan, N.C. Troops, 13: 665, 669.

35. Freeman was reported present through February of 1865 with his command in the 25th Regiment. In 1860, Freeman resided in Waynesville and worked as a merchant. His estate was valued at $1800 (real) and $8420 (personal). Manarin and Jordan, N.C. Troops, 7: 355, 378; and Federal Census of Haywood County: 1860.

36. Manarin and Jordan, N.C. Troops, 7:463; and Underwood, History of the 26th Regiment, 108.

37. Second Lieutenant Joseph G. Sudderth volunteered at age twenty. He was elected third lieutenant on March 15, 1862, and was promoted to second lieutenant on September 27, 1862. Manarin and Jordan, N.C. Troops, 7:574.

38. According to the report of Lawing, surgeon of Love's Regiment, the Union force consisted of the 3rd Indiana, 10th Michigan, a battalion of mounted infantry, and a two-piece artillery battery, with an estimate of two thousand total troops. Crow, Storm in the Mountains, 64.

39. At the opening of the battle, Major Stringfield advanced with about 250 men to reconnoiter on the opposite river bank. Stringfield discovered the flanking movement and withdrew his troops to an earthwork, then to a grist mill along the river where the Federals pressed them very hard; in fact men of Stringfield's command engaged the Federals in hand-to-hand combat. Crow, Storm in the Mountains, 65.

40. Manarin and Jordan, N.C. Troops, 2:5–6, 37.

41. Captain William Blair resided in Watauga County and volunteered for service on May 16, 1861, at the age of 28 as a sergeant. Blair was promoted to first lieutenant on February 3, 1862, and to captain on May 9, 1862. Blair served as commander of Company D, and led the "Watauga Rangers" through the large campaigns of 1863, and was wounded in action at the Battle of Brandy Station, Virginia, on August 1, 1862. Captain Blair was captured at Beaver Dam Creek, Virginia, on May 10–11, 1864. Manarin and Jordan, N.C. Troops, 2:36.

42. General John C. Breckinridge (CSA).

43. Within two weeks, the 21st was called on again to defend against a Federal attack, this time at Cold Harbor, Virginia. The major action of the battle, a Confederate victory, occurred on June 3, 1864. However, the two armies constantly skirmished and participated in many small-action fights. Private Denny was killed in such an action on June 6, 1864. Hester Jackson, Surry County Civil War Soldiers, 54.

44. Captain Robert Cotton Brown, commander of Company B, 44th Regiment N.C. Troops. Manarin and Jordan, N.C. Troops, 409–410.

45. D. Logan Warlick, a private in Lewis company, was killed at the Battle of Spotsylvania Court House, Virginia, on May 12, 1864. Sergeant William McGimsey survived his cramps and the war. Austin L. Parks transferred from the 41st N.C. Troops and served with the 11th until April 2, 1865, when he was captured at Petersburg. A. Pink Warlick was another of the brothers. Pink served as a corporal and survived the spring campaigns only to die of chronic diarrhea on June 30, 1864. Manarin and Jordan, N.C. Troops, 5:19–31.

46. Love apparently suffered a slight wound, but was hospitalized at Petersburg, Virginia, that following September due to the fact "He was just broke down and wore out." Love recovered and returned to the 56th N.C. Troops and soldiered on until he was captured at Five Forks, Virginia, on April 1, 1865. Love survived the war and confinement at Point Lookout, Maryland, where he was released on June 25, 1865, after taking the Oath of Allegiance. Manarin and Jordan, N.C. Troops, 13:665–666.

47. Samuel J. Smith, Company G, was wounded at Ware Bottom Church, Virginia, on May 20, 1864. Smith died prior to September 1, 1864, of his wounds. Manarin and Jordan, N.C. Troops, 14:669.

48. Captain Matthew Love, 25th N.C., and Samuel Ervin and George W. Love of the 56th N.C., all brothers of Robert Columbus Love. Federal Census of Henderson County: 1850.

49. Phillips, a 19-year-old farmer, enlisted on April 12, 1862. Phillips was killed in action at Bermunda Hundred on June 2, 1864, only three

days after attaching this short note. Manarin and Jordan, *N.C. Troops*, 14:667.

50. Manarin and Jordan, *N.C. Troops*, 14:557.

51. Possibly William A. Wagner, a private in Company A, 60th North Carolina Troops, also from Buncombe County. Private Wagner was listed as "detached on duty" during this time in the war. Manarin and Jordan, *N.C. Troops*, 14:514.

52. Refers to Eli Gross who was captured at North Anna River on May 24, 1864. Gross was confined at Point Lookout, Maryland, until he was paroled and transferred to Venus Point, Georgia, on November 16, 1864. Manarin and Jordan, *N.C. Troops*, 6:41.

53. Samuel Harrill, a private in Company D. Manarin and Jordan, *N.C. Troops*, 6:41.

54. Refers to George O. Griffin who died of wounds received at Ware Bottom Church, Virginia, on May 20, 1864, as a member of Company I, 56th Regiment. Manarin and Jordan, *N.C. Troops*, 13:685.

55. Also called Piedmont, Virginia.

56. During the Battle of Piedmont, William Stringfield was responsible for rallying the scattered Legion and leading them in an attack which checked the Federal advance and saved the command from complete rout. He also escaped personal capture. Crow, *Storm in the Mountains*, 74–75.

57. Cathey may have held a position in the Home Guard; however, the only officer identified with the 38th Battalion Home Guards (later 6th N.C. HG Regiment, 1st Brigade) was commanding officer Major W. M. Rhea. Cathey was asked by the adjutant general to recommend field officers for the Home Guard in a letter dated September 14, 1863. Bradley, *North Carolina Militia and Home Guard Records*, 3: 2, 15.

58. Love's Regiment was transferred to Jubal Early's command for the Valley Offensive of 1864. Sergeant William J. Smathers joined his unit on the triumphant march up the Shenandoah, into Maryland and Pennsylvania, to threaten the Union capital. Soon after the first of August, the Union began to attack Early's small and fatigued force. Sergeant Smathers was captured outside Winchester on September 17, 1864. After being initially detained at Old Capital Prison in Washington, D.C., Smathers was transferred to Elmira, New York. William Jasper Smathers died of dysentery at Elmira on November 2, 1864. He was interred in the national cemetery in plot number 824. William Best letter to author, April 1, 2002; and Moore, *Roster*, 4:157.

59. Second Lieutenant John H. Smathers and privates Jesse D. Smathers, Virgil H. Williams, John W. Bass, Edward D. Sharp, and John Redsleeve. All men enlisted in service in Haywood County on June 13, 1862. No Record of a Lieutenant Chavre (Shaver) could be found within the records of the Legion. Moore, *Roster*, 4:157–159.

60. Manarin and Jordan, *N.C. Troops*, 2: 289, 477, 544.

61. William Woods Holden, editor of the *Raleigh Standard*, a newspaper.

62. Alexander Stephens, Confederate Vice President.

63. Confederate cavalry general John Hunt Morgan.

64. Sergeant Leander Harmon Penland, a Macon County farmer was wounded at Chickamauga on September 19, 1863. He recovered from his wound, and after surviving the Atlanta campaign, was promoted to second lieutenant, a rank he held for the remainder of the war. Manarin and Jordan, *N.C. Troops*, 10:120.

65. Private James Jefferson Martin worked as a young farmer in Macon County before volunteering for service on October 19, 1861. Martin was wounded at Kennesaw Mountain, Georgia, in June 1864. Manarin and Jordan, *N.C. Troops*, 10:125.

66. Kirk's original plan was to take Camp Vance, then commandeer a locomotive and rush to Salisbury in time to liberate the prisoners held there. Following a brief skirmish with a small number of armed men at Camp Vance, in which ten conscripts and one officer were killed, Kirk burned the camp, sparing the hospital. By now the word had gotten to Salisbury, and Kirk decided to destroy the Morganton depot and return with his prisoners and many "new recruits" (conscripts who had joined the Union army) and return to Tennessee. On the way, Kirk first encountered resistance from a force under George Love at Brown's Mountian. Using several prisoners as human shields

and with his regiment's Spencer rifles, Kirk was able to thwart the spirited attack. Next, Kirk faced the Morganton Home Guard, commanded by William Waightsill Avery. With a loss of only ten on both sides, the Union troopers were able to cross back into Tennessee claiming an incredible victory 75 miles behind enemy lines, and taking 40 recruits, 132 prisoners, and 48 mules and horses. Sherman congratulated Kirk by saying: "This is the kind of soldiering I like to see!" As to be expected, the raid showed just how vulnerable western North Carolina was to Union incursions. Trotter, *Bushwhackers!*, 116–119.

67. All the names here refer to members of the Avery family. William W. Avery, Morganton Home Guard, Alphonso C. Avery, a staff officer, Clark Moulton Avery, who died of wounds received during the Spotsylvania campaign, and Lizzie Avery, Clark M.'s widow.

68. Thomas G. Walton, a former officer in the 3rd N.C. Cavalry, was appointed to command the Morganton Home Guard.

69. Privates William A. Collins and James T. Nichols, both of Company I, 39th North Carolina Troops. Manarin and Jordan, *N.C. Troops*, 10:174–178.

70. Captain Arthur M. Dyche and Second Lieutenant Harris Benjamin Whitaker of Company A, 39th North Carolina. Dyche a former trooper in the 2nd N.C. Cavalry, resigned as commander of Company A, to be effective from August 15, 1864. Whitaker either withdrew his resignation, or was rejected. Manarin and Jordan, *N.C. Troops*, 10: 112, 130.

71. Private Samuel Bell, Company H, 16th Regiment N.C. Troops. Samuel was Alfred's brother and was serving in the Army of Northern Virginia. Samuel Bell volunteered at age twenty-one on May 14, 1861. Bell was wounded in action at Mechanicsville on June 26, 1862, but rejoined his company after a brief absence. Bell was captured at Warrenton, Virginia, on October 1, 1862, and was transferred and exchanged at City Point, Virginia, on November 9, 1862. Bell was reported absent sick through February 1864, and present for duty through October 1864. Manarin and Jordan, *N.C. Troops*, 6:74.

72. The nature of the wound received at the Wilderness was confirmed in *N.C. Troops*. After the war, Alfred, the only surviving brother, would have ten children with his wife Sarah: Robert Lee (1871), Benjamin F. (1872), Augustus (1874), Lougerta L. (1874), Wade H. (1876), George H. (1878), William (1880), John (1883), Lovisa (1885), and Sarah (1887). Alfred and his wife are both buried at Lewis Fork Baptist Church in Wilkes County, North Carolina. Manarin and Jordan, *N.C. Troops*; 7:352; and Ruth Gregory, "Alfred N. Proffit," in *Wilkes County Heritage* (Winston-Salem: Hunter Publishing, 1982), 391–392.

73. Manarin and Jordan, *N.C. Troops*, 7:506.

74. Samuel L. Pryor had served as a sergeant in Company C since July 13, 1861. Pryor was captured at Falling Waters and was confined at Baltimore until exchanged on August 24, 1863. On September 1, 1864, Pryor was officially promoted to first sergeant. Pryor was reported present until captured along the Southside railroad on April 2, 1865. Manarin and Jordan, *N.C. Troops*, 7:303.

75. Manarin and Jordan, *N.C. Troops*, 2:476; and Josyln, *The Immortals*, appendix F, "Alphabetical Roster."

76. Thomas L. Gash, was the son of Leander (Uncle Lee) and Adeline Gash, also of Henderson County. Thomas was captured at Monticello, Kentucky, on June 6, 1863, and was confined at Camp Chase, Ohio, before being transferred to Point Lookout, Maryland, on November 11, 1863. Thomas was paroled and transferred to Cox's Landing, Virginia, for exchange on February 14–15, 1865. Manarin and Jordan, *N.C. Troops*, 2:473, 546.

77. Martin A. Young and Jasper H. Crawford, also members of the 6th North Carolina Cavalry. Manarin and Jordan, *N.C. Troops*, 2:545.

78. His brother Julius Gash.

79. The regiment returned to North Carolina in October 1864. Stringfield was promoted to lieutenant colonel and took over command of Walker's Battalion of Thomas' Legion on November 1, 1864. Stringfield was also assigned to patrol and work as a military administrator in several North Carolina counties. Shortly after the war, Stringfield was jailed in Knoxville until he was released on May 24, 1865. Shortly after, Stringfield moved to Waynesville and married Maria M. Love, the daughter

of Col. James R. Love, in 1871. Stringfield was trained as a civil engineer, but was employed as a secretary to Congressman Robert Vance in 1872, and operated the White Sulphur Springs Hotel in Waynesville as well as working as a land agent. Stringfield served in the N.C. Legislature in 1882-3 and was also a state senator in 1901 and 1905. William's work and kindness to the eastern Cherokee was appreciated, and the Cherokee gave him a name "Cho-ga See." Stringfield died on March 6, 1923, as a respected public servant, businessman, and friend. He is buried in the Green Hill Cemetery in Waynesville, N.C. Crow, *Storm in the Mountains*, 172–173.

80. Federal Census of Buncombe County: 1850, 1860; and Manarin and Jordan, *N.C. Troops*, 2:345, 508.

81. Manarin and Jordan, *N.C. Troops*, 2:36.

82. Sergeant David C. Davis who volunteered on May 11, 1861 and was mustered in as a corporal. Davis was promoted to sergeant in May–June 1862, and held that rank through December 1864. Manarin and Jordan, *N.C. Troops*, 2:30.

83. Adam's friend, and fellow sergeant, Bazilla McBride was admitted to a Richmond hospital on May 5, 1864, with "vulnus contusion-skull." McBride was reported as present through December 1864. Manarin and Jordan, *N.C. Troops*, 2:40.

84. William Cathey, a 25-year-old Jackson County resident had belonged to three units: Company A, 16th North Carolina; Company A, Thomas Legion; and Company K, 39th North Carolina. He was last reported present with the 39th North Carolina in October of 1863. In December 1864, Cathey could have possibly been serving with his old unit. By this letter, he certainly sounds like he is part of Stringfield's force. Manarin and Jordan, *N.C. Troops*, 6:15, 10:183; and Crow, *Storm in the Mountains*, 245.

85. William Holland Thomas.

86. William W. Stringfield.

1865

1. Virgil Lusk continued his career as an attorney, eventually attaining the position of state solicitor. Lusk served in that position for several years. Lusk was well respected in Asheville, his new home after the war, and in 1901 he was asked to write the history of the 5th Cavalry Battalion, which he commanded for nearly three-fourths of the unit's duration, for the Clark's Regiments series.

2. Corrupt, weak, and mentally disturbed Roman Emporer. To cover up his corruption and massive debts incurred by gambling, Nero is said to have had Rome put to the torch. "Nero played the violin while Rome burned."

3. "Parleir Letter Abstract," Box 85, Folder 28, Military Collection, North Carolina Division of Archives and History; and Manarin and Jordan, *N.C. Troops*, 13:314.

4. Noah B. Parlier, James' brother, also a private in company G, 54th Regiment N.C. Troops. Manarin and Jordan, *N.C. Troops*, 13:314.

5. Phoebe Cook Parleir, James's wife, Federal Census of Wilkes County: 1860.

6. Parleir would survive his wound and the war and return home to Wilkes County. Throughout his life, James was never a wealthy man, owning only $50 in property in 1880. James and his wife, Phoebe Cook, would have ten children by 1869. James lived in Wilkes until January 25, 1899, when he was stabbed in a fight and died of his wounds. "Parleir Letter Abstract," Box 85, Folder 28, Military Collection, North Carolina Division of Archives and History; Federal Census of Wilkes County: 1880.

7. Lawing, *Notes on Transcription*, 3.

8. Sergeant Harrison H. Galloway had been at home on furlough. Galloway returned sometime in January and was reported present until he was captured during Petersburg's fall, April 2, 1865. Manarin and Jordan, *N.C. Troops*, 5:25.

9. Privates W. Killian Morgan, Washington Thomas, John Hall and Robert Hall, Corporal James K. Polk Russell and Sergeant Marvel H. Shuman were all wounded at the Battle of Nashville. Private John W. Hall was captured. Manarin and Jordan, *N.C. Troops*, 10:126–129.

10. According to family history, as recorded in the Bell papers, during the war, Mary actually purchased a slave family. While the Bells were not slave holders, the Gray family were.

Despite troubles with disease, Mary was able to keep her farm running with the help of her slaves.

11. After the war, Alfred Bell returned home to Franklin and to his dental practice. During the war, Mary gave birth to two children, and lost one child to disease. Overall the couple would have six children. Bell lived in Franklin until his death on January 30, 1881. Manarin and Jordan, *N.C. Troops*, 10:120. Notes on *Alfred Bell*.

12. Corporal John D. Vanhook would go home on furlough and would remain there for the duration of the war. Manarin and Jordan, *N.C. Troops*, 10:129.

13. Corporal John Sidney Slagle, Company B, 39th North Carolina Troops, Manarin and Jordan, *N.C. Troops*, 10:128.

14. Captain Paschal C. Hughes, previously commanded Company H, 39th North Carolina. Hughes was never officially promoted to major; however, during most of 1865, he was the commanding officer of the regiment. Manarin and Jordan, *N.C. Troops*, 10:162.

15. Moore, *Roster*, 3:684.

16. Captain Lawson Harrill commanded Company I until he was captured at Fort Stedman, Virginia, on March 25, 1865. He was confined at Old Capital Prison in Washington, D.C., and Fort Delaware until being released on June 17, 1865, after taking the Oath of Allegiance. Manarin and Jordan, *N.C. Troops*, 6:41 and 116, and 13:682.

17. Private George O. Griffin died of wounds received on an unspecified date. Manarin and Jordan, *N.C. Troops*, 13:685.

18. Sergeant Amos Harrill one of the captain's two brothers in the company, was wounded at Ware Botton Church, Virginia, on May 20, 1864, and only escaped capture by crawling back to Confederate lines. Manarin and Jordan, *N.C. Troops*, 13:686.

19. No E. Jones was found among the rolls of the 3rd North Carolina cavalry; however, most records conclude in August of 1864, and further extant muster rolls are absent. For information on Coot Jones, the youngest of the Joneses of Caldwell County to serve, refer to Mildred Jones, "Captain Edward 'Coot'" Jones," in *The Heritage of Caldwell County* (Winston-Salem: Hunter Publishing, 1983), 393.

20. Jones in *Heritage of Caldwell County*, 393. Jones would also have a grandson who served in the United States Marine Corps in World War I.

21. Union General Henry W. Slocum, commander of the left wing of Sherman's Army operating in North Carolina.

22. Captain Elisha A. Perkins and First Lieutenant Hugh C. Bennett, both of Company F, 41st N.C. Troops (3rd N.C. Cavalry), and both from Burke County, N.C. Manarin and Jordan, *N.C. Troops*, 2:221.

23. Ruth Gregory, "William Proffit," in *Wilkes County Heritage* (Winston-Salem: Hunter Publishing, 1982), 392–393; and Manarin and Jordan, *N.C. Troops*, 9:352.

24. After the battle, Harper was promoted to major on April 9, 1865. In his later years, Harper became a prominent citizen of Caldwell County and western North Carolina. Some of Harper's accomplishments include building a section of railroad between Lenoir and Hickory in 1874, then operating it until 1892, and serving as the president of the Bank of Lenoir, trustee for the Charlotte Female College, and the director of the State Hospital in Morganton. In 1880-81, Harper was elected for a term in the North Carolina legislature. Hill, in Evans, *Confederate Military History*, 5:532.

25. This supposition was based on the fact that the only unit posted in Asheville was the 2nd North Carolina Mounted Infantry in early April 1865. Confederate units such as the 2nd Battalion Junior Reserves and senior reserves were checked for the initials or variations; however, by this time both battalions were operating outside Buncombe County. Photographic records show that the unit was present by April 9, 1865, in the western North Carolina city. The only man on the roster that seems to match the initials was Henry P. Evans, whose age would match up with the reference in this letter. The ambiguity of this identification is noted and those with knowledge of who this individual was should contact the author. Of course, this could also have been one big April fool and the writer could have written from Maryland, for all that can be confirmed.

26. John L. Swain became a Methodist minister after the war and served the church until his death circa 1900. *Archival Descriptor*, Swain

Papers, Southern Historical Collection, Wilson Library, University of North Carolina at Chapel Hill.

Appendices

1. The mountain counties comprised about ten per cent of North Carolina's population, with a proportionate number of men of military age. Below is a list of counties and the Confederate companies they provided. A list of Union troops was to be included; however, those companies in the Second and Third North Carolina and Fourth and Thirteenth Tennessee seem more a combination of men from three of four counties. This appendix also organizes the units by final official designation. For example, Company E, 7th N.C. Cavalry Battalion, would not be listed under Transylvania County; however, Company D, 6th N.C. Cavalry Regiment, would, after the formation of the 65th Regiment N.C. Troops from the 5th and 7th Cavalry Battalions. Also, Woodfin's Battalion and Coleman's battalions operated independently for a significant time; however, both those units became the core of new full-strength regiments, the 7th N.C. Cavalry (69th N.C. Troops) and 39th North Carolina, respectively.

2. From Johnston, Zeb Vance Papers, 342–344.

Bibliography

PRIMARY SOURCES

Manuscript Collections

Catawba College, Salisbury

Harvey Davis Diary

Duke University,
  Special Collections Department,
  Perkins Library, Durham

Alfred A. Adams Papers (19)
James H. Baker Papers (288)
Alfred W. Bell Papers (417)
Mary A. Council Papers (1259)
Matthew Norris Love Papers (3276)
John W. Reese Papers (4417)
Thornton Sexton Letters (4749)

North Carolina Division of
  Archives and History, Raleigh

Private Manuscript Collection

Isaac Erwin Avery Papers (1190)
Blair Letters (1206)
Todd R. Caldwell Papers (382)
Joseph L. Cathey Papers (214)
Cunningham Letters (1455)
Mary A. Gash Papers (59)
Gash Family Papers (1541)
James Gordon Hackett Papers (112)
George W. Griffin Papers (153)
Joseph L. Henry Papers (587)
Kimzey Letters (148)
Virgil S. Lusk Papers (717)
Edward G. Phifer Collection (1368)
William W. Stringfield Papers (109)
Harriet Espy Vance Papers (1255)
Stephen Whitaker Papers (36)
William M. Whitaker Papers (1034)
John Wright Papers (1594)

Military and Other Collections

Governor's Papers (Vance)
James B. Parleir Letter, Military Collection
Job Redmond Letter, Military Collection

Pack Memorial Library, Asheville

Veterans Collection Images

Private Collections

Robert G. Freeman Letters, Violet Marshbanks Cook
Asbury T. Rogers Letters, William R. Best, III
William J. Smathers Letters, William R. Best III

University of North Carolina,
  Southern Historical Collection,
  Wilson Library, Chapel Hill

Waightstill Avery Papers (33)
William J. Brown Papers (2603)
George Washington Finley Harper Papers (313)
Edmund Walter Jones Papers (3543)
Calvin Leach Papers (1875-z)

Laura Cornelia McGimsey Papers (2680-z)
Theodore Davidson Morrison Papers (2603)
James W. Patton Papers (1739)
Perkins Family Papers (3894)
Proffit Family Letters (3408)
John L. Swain Papers (3074)
Thomas George Walton Papers (748)

Newspapers

Charlotte Western Democrat, 26 January 1864

PUBLISHED PRIMARY SOURCES

Bradley, Stephen. *North Carolina Confederate Home Guard and Militia Records*. Four volumes. Virginia Beach, VA: by the author, 1989-1992.

_____. *North Carolina Confederate Militia Officers Roster*. Wilmington: Broadfoot, 1992.

Clark, Walter, ed. *Histories of the Several Regiments and Battalions from North Carolina in the Great War 1861-1865*. Goldsboro and Raleigh: State of North Carolina, 1901.

Evans, Clement A., ed. *Confederate Military History*. 17 volumes. np: Confederate Publishing Company, 1899; Wilmington: Broadfoot Publishing Company, 1987. Volume 5: North Carolina.

Federal Census of North Carolina Counties: Ashe (1850, 1860), Buncombe (1850, 1860), Caldwell (1850, 1860, 1880), Haywood (1850, 1860), Henderson (1860, 1880), Macon (1850, 1860, 1870), Surry (1850, 1860), Transylvania (1870, 1880), Watauga (1860), Wilkes (1850, 1860, 1900), and Yancey (1850, 1860)

Johnson, Robert and Clarence Beull, eds. *Battles and Leaders of the Civil War*. Four volumes. New York: The Century Company, 1888.

Johnston, Frontis W. *The Papers of Zebulon B. Vance*. Raleigh: North Carolina Division of Archives and History, 1963.

Manarin, Louis H. and Weymouth T. Jordan, Jr., comps. *North Carolina Troops 1861-1865: A Roster*. 14 volumes to date. Raleigh: North Carolina Division of Archives and History, 1966-.

Moore, John W., ed. *Roster of North Carolina Troops in the War Between the States*. 4 vols. Raleigh, NC: Edwards & Broughton, 1882.

War of the Rebellion: A Compilation of the Official Records of the Union and Confederate Armies. 130 Volumes. Washington, DC: United States War Department, 1880-1901.

SECONDARY SOURCES AND GENERAL REFERENCE

Arthur, John Preston. *A History of Watauga County*. Richmond: Everett Waddey Co., 1915

_____. *Western North Carolina: A History from 1730 to 1913*. Raleigh: by the author, 1914.

Barrett, John G. *The Civil War in North Carolina*. Chapel Hill: University of North Carolina Press, 1963.

Bowers, John. *Chickamauga and Chattanooga*. New York: Harper Collins, 1994.

Bradley, Mark L. *Last Stand in the Carolinas: The Battle of Bentonville*. Campbell, CA: Woodbury, 1996.

Burke County Heritage. Winston-Salem: Hunter Publishing, 1985.

Castel, Albert. *Decision in the West: The Atlanta Campaign of 1864*. Lawrence, KS: University Press of Kansas, 1992.

Cherokee County Heritage. Winston-Salem: Hunter Publishing, 1995.

Cotton, William D. "Appalachian North Carolina: A Political Study, 1860-1889." Ph.D. diss., University of North Carolina at Chapel Hill, 1954.

Cozzens, Peter. *No Better Place to Die: The Battle of Stones' River*. Urbana and Chicago: University of Illinois Press, 1990.

_____. *The Shipwreck of Their Hopes: The Battles for Chattanooga*. Urbana and Chicago: University of Illinois Press, 1994.

_____. *This Terrible Sound: The Battle of Chickamauga*. Urbana and Chicago: University of Illinois Press, 1992.

Crow, Vernon S. *Storm in the Mountains: A History of Thomas' Legion of Cherokee Indians and Mountaineers*. Cherokee, NC: Museum of the Cherokee Indian, 1982.

Dedmond, Francis B. "Harvey Davis' Unpublished Civil War Diary and the Story of Company D, First North Carolina Cavalry." *Appalachian Journal* 13 (1986), 368–407.

Ellis, Daniel. *Thrilling Adventures of Daniel Ellis, Scout.* New York: Harper and Brothers, 1867.

Fletcher, Arthur L. *Ashe County: A History.* Jefferson, NC: Ashe County Research Association, 1963.

Griffin, Clarence W. *The History of Old Tryon and Rutherford Counties.* Forest City, NC: by the author, 1937.

Hayes, Johnson J. *The Land of Wilkes.* Wilkesboro, NC: Wilkes County Historical Society, 1962.

Hennessy, John J. *Return to Bull Run: The Campaign and Battle of Second Manassas.* New York: Simon and Schuster, 1993.

Hickerson, Thomas F. *Echoes of Happy Valley.* Chapel Hill: by the author, 1962.

Horn, Stanley P. *The Decisive Battle of Nashville.* Baton Rouge: Louisiana State University Press, 1956.

Hughes, Nathaniel C. *Bentonville: The Final Battle of Sherman and Johnston.* Chapel Hill: University of North Carolina Press, 1996.

Inscoe, John C. "Mountain Masters: Slaveholding in Western North Carolina." *North Carolina Historical Review* 61 (1984).

____, and Gordon McKinney. *The Heart of Confederate Appalachia: Western North Carolina in the Civil War.* Chapel Hill: University of North Carolina Press, 2001.

Jackson, Hester B. *Surry County Soldiers in the Civil War.* Dobson, NC: Surry County Historical Society, 1992.

Josyln, Muriel. *Immortal Captives.* Shippensburg, PA: White Mane Publishing, 1996.

McDonough, James. *Chattanooga—A Death Grip on the Confederacy.* Knoxville: University of Tennessee Press, 1984.

____. *Stones' River: Bloody Winter in Tennessee.* Knoxville: University of Tennessee Press, 1980.

Mast, Greg. *State Troops and Volunteers: A Photographic Record of North Carolina's Civil War Soldiers.* Raleigh: North Carolina Division of Archives and History, 1995, second printing, 1995.

Medford, Clark. *Mountain Times, Mountain People.* Waynesville, NC: by the author, 1961.

Mosocco, Ronald. *The Chronological Tracking of the Civil War per the Official Records.* Williamsburg, Va: James River, 1993.

Paludin, Phillip Shaw. *Victims—A True Story of the Civil War.* Knoxville: University of Tennessee, 1981.

Phifer, Edward H. *Burke: The History of a North Carolina County.* Morganton, NC: by the author, 1977.

____. "Saga of a Burke County Family." *North Carolina Historical Review* 39 (1962).

Powell, William S., ed. *Dictionary of North Carolina Biography.* Four volumes. Chapel Hill: UNC Press, 1994.

____. *The North Carolina Gazetteer.* Chapel Hill: University of North Carolina Press, 1963.

Priest, John M. *Antietam: The Soldier's Battle.* New York: Oxford University Press: 1989.

Rhea, Gordon C. *The Battles for Spotsylvania Court House and the Road to Yellow Tavern, May 7-12, 1864.* Baton Rouge: Louisiana State University Press, 1997.

Russell, Mattie. *William H. Thomas: White Chief of the Cherokee.* Ph.D. diss., Duke University, 1956.

Sondley, Foster. *A History of Buncombe County.* Asheville, NC: by the author, 1930.

Stevenson, Alexander. *The Battle of Stones' River Near Murfreesboro TN: December 30, 1862, to January 1, 1863.* Boston: Osgood & Company, 1884.

Trotter, William R. *Bushwhackers!: The Civil War in North Carolina: The Mountains.* Winston-Salem: John F. Blair, Publisher, 1988.

Underwood, George. *The History of the 26th Regiment North Carolina Troops.* Raleigh: Edwards & Broughton, 1900.

van Noppen, Ina W. "The Significance of Stoneman's Last Raid." *North Carolina Historical Review* 38 (1961).

____. *Stoneman's Last Raid.* Raleigh: North Carolina State University Print Shop, 1966.

Warner, Ezra J. *Generals in Gray: Lives of the Confederate Commanders*. Baton Rouge, LA: LSU Press, 1959.

Watford, Christopher M. *North Carolina Regiments, Battalions, and Companies: An Order of Battle*. Unpublished manuscript, 1997.

Wellman, Manly W. *The Kingdom of Madison: A Southern Mountain Fastness and Its People*. Chapel Hill: University of North Carolina Press, 1973.

Wilkes County Heritage. (Volume one) Winston-Salem: Hunter Publishing, 1982; (volume two) Charlotte: Delmar Publishing, 1990.

Wooley, James E. *Early Marriages of Haywood County 1808–1870*. np: by the author, 1979.

Index

Numbers in **bold** are pages with photographs.

Abernethy, Robert 73–74
Adams, George F. 82–83, 140, 182–183
Allegheny County, NC 6, 201, 204
Anthony, George W. 10,
Ashe County, NC 5, 6, 33, 39, 52, 106–107, 131–132, 136, 147–148, 201, 204
Asheville, NC 7, **9**, 11, 24, 29, 38, 47, 53, 104, 116, 135, 143, 198, 208
Atlanta, GA campaign: 136, 139, 153–154, 160, 166–167, 171–172, 175–176
Avery, Col. Clarke M. 11, **35**–36, 114, 173, 215
Avery, Col. Isaac E. 66–67, 74–75, 87, 94–95, **114**, 212
Avery, William W. 172–**174**

Baker, James 25–**26**, 97, 212
Bell, Alfred 29, 87, 92–**93**, 125, 140, 149–150, 171–172, 175–176, 191–194
Bell, Mary G. 29–30
Bermuda Hundred Campaign 163, 165–166, 195
Bingham, Major Harvey 3
Blair, Albert 158–159
Blair, Robert M. 30–31
Blalock, Joseph **66**
blockading 44, 48, 148
Boone, NC 2, 36
Bragg, Gen. Braxton 69, 73, 85, 90
Brown, Col. Hamilton A. 18, **19**
Brown, Samuel **8**
Brown, William 8, 12
Brown, William J. 7, 8
Bryson, Goldman 2

Buncombe County, NC 5, 6, 8, 24–25, 34, 38–39, 53–54, 57, 61–62, 68–69, 72–73, 83–85, 89–91, 123–125, 137, 140, 142–143, 149, 159–160, 166–167, 182, 189–190, 199, 201, 204
Burch, Francis **66**
Burke County, NC 5, 6, 9–10, 12, 15–17, 21–22, 35–36, 44–48, 66–67, 74–75, 87, 88, 94–96, 98–99, 101–102, 105–106, 112–113, 114, 121–122, 163–164, 172–174, 191, 201, 205

Caldwell, Todd 112–113
Caldwell County, NC 6, 19–21, 30–31, 37–38, 54, 64–65, 114–115, 128–129, 135–136, 151, 157–159, 161, 186, 187, 195–197, 197–198, 201, 205
camp life 12, 20, 23, 37, 39, 45–46, 48, 53, 55, 56, 57, 67, 69, 72, 81–82, 83, 91–92, 96, 98–99, 103, 106, 110, 119, 120, 132, 136, 137, 141, 145, 152, 178, 183, 191, 193, 213
Camp Vance, Morganton, NC 2, 172–174
Carolina's Campaign: 187–188, 194–195; battle of Averasboro: battle of Bentonville 197–198
Carter's Depot, TN: 65, 118–119, 162; skirmish at 158
casualties 51, 52, 61–63, 65, 69, 89, 91, 93, 121, 126, 156, 158, 161, 165, 170, 180, 192, 198
Cathey, Benjamin **185**
Cathey, Francis **185**
Cathey, Joseph 156–157, 169–170
Cathey, William 184, **185**, 186

Centreville, VA 7, 28; skirmish near 29
Chambers, John **116**
Chancellorsville, VA, battle of 106–107, 108–109, 127
Chattanooga, TN 135–136, 142
Cherokee County, NC 6, 100–101, 108–109, 118–119, 133, 161–162, 201, 205
Chickamauga, GA, battle of 123–127, 135, 142, 153
Childers, Calvin 5, 39, 132, 136, 147
children 19, 25, 61, 66, 73, 84, 91, 98–99, 111, 159–160, 183, 194
Christmas 34, 80, 82, 84–85
civil unrest 3, 9, 12, 41, 64, 71, 72, 80, 88, 106, 119, 125, 126, 131, 140, 172–174, 183
civilians 12, 15, 27, 29, 34, 36, 38, 41, 44–45, 48, 53–54, 55, 57, 63, 64, 66, 69, 71, 73–74, 80, 88, 91, 96, 99, 112, 113–114, 117, 126, 128–129, 140, 142, 172, 174–175, 183, 187–190, 194–195, 198
Clay County, NC 6, 201, 205
clothing 12, 37, 38, 41, 52, 61, 65, 67, 73, 80, 84, 103, 120, 133, 145, 151, 153, 164, 171, 178, 184, 197
Coleman, David 126–**127**, 176, 194
Coleman, Robert A. **143**
combat experiences 62–63, 76–77, 90–93, 107–108, 115–116, 123–127, 136, 156, 158, 160–161, 163–164, 167–168, 172, 175, 180, 198

245

Index

Conley, Robert T. **181**
conscription 2, 38, 40–42, 56, 58–59, 64, 70–71, 79, 144
corruption 63–64, 73–74
Council, Jordan 33, 36–37, 42–43
Cumberland Gap, TN 68, 104
Cunningham, George 41–42

Dalton, GA 83, 91, 151
Davis, Harvey 55–56, 80, 97–98, 213
Davis, Tolivar 57–58
Denny, Azariah 56, 69–70, 100, 112, 133–134, 162–163, 212
Denny, Joel 112
desertion 3, 74–75, 80, 85, 88, 96, 99, 100, 106–107, 109, 119–120, 122, 132, 135, 146–147, 182, 196
discipline 21, 46, 54, 65, 68, 70, 73, 75, 79–80, 84, 85, 87, 110, 117, 118, 122, 132, 135, 144, 146–147, 182
disease 10, 14, 15, 22, 28, 30, 39, 43, 44, 47, 61, 65, 67, 69–70, 72, 82, 91, 108, 110, 118, 119, 127, 133, 141, 144, 173–174, 188, 192, 197
drill 20, 39, 40, 61, 63, 72–73, 96–97

East Tennessee, campaigns in 148
Eastern North Carolina and Southeastern Virginia Campaign: (1862) 45, 75–76, 1863– 96–97, 105–106; (1864) 149, 152
economy: inflation 3, 73–74; personal finance 54, 57, 61, 63, 84, 100, 107, 120, 122, 130, 133, 149, 151, 165, 180, 192, 197; real estate 89, 123, 192; shortages 3, 70, 73–74, 91, 102, 131
education 4, 5, 23–24, 92, 104, 153
enlistment 7, 8, 9, 11–12, 13, 16, 23, 29, 38, 40, 43, 48, 70, 170, 196
equipment 44, 53, 61, 62, 70, 74, 80, 81–82, 85, 98, 101, 122, 133, 153

farming 19, 29, 45, 63, 74, 91, 128, 131, 160, 174, 177
Folk, George N **179**
food: abundance 55, 56, 89, 132, 158, 159; foraging 34, 76, 80, 110, 117, 155, 181; prices 27, 54, 55, 73, 99, 100, 165, 177, 183; rations 20, 40, 46, 55, 56, 69, 99, 102, 106, 127, 135, 139, 141, 150, 153, 155, 166, 177, 181, 183, 184, 193, 196; requests 30–31, 54, 96, 106, 107, 120, 153, 197
Fort Fisher, NC 48
Fort Macon, NC 25
Franklin, NC 14, 29–30, 70
Frederick, MD 55; skirmish at 55
Fredericksburg, battle of 83, 89, 106, 109
Freeman, Robert 103
Freeman, Wesley 156–157
furloughs 34, 39, 40, 43, 57, 67, 70, 72, 92, 98, 117, 144, 145, 150, 153, 167, 176, 191–192

Gash, C. P. 7, 14–15
Gash, Harvey Y. 110–111, 139, 148–149, 179–180
Gash, Hattie 99–100
Gash, Julius 80–82, 99, 122–123, 187, 194–195
Gash, Martin M. 170–171
Gash, Thomas 150–151
Georgia units: 2nd Infantry 20
Gettysburg, PA 113, 114–115, 119, 121–122, 145, 158
Gordon, Gen. James B. 7, **18**, 28–29, 40–41
Gordonsville, VA 55, 127
Grant, Gen. U.S. 164
Greenville, TN 57, 81, 108
Griffin, Lorraine W. 109–110, 167–168
guard duty 33, 37, 65, 74, 77, 106

Hamilton, Hugh **199**
Harper, George W.F. 128–129, 135–136, 151, 160–**161**, 186, 187, 197–198
Harrill, Lawson 195
Haywood County, NC 5, 6, 41–42, 87, 103–104, 120, 141–142, 156–158, 168–170, 172, 174–175, 180, 184–186, 201, 205
Henderson County, NC 5, 6, 7, 26–28, 33, 40, 45–46, 47, 65–66, 103, 110–111, 135, 139, 148–151, 152, 156, 165–166, 170–171, 179–180, 198, 201, 205
Henry, Joseph L 125
Holbrook, William **126**
Horton, William 68, 153–154, 180–181, 183–184, 212
Hughes, Paschal **193**

"Immortal 600" 178–180
industry 4, 186, 208

Jackson, Gen. Thomas "Stonewall" 48–49, 55, 56, 107, 108
Jackson County, NC 6, 78–79, 132–133, 202, 206
Johnston, Gen. Joseph 117, 144
Jones, Edward 195–197
Jones, John T. 20–21, 37–38, 54, 64–65, 114–**115**, 157–158, 212
Jones, Walter 19–20, 212

Kimzey, John 26–27, 212
Kinston, NC 40, 42, 45, 47, 171, 179, 182, 187
Kirk, Colonel George W. 2, 172, **173**, 174

Leach, Calvin 15, 50–51, 59–61, 134–135, 152–153, 212
Lee, Gen. Robert 157–158, 163
Leventhorpe, Collet **77**
Louisiana units: 2nd Regiment 10
Love, George W. 156
Love, James W. 40, 152
Love, Matthew 40, 47
Love, Robert C. 165–166
Love, Samuel E. 135
Lowdens County, AL 38, 187, 189
Lusk, Virgil **129**–131, 154–155, 164–165, 168–169, 188–189

McDowell County, NC 6, 73–74, 202, 206
McElroy, Gen. John W. 3, 71, 79–80
McGimsey, Laura 9–10, 15–18, 75
Macon County, NC 6, 29–30, 70–71, 87, 88, 92–93, 125–127, 148, 149–151, 171–172, 175–176, 191–194, 202, 206
Madison County, NC 6, 129–131, 154–155, 165, 168–169, 188–189, 202, 206
Manassas, VA: first battle of 17, 67; second battle of 27, 56
marching 22, 28, 42, 51, 53, 56, 57, 59, 62, 67, 76, 90, 94, 105, 186, 187, 213
Meridian, MS 88, 126, 149, 192
military affairs (rumors on movements) 39, 42, 44, 47, 57, 67, 68, 78, 82, 85, 88, 95, 98, 104, 109, 110, 117, 142, 145, 162, 180–181, 186
Miller, Calvin **43**
Miller, Jesse 139–141
Miller, Stephen **75**
Mitchell County, NC 5, 6, 80, 202, 206
Mobile, AL 149, 193–194
Monticello, KY: skirmish at 110–111

Index

Morale: civilian 5, 14, 15, 17, 38, 48, 66, 70, 112, 126, 187; military 5, 10, 13, 15, 20, 24, 37, 42, 48, 49, 61, 82, 85, 88, 94, 97, 108, 119, 122–123, 130, 148, 162, 168, 188, 194–195, 196, 199
Morganton, NC 12, 35, 113
Murfreesboro, TN, battle of 85, 87, 89–91, 92–93, 215; camped near 34, 69, 72, 84

Nashville, TN 34, 85; Hood's campaign against 191–192
Neill, James R. 71–72
New Bern, NC 33, 36, 38, 39, battle of, 40
newspapers 77, 80, 158
North Carolina Confederate units: *cavalry:* 5th Battalion 129–131, 154–155, 164–165, 168–169, 182, 188–189, 203; 7th Battalion 80–82, 110–111, 122, 151, 170, 203; 1st Regiment (9th State Troops) 4, 7, 18–19, 28–29, 40–41, 55–56, 80, 82–83, 97–98, 140, 158–159, 182–183, 203; 3rd Regiment (41st State Troops) 44, 88, 101–102, 195–197; 6th Regiment (65th State Troops) 122–123, 139, 148–149, 170–171, 179–180, 182, 187, 194, 203; 7th Regiment (69th State Troops) 125, 203; Walker's Battalion, Thomas Legion 100–101, 108–109, 118–119, 132, 161–162; *Home Guards:* 2, 3, 125, 172–174, 203–207; 11th Battalion 3; *Infantry:* 2nd Battalion 25–26, 97; 1st Volunteers (Six Months) 9–10, 15, 21–22, 38; 4th Volunteers 11, 18; 1st Regiment State Troops 7, 15, 22–23, 49–52, 59–61, 89, 102, 119–120, 134–135, 153–154; 6th Regiment State Troops 66–67, 74–75, 87, 94–95, 114; 11th Regiment 47–48, 75–76, 95–96, 105–106, 121–122, 163–164, 191; 13th Regiment (3rd NC Volunteers) 74, 91–92; 16th Regiment (6th NC Volunteers) 4, 26–27, 41–42, 51–52, 109–110, 167–168, 203; 17th Regiment (2nd Organization) 137, 149; 18th Regiment (8th NC Volunteers) 56, 62–63, 107–108, 127, 155; 21st Regiment (11th NC Volunteers) 54–55, 69–70, 100, 112, 133, 162–163; 22nd Regiment (12th NC Volunteers) 4, 19–20, 110, 203; 25th Regiment 4, 27–28, 40, 45–46, 47, 140, 151–152, 156–157, 203; 26th Regiment 4, 20–21, 24–25, 30, 37–38, 54, 64–65, 111–112, 114–115, 145, 157–158, 178, 203; 29th Regiment 74–75, 193, 203; 33rd Regiment 35–36, 112–113; 34th Regiment 4, 203; 37th Regiment 4, 33, 36–37, 39–40, 42–43, 52–53, 83, 106–107, 128, 131–132, 136, 147–148, 203; 39th Regiment 29, 87, 88, 92–94, 125–127, 140, 149–150, 171–172, 175–176, 191–194, 203; 53rd Regiment 139–141; 56th Regiment 135, 165–166, 195; 58th Regiment 68, 128–129, 135–136, 151, 153–154, 160–161, 180–181, 183–184, 186, 187, 197–198, 203; 60th Regiment 34, 53, 57, 61–62, 68–69, 72–73, 83–85, 89–91, 98–99, 103, 116–117, 123–124, 131, 142–143, 159–160, 166–167, 203; 62nd Regiment 33, 65 66, 103–104, 203; 64th Regiment 203; Thomas Legion 78–79, 87, 120, 132, 141–142, 150, 158, 168, 170, 172, 174–175, 180, 184–186, 203; *Militia:* 105th Regiment 63–64; 111th Regiment 71–72, 79–80; 112th Regiment 104; *Union Troops:* 2nd Mounted Infantry 172–174, 198, 199, 203; 3rd Mounted Infantry 203

opposition to war 3, 7, 58
Osborne, Roland 13, 27–28, 45–46, 151, 212

packages from home 30, 41, 42, 53, 61, 76, 84, 90, 107, 120, 134, 171
Parlier, James 190–191
partisans 1, 33, 118, 139, 140, 148–150, 172–174, 183, 186, 197
Patton, Addie G. 13
Patton, Thomas W. 34, 38–39, 53, 57, 72–73, 84–85, 89–90, 116–117, 123–124, 142–143, 187, 189–190
Perkins, Elisha 44, 88, 101–102
Perryville, KY 68
personal matters 24–25, 28, 29, 35, 39, 43, 48, 53, 63, 68–69, 81, 101, 102, 106, 111, 113, 119, 140, 142, 150, 154, 160, 169, 171, 181, 189
Petersburg, VA 10, 45, 49, 65, 121, 171, 191; battle of Five Forks 140; campaign 171, 176–178, 183, 190
Pettigrew, Gen. James 20, 115
Phillips, John H. 33, 65–66
picket duty 50, 76, 85, 89, 98, 100, 134, 137, 147, 153, 159, 171, 177, 196
Piedmont, (New Hope) VA 168, 170
Plymouth, NC 156
politics 4–5, 58, 156–157, 170; elections (local) 44–45, 64, 156–157, 164, 170; elections (state & national) 183
Polk, Gen. Leonidas 84–85
Polk County, NC 6, 63–64, 202, 206
prisoners of war: Confederate 99, 107–108, 112, 121, 129–131, 143, 151, 154–155, 164–165, 168–169, 179–180, 188–189, 197; Union 46, 62, 94, 130, 156, 164, 186, 192
Proffit, Alfred N. 56, 74, 155, 176–**177**, 178
Proffit, Andrew J. 62–63, 74, 107–108, 127–128, 197, 212
Proffit, Calvin Luther 74, 91–92, 212
Proffit, William H. 7, 22–23, 34–35, 49–50, 89, 102, 119–120, 212

Raleigh, NC 10, 45, 47, 53
Ransom, Gen. Robert 19, 41, 47
Ray, Colonel John **124**
Recreation 96
Redmond, Job 182, 212
Reese, John W. 61–62, 68–69, 83–84, 90–91, 98–99, 131, 139, 159–160, 166–167, 212
religion: 96, 104, 165, 174; Catholicism 55; personal faith 13–14, 33, 45, 50, 52–53, 102, 128–129, 135, 174–175, 178, 182
Resaca, GA 160–161, 166
Richmond, VA 10, 25, 33, 41, 48, 49, 174, 197, 215
Rogers, Asbury 103–**105**
Rutherford County, NC 6, 57–58, 109–110, 167–168, 186, 202, 206–207
Rutledge, Henry M. **46**, 47

Saltville, VA 161–162
sanitation 183–184
Seven Days battles around Richmond 45, 49–52

Seven Pines, battle of 48–49
Sexton, Marion 33, 52–53
Sexton, Thornton 5, 39–40, 106–107, 131–132, 136, 147–148
Sharpsburg Campaign 55, 60–63; advances 55; Antietam, battle of 60–61, 65; Harpers Ferry 62
Shenendoah Valley Campaign (1864) 174–175; battle of Cedar Creek Shepherdstown battle of 62–63; battle of Winchester 180
Sherman, William T. 148, 172, 175, 180, 187, 192, 194, 197
Ship's Point, VA 7, 22
Shull, Phillip 83
Siler, David W. 70–71
slavery and slaves 13, 58, 71, 79, 84, 91, 189–190, 192
Smathers, William J. 87, 120, 170, 212
Smithfield, NC 198–199
society 14–17, 25, 38–39, 45, 99, 177, 189
South Mountain, battle of 59–60
Spottsylvania Court House, VA 152, 163–164, 197
Stokes, Col. Montford S. 15, 20, **49**
Stringfield, William 141–**142**, 158, 168, 172, 174–175, 180, 184
Surry County, NC 6, 25–26, 54–55, 69–70, 97, 100, 112, 133–134, 162–163, 202, 207
Swain, John L. 136, 149, 199
Sweetwater, TN, skirmish at 122

Tennessee troops: 16th Infantry Regiment 93
Thomas, William **78**–79, 118–119, 132–133
Tippett, William, 88, 125–127
transportation 4, 79, 166, 192
Transylvania County, NC 6, 13–14, 80–82, 99–100, 122–123, 151, 187, 194–195, 202, 207
Tullahoma, TN 90–91, 98–99, 103

Unionism 1–2, 8, 57, 126, 131, 165
United States Forces 2, 199; Colored Infantry (USCT) 152; 4th Tennessee Infantry 2; 13th Tennessee Cavalry 2
University of North Carolina 12, 21, 24, 113

Vance, Gen. Robert **11**, 72, 74–75, **143**, 215
Vance, Zebulon B. 8, 11, 21, 24–25, 57, **58**, 72, 155, 208, 215

Walsh, Phillip 128
Walton, Eliza M. 172–174
Walton, Thomas 44–45
Warlick, Lewis 9–10, 15, 47–48, 75–76, 95–96, 105–106, 121–122, 163–164, 191, 212
Warrenton, NC 15
Washington, DC 9, 108, 183; Early's raid 172
Watauga County, NC 2, 5, 6, 33, 42–43, 55–56, 80, 82–83, 97–98, 140, 153–154, 180–181, 182–184, 202, 207
weather 36, 41, 45, 50, 53, 82, 96, 101, 103, 104, 119, 151–153, 155, 172, 174, 186, 198
Weaver, James T. **167**
Weaver, Thomas 189–190
Whisenhunt, Isaac 44
Whitaker, Stephen 100–101, 108–109, 118–119, 161–162
Whitaker, William N. 140
Wilderness, VA 157, 176
Wilkes County, NC 6, 7, 15, 18–19, 22–23, 28–29, 34–35, 40–41, 49–52, 56, 59–61, 62–63, 74, 89, 91–92, 102, 107–108, 111–112, 119–120, 127–128, 134–135, 140, 145, 152–153, 155, 176–178, 190–191, 202, 207
Wilkesboro, NC 7, 18, 28
Wilmington, NC 44, 48, 88
Winstead, James **126**
women 7, 13–15, 16, 48, 53–54, 55, 57, 68, 71, 73–74, 91, 96, 98, 99–100, 104, 113, 117, 130, 140, 141, 154, 160, 167, 172–174, 177, 184, 188, 194–195
Woodard, John 12
Wright, James 111–112, 145, 178

Yancey County, NC 6, 71–72, 79–80, 202, 207
Yorktown, VA 12, 22, 41–42

Zionville, NC 2

www.ingramcontent.com/pod-product-compliance
Ingram Content Group UK Ltd.
Pitfield, Milton Keynes, MK11 3LW, UK
UKHW050702160426
5217IPUK00038B/1948